War and the Arc of Human Experience

War and the Arc of Human Experience

Glenn Petersen

Hamilton Books

Lanham • Boulder • New York • Toronto • London

Published by Hamilton Books
An imprint of The Rowman & Littlefield Publishing Group, Inc.
4501 Forbes Boulevard, Suite 200, Lanham, Maryland 20706
Hamilton Books Acquisitions Department (301) 459-3366

6 Tinworth Street, London SE11 5AL, United Kingdom

British Library Cataloguing in Publication Information Available

Library of Congress Cataloging-in-Publication Data

Names: Petersen, Glenn, author.
Title: War and the arc of human experience / Glenn Petersen.
Description: Lanham : Hamilton Books, an imprint of Rowman & Littlefield, [2021] | Includes
    bibliographical references and index. | Summary: "In this book, an anthropologist sets his experi-
    ences as a teenager fighting in the Vietnam War within the larger sweep of American culture and
    society. When his daughter is born decades after he returned from war the violence of those
    experiences, long suppressed, emerges from the shadows."—Provided by publisher.
Identifiers: LCCN 2021003749 (print) | LCCN 2021003750 (ebook) | ISBN 9780761872351 (paper-
    back) | ISBN 9780761872368 (epub)
Subjects: LCSH: Petersen, Glenn. | Vietnam War, 1961–1975—Personal narratives, American. |
    Vietnam War, 1961–1975—Aerial operations, American. | Vietnam War, 1961–1975—Naval
    operations, American. | United States. Navy. Carrier Airborne Early Warning Squadron 11—
    Biography. | United States. Navy—Aviation electronics technicians—Biography. | Radar opera-
    tors—United States—Biography. | Vietnam War, 1961–1975—Psychological aspects | Post-
    traumatic stress disorder—Patients—United States—Biography. | Vietnam War, 1961–1975—
    United States.
Classification: LCC DS559.5 .P438 2021 (print) | LCC DS559.5 (ebook) | DDC 959.704/34092
    [B]—dc23
LC record available at https://lccn.loc.gov/2021003749
LC ebook record available at https://lccn.loc.gov/2021003750

∞™ The paper used in this publication meets the minimum requirements of American
National Standard for Information Sciences Permanence of Paper for Printed Library
Materials, ANSI/NISO Z39.48-1992.

For Annette,
With more gratitude than words will express

Contents

Figures

Figures

Introduction

Just as I reached 40 and had begun imagining that I'd weathered most of the tough times, my daughter was born and I had the rug pulled out from under me. I was a tenured full professor teaching students I admired at a venerable university, head of my department, well respected by my colleagues, and publishing a steady stream of professional books and articles. I had established myself. As I understood it, a lot of this could be attributed to how well I'd put to new use the focus I'd honed as a boy fighting in the Vietnam War. I'd learned to harness my inner drive and ambition with a set of practical behaviors and to keep everything else blocked safely out of mind.

And I'd done it skillfully. Although I had only a 10th-grade education when I finished up my 4-year Navy hitch, I sped through college, earned an Ivy League PhD, and made a satisfying academic career for myself. How could anything be wrong? I was locked in. Until, that is, I adjusted to fatherhood by admitting I was an alcoholic and letting go of the comforting crutch booze had long provided me.

Then, boom! The war came roaring back, and it hasn't given me a day's respite since. My growing relationship with my daughter peeled back vast expanses of scar tissue and exposed a tangle of raw emotions. I found myself right back in the war, but this time I wasn't able to block out the turmoil. I don't know that it's ever going to leave me. And that's why I write this book, to tell veterans of more recent wars what may be lying in wait for them, too.

I flew 70 combat missions in Vietnam when I was 19, launching from an aircraft carrier out in the Tonkin Gulf, running the radar and controlling interceptors. There are few things hairier than getting catapulted off a carrier or making a night landing aboard one, but the flying was by no means the only daring part of my job. After we touched down I had to ready the plane for its next mission, working out on the carrier's flight deck in the dark, one of the modern world's most hazardous work environments. This all entailed weighty responsibilities I was eager to take on and hard work I wanted to do. But why? What did the cultural architecture of the society I grew up in have to do with the way I went to war?

I look at myself in the war from this anthropological perspective because that's how I've made my living in the years since I returned from Vietnam: it's how I see the world. There's never been much overlap between anthropologists who've fought in wars and anthropologists who write about war. Though many of my teachers served in World War II, they chose to remain silent about it, in print at least, and I can count on the fingers of one hand those I know who fought in Vietnam and then went on to become anthropologists.[1] These days, quite a few anthropologists write about the military and about war, but they do so from the viewpoint of researchers. The classic methodology of ethnographers, though, is what we call participant observation—a sort of total immersion—and that's what I'm bringing to the page here. I'm writing about a specific war from the dual perspectives of an insider and a researcher. And I'm doing what anthropologists typically do: I'm trying to find in the specifics of lived experience some larger conclusions about humans' social life in general.

Way out towards the front of the many reasons I've got for writing is my fascination with how my experiences in the Vietnam War came to shut me down for such a long time. That is, for a couple of decades following the war, I was unaware of what had happened to me there. My big fear is that the generation of young men and women who've been fighting the US military's wars in the early years of the 21st century, in Afghanistan, in Iraq, and in what's called the war on terror, are going through something quite similar. I want them to know what's in store for them.

The skills that allowed me to survive and thrive in combat, in particular the ability to focus tightly on the challenges directly in front of me, seemed to transfer really well to life after war. That same intense focus helped me pursue my career. I was successful, so how could anything be wrong? But slowly, surreptitiously, all the danger, the stress, and the trauma I'd managed to hide from myself found cracks in the brittle shell that held everything in. And then one day the whole damn thing broke apart and the war came spilling out. I know I'm not the only one who's experienced this. As an anthropologist I see a classic sort of pattern unfolding here: an adaptation to one set of conditions is put to a new and practical use when conditions change, but in time what had once been beneficial turns into maladaptive behavior.

During the war I developed a mindset that kept me oblivious to most of the perils I encountered and made it easy for me to imagine, in the war's wake, that nothing much had happened to me. Again, as an anthropologist I look at the ease with which I handled things like the exhaustion, sleep deprivation, and multiple threats to my life—hazards I faced as I worked nearly round the clock—and I see how this sprang out of influences that are a part of American cultural and social life. That's another of my goals: I'm hoping to shed light on how the reasons why we fight can produce a sort of amnesia, a forgetting of what happened to us while we fought. It can take a long time for the war and its legacies to return to mind, to force us to wonder both why we fought then and what it is we're struggling with now. This is what I think of as the arc of human experience.

I'm uncomfortable with some of the ways we generalize about my post–World War II Boomer generation and the Vietnam War. Those times were more perplexing than we may remember. Americans' self-confidence had probably peaked with the victory in 1945, but at the same time our self-satisfaction with our role as world leaders was disturbed by worries about the potential for a nuclear holocaust. Though some of us—the men, at least—possessed a sort of swagger as we stepped out onto the world stage, others began raising questions. As the 1960s unfurled, the generation's outlook shattered. Selective Service—the draft—meant that young working-class guys would have to spend time in the military, while those who could afford to attend college had other options. It's easy to speak in terms of all those young men growing up with the same social or cultural values, but that's not at all how it actually played out.

So my first task will be to explore how what we might think of as a shared cultural experience was in fact nothing of the kind, and how a lot of us—certainly myself—wandered around amongst the various possibilities we saw open to us. Although our generation is well-known for opposing the war, the overwhelming majority of Americans who served in the Vietnam War were volunteers. How did this affect the ways those of us who went to war experienced it? The flip side to many of the received truths about the war shows us there were quite contradictory ways of thinking about it; in turn the ways we thought about the war shaped the ways in which we experienced it.

More of these contradictions leap out at us when we look at American popular culture as a whole, especially in the movies and TV shows we took in through our pores as we grew. We watched what seemed like a nearly infinite number of westerns and war movies (which were pretty much the same thing, with little more than costume changes to distinguish between them). It's easy to toss around generalizations about these shows and about the messages we picked up from them, but the reality is more complicated. For one thing, the folks who produced them often intended to cast doubt on war and violence, but that's not at all necessarily how we kids understood them. For another, the military was the butt of endless humor. We saw the military and war portrayed both as great and glorious and in terms of pompous buffoonery.

Books and music had their impact on us, too. Some of the era's most successful novels painted the officers who commanded ships and squadrons and infantry companies as fools and sons of bitches. Popular song was mostly romantic up into the early 1960s, but then folk music, which had had an ambivalent attitude toward violence—it loved to celebrate fighting the good fight—began crossing boundary lines and, as the decade progressed, drove what had been relatively innocuous rock and roll into rock music and helped edge a lot of teens toward rebellion.

That rebelliousness coincided with the arrival of birth control pills and a sexual revolution. What were we learning when we learned to be young American men in that era? An ambiguous line from the antiwar movement had it that "Girls say 'yes' to boys who say 'no,'" and suggests to me that there was no simple answer to this question. The fact that people needed to have the notion explained to them tells us one thing, while the fact that it was said at all leads us to suspect something quite different. Was it an exhortation to folks who were otherwise hesitant or was it a report on how things actually were?

We speak today of "toxic masculinity," and the willingness of the millions of us who voluntarily crossed the sea to slay millions of Vietnamese certainly points to a deadly predisposition in young American males' worldviews. But it's equally the case that most of the young men who volunteered did so to avoid full-on combat. It was the guys who went unwillingly—the draftees—who were made into the infantrymen most immediately engaged in the killing. At the same time, though, the killing was possible only because of the millions of troops who worked at seemingly nonviolent duties, the ones who kept everything entailed in the violence working efficiently.

Modern wars grow out of complex mixes of an urge to violence and a relatively passive willingness to obey. It is this way because militaries and the wars they fight are driven much more by an overarching emphasis on order, obedience, and discipline, and by well-honed technical skills, than they are by outright violent behavior. Much about the military actually runs against the grain of simple or straightforward stories about war, and one jarring aspect of this contradiction lies in the claims commonly put forward by many of those charged with making war. They tell us how much they hate war, and that they fight and kill only in order to save lives.

This sort of contradiction can also be seen in what strikes me as a constant in military life and culture. Most rank and file members—the enlisted troops—engage in unrelenting criticism of the military. It's usually considered bad form among soldiers to speak positively about anything connected with their leaders or their units (unless they're bragging to those they're in competition with). At the same time, though, this cynical stance has little if anything to do with their performance.

It's often the case that the most gung ho troops are the most outspoken in their criticisms. I call this ironic detachment, an attitude that allows soldiers to shrug off responsibility for whatever happens. And this holds for veterans, too. Vets recall camaraderie and shared experiences with fondness, but they're also known to say they remember nothing good about war. What Vietnam vets have to say about the war and how they feel about it, for instance, depends on who they're talking to and the context of the conversation.

Because many ways of looking at the Vietnam War fail to notice more nuanced aspects of what was going on, then, I want to fill in behind and between the words that are usually spoken about the war. The cultural contexts were irremediably contradictory, and so were the outlooks of the men who were fighting.

EVERYDAY DANGER

The history of war, running back in time at least to Homer's *Iliad*, tells us that violence tends to attract and hold the eye. Stories about war aren't always dramatic or cinematic, but the ones that are, the ones that draw and hold attention, are far more likely to be told and retold. And so it is that it's the infantry company out in the jungle or the rice paddies that provides the iconic image of the war in Vietnam. Nevertheless, riflemen make up only a small part of the military and most of what goes on in a war doesn't happen in a rifle company.

In the same way that it's a mistake to draw too many generalizations about the Boomer generation's relationship to the Vietnam War, it's inaccurate to generalize too much about the face of the war itself. The conflict as a whole comprised multiple theaters, including the Mekong Delta, the Highlands, the cities, Cambodia and Laos, and the sprawling support bases, but also a very different sort of war, the one that was fought up in North Vietnam, prosecuted almost entirely by Navy and Air Force bombers.

For the Navy's part, this meant aircraft carriers and their battle groups. The camera lens focuses on kinetic action, and especially on explosions, gunfire, and wounded men being lifted out by helicopters. Or, when it comes to the Navy's role, on a few hundred aircraft and their pilots unloading bombs on the people below. Those bombers, though, are no more than the tip of the spear; thousands of sailors strained to keep their ships in position on the line out in the Tonkin Gulf, and to get those planes into the air.

The story I'm telling about combat as seen from carriers out in the Gulf, on what we called Yankee Station, deals with a big piece of the Vietnam War, and of all modern war for that matter. It's not well known, but it remains as relevant as ever. Even today, the admirals assure us, carriers are the mainstay that brings the fight to wherever the next battles are going to erupt. "Where are the carriers?" is, we hear, the first thing a president asks when told of a new crisis arising.

Much of the time there was little visual drama, but this hardly means that these activities were without impact. I've come to think of what so many of us did aboard the carriers and in dozens of other types of duties as instances of "everyday danger," and I'm struck by how much impact these seemingly innocuous duties had on us.

The many facets of everyday danger make up a substantial portion of what goes on in wartime and can inflict harm without ever being recognized. It's easy to be unaware of these hazards, or to ignore them, even as they wreak damage on the men and women who face them. The stress and trauma of war are experienced in all these many places, but they're much less likely to be recognized, given the ways our culture's war narratives prime us to think about what war looks like.

Bertel van der Kolk, a psychiatrist who treats traumatic stress, says that its effects are not always apparent, but that nevertheless, "the body keeps the score." What I'm speaking of as everyday danger can have just as much impact as more dramatic forms of traumatic stress, but it's harder to recognize, precisely because it's unexpected—it doesn't look much like what we've been led to think stressors look like. Those who carry it around in their bodies are less likely to recognize or understand it, and many of those who work in the Veterans Administration are so attuned to how trauma appears in infantrymen that they have little awareness of what to look for in others.

Troops in combat, in all its many forms, learn to speak about what they're doing in ways that make it hard to grasp just how they experience war, given the sarcasm and cynicism and ironic detachment that characterize most of what they have to say. They learn to downplay whatever they do and are alienated from everything. By bad-mouthing so much about the military they mask from themselves how much effort they put forth, and what it costs them. This in turn enables them to expose themselves day in and day out while the stresses continue to build. Then they continue to lug this burden around with them, oblivious to it until they're much older and can no longer bear the strain.

Perhaps no one captured the absurdity of this better than Joseph Heller in *Catch-22*. His novel excelled at making fun of fear and death and things that were otherwise thought of as entirely serious matters. It was his story that provided me a framework on which to hang my own experiences of the war and helped me understand how ironic detachment and cynicism had allowed my comrades and me to ignore what was happening. And so it was that we came back thinking nothing had happened, and were oblivious for years.

WHY WE FIGHT

I'd be exaggerating if I said that the farthest thing from my mind when I enlisted was being a hero, but it certainly wasn't high on the list of reasons I was thinking about at the time. I'm a prime example of how difficult it can be to pinpoint the reasons why we fight. I joined up with several things front and center in my mind: mostly I wanted training that would get me a promotion on the job I already held, along with a chance to travel and see the world. These were both typical motives, ones the military made good use of in their recruiting. But behind them lay images from the underlying culture I grew up with, which had schooled me in the male heroics I observed in that endless flow of westerns and World War II movies. Practical concerns like job training and the simple economics of survival intersected with the stories of valor implanted in young men. My personal experiences reflect my own character, of course, but they were equally a sign of the times. A lot of us turned against the war soon after we returned, not because of what we experienced in Vietnam, but because of the ambivalence we carried with us when we went there. Once we no longer had to explain to ourselves why the war was worthwhile—as we were fighting it—we could reclaim our generation's broader opposition to the it.

My story's neither typical nor atypical. Many young men and women imagine themselves as heroes (think of all those superhero comics), but not that many actually take up heroics as a career.

And then there's one more theme I want to explore, an ancient one, the oedipal contest between my father and me. It wasn't enough for me merely to excel in that struggle; I felt I had to *outdo* the man I wanted to become. In my early adolescence I wound up with the disturbing sense that I might well have to kill the man I wanted to be. So I ran away from home at sixteen and then went to sea, racing along every path I could find as a means of sublimating that terrible urge. More than that, though, this narrative lies at the root of another key theme in my story, the ache of betrayal that has never entirely left me. I realize that I cannot separate out my sense of my father's betrayal of me from my sense of having been betrayed by my country's leaders, the ones who sent me off to fight in a war they knew was unwinnable.

This underlying drive to be a hero, embedded in a lifetime of images of movie heroics, clouded my vision. I thought I knew what I was doing at the time, but as I pushed myself to the limits I failed to see what was going on. I subjected myself to stress and trauma even as I strained to remain unaware of them: oddly enough, embracing threats to your life means you learn to pretty much ignore them.

Because I wasn't paying a lot of attention to what I was actually doing, my ability to focus so closely on the job itself meant that I deliberately kept myself unaware of the dangers I faced (except, that is, when my plane mistakenly crossed into Red China). I didn't think much about the war, or perhaps I should say about the meaning of the war. Or maybe it's that I didn't think about why I fought; I just did it. I did as I was told. And as a result, I've spent the rest of my life caught up in a raging inner conflict. I feel bad about things I did in that appalling war, while at the same time I want to feel pride about having worked so hard at them. I am, it seems, deeply ambivalent about what I did in the war, even if I'm not ambivalent about the war itself.[2] This is the story of that chaos.

A NOTE ON WHO THIS FOR

I often speak with my students about the importance of writing with one's intended audience clearly in mind. Here, though, I'm not imagining *an* audience, a particular readership. I've written this for many different sorts of readers. And that's a problem. Things that are obvious and could go unsaid to one set of readers are opaque to others. What's likely to hold some readers' attention is going to bore others. There's rarely been a moment, or a paragraph, when I haven't worried about how off-putting it might be to one reader or another. In the end, I don't have a solution to this.

I'm not even sure what this book's genre is. It certainly has aspects of memoir in it, but I don't think of it as a memoir. It certainly has aspects of ethnography, but I'm not sure that that's what it is. As I've envisioned it, I use my own life experiences to talk about how war impacts individual lives and use an individual life—my own—to explain how wars shape human life in general.

It occurs to me, though, that my concern about nailing down just what genre I'm writing in may be misplaced. Memoirs are notoriously untrustworthy. Those who coach memoir writing often say that what's most important is emotional truth, but I'm not sure that's how I see this. I am interested in emotional truth, but I'm more concerned with historical truth.

I have a capacious memory and I've learned to trust it. My sister once laughingly said that "Before Google there was Glenn." To the extent that I've been able to cross-check what I've written here, I'm confident of my accuracy. I've gotten things wrong, I'm sure, but I doubt that these errors have much impact on the authenticity of the whole. I add to this the skills I've developed in a lifetime of working as a field ethnographer. When I'm doing ethnography there are times when I need—and have been able—to recall a 2-hour conversation among multiple Pohnpeians sitting around a kava stone almost verbatim.

The ethics of anthropology make two things imperative. First, that we protect the people with whom we work. That is, we must not write or speak publicly about things that would cause harm to the communities that generously allow us to live with them. Second, that as a means of honoring and respecting people's willingness to let us live and work among them, we strive to be as forthright and honest in reporting on what we've observed as we can possibly be. I'd like to think this is a credo that most of my colleagues would agree on. But I know that it's not.

The competitive character of academic and professional life leads scholars to embellish and invent, to manufacture out of whole cloth examples that support their own analyses and theories and to brush aside or cover over examples that might undermine their claims. They can be as susceptible to corner-cutting, embellishment, and outright cheating as professional athletes. There are places here where what I've written is an immediate, first-person account, and places where I'm standing way back, looking at things with a thorough-going scholar's perspective. But the whole is neither one nor the other. All I can say is that my career no longer looms over me, and candor prevails.

A NOTE ON USAGE

As a Navy man, I was a sailor, not a soldier. Marines don't like to be called soldiers either, and it's the same with the Air Force and Coast Guard. Soldiers are in the Army. A generic term for everyone in the armed forces (at least in the days when I served) is "serviceman," and members of the armed forces often speak generically of being in "the service." I think that "military" conveys what the armed forces are about better than "service," though, and when I'm speaking generically about men and women in the military I sometimes use the term "soldier" to refer to everyone in the US armed forces. I'm dismayed by the newly popular term "warfighter."

ACKNOWLEDGMENTS

My thanks to all those I flew with and all I served with, especially Nathan Terry and John Vega. To my daughter Grace, whose birth and life are at the pivot point of this story. My students, who keep asking me to tell them this story. Glenn Albright, who taught alongside me through much of this, and helped me navigate a lot of the blind spots. My mentors Robert Murphy, Eric Wolf, and Eugene Ogan, veterans who recognized things in me long before I could see them. My colleagues, who encourage me to keep protesting. Ken Guest, who reminded me of Ged's note: "Master, I go hunting." Sally Wright and Jeffrey Fine: among all the many psychologists and psychiatrists who've treated me, these two have done the most to help me live with my PTSD. My AA comrades for their empathy, tolerance, and understanding as I repeatedly unfurl my distress at our meetings. All the folks who've responded to my queries or offered support, including (and I know I've forgotten some of you) Andrew Bacevich, Marilyn Young, Edwin Moïse, Samuel Hynes, Tony Judt, Caroline Alexander, Nancy Sherman, Gregory Daddis, Michael Sherry, Leon Golden, David Price, Catherine Lutz, Alan Young, James Peck, Robert McDermott, Rebecca Lemov, Gian Gentile, Keith Taylor, Dan Duffy, Elizabeth Samet, Nick Turse, Yuval Neria, Elizabeth Anderson, Todd Gitlin, Paul Ehrlich, Piet Lincoln, Michael Staub, Hugh Gusterson, Martina Nguyen, Elizabeth Wollman, Brian Ferguson, Alisse Waterston, Sophie Barbasch, Michael Denneny, and the members of Christa Acampora's seminar on moral injury.

I've never met or conversed with Ron Kovic, but he's been an enormous influence. I've taught *Born on the Fourth of July* in my introductory anthropology courses for 40 years and while I never consciously tried to draw on it, when I look at what I've done it's clear that his approach to telling about the war permeates everything I've done here.

And most of all, Annette Barbasch, who's given me what I've needed (and that's been a lot) to sit and write this.

NOTES

1. In "Anthropology and Militarism," Hugh Gusterson observes that "Few contemporary anthropologists have much military experience" and that "anthropologists have written very little about Vietnamese culture or about the Vietnam War—the defining event for the generation of anthropologists now nearing retirement" (2007, p. 157). A piece I wrote many years ago on teaching about the war (Petersen, 1992) is one of the only two works he cites in this context. Among the reasons I've written this book is my desire to fill in what I see as a yawning gap.

2. In the end, of course, there's nothing much unique about how we experienced and remember the Vietnam War. Looking back at World War II from 35 years on, William Manchester wrote in *Goodbye, Darkness*, "My feelings about the Marine Corps are still highly ambivalent, tinged with sadness and bitterness, yet with the first enchantment lingering." During the war, he says, "I was transformed from a cheeky youth to a troubled man who, for over thirty years, repressed what he could not bear to remember" (1980, p. 398).

Chapter One

Why We Fight

The stairs running alongside the house passed just below my parents' bedroom, and I crept up to the street as carefully and quietly as I could. It was 3:00 a.m. Earlier that evening, before they'd gone to bed, I had wheeled my Vespa away from where it had been parked outside their window. As I look back now, those last few steps seem to mirror the passage into manhood I'd embarked on. I moved away from the house and passed out of one world and into another.

I was grappling with two nearly equal knots of fear, and I'm still amazed that I managed to overcome the terror and act, but my dread of what would happen if I didn't leave home finally outweighed my apprehensions about what lay ahead if I ran away. I've heard it said that to live freely is an immense act of will. For me, at 16, this was an act of will. But there was a lot more to it than that. As I walked the Vespa up the hill, to a spot where I could give it a noisy kick-start, I drew on resources I'd been cultivating in myself for years. I usually think of what I was relying on as toughness, but it might better be described as "spiritedness," a term the ancient Greeks knew as *thumos*, and there were many parts to the spiritedness that bore me away from home, including courage, awareness, ambition, and foresight.

When I look back, what particularly stands out is the connection between fear and foresight. I wasn't simply afraid; I also had a pretty clear sense of what lay ahead if I didn't leave. What my father might do, what I might do, what might befall me if I didn't escape. I'd thought through what I would have to do to make my escape and what my life might be like if I were free. It was the careful, thoughtful weighing of these alternatives, along with my willingness to act, that freed me.

And so I ran south, with no more certainty about where I was headed than that. It was October, and winter was coming. I'd be facing hard living conditions, so Southern California seemed to make sense. I drove down the Pacific Coast Highway and I was right—it was cold. I spent the first night sleeping on the floor in a dark corner of San Luis Obispo's Greyhound bus station. It wasn't pleasant.

Standing out on the street the next morning before getting underway again I thought for a moment, for just a very brief moment, about turning around. Perhaps my parents would acknowledge that there was a problem. And then I felt a second wave of toughness, of spiritedness, and of wisdom. I recognized that my parents would neither see nor concede anything. In a burst of insight that still astonishes me a half century later, I said to myself, "Glenn, if you turn around now and go back, then for the rest of your life, whenever you are unhappy with your life, you're going to remember this moment with regret and say to yourself, 'If only I had kept going when I had the chance, then everything would be different.' I'm not going to spend the rest of my life regretting a lost opportunity."

I kicked the starter, mounted, and pressed on. Highway 101, running south from San Luis Obispo, passes through Gaviota Pass just before it reaches the ocean. It was like I was reborn as I glided out of that narrow ravine, leaving the old behind and bursting into the sun of a new life.

I had only a couple of dollars left in my pocket when I reached Santa Barbara, where I decided to stop for a while. I slept in the backs of cars in used car lots, swathed in newspapers. I shoplifted food. And I began pounding the pavement looking for work. The anxieties I'd entertained before I took off about what would happen to me were reasonable, and it didn't seem at first that I was going to find anything. In a few days, though, I landed a job as a busboy in a restaurant, then found a rooming house. I quickly worked my way into the kitchen, where the pay was a little better. And then, as is my nature, I sought a better job. I went to work on an assembly line at the telephone company and got an apartment. In a few months' time I'd established myself.

And then, just as quickly, all the conflicting pulls in my makeup reasserted themselves.

Not long after I arrived in Santa Barbara I found a blue-collar tavern where I drank beer after work each day. Though I was 5 years under the legal drinking age, no one ever questioned me about it. I knew no one in town and that saloon provided the only friends I had and a spot where I could steep myself in the world of working men. Many of the anxieties and fears that had beset me since I'd run away quieted down while I was drinking, and that's where I could relax a bit. I paid close attention to the way these men talked and carried themselves, was soon crafting a mask for myself, and in a short time I'd figured out how to pass myself off as a lot older than I was.

In one of those curious turns life takes, though, it was in the Canteen Tavern, a hole in the wall joint if ever there was one, that my horizons radically expanded. Don McPherson, a young artist—an aspiring painter—whom I'd met there, began introducing me to the realms of art and culture. Don and I got that first apartment together and we shared a place filled with books and records from the library, the walls covered with paintings and prints and poetry. I was making my first steps toward becoming an intellectual and I took to the new world before me like the proverbial duck taking to water.[1]

There were, of course, other sorts of growth. While I was still washing dishes and scrubbing pots in the kitchen at the Copper Coffee Pot, I'd clashed with the younger of two brothers who worked there. For some reason, tension had been building slowly between Danny Romero and me; we exchanged words one day and the tension flared suddenly into confrontation. He was preparing vegetables and held a long and razor-sharp chopping knife in his hand. He pointed it at me and stepped forward. I had nothing but the heavy iron ladle I'd been washing. I knew perfectly well that I was at a terrible disadvantage and was going to get badly cut, but I also understood that I needed my job to survive and that if I backed down there was no way I could continue working there. I turned from the sinks to face Danny, the ladle cocked to defend myself. I was scared.

And then Danny's older brother Eddie intervened, grabbing him, calming him, pulling him through the door out into the alley. When they returned a few minutes later, Danny had quieted down. Though he'd been antagonistic toward me ever since I started working there, his attitude now changed radically. He was friendly and cooperative, and I was able to work in peace. I learned a huge lesson about what it took to be a man in that world.

I see myself advancing through the stages of what was in many ways a young American male's normal development, but at a very high velocity, seemingly bolting from age 16 into my early twenties almost overnight. And then I ran up against a barrier. As always, I wanted to advance myself, but at the phone company where I'd gone to work I'd need a driver's license in order to move out of the repair shop to the job I wanted as a lineman. I had a motorcycle license to drive my Vespa, but not to drive a truck.

The guys who worked beside me had served in various branches of the peacetime military. Much of the talk as we worked was about their experiences, stories of where they'd traveled and what they'd done and seen. It all sounded a lot more attractive than what was already beginning to feel like a dead-end job on that assembly line.

Seven months of life as a free man in Santa Barbara got me past my initial fears; I gained my footing, my imagination broadened, and my confidence carried me forward. I was seized by a sense that I could do whatever I wanted, and by new ideas about what I might do. If I enlisted in the military, I discovered, I could return to the phone company when my hitch was up, and my time in the service would count toward seniority there. If the military trained me in electronics, I figured, I could return with skills and seniority and spring past the barriers that held me back. I could become a lineman.

Making sure that my call could not be traced, I phoned my parents and asked them to sign the enlistment papers for me. Relieved to learn that I was alive, they agreed. Days after my 17th birthday I joined the Navy.

Four years of training, travel, and war would so thoroughly transform my horizons, though, that I soon lost any interest in returning to the phone company.

WHO KNOWS WHY WE FOUGHT?

It should be clear that a sense of patriotism didn't play an obvious role in this decision. It's not that I was any less patriotic than other kids my age, but in those days young men didn't talk that much about patriotism—it was there, but it was taken entirely for granted. Because of the draft, the military always loomed directly ahead of teenagers who didn't go to college. But there was a trick. If you seized the initiative and enlisted, rather than waiting to be drafted, then you could try—if you qualified—to join the branch of your choice and seek out an assignment that got you training in a field where you thought you might want to work afterwards. For a lot of us the military was our higher education. And for this reason some of the branches could afford to be selective. The Air Force and the Coast Guard had turned me away because I lacked a high school diploma. But like many others, I set my sights on something at least a little more glamorous (if that's the right word) than the job of an infantryman—a grunt—in the Marines or the Army. And that meant the Navy.

Let's face it, I joined the Navy to get off the assembly line, to get some valuable job training, and to see the world. And though I'd grown up with TV shows and movies about the Navy's role in World War II, and understood some things about its role in battle, as I signed the recruiter's forms it never occurred to me that I was about to go to war.

When war did come, though, all that history and familiarity asserted itself. The only surprising thing is how quickly it came. My timing, I often say, was impeccable. I was still in boot camp at the beginning of August 1964, when what's called the Tonkin Gulf Incident took place and our aircraft carriers began launching bomb runs over North Vietnam. Though the United States had been dispatching troops to South Vietnam for years, the government called them advisors and maintained the fiction that our soldiers were not engaged in combat. The Tonkin Gulf Incident is notable both for the fact that it marks the beginning of direct, open warfare by our forces against North Vietnam and for the multiple ways in which our leaders misrepresented what happened. They used a brief, chaotic episode at sea, the details of which no one seemed sure, as a pretext to begin the bombing they had in fact been planning for months.[2]

Like so many other guys in my generation, I went to Vietnam willingly, not because I was eager to fight, but because it seemed like it was what was expected of us. This is easy to say, but it's harder to believe, since so many others in my generation, growing up in the same cultural realm as those of us who did go, defied the draft and refused to serve. How did American society produce such completely different results within a single generation of men? It's easy to say that I was young and naïve, and that our leaders took advantage of me. That is, in fact, just what I've felt and said for years. But as I think this through now I see it differently.

It's not that I no longer fault the government and the military—I still do—but that I can now see how eager and willing I was to participate. I understand something of how these small bits of my history describe the path I took to get to Vietnam, but they really don't *explain* much about how or why I wound up fighting there.

WAR, EVERYWHERE

When we were little and shared a bedroom, my brother and I hung the ceiling with model planes we'd built from plastic kits, every one of them a warplane. I can still identify that era's planes, and distinguish a Cougar from a Panther, a B-25 from a B-24, and a PBY from a PBM (and I had my favorites, the Cougar, B-25, and PBY). But I recall no civilian aircraft; as a boy, my playthings were the weapons of war and I grew up understanding them and what they were for.[3]

In the same way that our room was festooned with these warplanes, my imagination was littered with images of combat. It's important to understand that in the late '40s and '50s the Navy felt its future was mortally threatened by the Air Force's strategic bombers and long-range missiles, which were intended to deliver nuclear weapons anywhere in the world. Part of the Navy's scheme to fight back included major support for a number of movies and television series, some of which I remember vividly. *Victory at Sea* (with its celebrated theme music by Richard Rogers) was first and foremost; it aired when I was 5, I watched every episode on TV alongside my father, and it shaped my early understandings of the world as surely as the Catholic school I'd entered at the same time. *Navy Log* and *The Silent Service* (and a few forgettable other series) followed in its wake. Watching them, I learned about the differences between the Navy and the infantry, and that our Navy had been as important to winning the war as the ground troops.

It was the same at the movies. For every *Guadalcanal Diary*, *Sands of Iwo Jima*, or *The Longest Day* on the big screen, I also saw *They Were*

Expendable, Away All Boats, or *Run Silent, Run Deep*. But the larger point here is that my generation's childhood was beguiled by two kinds of stories, those about cowboys and those of World War II. They focused equally on bravery and morality, and many dealt with these qualities pretty simplistically. But when I return to these movies as an adult, I also find that at least a few—and probably more than a few—actually told stories that were nuanced, shaded, and complex. I'd like to blame these shows for my naïve views of war, but the fact is that as a boy I was hardly capable of taking in many of the messages they were meant to convey. I saw them not only in literal black and white, but also in moral shades of black and white. I now understand, too, that some of the films that I took to glorify war did no such thing.

The news I heard on the radio seemed to echo these themes. Ours was an ancient floor model, much taller than me when I was young. I still recall hearing about concerns that the Korean War would turn into World War III and running into the kitchen to tell my mother. This was probably in late 1950, before I turned four. I recall hearing as well, when I was five, about the hydrogen bombs and cobalt bombs that were said to be superseding the atom bomb.

When I was three, the parish built St. Lawrence O'Toole School in our backyard, literally, chewing away at places where I played and displacing our chicken coops. The school and its asphalt playground paved over a cherished piece of my mental geography. Along with it came the nuns who converted a house three doors down the street into their convent, simultaneously adding to that geography. These new apparitions, seemingly arriving from outer space, scared the hell out of me (my father described with glee how I raced home screaming in terror the first time I saw "The sisters, the sisters!"). At age 5, I began kindergarten at St. Lawrence, and stayed there until I graduated from the eighth grade. There are plenty of stories about Catholic school life in the '50s, and there's no need for me to rehash the experience, but the impact those institutions had on us when we were small and impressionable can hardly be ignored.

This was at the peak of the baby boom and 50 or more of us—rambunctious little boys and girls—were in each classroom, with one fierce nun exercising iron discipline. The sisters marched us in and out of the building and enforced silence and order at almost all times. Verbal, emotional, and physical punishment were routine. We were right to fear them, and my father's story about how frightened I'd been the first time I saw them was followed a few years later by his complaint that my siblings and I feared the nuns more than we feared him. He said he wanted us—and this is not a snidely mocking observation, it is gospel truth—to fear him at least as much as we feared the nuns. The nuns beat the fear of God into me; my father simply beat fear into me. The discipline at St. Lawrence was as effective as that of any military school but drilled much more deeply into our being: everything we did and learned was couched in terms of its impact on our immortal souls.

These sisters dressed in black and white uniforms (or as they called them, habits) of the Dominican order that mirrored exactly the black and white understanding of the world—of morality and virtue and humanity—they imparted to me and my fellow inmates. The world in those days was no more black and white than it is today, and so the worldview they drummed into us did not help make sense of the real world we were living in.

Our school days were punctuated by air raid drills that sent us diving beneath our desks.[4] These premonitions of Armageddon were coupled with the nuns' daily exhortations to say our prayers before going to bed at night. They assured us that saying our prayers would allow us to die in a state of grace (meaning we would go to heaven) and that the odds of being killed by a nuclear attack while we slept were high. It's easy to chuckle at this now, I know, but I need to put it into context.

The new school had literally paved over parts of my world. I was terrified of the nuns, who were telling me I might be killed in the night by one of the bombs I'd heard about on the radio. They were instilling in me the notion that I have a soul, that they wield power over it, that it is imperiled, and that I must work hard to save it. Stepping back a bit, it's not difficult to see what I've been reacting against for most of my life. If I step back a little further, though, I can also see how all this makes up a fundamental part of who I am, and how I experience life. The world is a dangerous and threatening place, yes, but the much more meaningful lesson I learned was that I am charged with battling it.

When I went off to war a few years later I carried with me some things I'd integrated into my being at an early and very impressionable age. If I die in a state of grace, good, but it is even better if I die while actively resisting a threat to my soul or to my faith. Though the heroes of my early childhood seemed on the face of it to be of two distinct types, cowboys and soldiers on the one hand, and the church's martyrs on the other, they represented a common theme in American life in the years following World War II. We Catholic kids were schooled in the theology of martyrdom. Martyrs are those who die in defense of their faith; they go directly to heaven, where they sit by the side of God; and they immediately become saints, whether officially canonized by the pope or not.

When I reflect on it, as I often do, I cannot make any clear-cut or logical distinction between the Catholic Church's martyrs and those who die violent deaths today in the name of defending their faith. This isn't an abstract theological matter of angels dancing on the heads of pins. The deaths we learned about in school (and we spent a lot of time studying the lives of the saints), and which were portrayed everywhere around us by statues and paintings, were brutal, bloody, and capricious. There was in our church, for instance, a statue of St. Lucy, holding her eyes (which had been plucked out before she was executed) in a dish.

I still have difficulty finding a clear moral distinction between modern-day accounts of suicide bombers in the Middle East and the morbid tale of the first St. Lawrence, namesake of the bishop after whom our school was named, who was roasted over an open fire on a gridiron. Midway through the proceedings he said to his executioners, "I'm well done. Turn me over!"

There was, of course, more to it than this. I picked up some useful things, some things worth remembering, at St. Lawrence, along with all the neuroses. Chief among them, perhaps: "Actions speak louder than words," a notion that probably describes my outlook as well as anything else I might say.

Back in those days of unwieldly, temperamental movie projectors, we rarely watched films at school, but occasionally classes would file down into the basement "auditorium" for a screening of something the nuns could agree on as uplifting, ones they screened again and again for us. They were a welcome treat.

I remember only a few of these movies, but three stick in my mind. *Sergeant York*, starring Gary Cooper, told the story of a World War I pacifist, Alvin York, who is drafted despite his bid for conscientious objector status. He drops his opposition when he has what is portrayed as a divine revelation and decides that killing the enemy on his government's orders is acceptable in God's sight. It includes several noble speeches about doing one's patriotic duties, won Cooper an Oscar, and was the most successful American film of 1941. The timing had been perfect—it appeared while the United States was gearing up for a war that was beginning to seem inevitable and was still in theaters when Pearl Harbor was bombed. And it remained entirely relevant during those early years of the Cold War.

Then there was 1940's *The Fighting 69th*, about a mostly Irish-American infantry regiment in World War I, with Fighting Father Duffy, played by Pat O'Brien, as their chaplain. If it's possible for there to be a war movie with a priest as the hero, this is it. In a climactic scene, James Cagney throws himself on a hand grenade, an act I saw reprised in a television drama a few years later, one that really lodged in my imagination.

The Miracle of Our Lady of Fatima is a third. It appeared in 1952 and while it's ostensibly about three children in early 20th-century Portugal who have visions, much of it centers around an anticlerical government's attempts to suppress religious belief; it was very much a Cold War allegory. The scene that most powerfully etched itself into my memory portrayed the children being taken one by one into an adjacent room, where they were supposedly tortured by being dipped in boiling oil (or so I remember it), in an effort to force them into renouncing their visions. Reading the synopsis now, I see that this was a ruse, but my own memory is that they were indeed horribly tortured for their faith but would not recant.

As I said, we were taught, consistently and in dramatic fashion, about our duty both to fight and to kill for our country and to die for our faith.

We were also well-versed in the mathematics of sin—original, venial, and mortal—and what it took to guard our souls from the wages of sin. I'm not sure whether I really flunked Catholicism, but if I did it has to do with my inability to grasp one of its central tenets, absolution. I've never managed to believe that when I've done wrong the stain can be washed away simply by confessing it to a priest. This may be something I was born with or learned in the cradle (or perhaps both); at any rate, I had no sense that my parents would ever overlook something I'd done wrong, and to the extent that God was simply my parents writ large, I had no expectation that he would absolve me. And yet . . . a central theme in the story I'm telling here has to do with all my attempts to atone for having fought in a war I came to think was wrong.

I was 10 when I got my first after-school route delivering the *Oakland Tribune*, a boy nearly buried beneath the canvas sack of newspapers hanging round my shoulders, struggling doggedly up East Oakland's steep foothills. Especially on Wednesdays and Sundays when the paper was stuffed with all the extra advertising materials, the load I hauled seemed to weigh as much as I did. It was a small thing, that first route, but that's what started my journeys, and there was a lot more to it than meets the eye. I continued carrying the *Tribune* until I was 16, getting a series of longer and longer routes until at the end I was delivering two routes back to back each day.

My father was a mail carrier, and by toting a heavy sack door-to-door I was in some ways trying to emulate him, a practice that wasn't going to pay off very well—at least at the time. I did read the paper as I walked my rounds each day, though, and grew increasingly aware of the wider world. (I distinctly remember, for instance, reading about President Eisenhower deploying American troops to Lebanon in 1958, when I was 11.) At the same time, I was discovering ways of looking at and puzzling about the world that were sharply at odds with everything I was learning in school. Much of this new influence came from a couple of the comic strips I read every day, *Pogo* and *Lil' Abner*. Their bizarre and sometimes crazed casts of characters and the anarchic language they spoke introduced me to a beginners' skepticism and satirical ways of looking at the wider world I was coming to know. Those guys were ironic about everything.

This may well be where I first found out about seeing things not simply as they seem and got into the habit of looking behind and to the side of things, and perceiving folly almost everywhere. Like every other American boy my age, I was also reading superhero comics, with their clunky confrontations between good and evil and their stodgy dedication to truth, justice, and the

American way, but I think I may actually have been more influenced by Donald Duck's "Uncle Scrooge" in a series of comic books slyly but relentlessly poking fun at contemporary American life.[5]

Soon I was seeking out cartoons wherever I could find them and quickly advanced to *Mad Magazine*, which contributed more to my education than any schoolbook. Later, when I picked up Joseph Heller's novel, *Catch-22*, it seems that I was merely taking one more step into a world I'd been preparing to enter for years. I recall very little of school during those days, except that it felt like prison and that I wanted desperately to escape it. Though a paper route may not sound like much of an education, that daily routine of responsibility, hard work, and paying attention to the world helped me piece together a persona that would consist of roughly equal parts seriousness, irony, and something that borders on skepticism and cynicism, without ever being quite conscious of it. I threw myself whole hog into things, but this never got in the way of doubting them.

And it was while reading the *Tribune* that I discovered summer youth work programs run by the city's parks department. By the time I was 16 I'd made my way to a job as counselor at Oakland's boys' camp high in the Sierras, where I spent the summer teaching nature study, archery, and canoeing.

HEROES

Boys in the 1950s admired a handful of star athletes and fictional superheroes, like Mickey Mantle, of course, and Johnny Unitas, but we were most in awe of the cowboys and soldiers who seemed to own the TV and movie screens. There were so many cowboys on TV that it's hard to think of one that we would all agree on as a favorite. But even before we got a TV at our house, when I did my viewing on the neighbors' sets, I idolized Hopalong Cassidy. There are photos of me at age three, dressed from head to toe in a black Hoppy suit, pointing my six-gun at Mrs. Rogers, the nurturing widow who lived next door. She and other neighbors gave me this rig when I got home from a hospital stay brought on by pneumonia and an allergic reaction to penicillin. The image of her smiling benevolently while I point the pistol she's just bestowed on me directly at her is striking.

Cowboys and Indians is what we called the game we perpetually played outdoors, but there wasn't a lot of difference between the westerns and the war movies; John Wayne, who seemed to be in most of them, changed little more than his shirt as he wove his way from one genre to the other. To be sure, though, there weren't many cattle in those stories about cowhands, as they evolved in the '50s from horse operas to adult westerns. Instead, the stars spent their time fighting one another, outlaws, and Indians, or else

Figure 1.1. The author, age 3, in his Hopalong Cassidy outfit with his neighbor, Mrs. Emma Rogers. *Author's personal collection (photo presumably taken by my mother in 1950)*

hanging out in barrooms. To a young boy they were really about gunfights and about gunfighters like Paladin, the hired gun in one of my favorites, *Have Gun, Will Travel*. But the one I enjoyed most as I was entering puberty was *Maverick*, about a gambler with a sense of humor and a notable desire to avoid gunfire. As I was learning to laugh at the world's follies, his ironic detachment was taking the edge off the thrill a minute shoot 'em up shows that had so appealed to me when I was younger.[6] Even as I immersed myself in the code of the gunfighter, the righter of wrongs, I was drawn to the guy who could laugh at himself and the rest of the world.

One heroic figure in particular loomed largest for nearly all of us, at least for a time: Davy Crockett. Walt Disney's version of Davy, played with simple sweetness by Fess Parker, truly swept the nation. The story actually involved a lot more than just the usual clichés that filled adventure tales in those days. Davy fought Indians, bravely and cleverly, of course, but unlike

Figure 1.2. The author, age 3, in his Hopalong Cassidy outfit pointing his pistol at Mrs. Emma Rogers. *Author's personal collection (photo presumably taken by my mother in 1950)*

other heroes, he went much further in modeling good citizenship and even martyrdom for us. After fighting Indians in the first of the three 1955 TV episodes, Davy headed to Washington to represent Tennessee in Congress. His guiding principle couldn't have been nobler: "Always be sure you are right, then go ahead." And then in the final episode, he sacrificed his life to prove the strength of his convictions. He rode to Texas with a band of Tennessee volunteers and died fighting at the Alamo. At its most obvious, Davy's legacy for us lay in that splendid act of figuring out what was right and then going on to fight to the death for it.

For a kid like me, though, there's much more to this story. The Davy Crockett series ran when I was in second grade, preparing for my first communion and being drilled in the basic tenets of the Catholic faith. In Disney's telling, Davy was much more than just another gunfighter with a white hat, and this is why we found his story so riveting. The legendary frontiersman was modeling not only typical western bravado for us: he embodied what politics and good citizenship should look like. This was at a time when Washington was filling up with veterans who'd returned from World War II. President Eisenhower was sort of a warrior-saint and future presidents Kennedy, Johnson, Nixon, and Ford were among the many veterans moving through Congress at the time. Senator Joseph McCarthy, famed as a communist hunter and known as "Tail-gunner Joe," was a hero to the nuns. We kids had little grasp of what politicians were up to, but still, we got the message loud and clear as we pulled on our coonskin caps.

In that Disney version, Davy is three times a hero. He doesn't simply go to Congress, he acts out the role of the decent, common man using unpretentious moral wisdom to defeat the scheming professional politicians. I don't think we really understood the line from the show's theme song, "He patched up the crack in the Liberty Bell," as a metaphor for fixing the government, but that was certainly what we were seeing on the screen. Not satisfied with merely teaching us about good government, though, Davy makes an even greater leap. Dying in battle against the Mexicans at the Alamo, he achieves immortality as a martyr spreading democracy in the same way that so many martyrs had given their lives bringing the Catholic faith to the heathens. Davy Crockett, in the mind of a young boy, was a secular saint.

But other, more complicated strands are also woven into the Davy Crockett story, especially that battle at the Alamo. Davy and his band, heavily armed, rode into a foreign country and fought against its troops, soldiers who were merely trying to protect their homeland from the historical equivalent of terrorists. Think about it.

It occurs to me that should this be read in Texas or Tennessee, I might find myself in big trouble. But surely William Travis, Jim Bowie, and Crockett and the ragtag bands that traveled to Mexico expressly to rip it apart must have provided my generation with a mythology that explained why going off to kill Vietnamese in their own land was a good and glorious thing to do. And it raises serious questions about just why we're now so shocked that outsiders seek to come to the United States and wreak havoc for political purposes. It may not have been entirely coincidental that it was a Texan, Lyndon Johnson, who chose to make a stand in Vietnam, and who urged the troops there to "nail the coonskin to the wall" (Beschloss, 2001).

I realize now, looking back with the clarity of hindsight, that in my young mind fighting, serving, and dying were all bundled into the same neat package, and I can see that my religion was as much about the cowboy way as it was about theology. Rugged frontiersmen were America's martyrs, bringing peace, justice, and the American way to an untamed continent. I never really separated these themes out from one another as they intertwined themselves in my psyche and my soul.

Figure 1.3.   Davy Crockett at the Alamo. *The Fall of the Alamo* **by Robert Jenkins Onderdonk depicts Davy Crockett swinging his rifle at Mexican troops who have breached the south gate of the mission. Robert Jenkins Onderdonk.** *Transferred from en.wikipedia, original is at the Texas State Archives; A Glimpse of History in Modern San Antonio*

When the nuns did direct our attention to what was happening in the world around us, what we learned usually had in some way or another to do with the evils of communism and the heroism of Catholics struggling against it. They taught us about Cardinal József Mindszenty, imprisoned and tortured in Hungary and then holing up in the US embassy in internal exile. About Dr. Tom Dooley, providing medical care and resisting communism in Southeast Asia. And an endless flow of magazine stories about Maryknoll priests dying in China as they struggled to minister to Catholics after the revolution. As we grew aware of it, contemporary history was almost as much about modern-day martyrs as it was about anything else; it's no surprise that they became our role models.

WHY SO MANY DIDN'T FIGHT

It's easy to imagine a neat, straight line linking all those cowboy and war movies to our willingness to fight in Vietnam, but the reality is vastly more complex. Most men of my generation never served in the military, and of those who did, most didn't go to Vietnam. The exact figures aren't crucial here, but a reliable set of numbers reports that between 1964 and 1975, 27 million of us were of the right age for the draft. About 2.2 million were drafted, while 8.7 million more or less voluntarily signed up for service. About 11 million of the 27 million eligible, roughly 40%, were in the military during the Vietnam era. About 3.4 million served in Southeast Asia, that is, 31% of those in the military, and about 12% of the total pool (Baskir and Strauss, 1978, p. 5).[7]

A great many of the nearly nine million of us who volunteered did so because we knew the draft would eventually catch up with us, and that by enlisting we'd have a better chance of choosing the kinds of duty we'd be assigned. I find myself fascinated both by the large numbers of us who thought going to war was acceptable, or even a good thing, and by the even greater numbers of our generation who avoided going to war. The real minority, it's clear, were those who actually got drafted. It's easy to point to convenient cultural explanations for our aggressiveness, but I'm not sure how much they really explain.

In trying to understand just what those cultural influences on me were, I've gone back and watched some of the shows and movies on TV, on disks, and online and I am astonished by what I've seen. A lot of these follow fairly complex story lines. Characters are often conflicted about the choices they must make. War and violence are often portrayed as brutal and stupid. This is not at all how I remember viewing them as a boy, when what *I* saw were stirring accounts of brave soldiers and sailors and fliers prevailing against terrible odds or dying gloriously in the name of fighting for the right.

Let me give you one memorable example from my own experience, an episode on the *General Electric Theater* television series in 1960. I've never seen it again, but the story remains etched in my mind all these many decades later. When I recall how I understood it as a boy and compare this with what I now see when I reflect on it, it's almost like two different stories. Sammy Davis, Jr. (an accomplished African American actor and singer), plays the title character, "The Patsy," that is, a soldier who is the butt of jokes, who is taken advantage of, and is mercilessly hazed by the rest of his platoon. It's a peacetime drama, set during routine training exercises. One of the troops tosses a practice (dud) hand grenade among his squad, pretending that it's an accident and that it's live. Everyone but Davis is in on the joke. Davis, believing that it's about to explode, acts spontaneously to save the others. He throws himself on top of it, clasps it to his belly, and yells for everyone to run. He gains some respect for this selfless act.[8]

What I recall understanding from this story as a 13-year-old boy was how wonderful it was to be brave and selfless and ready to sacrifice your own life for the good of the platoon. All noble sentiments, to be sure. The fact that I still remember the episode so well 60 years later says a lot about its impact on me. Not only do I remember the title and the starring actor, but the image of Davis lying doubled-up on the ground screaming, "Run, y'all, run!" is seared into me. As I summon the episode to mind now, though, to retell the story, I find myself contemplating a whole series of other things that I might have reflected on had I been an adult watching it.

First and most obviously, the callous racism. The mean-spiritedness with which soldiers are prone to treat those they don't like for one reason or another. The stupidity of some. The frequency with which troops are injured and killed during routine training. The dangers of what is called "friendly fire." And the compromised value system of military life, where the deadliness of everyday dangers is ignored, diminished, or derided. Within this framework, the simple act of heroism is even more remarkable, I suppose, but it's also the act of just one man, as opposed to the thoughtless cruelty of all the others. As an adult I understand the lessons to be learned here in ways that run entirely contrary to the way I viewed them as a boy.

As I now understand all this, we see an issue here as old as time, or at least as old as Homer's *Iliad*. Storytellers usually mean to accomplish several things. They want to draw and hold people's attention—they are performers. But they also hope to impart lessons about things people in the community care about. Stories differ in their complexity; storytellers differ in their desires to convey complex messages and in their abilities to do so effectively. But there's got to be a *story* in the dramatic sense of the term—that is, conflict, excitement, tragedy, or glory—if the audience is going to pay attention. But as in any sort of human communication, the message the speaker thinks he or she is conveying is not at all necessarily the message that listeners will hear or comprehend.

I struggled through a lot of old films to gain this understanding, but according to film critic Adam Nayman the French film director Francois Truffaut said in 1973 that he'd never "really seen an anti-war film . . . every film about war ends up being pro-war." That is, "even the most skillful and poetic attempts to use the medium as a form of protest become weaponized against themselves" (Nayman, 2020).

And so it is that young boys are likely to notice little in a story beyond the clash of swords or the flash of gunfire, and to identify not with the emotional or moral conflict that is tearing a beautiful soul apart, but with the thrill of a cavalry charge. It's not that these stories don't explore death and the brutality of war—they do—but that that's not what the boys come away with. In simple terms, I can tell you what I remember from a great many movies I watched as a boy, and nearly all of it is about glory and manhood and the way one establishes one's manhood by achieving glory.

And it wasn't just the movies. We lived with an endless stream of gallant Americans fighting the good fight, including the newspaper comic strips *Terry and the Pirates* and *Steve Canyon*, and comic books like *Blackhawk* (with its United Nations–worthy cast of characters) and *Sgt. Rock*. I vividly recall images from all of these.

In what I think is one of the finest books about the Vietnam experience, *Born on the Fourth of July*, Ron Kovic shows himself as a boy returning home from watching the World War II classic *To Hell and Back*, reenacting it first with toy soldiers in his yard, and then again a decade later during a firefight in a South Vietnamese village. The example is one I identify with entirely, and it's easy to assume that what he portrays is shared by all the boys of our generation. But it's simply not true. No matter how many of us did reenact those battle scenes at home with our friends and toys, most outgrew that childish stage. The guys who resisted the draft watched the same shows and played the same games; that's what boys did then. But as they passed through late adolescence and into young adulthood their understandings of war and violence evolved.

The point I'm trying to make here is that even though I can show you what happened to me and many others, and how it happened, it's difficult to say why it happened to *us* and not to millions of others of my generation. The fact is that the culture we grew up in wasn't simple. A line from Immanuel Kant tells us that nothing straight was ever fashioned from the crooked timber of humanity (1991). For all we had in common growing up in the fifties and early sixties, we followed some startlingly different paths as we grew. Some fought eagerly, some fought reluctantly, some found ways to avoid the war, and some actively resisted it.

HOLLYWOOD, THE WAR, AND THE MILITARY

Standing out among all these stories is an especially thrilling image I have of Van Johnson as pilot of the Ruptured Duck, one of the B-25 bombers launched from the aircraft carrier *Hornet* early in 1942 to bomb Tokyo. I first saw *Thirty Seconds Over Tokyo* as a boy of 7 or 8 years old. I know little about the art of moviemaking, but I know that the drama of the scenes building up to the takeoff from the *Hornet* had a huge impact on me. Bombers of that size were never meant to fly from the heaving deck of a carrier, and no one was sure they'd succeed. I can still feel the tension rise as the engines are pushed to full power and the pilots salute, and then the awful suspense as we waited to see whether the planes get airborne or crash into the sea.

There's another piece of the story as well, though, that gives that movie special resonance for me. After the squadron finishes attacking Japan, the planes, desperately low on fuel, crash along the China coast. The flyers must evade Japanese troops. Some do and are saved by kindly Chinese. Some don't and are executed. Years later, when I went through prisoner of war (POW) training before shipping out to Vietnam, and then later when my plane flew into Red China, those scenes from the film came echoing back.

I'd grown up with a very clear notion of what would happen if I were shot down and captured, one that was underscored by the many POW films I watched, like *Stalag 17*, *Bridge on the River Kwai*, and *The Great Escape*.

Almost everything about those films and TV shows had an impact on me. Hollywood and the Pentagon teamed up, combining their skills to embed air power into our daily lives. James Stewart, one of America's most beloved stars, was a World War II pilot whose experiences were grist for the mill. In 1955's *Strategic Air Command* he's a ballplayer who sacrifices his career to return to flying nuclear weapon-laden bombers. Like so many other films about the armed forces in those years (and in war stories in general, for that matter), a crucial plot line has to do with conflicting pulls between love and duty, as flyers are torn from their families to meet the goal of having bombers constantly in the air, ready to strike Russia on a moment's notice. *Bombers B-52* celebrates not only duty and love but also the newest and most powerful of the heavy bombers itself.

The love interest, it was said, was to draw women into the movie theaters, but what the young boys who absorbed them were learning was the imperative of putting everything—wives, children, and even baseball—aside in order to defend the country. That's not why we boys went to see these films— we went to see jet planes and bombs and explosions and dramatic cockpit scenes and crash landings—but always the subliminal message was there. In the ancient tension between love and duty, red-blooded American men were expected to put their responsibilities as warriors charged with defending their country, and thus their families, first. [9]

Not to be outdone, the Navy matched the Army and Air Force films on the big screen with *They Were Expendable* (PT boats), *Away All Boats* (an attack transport) or *The Bridges at Toko-ri* (carrier pilots in the Korean War). *Run Silent, Run Deep* and *Destination Tokyo*, among a dozen others, featured nearly identical sequences of submarine captains lining up torpedo shots through their periscopes and then ordering their crews to "Rig for depth charges." Kill or be killed was clearly the message. The endless streams of gunfighters on the screen were matched by endless streams of war stories, but the real point is that my generation's childhood was immersed in what seemed to us like variants of the same of story, violent struggles between right and wrong or good and evil, with the good guys always prevailing. All the stories focused on bravery and morality, and sometimes dealt with them simplistically; in my mind stories about cowboys and soldiers were inextricably linked to one another, if they weren't essentially the same thing.

There's more, though. "The Patsy" was hardly alone in its challenging portrayal of the military. *The Caine Mutiny*, which won a Pulitzer Prize as a novel and then an Academy Award for Humphrey Bogart as a film, gave me a broader sense of just how brutally arbitrary the military could be, and of its leaders' frequent failures to exemplify the best traditions of the service. But it was *Mr. Roberts* that loomed largest in my imagination. It explored the boredom that makes up such a large part of warfare, the restlessness and distrust that beset the troops, and the antagonism between the captain, as the face of authority, and his crew. It did it so well that it, too, went from novel to Tony Award-winning play to popular film. Like *The Caine Mutiny* and *From Here to Eternity*, another classic, it placed front and center the pettiness that characterized so much of military life. In his book *Wartime*, Paul Fussell (1990) described the military's propensity for "chickenshit" to a T, but I can now see that I was aware of it long before I experienced it firsthand.

By the time I actually joined up, my expectations were already jaundiced. Although I wanted to do something heroic, I understood that the military wasn't entirely, or maybe even mostly, heroic—that it was at least as much about putting up with absurdity and uncalled-for cruelty as it was about doing anything glorious. My real exposure to what the military—rather than war—was like came from one of television's classic situation comedies, *Sgt. Bilko*, known also as the *The Phil Silvers Show*.

Bilko is said to have been the most popular comedy on the TV in the late 1950s, and it undoubtedly shaped the outlooks of most of us who served in Vietnam. It still occupies a sizeable piece of my memory, and even today I can walk you through the basic premises of a half-dozen episodes. It was set in the motor pool at imaginary Fort Baxter in rural Kansas, but we understood that its stories were about the peacetime military as a whole, and the Army we were expecting to be drafted into. My own favorite episode told the story of Private Harry Speakup ("Hurry, speak up!"), who makes it through the entire Army induction process without anyone noticing that he's a chimpanzee. I could offer some wry commentary on what this was meant to say about the military bureaucracy's clumsiness, but I think I'll let it speak for itself.[10]

This humor proved strikingly successful and TV producers were soon cranking out a steady flow of wartime and military comedy series in its wake, including *McHale's Navy*, *F Troop*, *Ensign O'Toole*, and *Gomer Pyle U.S.M.C.* One of these, *Hogan's Heroes*, had the distinction of both softening the travails of a prisoner of war camp *and* making Germans the butt of most of the jokes, even before Mel Brooks brought the Nazi-lampooning genre to its pinnacle in his 1967 film *The Producers*.

Bilko's army didn't spring out of nowhere, of course. Satirical accounts of our fighting forces have been around for a long time. Bill Mauldin's celebrated Willie and Joe cartoons, drawn for the Army's *Stars and Stripes* newspaper in Europe during World War II, featured two long-suffering infantrymen. They commented sardonically on how bad conditions were—mostly about their officers and the army as a whole, not about combat itself. Their sense of the military's inherent incompetence ran squarely against the grain of most visions of the war we'd been exposed to, paving the way for *Bilko* and then *Catch-22*.

As kids, we read Mauldin's successors, the *Beetle Bailey* and *Sad Sack* comics. I recall watching a long string of shows at Saturday matinees, movies like *Don't Go Near the Water*, *The Wackiest Ship in the Army*, *No Time for Sergeants*, three less than memorable slapstick films about soldiers, sailors, and paratroopers starring Dean Martin and Jerry Lewis, and a whole series of absurd flicks about *Francis, the Talking Mule*, and these are just ones *I* remember seeing as a boy. They captured the ongoing transition from fighting a war to surviving in the peacetime military. I suspect that as the chances for conspicuous gallantry in the face of the enemy grew fewer, there was a deliberate attempt to make the armed forces seem attractive by painting them as a fun destination (a ploy that was explicitly spelled out in the 1980s film *Private Benjamin*, which featured Goldie Hawn enlisting in the belief that she's signing up for something a lot like Club Med).

The pinnacle of the collusion (and there was a lot of it) between the Pentagon and the motion picture industry in the business of making money by making the peacetime military attractive came for me when at age 14 I saw Elvis Presley's *GI Blues*. I don't know that the Army has ever looked quite so glamorous or appealing as it did there in occupied Germany. Those soldiers thought at least as much about sex as about war and the greatest lover among them (played by Elvis, of course) is the guy who wins a very large bet by successfully courting a famously unattainable female; he's sexy, honorable, talented, and mans a tank.

And then, arising out of all this farce and the military equivalent of horse operas, the black humor of Joseph Heller's *Catch-22* struck (1961). It managed to convey the honor, the horror, and the absurdity all at once. In it, I read about men who were heroic not only in battle, but in their unrelenting hostility to military leadership. They were, for me, existential heroes, and they did more than anything else to shape my own relationships with the military.

Catch-22's sardonic perspective on war wasn't entirely new but it was different. Its storyline turns in part on the death of a B-25 gunner in the arms of Yossarian, its bombardier, and the ways this shapes Yossarian's grasp of his place in the war. But it also serves as the last straw in Yossarian's deteriorating relationship with the Army Air Force in Italy. Most of the book shows us, through Yossarian's eyes, just exactly how absurd, loathsome, and stupid the military can be.

Catch-22 is much more about the military than it is about the war. In later years Heller (1998) repeatedly insisted that he was commenting on American society in the 1950s, not on World War II, and that's one of the things that gives it so much power. It is also a big part of why the tale had so much influence on me. *Mad Magazine* had already introduced us to the systematic poking of holes in authority figures. *Bilko* and others had paved the way for us to understand how inane life in the military could be. And so when I stumbled across *Catch-22* on a drugstore paperback rack in Santa Barbara, I dove into it. But it was the intersection of the violence and the gunner's gory death with all this absurdity that gave the book its path-breaking character and worked impossibly bizarre magic on me.

Catch-22 was hardly alone. Although its deeply subversive viewpoint seems to have had a much greater impact on me, looking back I can see its place in the spectrum of war stories popular enough to have gone from novels to plays and then film, all demonstrating the chord they struck in postwar America. They all shaped my perspectives on the military, and especially on the Navy. Both *Mr. Roberts* and *The Caine Mutiny* emphasized the mindless and often unnecessary discipline and command authority on ships in the western Pacific. Both made heroes out of those who resisted their captains' abuses. I joined the service having already grasped the elemental premise that the brass would act arbitrarily and foolishly and that the men faced double duty: they both fought the war and resisted their own leaders. When I reflect on it now, I can see how I came to believe that pushing back against leadership is a fundamental part of fighting the good fight.

I can see, too, that *Catch-22* was in fact just one of many rebellious and absurd takes on contemporary American society that influenced me during my teens, starting with *The Catcher in the Rye* (Salinger, 1951), which played a big part in my decision to run away, and soon followed by Jack Kerouac's *On the Road* (1957), Nikos Kazantzakis's *Zorba the Greek* (1953), and then the tidal wave of Bob Dylan's music.

Catch-22, more than any of the others, though, sparked the transformation. It got to the heart of what rebellious young men like me were rebelling against, but at the same time it conjured up an image of the topsy-turvy heroism that seemed to characterize men like Yossarian, flying missions despite their bitter antagonism toward the ways the military treated them. Something in this web of contradictions seized hold of me. I spotted a way to be heroic and to rebel at the same time. This sounds contradictory, I know, but everything that followed for me in the next few years erupted from that crucible.

I enlisted in the Navy just weeks after reading *Catch-22*, taking with me a set of attitudes that were simultaneously gung ho and ironic, motivated and detached, heroic and skeptical. People often find this hard to understand, and I need to think out loud for a moment about what happened to me when I read *Catch-22*, and about what it triggered in me.

I had a decent job with the telephone company in Santa Barbara, but I was stuck in the shop, and without a license to drive a truck I was going to stay there. I was ready to move. I'd escaped from home and gained my freedom to grow, but now I was spinning my wheels. In some ways, the military was an obvious choice, and in others it was odd. As I listened to older guys on the assembly line swapping tales of their time in the service, what I heard pretty much affirmed what I'd already figured out. Although the military was characterized by authoritarian nonsense, it also provided opportunities to travel and gain exotic life experiences not readily available anywhere else. There wasn't much glory to be earned during peacetime, but if I played my cards right, I could get training that would advance me quickly when I returned to my job at the phone company after I was discharged. What I had to gauge— and again, I'm struck by how well my native wit made the decision—was the degree to which enlisting would allow me the freedom I wanted to keep on moving versus the discipline that would place me back under a brutal thumb much like my father's. Thinking about it now, I see that *Catch-22* showed me just how I could achieve a tolerable, livable balance.

FATHERS AND SONS

When I was 5 or 6 my mother gave my father binoculars for his birthday. Our family's precarious budget made this a big deal, which is partly why I remember it, but I also recall her telling him they were for birdwatching. I understood early on that my dad, who'd worked with the forest service before he married, held onto his interest in nature. When I was ten or so, I asked him about an unfamiliar bird I'd spotted while delivering my newspapers. It was a mountain bluebird, he explained, not often seen where we lived. My mother said something about me taking after my dad, and in the context of my family's starved emotional economy, I heard this as approval. I began paying more attention to birds, and within a year or two, certainly by the time I was in eighth grade, I'd become a birdwatcher. It turned out to be a dangerous choice.

It's easy to see how I began following in my father's footsteps, but it's taken a lot of introspection to understand how this wound up leading me into treacherous territory. If I had simply watched birds with my father, I suspect, it wouldn't have been such a problem. But I'd stumbled onto the first terrain where I could I really pour my heart and soul into exceling and mastery. I had zero talent for the pursuits most boys engaged in, but as a budding naturalist I began at last to thrive.

I joined the Audubon Society, the birdwatchers' national organization, and along with closely studying their monthly magazine I began subscribing to technical ornithology publications. I started hanging out with the rangers at Oakland's natural science center on Lake Merritt and at Audubon's nature center in Berkeley. Getting to both places entailed long trips, either on my bike or the bus; obviously, I was working hard at this. It wasn't long before I could tell a bluebird from a bunting, a swallow from a swift, and distinguish among the seemingly infinite varieties of sandpipers and plovers.

Building all those model airplanes a few years earlier, it turns out, helped me spot crucial differences among birds. The B-24 and the B-25 bombers, after all, had similar high wings and twin vertical stabilizers; I had to learn to count their engines. The Cougar and the Panther were essentially the same aircraft with distinctly different wings. Though the PBY and the PBM looked alike, the PBM was much larger.

Soon I was making the transition from birdwatcher to "birder," going on Audubon fieldtrips, and participating in their Christmas bird-counts. One of the Audubon leaders told my parents, when I was no more than 14 or 15, that I wasn't just a birdwatcher, I was a "student of ornithology." And there's the rub. At 15 or so, I was on the brink of surpassing my father at his avocation. This was not a good thing to do, not with my father.

There were many reasons why the tensions between my father and me grew to a boiling point, and birding was just one of them, but it captures the conflict very clearly. I wanted to be like my father, but because I had so much ambition and drive, I wasn't going to be satisfied with merely being like him; I was driven to surpass him. And because I was keen and intelligent, I'd found something that would allow me to surpass him while I was still young. He was defensive about having only a tenth-grade education. This meant he was growing uncomfortable with me; I recall making a joke once, something that he took exception to, and it provoked him. He snarled at me, saying he didn't "have to take any crap from a snot-nosed kid." The conflict was beginning to surface.

I'd never been athletic and lacked the hand-eye coordination called for in basketball and baseball. I tried tackle football and boxing, but quickly figured out that getting knocked down wasn't much fun. I took guitar lessons but lacked musical talent. I was too young to have a conscious plan, but I can see how it worked. In taking up birding I was emulating my father, doing well, and reaping praise from the experts. Birding was hardly a way to impress girls, of course, and it generated mild ridicule from the other guys, so I wisely refrained from broadcasting what I was doing. But still, it gave me my first good shot at what I think of as sort of a natural progression: We find something we like, and if we're able to do well at it, we get the pleasure that comes from performing well and impressing others with our skill. The more we work at it the better we become, and the more we impress others. Unfortunately, I was getting good at something that wasn't impressing anyone my own age but *was* pissing my father off. I was, let's face it, a nerd, but I was also rebellious and drifting toward defiance. The hole I was digging myself grew deeper and deeper.

The more I became like my father, and the better I got at it, the farther we grew apart. The strife ratcheted up. By the time I ran away, I wanted to kill the man that I also wanted to be. There, I've said it. It's hard to make sense of, but it's true. It's the only way I know to explain the intensity of the emotions that led me to run away. In my own mind, I had to choose among withering away, killing my father, or leaving.

Like a lot of what happened in the war itself, my relationship with my father was stained by so much fear that it's hard for me to see it with any sort of clarity. I think of it as a black hole that absorbs all the surrounding light. Or maybe it's like the sun—it's so intense that you can't look directly at it. At any rate, I know a lot about my fear of my father, from a variety of sources, but even after all these years I can't see it directly, only its roughest outlines. In the last couple of years before I ran away, I often imagined my parents dead, and after I left I always said my parents had been killed.

I trembled with fear each night when my father came home. My cousins now tell me that he *was* terrifying—that they were terrified of him. One told me her mother, my aunt, said when I ran away that my father got just what he deserved for the way he treated me. And he knew how I felt: I remember him telling me to wipe the look off my face, the glare, that is, that must have conveyed hatred. It's difficult for me to say with complete conviction that I wanted to kill him, because to have clearly and consciously conceptualized it that way at the time would have been too frightening and too morally challenging. But that doesn't mean that the underlying feeling wasn't there.

I had a premonition of all this when I was ten or so, standing on the back porch after dumping the kitchen garbage into the big trash barrel, following a scolding for having failed to do the task without being reminded. I was pondering my existence and my fate when I suddenly understood the problem: My father did not see me as a separate and autonomous individual. Instead, I was to him nothing more than an extension of himself.

I recognize this now. My father's father died in the world influenza epidemic of 1918, when my father was a boy, and he grew up without a father. He'd had no experience of needing to separate himself from his father. And so as I entered my teens, he blindly stifled my drive to become my own person. There was no space in our home for me to grow, to expand, to become something new and different. The night I ran away, my father had just grounded me—restricted me to my room—for 6 months. If he found me trying to sneak out, he said, he'd lock me in. I'd seen this coming and had already practiced climbing out the window on a rope, so I was hardly surprised. (Our house was built on a steep slope; my room was down below the rest of the house, but there was still a 12-foot drop beneath the window.) My dad was a man of his word and the next step in our clash of wills would have had him chaining me to my bed. In that last confrontation the die was cast.

In the months after I ran away, I didn't simply find a job. Within weeks I got a promotion, and then sought out a different and much more demanding job. When I saw my progress stopped, I joined the Navy as a way of opening new avenues for myself. And in boot camp I was appointed a regimental commander and led the entire brigade in the parades. My father had nothing to say when he learned about this, but I'm guessing that he was choking on his rage rather than swelling with pride. I liken myself to a seed sprouting: when I hit the light, I grew rapidly, and then burst into bloom. Had I not left when I did and let off the head of steam that was building, to mix metaphors horribly, there would have been some sort of tragic explosion.

We often hear that it's the old men who start wars while the young men are sent to fight them. I've spent far too much time, though, living among Pacific islanders who think Americans are barbarians for sending their children—their "babies"—to war. For them, war is properly the business of mature men. To some extent, I suppose, it's the lifetime I've spent as an anthropologist that makes me believe that war as we know it in the United States reflects our culture at least as much as it does human nature. This is why I see a great deal of what happened with the Vietnam War through the perspective of deeply strained father-son relationships. I'm not suggesting that it was deliberate or malicious, but the men who fought World War II impressed upon their sons a skewed version, and in some ways a myth, of their own experience. Some of us went to war because that's what our fathers did and because we wanted to emulate them. Some went to war because our fathers told us that we had to, in order to live up to their expectations. Some of us refused to go to war in order to spite our fathers, to assert our independence and individuality. Some fathers advised their sons to avoid the war. And some of us loudly resisted the war, telling our leaders they were wrong in steering us into it.

Though my relationship with my father played a huge role in the choices I made during the Vietnam era, there was nothing straightforward about it. As an anthropologist, I know that relations between sons and fathers (and older male authority figures in general) are problematic in the human species. Fathers try to pass on to their sons a certain amount of competitive spirit as a means of helping them survive, but when the son's competitive drive and abilities thrive, father and son may well find themselves competing against each other. Some dads deal with this with grace, or even pride, while it threatens and sometimes overwhelms others.

AND THEN THERE WAS THE MUSIC

Music was a building-block of the culture I grew up in, especially as it began to change so starkly in the 1960s. The music I listened to says a lot about what was on my mind during those years, and it seems like it played a big part in pointing out the paths I would take. One of the themes that grew out of young men's experiences in the Depression years of the 1930s and went on to become a pattern for us to emulate in the 1950s and '60s was "moving on." There were scores of songs about rambling and I listened to them all. When I hear Kingston Trio recordings from those days I'm stuck by just how pervasive that theme was in their music, but they weren't the only ones. One song in particular, sung by Bud and Travis, "Joey, Joey, Joey," from a Broadway musical of all places, captured my spirit with the lines, "You've been too long in one place, / And it's time to go, time to go!" I listened to this again and again during my Santa Barbara days, and it was this refrain as much as anything else that moved me to join the Navy.

I'd always been drawn to whatever it is that we call "folk music." From the moment I heard the Kingston Trio's first radio hit, "Tom Dooley," I was hooked. I gravitated to the soulful sound of Joan Baez, Bob Dylan, and Judy Collins, to the topical commentaries of Phil Ochs and Tom Paxton, and to the soaring harmonies of Peter, Paul, and Mary, Bud and Travis, and Ian and Sylvia, on the one hand, and on the other, to the gravity of old-timers like Leadbelly, Sonny Terry and Brownie McGee, a host of bluesmen, and the wonders of bluegrass. Two of my life's trajectories in those years flowed out of my immersion in that music.

One of these is simple. My sympathy for underdogs, for relentless pursuit of social justice and equality, and my political outlook in general are all rooted in the messages this music bears. The other track isn't at all simple, though, and I've long puzzled over it.

It has to do with ways that contradictions in my own mind mirrored some of those in the music. The impact folk music and the sixties folk scene—what Dave Van Ronk (2005) liked to call the "folk scare"—had on me are obvious, but for a long time I thought these contradictions would drive me mad.[11] What had seemed to me a sort of homogenous scene in the 1960s, it turns out, was really riddled with discord. From all these many decades away, it's easy to suppose that the music moved seamlessly from pop renditions of traditional styles toward the more traditional forms themselves (a contrast known at the time as urban versus ethnic), then into protest music, and finally on to full-throated antiwar ballads.[12] I've made myself crazy over the years, asking repeatedly how it was possible that someone as thoroughly immersed as I was in the folk scene and its general mindset could have gone off so readily to war. It may not seem like a big deal to you, but for me it's been an unrelenting component of my guilt, my sense that *I should have known better.*

I have at last found an answer to this question, and it lies in the ways in which the things we were singing about evolved during the time I was in the Navy. In the early sixties, in the years before I enlisted, folk music hailed both peace *and* fighting the good fight. One of the songs that most stirred my soul is Peter, Paul, and Mary's rendition of "Rising of the Moon," just one of dozens of tunes celebrating the long Irish struggle for independence. There were songs of the Spanish Civil War and of fighting fascism in World War II, and Woody Guthrie painted "This machine kills Fascists" on his guitar. The fight for justice was a central theme in those songs, and oddly overlapped with all the cowboy and war movies we watched so avidly, the ones urging us to fight the good fight. And Pete Seeger, of course, sang "If I Had a Hammer" about fighting for justice and freedom.

There were plenty of songs about peace and pacifism, too, like Pete's "Where Have All the Flowers Gone" and Dylan's "Blowin' in the Wind" (both covered by hundreds of performers). But they were directed at over-arching concerns about nuclear weapons and mass destruction rather than fighting guerillas in the jungle.

For me, this contradiction is sharply etched in a story Todd Gitlin tells of going to watch *Casablanca* with his college friends at the start of the sixties. *Casablanca*, a war movie with virtually no fighting in it, made opposing the Nazis both glorious and glamorous. Gitlin tells of watching the film with his "peace group—anti-atom bomb, anti-cold war" and how loudly they cheered when one of the heroes praises the other: "You fought against the Fascists in Spain" (Harmetz, 2002, p. 344).

When I first read this passage, and I read it because *Casablanca* has more dialogue that stirs me than just about any other film I can think of, I was immediately struck by what seemed like a glaring contradiction, peaceniks celebrating someone going to war. Gitlin has told me in conversation that this contradiction is not so readily apparent to him. In my struggles to understand how someone as attached as I was to folk music and its message of peace could march off so willingly to war, I continually confronted quandaries in the opposition between peace and war. But here is one of my generation's intellectual leaders with his peace group cheering the fight against fascism.

In the early '60s, *fighting* for peace and justice wasn't simply okay—it was an imperative. As odd as it sounds now, peace didn't necessarily mean an absence of war. It could also mean fighting the right war—that is, fighting the good fight. This wasn't really out of synch with all those cowboy movies we were watching. Not until the Vietnam War exploded onto the scene in 1965 and had become nearly synonymous with widespread killing of civilians, did "peace" come to mean opposing war in general. When I finally grasped that this radical shift in the meaning of "peace" had taken place after I was already involved in fighting the war, I was at last able to comprehend why I'd been so willing to fight, despite my attachment to all the values of folk.

This may not sound like a big deal, but the guilt I've shouldered for having fought in the war has made it a major philosophical puzzle for me: Given my immersion in folk, how could I not have known better than to go to war? In this light, though, it makes complete sense. I was full of *thumos*, the impulse to fight the good fight.

In *Dylan Goes Electric*, Elijah Wald (2015) writes of the pivotal moment at the 1965 Newport Folk Festival when Bob Dylan pulled away from the role in which he had established himself, as a solo acoustic troubadour singing commentaries like "Blowing in the Wind" and "The Times They Are a'Changin'." Dylan picked up an electric guitar and a blues band to jump start what would soon become a new genre of rock music. Wald points to a clash between twin streams in the folk scene that mirror many of the contradictions in my own consciousness. There was, on the one hand, the thread that honored traditional music forms and musicians. On the other, there were the angry cries of protest. The first emphasized continuity and community, while the second celebrated individualism, rebellion, and nonconformity. They managed to coexist for quite a while, but as youth culture made its radical shift in the mid-'60s, the tensions between them grew, and Dylan's first electric performance served as a flashpoint.

I might well have been there at Newport if I hadn't already been a year into my Navy hitch. As it was, these diverging themes had already rooted themselves in my own psyche. I began adding a new layer of complexity into my life, building on the contradictions that had attracted me to Yossarian, and then urging me forward. Zorba the Greek, the deeply thoughtful and wildly independent protagonist of the film named for him, released in 1964, soon joined Yossarian in my pantheon of heroes. And then in a bookstore in San Diego, where I was stationed, I stumbled across Jack Kerouac's recently published book about Big Sur, one of my favorite places on the face of the earth. We'd camped there when I was very young and I recalled it as time spent in Eden.

Today, Kerouac is treated as a cliché when it comes to young men in the sixties, but I'd never heard of him when I first picked up that book—I'd already entered the cloistered barracks, where the Beats were barely known. I soon made my way through Kerouac's *On the Road* and *Dharma Bums*, spilling volatile fuel onto the embers I'd banked when I left Santa Barbara. When I finally left the Navy, my consciousness nearly exploded, partly because all this had been incubating inside me, and the threads of folk and rock, the music that made the journey with me during those years, would play a huge part in hurtling me through those changes at flank speed.

NOTES

1. I've described these joys as well as some of the practical lessons I learned living there in Santa Barbara in "When Santa Barbara Was My Paris" (Petersen, 2013).

2. I discuss the Tonkin Gulf Incident's contexts, repercussions, and ramifications in Chapter 9.

3. Several companies manufactured these plastic airplane model kits, but Revell was very much the most popular on the West Coast when I was growing up. These kits were created specifically for the generation of boys who grew up in the early postwar years; they literally grew with us. Two of Revell's first issues were the Navy's Cougar and Cutlass fighters, planes I quite explicitly recall building. Revell's series represent a triumph of marketing as well as of design and execution. One set of three ships sold together—an aircraft carrier, a destroyer, and a patrol torpedo (PT) boat—were billed on the box cover "As inspired by NBC's award-winning series 'Victory at Sea.'" Another set celebrated the introduction of the Navy's entries into the rocket age; this was the "Guided Missile Fleet." This set's box featured the logo from a second TV series, *Navy Log* on CBS, and included a cruiser, a submarine, and a seaplane tender converted into a missile-launching platform. The Navy actively aided production of these models as part of its efforts to obtain and hold onto a vital role as the military was shifting to missile technology and nuclear weaponry. A detailed, and exceptionally well-illustrated, history of Revell's models is *Remembering Revell Model Kits* (Graham, 2008).

4. Alex Wellerstein, a historian of science at Stevens Institute of Technology, has a web site devoted to the history of the US government's "Duck and Cover" campaign. It includes the 1951 animated cartoon produced to teach schoolchildren how to cower beneath their desks during air raid drills. http://blog.nuclearsecrecy.com/2012/12/21/duck-and-cover-all-over-again/.

5. Ariel Dorfman (2018) wrote a celebrated critique of *Donald Duck* comics and the American imperialism they seemed to endorse. I don't mean to challenge this analysis, only to say that for my part I gained a certain critical perspective on American society and culture from reading about miserly Uncle Scrooge.

6. *Maverick*, James Garner (the actor who portrayed him) wrote in his autobiography, "just believes in self-preservation. His attitude is, why risk your life over something trivial, like money? Or 'honor'?" "Maverick," he says, "is often portrayed as an anti-hero, but I don't think that's true. I'd call him a *reluctant* hero" (Garner, 2011, p. 55).

7. George Flynn's book *The Draft, 1940–1973* (1993) provides the most comprehensive look at military conscription during the World War II and Vietnam eras. *Chance and Circumstance* by Baskir and Strauss (1978) is a classic examination of the draft during Vietnam War. Wikipedia's entry on "Conscription in the United States" also provides detailed figures.

8. The IMDb website provides an overview of this episode: https://www.imdb.com/title/tt0586346/.

9. Many books have been written about the close ties between moviemakers and the US military, including Lawrence Suid's *Sailing on the Silver Screen* (1996) and *Stars and Stripes on the Screen* (2005). These explore both the technical aspects, which require the military's cooperation, and the propaganda themes, which are necessary to get the military's cooperation.Wikipedia has a lengthy list of war films, broken down by country and era: https://en.wikipedia.org/wiki/List_of_war_films_and_TV_specials#Cold_War_(1945%E2%80%931991).

10. Video clips of this Bilko episode are occasionally available on YouTube, but the complete script can be found at https://www.philsilversshow.com/best-show.

11. *Folk Scare*, for those who don't recognize it, is a play on what was known in those days as the "red scare," the fear that communists and the Soviet Union would at any moment act to destroy our way of life. And to this day, when "America the Beautiful" is played during the seventh inning stretch at Yankees games, the announcer tells us we're celebrating our troops abroad who are defending "our way of life."

12. Many writers have tackled the interrelationships among the '60s generation, its music, and the Vietnam War, including Andresen's *Battle Notes* (2003), Bradley and Werner's *We Gotta Get Out of This Place* (2015), Bradley's *Who'll Stop the Rain* (2019), and Kramer's *The Republic of Rock* (2017).

Chapter Two

Becoming a Warrior

BOOT CAMP

I was just days past my 17th birthday when I marched into the Navy's Recruit Training Center—boot camp—in San Diego. It was the spring of 1964. Within a few weeks I was learning to lead the parades there, and I have absolute recall of bracing myself in front of the salty old chief petty officer who drilled our parade formations. He was interviewing those of us who'd volunteered to serve in the color guard—the group of recruits who handled a series of formal roles in these parades. Eyes boring into me, the chief asked for my combined scores on two of the classification tests.

"GCT/ARI?"

"One hundred thirty-seven, sir" (which was high).

"College?"

"No, sir."

"High school?"

"Tenth grade, sir." (And I don't know whether he noted the gusto with which I said it, but it must have been the first time I felt pride in my lack of formal education; it certainly wasn't the last.)

And that was it. Not only was I chosen for this special color guard company he'd recently formed, but the chief assigned me to lead the Second Regiment. Since there was no First Regiment, this placed me out in front of the parades, barking orders across the drill field, and presenting the brigade to the combined brass and visitors.[1] I tell this story partly because it pleases me to recall it, but mostly because it illustrates one of the ways in which the Navy spotted young men willing to stretch themselves and plied us with rewards meant to draw maximum performance out of us. I was a young racehorse, straining at the bit, and they let me run.

41

If I had to pick the point at which I gave myself over to the Navy—at least the part of me that I gave them—this might be it:

I march at the head of the parade and I'm presenting the brigade to the admiral. I've got a saber in my right hand, its blade resting against my shoulder. As the band's volume falls away to a single drumbeat, so that my voice will be heard across the parade ground, I order the regimental and battalion commanders forward to the reviewing stand. As loudly and as clearly as I can, but without screaming, I bellow,

"Officers and guidons, POST."

Then, catching the drumbeat, "Forward, guide center. . . . MARCH."

"Officers and guidons, HALT."

"Officers . . . PRESENT . . . SWORDS." As I sing out "present," my right arm swings up smoothly, the saber flashing in the sun. Twisting the blade to the horizontal, I pause the pommel just in front of my chest, the blade's tip pointing to the sky. At "swords," I drop my arm down and back, past my side to a position a few inches behind me, the saber's tip now pointing slightly downward. I may well be the youngest man on the base, but I'm out in front of everyone, leading them all.

I was very much a man-child then, and that saber represented a lot of responsibility. To this day there are times when in my mind I find myself striding about with its ghostly image resting against my shoulder, saluting with it, bending my back stiffly into a brace and singing out orders across the parade ground. It wasn't that I'd been given actual command of all those troops—I was simply orchestrating a performance—but I did incorporate that image of myself out in front, not only of the corps of recruits, but of my father, who was in the crowd watching me. Less than a year after fleeing his home in an act of self-preservation, I was in the commanding role and I've never forgotten it. The Navy was telling me I could do anything, and I believed them.

I think, though, that the biggest lesson I learned in boot camp was that first and foremost our goal was simply to get through and be done with it. Within days of arrival—probably hours—we were already singing out a hallowed marching cadence:

> Ten more weeks and I'll be home, Honey, Honey.
> Ten more weeks and I'll be home, Babe, Babe.
> Ten more weeks and I'll be home,
> Drinking beer and pissing foam, Honey, oh Babe of mine.

We counted down the weeks and the days wherever we marched. And in almost no time we were letting others know not only how bad things were but how resigned we were to them, calling out to those who arrived after us, the "mothballs," as the newest bunches of recruits were called,

> Mothball, mothball, don't be blue.

My recruiter screwed me, too.

We spent far more time pissing and moaning about how bad things were than we ever did talking about anything we might be looking forward to. I found this confusing. The regimen was so much simpler and more benign than living with my father's unpredictable temper and discipline that I had trouble understanding what the fuss was about. At one point I even asked our company commander if I could see a psychiatrist.

"Why? You think you're crazy?"

"No, sir, I think everyone else here is."

He assured me there was nothing to worry about, but looking back, I can see that I was disoriented by the stark contrast between what I was experiencing firsthand and what everyone else was saying about what was going on.

The extraordinarily close fit between what both the Navy and I wanted continued when it was time to figure out what sort of training I'd get. I really had been influenced by reading *Catch-22*, and in taking Yossarian not simply as a hero, but as a role model, a figure I hoped to emulate, I clearly had flying on my mind when I enlisted. At the same time, years of watching *Sgt. Bilko* had prepared me for the inevitable confusion as I sought my assignment, but we actually resolved it quickly.

The clerk asked me what sort of duty I'd like (and I emphasize that I was being offered a choice), and I said I wanted to fly. Because I wore glasses, he said, I wasn't eligible. I'd meant only that I wanted to be on the crew of a plane, like Yossarian, but he thought I was saying I wanted to be a pilot. After hearing that I couldn't fly, I turned to my other priority, electronics. At that point it was still my plan to head back to the phone company when I'd completed my hitch, and I was looking for training that would help me advance. Since I'd scored high on the classification tests and was interested in aviation, he suggested that I become an aviation electronics technician, and then I could fly as an aircrewman, which is exactly what I'd wanted in the first place.

I'd heard plenty of stories about the glowing commitments recruiters make to attract customers, promises that seemed to never come true, and I often joked that as a dropout all *I'd* been promised was boot camp, but there I was: within a couple weeks of enlisting, I was already headed toward two of my main goals. Despite what I think of as my already high level of cynicism, the fact is that the Navy and I were mostly on the same page. I wanted to excel; they thought that I could and gave me opportunities to do so. They gave me exactly what I sought. Though I could never have conceptualized it at the time, they needed me—that is, they needed recruits who were not only talented, but also ambitious and driven, and willing to take on dangerous duties. Guys with *thumos*, in other words. I knew what I was asking for, and they understood who was asking for it, and this is one of the reasons why I'm reluctant to portray myself as a victim.

THE TONKIN GULF INCIDENT

I was still marching and drilling in boot camp when the Tonkin Gulf Incident unfolded during the first week of August '64.[2] As the story was relayed to us, over the course of several days North Vietnamese torpedo boats launched two unprovoked attacks on US warships in the Tonkin Gulf. (Military historians generally agree that there was just one attack, provoked by the United States, with no damage done to the American vessels, though North Vietnam's boats fared much worse.) I actually remember my first thought on hearing the news, something along the lines of, "This is great. Maybe they'll declare war, we'll be mobilized, and we'll get the hell out of this place sooner than we expected." Ah, youth.

Although the American public knew next to nothing about Southeast Asia at the time, the Navy's 7th Fleet had been engaged in operations there since the early 1950s. Precisely because its ships had been so actively patrolling in the South China Sea, the Navy's buildup in Vietnam wasn't as noticeable as that of the Army and Air Force. The Navy simply began doing more of what it had already been doing, with the notable addition of live bombs and shells. American carriers launched the first air strikes on North Vietnam in the immediate wake of the Tonkin Gulf action, and all my subsequent training was in preparation for flying off those same carriers in the Gulf.

Some of my ambivalence as I look back on fighting in the war—and ambivalence is central to everything I have to say in this book—has to do with my initial response to that first news. There's hardly anything novel about young men in the military looking forward eagerly to combat, I know, but as someone who's spent a lot of time trying to make sense of just how willing I'd been to fight, I'm struck not only by how ready I was to leap into the fray myself, but that I envisioned the battle solely in terms of how it could benefit *me*.

TECHNICAL TRAINING AND FINE-TUNING CYNICISM

That first stage of my transformation, as I bought into this new world I'd entered, was followed by a long stint in technical training, where my outlook continued to evolve. The process was almost imperceptible at the time, and it's only in looking back from this great distance that I get some hint of what was happening to me.

Although the Navy had been operating in Indochina and the South China Sea for years, this was still a time when most of us thought "war" meant tangling with the Russians. And though the Navy was already bombing North Vietnam as I completed boot camp, we were still operating, in effect, in the Cold War order of things; there was as yet no great urgency to deploy more men and arms, and I continued on a long, well-paced path designed not simply to train men, but to observe and select them.

This is in some ways one of the harder pieces of the story for me to call to mind. At 17, fleeing in desperation from a world in which I was convinced no one was paying attention to me, it never occurred to me that I was being closely observed and evaluated. But each time I saw a new and possibly rewarding opening on the path ahead of me, I took it, and each time I set my sights on a new goal they gave me the opportunity to pursue it. The Navy had a pretty good idea of what it was doing. What I'm talking about here is the integration of my own ambitious and driven personality with the needs of the system into which I'd jumped.

In exactly the way that I'd found myself wanting to do what Yossarian (and in fact Joseph Heller, who created him) had done, I began wanting to do what some of the older men around me were doing. From the outset I'd pursued aviation, and I figured out which enlisted men got to fly and how they'd gone about doing so, then set out to do the same sorts of things. And that is, I suppose, something the military understands and relies upon. They depend on the ones who are ambitious and competitive, and they design programs and pathways that are competitive precisely in order to gain and hold their attention.

The first training programs I went through, called "A" schools, were set side-by-side with the more advanced programs, the "B" schools. Older, experienced enlisted men who'd been serving in the fleet were all around as I progressed through my training. I listened to their stories and grew to understand what lay ahead and what I had do in order to get to where I wanted to go. This is an old and well-thought-out way of doing things in the military: seasoned, experienced men are sent back not to simply train the new ones, but to work alongside them and inculcate a professional mentality.

I listened to an endless flow of what the Navy calls "sea stories," rather than the "war stories" the infantry tells; they're not exactly the same but they serve the same function. Sea stories are known for their humorous exaggeration, but they do an effective job of conveying the Navy way of life. In what is probably the best known and most widely admired work of American fiction from the Vietnam War, Tim O'Brien's *The Things They Carried* (1990), there's a piece entitled "How to Tell a True War Story." It's actually about how much fiction there is in these stories, and it suggests to me that the Army's war stories serve pretty much the same purpose as the Navy's sea stories.

Many of the tales I heard early on weren't much more than jokes, meant to do little more than entertain us while they imparted a sense of the Navy's culture. But I've still got very clear recollections of stories our instructors told us in the first of my schools, A-Fam, that is, Aviation Familiarization. These yarns and the lessons I learned from them shaped everything that came after. The ones with the greatest impact, judging from how they stick in my consciousness, had to do with aspects of working on carrier flight decks during operations. They were about the aircraft and the other equipment, and the kinds of damage they're prone to and how to avoid it.

Even more deeply embedded in my consciousness are stories about the harm the planes and equipment can wreak if the men working around them fail at any moment to exercise the utmost awareness and caution. The slightest lapse or slip can lead to death or dismemberment. It's hard to exaggerate the degree to which these lessons were drilled into us. Among the most common and frequent hazards—the stories that formed the basic framework of everything I was going to be doing in the next few years of my life—were the perils presented by propellers and jet engines. We heard story after story about men whose attention wavered for just an instant and who then proceeded to step into a turning prop, get sucked into a jet intake, or get blown off the deck into the sea far below. We internalized a sense of flight decks as places where death constantly threatened.

When I think about the time I spent talking with guys at that early stage in particular, but in the Navy in general, I don't recall much being said about why we signed up, but there was a basic, intrinsic hostility to the military from day one. This had something to do with a usually unspoken sense of coercion, a shared understanding that we wouldn't be there if it weren't for the draft. At the same time we knew we were getting incredible training, which was what we all wanted badly. I have little sense, though, that we were conscious of or cared about the fundamental contradiction that now leaps out at me. We intensely disliked the military and had almost nothing good to say about it. If you've been in the military, you will understand this, but if you haven't, this is likely to surprise you: all that hostility had very little impact on how we actually performed. We worked hard and did what was expected of us.[3]

It turns out that the burning desire to get through training, interlaced with unremitting hostility toward it, wasn't only about boot camp. When I arrived for my avionics (i.e., aviation electronics) training, I began learning that these themes were woven into the fabric of navy life. Wherever we were, we keenly anticipated the completion of whatever we were engaged in and talked endlessly about our ETD—our estimated time of departure—in the same way that soldiers did. It wasn't just about leaving the war, it was about everything. Though I'd been puzzled in boot camp about how much everyone disliked everything, I soon got with the program. It was during that year on a small base in Millington, a dozen miles outside Memphis, Tennessee, that I took to heart what I think of as the Navy creed: unremitting hostility toward nearly everything about the Navy. It all "sucked."

This attitude drove our overwhelming desire to be done and gone. We counted the days till we shipped out. "Ten days and a wake-up," someone would say. "Two weeks and a wake-up," "Three days and a wake-up," others would respond. The wake-up was the day you departed, and it was filled with so much joy that it didn't count. Being "short," that is, having a short amount of time left, was the goal. I remember guys saying, "I'm so short I need a ladder to climb over the doorstep."

Accompanying this wish to be done and away was an equally intense cynicism. It seemed that every conversation included, along with comments about how much whatever we were talking about sucked, guys speaking of how little they cared about things. "Like I give a shit." "I could not care less" or "I could care less," both said with the same inflection, as was "Give a shit, give a shit, care, care, care."

We were, mind you, at what was one of the finest technical schools in the country, the Naval Air Technical Training Center, Memphis. More often than not it was referred to as the Naval Air Testicle-Twisting Center. Abbreviated as NATTC Memphis, pronounced NattCenter Memphis, it was also known as Rat-Center Mucus. At the last of my many training programs there, Airborne Radio Code Operator school, or ARCO, we even had a cheer in radio code: "Three dits, four dits, two dits, dah! ARCO, ARCO, rah, rah, rah!" That's ··· ···· ·· —, or S-H-I-T. If we had anything good to say about the Navy, I don't recall it.

It was there that I became truly steeped in the Navy worldview. I can't define it or describe it in a single word. It included, but wasn't limited to ironic, sarcastic, skeptical, cynical, subversive, mordant, jaundiced, sardonic, satirical, derisive, hostile, mocking, and distrustful. I haven't folded in things like anger and hatred for a reason: it's not that these weren't to be seen, but that they imply a level of intensity that was encountered only occasionally. This overall attitude or outlook, which I'll variously call cynicism, skepticism, or irony, was, more often than not, essentially rote. It characterized the general feeling, the atmosphere we lived and sailed and flew in, rather than explicit outrage directed at specific situations or events.

At some level our attitude was a response to what the military knows universally as chickenshit. In his book *Wartime*, Paul Fussell (1990) devoted a memorable chapter to chickenshit in World War II. It's a fundamental building-block of military life, but it's also a preoccupation of almost anyone who works in a large bureaucracy or organization. It's often spoken of as bullshit, too, but chickenshit is meant to express how petty it is, and this is particularly characteristic of the military.

In World War II this cynical attitude towards the military's inevitable incompetence was immortalized in the term, "snafu," which I learned as a boy meant "situation normal, all fouled up," but is really, with classic military inflection, "situation normal, all fucked up." It speaks not simply to bureaucratic ineptitude, but to everyone's expectations that this is how things will always turn out. Stories and movies about the military, both the comedies and the dramas, invariably draw on the confluence of snafu and chickenshit, and *Catch-22* is to my mind the greatest of them all. Writing about his book in the years after it became a hit Heller (1998) insisted that his book was about the "organization man" bureaucratic culture of the United States in the 1950s at least as much as it was about World War II.

But I also see that I learned during that first year of training that the unceasing spew of complaint, of cynical hostility, and of what nowadays days gets called ironic detachment, in no way affected the actual performance of our duties. To put this another way, it's difficult, if not impossible, to gauge much about morale based merely on what the troops are saying. I think this is one of most important things we have to keep in mind about the military: the quality of performance isn't at all necessarily related to the intensity of the complaints.

In the course of my training in Tennessee I grew thoroughly accustomed to this odd disparity and looking back I see one of my early introductions to what social scientists call cognitive dissonance. What I was fully in the midst of, and fully engaged in, was a perfect example. Large numbers of young men in their teens and early twenties were working long hours each day to gain complex technical expertise. We were pushed through our classes at a rapid clip, tested weekly and sometimes daily, and swiftly weeded out if we faltered.

It was a good deal. In return for our concentration and hard work we gained skills that would allow us to get promoted quickly and serve us well when our enlistments were done. Everyone understood that that was the bargain we'd struck. I don't recollect anyone who didn't apply himself, who wasn't eager to complete the programs.

Along with all the technical training, we were exposed to a whole lot more from the older and more experienced sailors training in the advanced B-school programs. We were being schooled not only about avionics and the different kinds of equipment, aircraft, and the missions they flew, but about the many kinds of squadrons and ships and duty stations. Guys talked continually about what was the best sort of duty and what were the best locations for naval air stations. The worst places were known collectively as NAS Bumfucked, Idaho, and we wanted to avoid them at all costs. There were a few, like Mildenhall in England and Rota in Spain, that were reputed to be superb.

While Navy pilots sought glory in flying fighters off attack carriers, enlisted men overwhelmingly preferred to serve on land. Over the years I came to characterize this outlook as "the Navy would be okay, if it weren't for all the damned ships." Most of us sought assignments to patrol and transport squadrons and any other units that flew heavy, land-based planes.

The men I trained with and worked beside were highly motivated, well-disciplined, and obedient. We were for the most part guys who could have gone to college, but for financial or other reasons did not. We thought ahead, controlled our impulses, and were cooperative. Fights were rare. There was a bit of drunkenness, but not much, really, since so many of us weren't yet 21 in a place where drinking was well-monitored. For the most part, our superiors told us what we had to do and we did it. We wanted to get the hell out of there and out into the fleet.

By civilian standards, my experiences trying to leave the Memphis training center were bizarre, but they were nothing more than routine snafu in terms of Navy expectations. As my class completed radio operators school, we received the orders that sent us on to our next duty stations. No orders arrived for me. Wait, I was told. Having no alternative, I did. The Mississippi Delta region is hot and muggy most of the time, and is especially so in July and August, but other than the weather, I didn't mind much at first. Each morning I spent an hour or so cleaning the latrines and showers, but most of that work went to guys who'd just reported and hadn't yet begun training. The rest of the day I was free.

After two weeks of this, though, I'd grown increasingly restless. The whole point of boot camp and all that avionics training had been to get through it and away from it, and there I was still spinning my wheels at Rat-Center Mucus. I went to the personnel office and explained my situation and was told to wait some more. I did. After two more weeks with no orders, I returned and spoke to the chief who ran that section of the personnel office. Acknowledging my eagerness, he did something almost unthinkable in those days. He picked up the phone and made a long-distance call on the spot. They found my orders and he informed me that I'd be heading to Carrier Airborne Early Warning Squadron Eleven (VAW-11) in San Diego. I shipped out a few days later, after the proper documents finally arrived.

It seems entirely possible, and maybe even likely, that if I'd kept my mouth shut I could have spent the next three years doing nothing there in rural Tennessee. I would have avoided sea duty. And no one would have noticed. It wasn't simply that my orders never got sent, even after I inquired about them, but that no one noticed. If I hadn't spoken up, I would have fallen through the cracks. Anyone who's spent time in the military recognizes this aspect of bureaucratic chaos. As long as I didn't make waves and kept my head down, I would have been left alone for the duration.

When I finally did get my orders, of course, I ran smack into yet another classic form of snafu. I'd trained at length as a radio code operator because they flew only in the big, long-distance planes, the ones that *didn't* go aboard carriers. I'd done my avionics training in radios, precisely in order to get into code school. And so where was I being sent? To what's called a tailhook outfit, a radar surveillance and reconnaissance squadron that flew its planes, so awkward looking they were called Willy Fudds, off aircraft carriers, exactly what I'd taken so much care to avoid. It made little sense, but one of the main outcomes of our immersion in all that chickenshit was that we became more or less resigned to it.

OFF TO THE FLEET

I've always thought of it as no more than everyday incompetence that the Navy trained me to be a radio operator and then ordered me to a carrier-based radar squadron. As I write, though, I find myself wondering whether it was a mistake at all. It was really difficult to find enlisted flight techs to man those Fudds. It required the intersection of intelligence, ability, ambition, and more than a little recklessness. In the same way that the drill master had spotted me as a guy who would do the job right, and the personnel clerk who directed me into avionics saw where I could best plug a need, someone at the Enlisted Personnel Distribution Office Pacific (EPDOPAC) center may well have taken all the material they had on me and figured out that I was a guy who could and would do this. (I think we all assumed that EPDOPAC, where these assignments were made, did its work in an entirely random fashion, but like so many other things I find myself now comprehending in the light of all this reflection, they may well have been just as skilled and dedicated as I was.)

There was a winnowing process for enlisted men who could and would serve as aircrew in the same way that there was for pilots. I have no idea what the actual figures look like, but I know that many young men want to be pilots. Some portion of them want to be military pilots, and some of these want to be Navy pilots. Some make it into training programs, some make it through. Some are assigned to be carrier pilots, and of those, some make it as attack and fighter pilots. Of all those who start out wanting to fly, no more than a few percent achieve the pinnacle. And the Navy must have faced a somewhat similar problem finding enough enlisted men to fly. When I think of all those who went through basic training with me, only a handful went to avionics schools, and of all of us in avionics schools, only a very few showed much interest at all in flying. Of those who did, the clear preference was to serve in land-based aircraft. And then there were the very, very few of us willing to fly in tailhook squadrons. And even then, there were many fewer who could make it through the rigorous training and still remain willing to serve in combat.

What surprises me is that I was so unaware of all this as I was passing through the stages of the sorting process. I understand now that there always seemed to be what I saw as some sort of glamorous prize dangling before me. These were opportunities that guys like me looked upon as rewards, but I had little if any sense that most others didn't find these options nearly as attractive as I did. I see myself continually jumping through the hoops, and when I'd made it through all the preparatory stages, actually performing the tasks in combat just didn't seem like that big a deal.

Even more surprising is that I was as cynical about it all as anyone else, even while I was throwing myself into it. As I say, this is one of the fundamental contradictions that puzzles me about my time in the military. How could anyone be simultaneously as gung ho *and* as cynical as I was? This explains it. Even as I was immersed in a sea of skepticism—the ironic detachment that almost all enlisted men exhibit toward the military—my *thumos* was driving me full speed ahead in pursuit of my own ambitions.

I'd arrived in Memphis for training in August of 1964 and I reported to San Diego's North Island Naval Air Station in August of '65 assuming that I'd be put directly to work after a full year of nonstop training. I found myself instead facing an entirely new round of schooling. Among the greatest lessons the Navy had taken away from World War II was the absolute importance of training. We trained and drilled endlessly.

Now that I'd joined a fleet early warning squadron, my horizon was no longer limited to electronic circuits; I was now going to be taking responsibility for keeping aircraft in the air, for the ships our squadron protected, for aircraft under my radar control, and for the aircraft that I flew in. I also had to master the art of surviving on a carrier's flight deck during operations and to work on and inside powerful, dangerous equipment.

If the US Navy learned anything in World War II, it was about how vulnerable warships are to attack from the air. That's what happened to the US fleet at Pearl Harbor, and in the celebrated battles in the Coral Sea and at Midway. You have to know where your enemy is, where its forces are coming from, and where they're heading; in the age of aviation, new speed became essential as well. This is why radar was developed, but in its early years it was limited to "line-of-sight." Because it worked by bouncing electronic pulses directly off objects and then using the returning pulse to measure their bearing and distance, radar was limited by the earth's curvature, and the relatively primitive nature of the technology made it impossible to spot things beyond the horizon. A ship on the water has a very limited horizon, and in the years following the war, radar still could not spot low-flying, rapidly approaching aircraft until they were much too close.

And so it was that the E-1B Tracer was developed in the 1950s.[4] It was originally designated a WF-2, and that nomenclature and the plane's ungainly appearance earned it the nickname "Willy Fudd." No one ever called them

Tracers; they were always and everywhere known as Fudds, and we who flew them were Fuddmen.[5]

Its tasks were many, but they all centered around what was for the time a state-of-the-art radar system. The Fudd was, simply, a flying radar platform, and everything it did depended upon the massive antenna in its radar dome or radome. Unlike any aircraft that came before it, the Fudd's antenna was housed not in a bubble jutting out from the plane's fuselage but attached separately above it (and establishing the fundamental premise for today's AWACS planes). Aerodynamically shaped, so that it lifted its own weight, the radome looked something like a teardrop sliced lengthwise, but at a glance it looked more like a mushroom that had popped out of the plane's roof. With its radar's range of 200 miles, a Fudd in the air enabled an aircraft carrier to see far beyond its own horizon. Its two radar operators' primary tasks were to control the carrier's aircraft, directing its fighters to intercept enemy bombers long before they could approach the ship, and guiding its own attack aircraft to where they would deliver their payloads.

The heart and soul of the Fudd and our early warning squadron, then, was the radar. The point of the Fudd was to get its APS-82 system high into the air. The Navy in those days was still run by World War II veterans, men who'd fought in—and whose careers were shaped by—those epic battles in the Pacific, and in their minds protecting carriers and the rest of the fleet from dive bombers, torpedo planes, kamikazes, and submarines was every bit as vital to naval aviation as the ability to launch attacks. We were engaged in

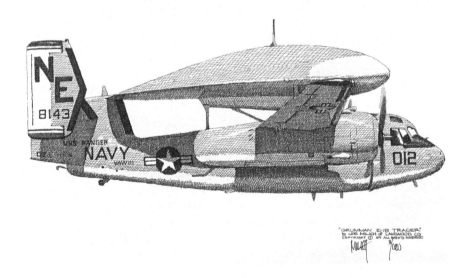

Figure 2.1.   E-1B Tracer, better known as a Willy Fudd. *Print by Joe Milich, Aviation Art. Used by permission. Photo by Sophie Barbasch, by permission.*

the mid-'60s in procedures that had been developed in the 1950s to solve problems the Navy faced in battles fought in the 1940s. Generals are often accused of fighting the last war, and admirals aren't much different.

In the same way that my performance in basic training got me into the intense naval air technical training program, my successes there sent me to VAW-11's radar shop. Looking back, I can see how my squadron must have understood me. The squadron was huge; we placed small units, called detachments, of three or four planes on every carrier in the Pacific. But despite the radar's central importance, there were only a handful of us who worked on it. Out at sea there's no place to turn for help, and with fewer than a half-dozen techs to maintain these systems, each detachment desperately required diligent, creative, and dedicated men. They simply couldn't find enough guys with the aptitude to handle all the training, not to mention the operations. Only five of us were in my two-month program of instruction on the Fudd's radar system, two older, career sailors and three of us youngsters who'd recently arrived from A school in Memphis. That meant no more than twenty or so qualified techs were coming into the entire Pacific fleet each year. Our Fudds were meant to be a temporary expedient and were slated to be replaced by the much more sophisticated E-2 Hawkeye in the mid-1960s, and the Navy was expending few resources on a system it was expecting to soon replace.

Although the Fudds' technology was fast becoming obsolete, the first E-2 model was a failure and Grumman's engineers were still a long way from working the bugs out of the revamped technology.[6] (They ultimately succeeded—the Hawkeyes remain a mainstay in today's fleet.) This meant that the detachments still flying the Fudds faced a sort of catch-22. The Navy wasn't keen on providing resources for a plane it was planning to get rid of, but suddenly found itself in a war its leaders were eager to fight, with a fleet to be protected, and it couldn't get along without us. So we kept sending our Fudds to Vietnam, and kept them flying, even as the flow of material support for them was steadily diminishing. This basic contradiction explains why we had so much difficulty getting personnel to operate and maintain the radar and obtaining the parts we needed to repair it.

From the outset I was put to work repairing the individual components that made up the radar system as a whole. We did this on workbenches in the avionics shop, where we slipped off the black metal casings (which is why they're called black boxes), trouble-shot the intricate webs of circuits within, repaired them, and sent them back out to the planes.

After I'd managed to combine what I'd learned in my training classes with day-in and day-out, hands-on experience working on all those different subsystems, and gained some sense of how all the pieces fit together, I reported to a unit preparing to deploy to Vietnam, Detachment Q (Quebec). I began to grasp how the system as a whole functioned inside the aircraft itself:

all the complex webs of wiring and waveguides, the precariously balanced antenna in the radome, and the inherent difficulties of figuring out just which black box or set of cables was causing a problem when every piece was interconnected with every other piece. Each of our detachment's four planes had its own personality, and as the flight technician responsible for keeping the radar functioning during our long missions I had to know how to coax the best performance out of each.

This is when I first encountered and learned to appreciate "Murphy's Law," the notion that anything that can go wrong, will go wrong. My thorough grasp of Murphy's Law helped prepare me for the rest of my time in the military, and for life itself.

As my familiarity with the electronics system progressed, I was also training as one of the small handful of men who operated it, a radar intercept controller/flight technician. A crew of four manned the Fudds: pilot and copilot, radar officer, and the enlisted flight tech. The radar officer and the flight tech received exactly the same training in operating the radar and controlling other aircraft, did all the same tasks during the missions, and shared responsibilities. But that was where the officer's job began and ended. The enlisted tech, on the other hand, was also responsible for making sure the radar system kept functioning optimally and for attempting repairs in-flight. The Fudd's radar was fragile and persnickety and required constant tending. What's more, though, the enlisted tech worked a regular maintenance shift back aboard ship, repairing each aircraft as swiftly as possible to turn it around for its next mission, which was just a few hours away.

I haven't yet let go of the sense of unfairness I felt about this. I was paid some small fraction of what officers received and had few of their privileges. But I did three jobs to their one. I remember groaning silently to myself once when one of the radar officers, sitting to my left, complained to the pilots about inequities between the first few feet of the plane, where they sat, and the next few feet, where we sat. I wanted badly to point to the disparities between the left and right sides of the plane (that is, between him and me), but I understood military protocol well enough to think twice about speaking my mind.

This disparity wasn't exactly chickenshit, but it's a good example of how in hierarchies we tend to be much more sensitive to the perks of those above us than to whatever privileges we hold over those below us.

As time went by I became so deeply immersed in using the radar to control interceptors and to protect the fleet that I no longer thought of it as merely a collection of black boxes. I grew to be a living part of the APS-82 when we were in the air, and as I progressed through all this training an intense attitude of responsibility took root in me. I had little awareness of this at the time, but I now see that I was saddling myself with a burden that included moral, intellectual, and emotional, as well as physical aspects. Every feature of the work weighed heavily on me because every piece of it was integral to protecting the fleet. I took to it readily, though, at least in part because of the skills I'd already developed as a birder.

Birding strikes many people as an eccentric pastime, without much relevance to practical concerns and hopelessly nerdy, but with the advantage of hindsight I see how it prepared me for the tasks I needed to master. Guarding the fleet and controlling a half-dozen aircraft while flying off North Vietnam's coast were among the most demanding of the many things I did in the war, and I can now see that there wasn't much in that work that didn't draw on skills I'd honed while birding.

I'd learned as a boy to sit nearly motionless for long periods in uncomfortable conditions, watching intently, looking for small, tell-tale movements, waiting for things that might never appear, and noticing instantaneously when something new did show up. I learned to recognize tiny differences in silhouettes and relative sizes (a skill I'd first started acquiring as I built those model airplanes), to keep my eyes on multiple objects simultaneously, and to have a sense for where something that disappeared from view was likely to reappear. I learned to estimate flight trajectories and vectors. To recognize flight patterns. To single out the odd species in a flock. To keep a close record of what I saw and to report on where it was and where it was heading. To recognize things that were where they weren't expected to be. All these are among the practices birders cultivate.

Skeptics will ask how birdwatching could possibly be of practical use in the war, so here's an example: Among the habits I picked up while birding as a boy was always to scan flocks of Brewer's blackbirds on the off chance that a starling might have joined them, at a time when starlings (which had been introduced to the US east coast from Europe in the 1890s) were occasionally showing up in central California. One of my responsibilities in the Tonkin Gulf was to "delouse" flights of bombers returning from raids in the north, that is, to study the radar patterns and ensure that no North Vietnamese MiGs had tucked themselves in behind them, thus enabling the enemy to sneak up unobserved on our fleet.

The first stages of training to control interceptors will look simple to some. Using radar simulators, I had to spot intruding planes—"bogeys"— that might potentially attack the ship, and direct jet fighters to intercept and then knock them out of the sky with air-to-air missiles. This sounds a lot like what one does with simple video games, I know, and so it hardly seems like a big deal. But there were crucial differences. First, this was long before these sorts of games came along and was entirely novel. Second, if I did my job right in combat, that is, under the conditions I was being trained for, someone was really going to get killed. Third, if I failed to do my job right, lots of people were going to get killed. And the difference didn't lie in merely doing my job, but in how well I did it.

Guiding a jet fighter into place for a successful intercept while staring at nothing more than a few blips on a glowing screen is a demanding task. Unless it is done perfectly, either the bogey escapes and completes its attack, or the interceptor you're guiding gets shot down. You don't vector your interceptor directly at a bogey, of course, but at the spot where you calculate the bogey will be when the interceptor reaches it. A vector off by a degree or two will either put the interceptor too far behind the bogey and force it into a fruitless "tail-end chase," or out in front, in position to get shot down.

These alternatives to a successful intercept were drummed into me, and success, I was taught, was the only acceptable option, given the likely consequences of failure. I got no—and I mean absolutely no—sense that there was anything remotely like play in what I was being trained to do. We worked in what the Navy called Hunter-Killer Groups. I was the hunter and the aircraft under my control was the killer. If I did my job right my pilot killed; if I failed, he got killed . . . and then maybe we all got killed.

Our radar system included primitive computers meant to help calculate the best course for the interceptor to fly, but by the time I joined the fleet we'd abandoned them. They simply weren't adequate to the task. Most of my training, then, was in learning by trial and error to mentally calculate the best vector. After grasping the rudiments of directing intercepts in the simulator, I started flying training missions, doing the real thing: directing live intercepts, lacking only the missiles.

It was, as I say, a gradual process, and the changes it worked on me weren't obvious. But as I made the transition from long sessions in the ground training devices to actual missions, flying and taking control of other aircraft, the changes penetrated more deeply into my being. Directing interceptors while sitting in a chamber on the ground was serious work, but it was quite another thing to be in the air giving commands to a fighter pilot. One with loaded guns and armed missiles. It wasn't exactly Tom Cruise in "Top Gun" on my end, but in terms of the responsibility saddled on an 18-year-old kid being trained to understand that what he's learning will become the real thing in a matter of months, it was huge.

What I'm most interested in at the moment, though, is how my mindset developed as I came to understand that everything I was doing was real, made a difference, and was for keeps. What happened to me, that maybe didn't happen to everyone, is that everything became much more serious, much more important, much more a matter of life and death. I immersed myself in my tasks. This is a crucial piece of the puzzling traumatic stress I experienced, but it's not very apparent to the naked eye, and it grew radically more intense out in the Tonkin Gulf, where we assumed attacks on the fleet were imminent and my body and mind were on high alert virtually all the time. I was training not simply to do a series of tasks, but to assume responsibility for my own plane and the others I controlled, as well as for the fleet we were guarding.

It's easy to see in hindsight that North Vietnam's forces did not constitute much of a threat to the fleet out in Tonkin Gulf, but we didn't understand that at the time. Most of the Navy was unaware of how our military command structure had misrepresented (or, if you prefer, lied about) the Tonkin Gulf Incident, which had first put the Seventh Fleet to work bombing North Vietnam. Navy leadership believed, even if they weren't entirely convinced, that North Vietnam had launched a third torpedo boat attack on its destroyers in September 1964, and the fleet remained on edge, assuming that yet another surface attack could take place at any moment (Marolda and Fitzgerald, 1986, pp. 454–459). After all, most of the Navy's losses in World War II had come from air and submarine attacks, not from men-of-war slugging it out against one another with heavy guns, and the fact that North Vietnam had no subs or surface fleet beyond the torpedo boats that had been involved in the Tonkin Gulf Incident in no way precluded the MiGs in its air force from striking. And there were reports of unfriendly subs operating in the area. We were on constant alert once we entered the Gulf.

When we took up station in Vietnam, our Fudds assumed full responsibility for airborne early warning. We were guardians of the fleet. And that meant to me that I would be responsible for spotting anything heading for the fleet and for intercepting it. I'd direct my own plane and the six S-2Fs we'd have under positive radar control. That's why the pilots I flew with, and not my trainers, took the most active hand in seeing that I developed proper radio transmission (R/T) procedures. They spoke to me about how closely they relied on the voice guiding them and stressed how crucial it was for me to sound confident when I gave commands. They got me to understand how much more confident they felt when they were directed by a clear, calm, and steady voice, and worked with me to develop mine. (I'm aware that I have a manner that projects a lot more confidence than I usually feel and this is where I developed what some call my public radio voice, deep and resonant and well-paced.)

I was also charged with navigating my own plane, which entailed an odd allocation of responsibility. The plane commander—ordinarily the pilot—is, as his title makes clear, in command. But he relies on his radar operators to navigate—to tell him where he is and where he's going. In essence, he took orders from me. And so I bore not only the responsibility for the interceptors and the fleet, and any other duties we might be discharging (like locating downed pilots), but also for ourselves.

I spoke at the beginning of the ancient Greeks' notion of *thumos* as I described what it was in my character that led me to run away from home. A common translation is "spirit"—in the sense that a horse is said to be spirited, that is. Another translation is "heart," as in the old song, "You gotta have heart." Scholars debate the range of its meanings, of course, but I think the broad concept has a lot to tell me about myself. *Thumos* is said to refer to an intersection of ambition, bravery, desire for fame, the capacity for righteous anger, and a willingness to stand up for or insist on what is right. It is simultaneously about the self, the assertion of the self, and the larger good of the community. *Thumos* drives one to excel, not simply in terms of self-aggrandizement, but in the sense of doing the right thing. It is a human drive, and it plays a role in making society possible, but it's distributed unevenly among us. I have no idea whether it actually exists: it is a way of talking about something that we want to believe moves humans to action, and in that sense it's not a whole lot different than other sorts of abstract qualities, virtues, and character traits I'm talking about here, such as pride, guilt, responsibility, ambition, diligence, et cetera. We've got a gut sense of what these things are, as long as the philosophers and linguists don't push us too hard.[7]

I see what was happening to me in those early days in the Navy as the unleashing of my *thumos*. I don't think I'm arrogating too much to myself to speak this way. My willingness to run away as a way of gaining autonomy and insisting on my right to exist on my own terms, and then my insistence on staying away, on taking care of myself, and on joining the military all demonstrate a measure of internal spirit, of *thumos*. I wanted to be a flier, like Yossarian. I wanted to train in a demanding field like aviation electronics. I wanted to fly so badly, in fact, that I cheated on my flight physical. My eyesight was borderline and, worried that I might fail the vision exam, I snuck in and memorized the first few lines of the eye chart. I still remember them:

NS
RZOK

I didn't have a clear idea of where exactly I wanted to head, but always, I chose flying.

While I was earning my gold aircrew wings (which marked for me a peak of personal achievement and a visible sign of my *thumos*), I was simultaneously learning the ropes of working on the carrier deck during flight operations. In the overall scale of doing dangerous work in a dangerous place, day in and day out, the barely controlled chaos on a flight deck ranks impossibly high. Not only are all kinds of dangerous things happening, and dangerous equipment conspiring to kill you, but the ambient conditions obscure your perceptions of just what the hell is going on.

FIRST ENCOUNTERS WITH EVERYDAY DANGER

Along with being one of the world's most hazardous work environments, a carrier's deck is probably the noisiest. Today, everyone wears sound-attenuating headgear on the flight deck. But back then—as we used to say, back in old navy, in the days of wooden ships and iron men—headgear was optional, and iron men thought it unmanly. And when I was in the air, the Fudd's massive number 2 engine was just outside the uninsulated sheet metal airframe, a couple of feet from my head, roaring in my ears 7 hours a day.

It's hardly surprising that I lost a lot of hearing. Like the PTSD I'd eventually be diagnosed with, I didn't recognize it for years, but my hearing loss has caused me tremendous problems—it's hard to be comfortable with people who seem always to be mumbling.

To my mind, the most basic things to understand about the flight deck are that in combat it's almost constantly operating at full pitch and that in its own way it replicates, within the confines of a little more than two acres (today's carrier decks are twice this size), the notorious conception called the "fog of war." In daylight it's a bad place. In the pitch black of nighttime combat conditions it's something akin to hell. It's not that people are trying to kill you, but everything that happens there combines to create conditions likely to kill you.[8]

In the Tonkin Gulf we operated under full wartime combat-readiness conditions. This is a step down from general quarters, when all hands are manning their battle stations, but it means that no lights are shown at night. Given the heavy overcast in the Gulf, this meant total darkness on the flight deck.

During flight operations, when planes are launching or landing, the ship is steaming at full speed into the wind, to increase lift over the deck and improve handling for the aircraft. The deck is pitching and rolling. Engines are screaming, and with the wind whipping across the deck it's nearly impossible to hear. Propellers are whirling everywhere. You can't see them. You can't hear them. You barely notice the prop and jet wash for all the wind. The planes are moving constantly, being re-spotted as they head toward the catapults or away from the arresting cables. Danger is everywhere you turn, except that you can't see it. In the sense that there's a logic and order to what's happening, it's not chaos, but because the hands are continually racing about among the planes, it's nearly impossible to keep track of the order of things as they unfold. For most intents and purposes, then, it's about as close to chaos as one can get. And the crews must get their work done amid this array of things trying to kill them. I think of all this routine chaos as "everyday danger," and it's a notion I'll be grappling with it at length in the following chapters.

While all this is underway, the various crews working on the deck—maintenance, fueling, ordnance, and plane handlers—each in their distinctively colored jerseys, race about, responding to deal with each new problem. The entire point of all this frenzy is to get the planes up into the air and then to get them back down onto the deck, where they'll be readied for the next launch. Urgency is at a peak, and it prevails. Everyone's preoccupied with doing all that's required to keep launching and recovering the birds. And the hazards are multiplied by the facts that the activity is unending and that everyone's exhausted.

In the same way that even the most vivid portrayals of infantry firefights in movies, novels, memoirs, and journalism can't capture a battle's essence, descriptions of a working flight deck are inherently compromised. In a film or story the pieces have to be rendered sequentially and have to be made visible. In real time, though, this is all happening simultaneously and in the black of night, and there is the constant tension, just micrometers below active consciousness, between giving all of your attention to getting the job done and to preserving your life. As in a firefight, however much you may want to save yourself, you understand that that's not the point—that's not why you're there. You've got to get the job done, and that means putting your own survival second. You're as careful as can be, but "as can be" starkly limits "careful."

It's not just the flight deck during operations. There are a multitude of tasks aboard a warship—or on an airbase handling warplanes, for that matter—that are hazardous enough to be called life-threatening. And that's not even considering all that's entailed in flying warplanes in combat. For the life of me, I cannot figure out how to make lucid distinctions between "combat arms" and "combat support." It's not that they're identical, but that there's so much overlap. Whenever you're working with materials or equipment designed to kill people, you're flirting with danger.

At the root of the difficulty in regularly facing peril as you carry out your duties is this basic problem: You can't accomplish your work effectively, and as quickly as it must be done, if your main concern is your own safety. So you've got to suppress—hide away inside your being—awareness of all the hazards. You don't think consciously about what can happen to you if someone makes the slightest mistake. And this has long-term consequences. Let me illustrate with what is in one of most deeply lodged features of this, at least for me.

I'm talking about avoiding the prop arc, the circular area encompassed by a propeller as it turns. Stepping into a turning prop means being hacked instantly to death. And so one of the first things drummed into us as we began working around aircraft was that avoiding prop arcs is imperative. But it's not that simple. Under optimal conditions, it can be difficult to see a whirling propeller. Under nighttime flight deck conditions, with engines roaring all around, wind whipping across the deck, and virtually no visibility, it's impossible to know whether the prop of any given aircraft is turning. And so we learned from the very outset that one never, ever, steps into or through that arc, under any circumstances or conditions. To this day, I would never, ever step into a prop arc, even around museum aircraft that haven't turned their engines in decades.[9]

Sailors who begin working on flight decks must master many lessons like this, but there's a great deal of difference between being merely exposed to instruction and thoroughly learning the lessons. While I was preparing myself for the war I wasn't simply training to operate and maintain the Fudd's radar. I was learning how to live within a web of responsibilities and life-threatening dangers and lodging them so completely in my being that the fears and anxieties embodied in me didn't interfere with my ability to get my jobs done. All this took place gradually, so gradually that I was hardly aware of what was happening. By the time we were on Yankee Station, though, and I was flying in Vietnamese airspace and working on the flight deck under nighttime combat readiness conditions, I'd been trained well. I was able to block out most concerns for my own safety in order to perform all those jobs.

The military devotes a huge amount of time and expense to training. Some of this is obvious: as equipment grows more and more complex, the skills to operate it become increasingly demanding. But much of the training has little to do with any specific skill. Rather, troops are learning how do their jobs effectively by ignoring the obvious threats to their own lives. This is fairly straightforward when one thinks of what rifle companies do. It is not so obvious when one thinks about other sorts of work. But it's the same process of habituating servicemen of any sort to be as oblivious as possible to threats to their own safety. All this changes a person, but precisely because one learns to do one's job well while ignoring the threats, these changes can be quite invisible to the naked eye.

We learned to do our jobs well under the most adverse conditions. At some level, this is a good and necessary thing, so, we might ask, so what? On another level, though, it's deeply problematic. After combat, it's all too easy for veterans to continue drawing on that same capacity to ignore what's happening to them. When we ignore these threats to our safety and to our bodily integrity, they build up, and consequences follow.

What's at stake, then, isn't just the massive amount of technical knowledge necessary to operate a modern navy. It's the ability to do so as effectively as possible under conditions of great strain. In the wake of the World War II naval battles at Guadalcanal, when Japan's southward advance was finally halted, Admiral Chester Nimitz, Commander in Chief of the Pacific Fleet, said the key to the Allied forces' victory there had been "training, TRAIN-ING, and M-O-R-E T-R-A-I-N-I-N-G," and his successors took it to heart (Hornfischer, 2011, p. 427). As we readied for deployment to Vietnam, my detachment repeatedly sailed aboard our carrier, engaging in exercises off the coasts of California and Hawaii. We were operating continually, and I wasn't simply learning to maintain the radar and to master my intercept controller technique, I was shouldering a series of new responsibilities and acquiring a certain sense of command.

A detachment with four E-1Bs was quite small. Ours had 45 enlisted men and 19 officers. To keep the planes flying while we were at sea, roughly 20 men worked maintenance on each of two 12-hour shifts. Between the catapult launches, arrested recoveries, and the long missions (all of which I'll be describing), the battering our planes underwent was brutal, but there were only a couple of men at any given moment responsible, respectively, for each of the tasks required to keep the engines, the airframe, the hydraulics, the controls and wiring, the instruments, the radios, and the radar up and running, and to service and clean the planes. It wasn't just the aircrews themselves that had to learn to work together as a tightly knit, closely coordinated unit. The ground crews had to come together in the same way.

We all did our jobs, and to the best of my recollection, we did them well, even if there were normal tensions, dislikes, and disagreements among men of disparate backgrounds. Though we complained continually about everything, everyone worked together to keep our birds in the air. I can't stress this enough. Whatever we were going to be doing in Vietnam, and this wasn't entirely clear to us before we sailed, we recognized it as deadly serious work. I recall no one who wasn't committed to the job or was unwilling to work as long and as hard as necessary to get it done. We took the missions seriously; a few of us took them personally.

POW TRAINING

I've been trying to explain why training for combat entailed much more than just skill and knowledge. It was also meant to instill in me ways of seeing and understanding things, and ways of thinking about myself and my duties. Much of this had to with my job running the radar and controlling interceptors, and much of it had to do with working on the flight deck and keeping the aircraft operational, but the training that had the deepest impact on me was my experience with the Navy's SERE school, that is, its Survival, Evasion, Resistance, and Escape program.

I tread a very fine line as I write this. I want to be as honest as I possibly can. I want to avoid hyperbole and overdramatization. I especially don't want to make myself out to be a victim. But this is where opposing trajectories collide. What I find is that in the end, I cannot speak honestly about this set of experiences without screaming in pain, in rage, in indignation, and in protest.[10]

Everywhere in my notes and drafts I find passages when this topic in particular has upset me to the point that I can't write. It's nearly impossible for me to remember just how intense these feelings actually can be, but when I'm experiencing them and note what it's like, it's almost always the same. I leave my desk, and stagger out of the room, barely able to walk. I collapse onto my bed and pass out. A deep and powerful residue of violence, of nearly unspeakable distress flows over me. It is so emotionally painful that I'm not capable of holding it in mind for long, and a while later I'm trying to convince myself that it wasn't all that bad, really. If I didn't have page after page of my own descriptions of it while it's happening, I wouldn't believe it.

This raw disruption lies at the intersection of everything I experienced in the war: it's physical, it's emotional, it's intellectual, and it's moral. Standing by itself it is painful but bearable. When it is combined with the subterfuge, lies, and what I see as the outright criminal behavior of some of those who led us, then the acid wash of betrayal embedded in it and the sheer moral perfidy that magnifies it are transformed into a white-hot poker that is thrust into my bowels.

SERE training intensified all the experiences that shaped the contours of my psyche before I went to war. It taught me why it was my patriotic duty to resist torture, that is, to allow myself to be tortured. And in turn, it underscored my awareness that at any point while I was in Vietnam I was liable to be shot down, captured, and thrown into a POW camp for the duration. It raised the stakes of what I was doing and gave everything I did heightened meaning. This experience, more than anything else outside of Vietnam itself, impressed on me that what I had volunteered for, what I was giving everything I had to, was not a boys' game, nor a movie. It was real, and its consequences would be just as real.

The SERE training I went through was a program the Navy ran for troops whose duties placed them in particular danger of being captured in Vietnam. It was mostly aircrews and river boat crews who went through it, and I did my stint before I headed overseas. For those of us on the West Coast, the training took place at an isolated camp in the mountains of Southern California. At the time, we referred to it simply as "survival school" or Warner Springs, but nowadays the program is better known by its SERE acronym. Members of the public who pay attention to these things now know a lot more about SERE training than they used to. We've learned that the military used aspects of this training to develop its expertise in what it likes to call enhanced interrogation, but which laymen know as torture. I'm not quite sure why we emphasized the "survival school" part of it when we talked about the program, as opposed to the POW camp part of it, especially because it's the training to withstand torture that remains indelibly impressed on me.

I use the word "torture" pointedly. In April 2009, as more and more was coming to light about American treatment of prisoners of war in the Afghanistan and Iraq wars, the *New York Times'* public editor, Clark Hoyt, wrote a column ("Telling the Brutal Truth"[11]) about the debate over how to describe what was being done to them. He quoted various readers who objected to the *Times* calling the treatment "harsh," "brutal," and "torture"; they claimed that this demonstrated the paper's political bias.

In his next column (May 2, 2009), Hoyt included the letter I wrote him commenting on the issue, and it's worth noting that the *Times* has continued using the word torture in its pages.

Here's what I had to say at the time:

> When I went through the Navy's Survival, Evasion, Resistance and Escape training program in 1966, before shipping out to Vietnam where I flew many combat missions, everyone—those who ran the program and those who underwent the training—referred to what was done to us as "torture."
>
> We operated on the assumption that that was the whole point of it, to prepare us for full-scale torture by subjecting us to a smaller-scale version of it. There would have been no point to it if we hadn't understood the direct connection between what was done to us at the SERE camp and what we could expect if we were shot down and captured.
>
> To the extent that these recent activities have been adapted from SERE practices as they were developed in the 1960s, they should be called what those intimately familiar with them called them: torture. [12]

I haven't changed my opinion, but I have given a lot more thought to the impact that torture had on me. Two things loom largest in my mind. First, I now understand that when my plane strayed into Red China (a story I'll soon be telling you), that POW training did a lot more than just prepare me for what would happen if I were captured. It added an additional element of icy fear as I waited to be shot down. Indeed, on every mission I flew in the Tonkin Gulf, I was intensely aware of what lay in store if something went wrong. I'm not suggesting that some sort of training wasn't necessary, but I now understand one of its unforeseen (at least by me) consequences: it made everything I did a lot scarier. I wasn't dealing with just the dangers of carrier flying, but with the promise that if something went wrong, and if I managed to survive, my troubles would be just beginning. This heightened my apprehension on every mission I flew and added to the stress. It's fair to say that a big piece of what I've carried with me ever since has to do with the ways I was tortured when I went through that POW training.

We began by trying to live off the land in a place where there was almost nothing to eat and were soon weak from hunger. We were hiding, running, crossing fields strung with concertina wire and swept by machine gun fire. Wrapped in parachutes, we slept on the ground—barely. It was only after we'd been suitably weakened that we were thrown into the POW camp and put to work hauling heavy stones back and forth across the compound for much of each day.

I was punched and kicked by guards. At first, I tried to stand up to the punches, but as they continued to rain on me I began to roll with them, falling to the ground. I was ordered to stand and when I was slow in complying heavily booted feet kicked at me.

I gradually found a rhythm, falling when hit, standing when kicked. This went on over the course of a few days, with the guards singling us out one by one for individual treatment. The guards were well-trained to act entirely in the role of foreign, generically eastern European soldiers. (At that early stage of the Vietnam War the US military was still operating with a Cold War mentality.) I found it difficult to keep in mind the play-acting aspects of the experience and increasingly began to experience it as real. The beatings and the hunger were entirely real and physically immediate and loomed larger and larger in my consciousness; the parts that understood that this wasn't for real receded into the background.

The object was to prepare us for prisoner-of-war camps if we were shot down over North Vietnam. In the early stages of the training, we were taught that during the Korean War US troops had fared poorly in POW camps, with their brainwashing programs (made famous by *The Manchurian Candidate*). The military was concerned that too many men had broken down under torture and confessed to war crimes. After the war our military compared the performance of Turkish soldiers in these same POW camps and determined that the Turks had held up much better than American troops had; they set out to learn what had produced this resiliency. (I have since learned that the CIA undertook large-scale research on this problem and that the training I went through was part of that work.) The official rationale was that if we could withstand the torture at the outset, and bond together with other POWs, we would convince our captors that we weren't worth the trouble of breaking.

It was to that end that the SERE camps were created, as proving grounds where we would be subjected to a POW experience as realistic as could be achieved without causing us major physical harm. These camps were the only place in the US military where troops could deliberately be physically harmed as a matter of legal, official policy, and we were beaten and tortured. It's a matter of record that some of us underwent waterboarding there, while others were forced to watch.

I can't speak for the other branches of the armed forces, but for the US Navy the issue was preparing its fliers for the possibility of being incarcerated in one of North Vietnam's POW camps, the most famous (or infamous) of which was the Hanoi Hilton (officially Hoa Lo Prison, built, incidentally, by the French), where Senator John McCain spent 5 years. Most of those who passed through the program were bomber and fighter pilots, but there were a handful of us enlisted crewmen on these missions in the North, and we went through the training alongside our pilots.

The guards deliberately broke one man right in front of us, as an example. They first reduced him to sobbing, bawling tears, then seated him in the shade beside his comrades, who were laboring in the sun, and gave him extra food and water. As we understood the program's protocol, he would be made to sign papers stating that the United States was engaged in biological and chemical warfare in Vietnam and that these would be placed permanently in his service record. It was a distressing, disturbing sight, seeing him there, and I was deeply afraid that the same thing would be done to me. I don't believe there was anyone in the camp who hadn't volunteered for duties that would expose us to the risk of being captured, and we were, I think, of a shared mindset that the last thing we wanted was to have documents like these, with our signatures on them, follow us about for the rest of our lives, which is how we envisioned the process.

After a day or two, a guard singled me out. He marched me through the gate, out into the open land—the area surrounding the camp was devoid of any features at all, creating a completely bare field of fire—and then toward the only objects in immediate view, a couple of black wooden boxes sitting on the ground and tilted at about a 30-degree angle. He swung open the lid on one of them and motioned for me to climb in. I stepped over the edge and into the box. Then he pushed me down, forced me down, crammed me down. I folded up into a fetal position as he swung the lid closed on top of me.

It was stifling—it sat out in the direct sun. There wasn't room enough for me inside it—it was clearly meant for someone smaller than me. I panicked for a moment. "I can't do this," I thought. Every part of my body seemed to stiffen, and I began to ache within minutes. "I'm going to die in here." "Let me out," I screamed in my mind, but without making a sound. "I'll confess to any war crimes they want me to sign," I thought, "if they keep me in here long."

And then, realizing that I had no idea how long I was going to be in there, I relaxed. Not much. Just a little bit really, but enough for me to understand that I wasn't going to die on the spot. It would take a while. I tried to focus my mind on something else, on anything else, anything that would keep me from thinking about how painful it was, how difficult it was to breathe, how hot it was, how long I was likely to be in there. Again and again the panic would bubble up and again and again I would fight to relax just enough to let it pass by, and to allow me to turn my mind elsewhere.

I think I passed out a couple of times, whether from the fear, the lack of oxygen, or the failure of my blood to circulate, I can't say. And then slowly the fear of dying started to ratchet up. I kept reminding myself that this "wasn't for real," that it was a mock POW camp, and that they wouldn't let me die. But they actually had no way of knowing whether I'd died already.

The notion that this wasn't for real did nothing to alleviate the fear, the pain, the sense that I wasn't going to make it.

I wanted desperately not to break and was hanging on the best I could. When I was finally hauled out of the box by a guard and marched into an interrogation chamber, my legs were so numb that I had to be dragged much of the way before I regained the circulation I needed to walk on my own. I was thrust into a darkened room and fell stumbling onto the floor. As I gradually became aware of my surroundings, I saw a table with a man seated behind it and two or three guards standing near me. I was yanked to my feet and faced toward the table. Powerful lights shone in my eyes. I was marginally aware that my glasses were so filthy at that point that they blocked out some of the glare. Questions were shouted at me. I gave my name, rank, serial number, and date of birth, as I had been instructed to do, but nothing else. My interrogator ordered the guards to begin to torture me. I was punched and kicked a bit as they moved me into position, then bent me over backwards, into an awkward position and strapped into place.

I really don't remember much of this part. They stopped with the physical punishment and questioned me again. After a while I gave up some inconsequential information but refused to speak more. There was more torture, but I don't recall it. After a time, when I wouldn't speak, the interrogator ordered the guard to throw me back into the black box. I'm not quite sure how my legs had the strength to carry me out of the room.

As I was marched from the interrogation quarters toward the boxes, I was aware that I had been on the brink of cracking when I'd been released from my first stint in the box. I was sure that I wouldn't last long at all the second time around, but I made up my mind to endure as long as I could before I began screaming to be let out. It was terrifying. I knew I wasn't likely to last, that I would crack, that I would be forced to undergo the same humiliations as the fellow I'd seen broken earlier. I wanted desperately not to do that, and I was preparing myself to climb back into the box. The guard marched me up to the boxes, then past them, up to the prison compound entryway. As the gates opened, I was shoved sprawling into the dirt. Lying face down on the ground, my mouth full of grit, I thought to myself that that moment might just prove to be one of the happiest of my life. I had survived and prevailed. At least for moment, and that was all the mattered to me right then.

I was 18, a man-child. I was full of *thumos* or spirit, well-endowed with testosterone, I suspect, and well-nurtured by all the stories of toughness that a youth in 1950s to 1960s America took in like mother's milk. I'd seen the POW camp movies, and I thought I knew the drill. But when I step away from the immediacy of my own mindset, from the way I consciously experienced this at the time—that is, what I thought was going on, what was happening to me—what leaps out at me has mostly to do with how young I was in comparison to the others who were going through it with me. I'm talking about the pilots who were most likely to get shot down in Vietnam. The Hanoi Hilton held mostly fliers. In 1970 the average POW there was a 32 year old pilot with a wife and two children. They were, for most part, Navy lieutenants or Air Force captains, with college degrees (Tucker, 2000, p. 337).[13]

They were also guys who'd explicitly sought out duty like this—they pursued the heroic. I have to say much the same thing about myself, but the difference is that for all my bravado, I was pretty much still an unformed lad, 15 years younger and without much of the life experience these older men had. I suspect that the mock POW training, especially the torture, may have had a different sort of impact on my psyche, on my self.

Oddly enough, over the years I've held a strangely positive view of what happened to me when I was locked in that black box and interrogated. I've heard myself explaining to others that when I'm deeply stressed, and unsure about whether I have the strength of commitment to continue on despite adversity, I recall that afternoon. I was certain that I about to break when I was pulled out of the box and taken in for interrogation. The torture there was relief. When my interrogator said I hadn't provided enough information and ordered the guard to shove me back into the box, my immediate thought was that I wouldn't be able to withstand it. I knew I'd been close to cracking already, so how would I manage to handle any more of it? And then I said to myself that I'd get back in and stand it for as long as I could. For the rest of my life, when I've been in doubt about whether I could persevere in some difficult situation, I've remembered what I did then. I resolve to continue on until I can simply go no further.

Once, when I was explaining this to a friend, he pointed out that I might be drawing the wrong conclusion. It's just as likely, he said, that this all was part of my makeup before the POW camp incident, and that that's what enabled me to bear it then, when I was 18. I don't know, but I suspect there's not a lot of difference—it's just that the black box version gives me something concrete to hold onto when I need to encourage myself.

After two years of constant training, learning what it means to work around aircraft and on a carrier's flight deck, learning to operate a massive radar system, control other planes, direct interceptors, and cultivating a mindset that told me I must be prepared to be shot down and held prisoner, in the fall of 1966 I went to war.

NOTES

1. Video clips of recruit parade formations from both the 1960s and the present can be seen on YouTube.

2. Among the general Vietnam War histories I've found particularly useful I would include the following titles, in addition to the more specific studies I refer to throughout this work: Max Hastings' *Vietnam: An Epic Tragedy, 1945–1975* (2018); George Herring's *America's Longest*

War (2013); Frederik Logevall's *Choosing War* (1999) and *Embers of War* (2012); Stanley Karnow's *Vietnam* (1997); Edward Marolda's *The U.S. Navy in the Vietnam War* (2002); John Nichols' *On Yankee Station: The Naval Air War Over Vietnam* (1987). The most complete account of the Tonkin Gulf Incident is Edward Moïse's *Tonkin Gulf and the Escalation of the Vietnam War* (2019). A quick glance at the comments sections for these books on Amazon will make it clear that a vocal minority sharply disagrees with each of these works.

3. It's my sense that this ironic detachment, leavened with unremitting animosity toward the military, has been a constant since at least World War II. In his classic *Battle Cry*, Leon Uris (1953) captures the ambivalence in his Marine battalion; the men mix their pride in the Corps with nonstop bitching about *everything* they experience. These days, without a draft to chase young people into the military, it's possible that the hostility has ratcheted down a bit, but based on my own conversations with many of the veterans on my campus I don't think a whole lot has changed. Geoff Dyer's (2014) vivid account of a carrier in the Persian Gulf suggests a Navy that's somewhat less ironic and more gung ho than the one I remember, but I suspect that a lot of what he reports reflects both his own outlook and attitudes staged for the media as much as it does any real diminution of the virtuoso hostility I remember.

4. Edwin Armistead's book *AWACS and Hawkeyes: The Complete History of Airborne Early Warning Aircraft* (2002) provides a comprehensive look at the evolution of these early warning planes.

5. The Navy's official history magazine ran a short piece on the Fudds: Polmar (2010), "Elmer Fudd's Flying Cousin," https://www.usni.org/magazines/naval-history-magazine/2010/april/historic-aircraft. A concise account of the Fudd's development and history appears in René Francillon's *Grumman Aircraft Since 1929* (1989, pp. 401–405).

6. The E-2s' radar was looked on as superior to the Fudds' "when all their systems were working to specifications. Reliability, however, was poor, and maintenance personnel had a difficult time keeping the systems operational." It wasn't until the E-2B, the Hawkeye's second iteration, was deployed in late 1970 that many of its "reliability and maintenance problems" were solved (Francillon, 1989, p. 458).

7. In *Manliness*, Harvey Mansfield (2007) discusses what he thinks it means—or should mean—to be a man in today's society. A lot of what he says strikes me as bombast, but his commentaries on *thumos* have helped me as I've tried to develop some perspective on my own sense of the concept.

8. In *Another Great Day at Sea*, Geoff Dyer (2014) captures the chaotic flavor of operations on modern carriers as well as anyone has.

9. It's easy to suppose that this is no longer relevant on today's carriers, given all the emphasis placed on their main force, the F/A-18 Hornet jets. But every carrier is still outfitted with an E-2 Hawkeye squadron and a couple of C-2 Greyhounds, the passenger- and freight-hauling aircraft, all of which are propeller-driven.

10. Appendix A includes an opinion piece I wrote in response to these reports.

11. http://www.nytimes.com/2009/04/26/opinion/26pubed.html.

12. http://www.nytimes.com/2009/05/03/opinion/03pubedlet.html.

13. Enough POW camp movies have been filmed for the IMDb movie data-base site to have a "Top 35 prisoners of war movies" list (which actually lists 37 films). Half of these appeared during my youth. https://www.imdb.com/list/ls054603419/.

Chapter Three

Everyday Danger

And then we were in the thick of it, a part of what Navy hands called the Tonkin Gulf Yacht Club, out on Yankee Station. I'd like to begin with a thoughtful account of what we were supposed to be doing in Vietnam, but it wasn't entirely clear to us, even at the time. The USS *Bennington* (CVS-20) was a World War II–vintage aircraft carrier, one of the 24 "Essex class" ships built at top speed in a 3-year sprint during the war (and named for a Revolutionary War battle fought in Bennington, Vermont, not what was in those days the women's college there). Benn's aircraft fought in the last battles of the Pacific war, helped sink *Yamato*, the most powerful battleship that ever sailed, and bombed Japan's home islands, but by the 1960s it was assigned to anti-submarine duties in a war theater where submarines played a limited role. On some of its Vietnam tours Benn carried a detachment of A-4 attack jets, but when we departed for the Tonkin Gulf in 1966 our air group consisted of two S-2F (known to all as "Stoofs") anti-submarine squadrons (VS-33, VS-38), a helicopter squadron (HS-8), and my unit, VAW-11's Detachment Q.

Like the other carriers fighting the Vietnam War, we steamed constantly in the mouth of the Tonkin Gulf, in the expanse of open water a hundred miles or so off the North Vietnam coast that the Navy had designated as Yankee Station. Our Fudds flew daily missions that were part radar picket line guarding the fleet, part surveillance of coastal shipping, part reconnaissance, part control of attack aircraft, part search and rescue, and part general utility work. We scoured the Gulf, the southern coast of North Vietnam, and the northern coast of South Vietnam. The work was unrelenting—literally. *Bennington* put six of its Stoofs and a Fudd into the air five times a day (the choppers seemed to fly on their own cycle). Each of our missions was 7 hours long; given the hour of overlap with both the preceding and following

sorties, these five 5-hour spans on station resulted in round-the-clock cover-
age of the waters and skies we'd taken charge of.

Much of what we were doing carried over as standard order of procedure
(SOP) from before the Tonkin Gulf Incident, but as the war progressed our
duties took on greater intensity. Our detachment carried the four Fudds normally allotted to an antisubmarine carrier, but because one of them, 762, was
permanently grounded by an antenna problem and became what we called a
"hangar-bay queen," we had to fly all those sorties with only three operational aircraft. With just those three birds available to us, we were responsible for
keeping an aircraft on station 24/7. We did it, but it placed an unanticipated
strain on all of us, especially on the radar technicians and the enlisted aircrewmen. We also lacked the sixth aircrewman we should have been assigned, and yet, short a plane and a flight tech, I don't recall that we never
missed a sortie; in retrospect, I have no idea how we pulled that off. We
fulfilled our primary mission with aplomb, continuously screening the fleet
from attack, whether by subs, bombers, or surface craft.

**Figure 3.1.   USS *Bennington* underway. The US Navy aircraft carrier USS *Ben-
nington* (CVS-20) underway at sea on 5 March 1965.** *PH3 Rassmussen, US
Navy—US Navy photo NH 97581*

Our task wasn't as conspicuous as an attack carrier's, if that's the right word, but our Fudds' responsibilities were at least as demanding and exhausting as those flying from the bigger and newer attack carriers (the CVAs). The Fudd outfit on the USS *Shangri-La*, for example, steaming on Yankee Station with us, lost some of its planes to crashes and had only one aircraft operational during parts of its deployment and only two for much of it. How many missions could any of their crewmen actually have flown? I can hardly conceive of it.

It's not fair for me to say that those guys had it easy. But then again how can you say that you had it harder than someone else without there being at least some implication that the others had it easier, and thus hinting that it was easy for them? I don't know. But this is what comes immediately to mind.

Here's another contradiction, at least for me. There's always been a part of me that has felt in some way diminished by having been aboard an antisub carrier rather than an attack carrier. I'm not arguing that this makes much sense, yet the perception lingers. Our primary task was to defend the fleet from attack, not mount attacks. Defense rarely seems as glamorous as offense. But this is precisely what made our duties more exacting: If weather or other factors should keep a unit from launching a bomb strike, as it often did, they didn't launch, but there have got to be aircraft out guarding the fleet no matter what's happening.

Having only one or two operational aircraft for much of a deployment wasn't the rule, but the *Shangri-La*'s experience tells us the attack carriers could actually operate without their Fudds because they were relying on us to screen them. On our anti-sub carrier, though, there was a very clear understanding that we couldn't function without our Fudds. That's why we drove ourselves so hard.

This isn't just my own subjective recollection. An item in the report my skipper filed as we finished our final tour on Yankee Station comes to mind. We needed more enlisted aircrewmen, he wrote, because operations were far too demanding for the five techs we carried. It's clear that the issues lodged in my mind were really there: I'm not making them up.

What most strikes me, though, is still another contradiction. I was well-trained to handle all my jobs. I was prepared to maintain the radar and to run it. What I was not prepared for was the sheer intensity of what we were doing, and because I had no idea of what was in store for us, I didn't really grasp what was happening to me. I can describe what I did quite clearly, but at the time, I was oblivious to how it was affecting me because it just wasn't something we talked about. I assume this is because none of us really understood what was happening.

Chapter 3

ON THE LINE

Now I can tell you what *I* was doing out there. While engines are what get the planes into the air and keep them there, our Fudds' purpose was to provide radar platforms. The engines performed well and weren't prone to breaking down, but this was not the case with the radar, which was in constant need of repair. Five of us were assigned to maintain the radar and our duties were distributed among three distinct sorts of jobs. Three of us were teenagers serving our first and only tours of duty; two were older men (in their 30s) who were career Navy.

Maintaining the complex interconnections among the APS-82 system's two dozen plus different components and the vast webs of circuitry that linked them lay at center of this task. All five of us worked on the system as a whole within the planes themselves. Three of us, the two older guys and I, repaired the individual radar components—the black boxes—in the avionics shop. And three of us, one of the older men and two of the younger men, including me, did the third job, which was flying missions in the combined role of radar intercept controller and flight technician. Only two of us, one of the older guys (Jim Bates) and I, did all three tasks. There were also two radio technicians who flew as flight techs; they did radio repair work on the aircraft, but not in the shop.

Only two of us, then, worked at all three of the distinct jobs associated with the radar: a career first class petty officer in his 30s and me, a teenager on his first tour. I was, as always, determined to take on as much responsibility as I could, and I understand this in terms of my thumos, of my ambition and drive for mastery. I pursued expertise in every facet of the radar system. Until the E-2 Hawkeyes ultimately replaced them, our Fudds were one of the most technologically-advanced aircraft the Navy had, not in the sense of aerodynamic flight characteristics, but in their sophisticated electronics systems, and I wasn't content with simply taking on one or two facets of the job. By the time we returned from the Tonkin Gulf I was skilled—if not expert—at everything. Well before I was 20, I'd earned my gold aircrew wings and been promoted to second class petty officer (Aviation Electronics Technician Second Class or ATR2 AC, in our jargon; an E5 in shared US military parlance) and was one of the world's leading E-1B radar technicians. A small arena, to be sure, but a difficult and responsible one just the same.

The dangers inherent in flying off aircraft carriers were—to an extent that astonishes me now—cloaked by the routine of the missions we flew. It's a commonplace notion that war entails long periods of boredom interrupted by bursts of intense terror. I understand the truth in this, but I wonder if it's really the case, in the sense that when I look back now I see that the boredom intertwined with the tension and terror; it wasn't one or the other, but the two coexisting. I still have nightmares about flying—about what we sometimes called boring holes in the sky, just flying on and on and on. But my nightmares capture the stress of responsibility and watchfulness I experienced throughout those long flights.

What really amazes me, though, is that what seemed at the time to be the *routine* maintenance work would turn out to have a greater, and more lasting, impact on me that the flying itself did. Let me explain.

EVERYDAY DANGER: MAINTAINING THE FUDDS ON YANKEE STATION

Up in the Radome

When I stop and think about it, it strikes me as odd—absurd, even—and yet somehow typical that although the Fudd's radome was its reason for being, it was designed as an afterthought, and almost casually slapped onto the back of the newly-designed S-2. I imagine that the last thing the engineers were thinking about as they designed it was how the men who maintained and repaired the radar could possibly do the work that needed to be done within the radome itself. And I was one of those guys.

Because of its aerodynamic shape, the radome was asymmetrical and higher in some places than others; at the highest point the clearance between floor and ceiling was a bit over four feet. The antenna was a huge, elliptical steel crescent, curving in a sweeping parabola, 17 feet from end to end, tapering to blunt points at the tips and about three feet high at the center. It rested at the end of a long boom that was in turn mounted on a low pedestal bolted to the radome's floor.

In order to keep the antenna on a level plane, as the aircraft itself climbed and banked (and because it hung in the air at a slight angle even when it was flying straight and level) the dish tilted continuously up and down as it revolved. Inputs from various instruments flowed into the system in order to feed the antenna the information it needed to keep itself in its even plane, and the machinery that accomplished this was delicate. The circuitry controlling the antenna regularly went out of whack and had to be repaired and recalibrated. Since virtually everything in the Fudd's radar system was fragile and in need of continual mending, we took for granted the work we did on the antenna.

Except for one major task: the only way we could be certain we had successfully repaired an antenna problem was to climb up into the radome and directly observe it as it rotated, to make sure that the dish was tilting precisely as it should.

And this is why I say the entire system was designed with no thought given to just how we were going to do this work. There was no light in the radome—it was dark up there in broad daylight, when at least a little light filtered in from the hatch in the floor, but totally black at night or when the plane was on the carrier's hangar deck. A series of metal struts crossed the floor to strengthen it enough to bear our weight as we worked up there. The only way to know if the dish was tilting properly was to watch a simple gauge—an arrow pointing at a ray of lines marking the angle of tilt—as the antenna revolved. And because it was dark, the technician had to focus his flashlight on the gauge. [1]

Now comes the tricky part. This hulking antenna rotated at six revolutions per minute. Period. It turned either at full speed or it was stopped, with nothing in between. There was no way a man up inside the radome could run alongside it at 6 rpm while still watching the gauge. The solution we arrived at, in order to "walk the antenna," which is how we described the process of checking its operation, was for one man to sit below in the aircraft, at the antenna motor's on-off switch. The man up inside the radome had to signal his partner to switch the antenna motor on and off at a speed slow enough for him to scuttle alongside the antenna while gazing intently at the gauge. Lacking any built-in technology, we signaled with a series of stomps on the floor of the radome. Under optimal conditions this was fairly effective, but because aircraft engines were constantly roaring everywhere around us as we worked, it was often impossible to hear clearly. It took enormous concentration simply to turn that little switch on and off at the right pace.

The attention of the man up in the radome is directed entirely at the gauge as he tries to keep his flashlight pointing at it. The antenna is huge and powerful and threatens at every second to go too fast. The technician must stomp his foot at the right pace and in the right rhythm to keep the antenna turning at a rate that ensures he can move with it. But the radome roof is low and asymmetrical, and so he is bent over, at some points nearly in two, as he scrambles beside the boom. And the hash-work of exposed metal struts on the floor grab at his feet as he scuttles along, curled into a near-fetal position. There in the dark, with his entire concentration aimed at the gauge, while keeping his flashlight aimed at it, he dances over the latticework grabbing at his feet.

If the antenna starts turning too quickly, it will smash into the man walking it. It is massive and can easily kill him. A shipmate was killed when one of Benn's antennas crushed him against a steel bulkhead. We understood the danger, but what else could we do? The Fudd was only as valuable as its radar, and the radar simply didn't work unless the antenna was reliable.

Once, when I was at the controls inside the plane and my buddy Gene Warden was up in the radome, I missed the signal as he stomped, and let the antenna revolve for a split second too long. It gained speed and momentum, and Warden saved himself only by diving headlong into the narrow space at the trailing edge of the radome. He was fortunate; if he'd been at the front or the side, there would have been no clearance and he would have been smashed. When he clambered down he blasted me for my incompetence, which had nearly killed him. I don't know what happened, whether I couldn't hear his stomps above the roar of a jet engine beside us, or if I had momentarily dozed off, a much-too-frequent occurrence since I often worked around the clock, sometimes for days on end. But it scared me so much that from then on I refused to work at the controls below, insisting instead that I be the one walking the antenna up in the radome.

Once while I was up there, I was just a fraction of a second late stomping the signal to halt the antenna's rotation. My boot caught on a strut on the floor, then jammed against it, and the dish came to a stop, pinning my leg in place. I could not move. Had the dish revolved any further than it did, it would have ripped off my leg before hurling me through the side of radome. It took three men to pull the antenna back (there was no way to reverse it) far enough for me to slip my foot out.

See this with me: There I am, up inside that black hole, bent nearly into a fetal position, attention riveted on a gauge illuminated by my hand-held flashlight, scuttling around sideways, trying to time my stomps properly to keep the antenna slowly rotating, all the while dancing over metal work I can't see in the dark. My attention is focused on the task at hand, making sure that the antenna is tilting properly as it revolves. Only the edges of my attention are concerned with stomping at the right pace to signal the man at the controls below, who can see nothing of what is taking place above him. And nothing but my attention's most residual pieces are left for maintaining the proper crouch and avoiding the struts grabbing at my feet.

The darkness, the confinement, the crouch. All of my consciousness devoted to the job at hand as I stay in that fetal crouch, scuttling crabwise. When I began writing about these experiences, I framed them in terms of confronting "the womb and the tomb," right there in the radome, and I thought about how both womb and tomb are usually out of harm's way. Not so in those E-1 radomes, which were designed only for the purposes of the mission, with no concern given to the safety of the men who had to maintain them. And so to climb up into one and walk the antenna was like crawling into a womb that was womb-like only in its confinement. I can feel, as I write, the terrible hunching over, the need to shrink myself for safety's sake, the utter confusion about how to keep all my attention focused on the gauge while still trying to preserve myself. All this is imprinted on me.

Since then, however, I've encountered an even more disturbing way of perceiving all this. Michael Graziano, in *The Spaces Between Us*, describes a human stress response or startle reflex known in German as "das Zusammenschrecken." The term, "roughly translated as a 'whole body shrinking,' is actually a good description of the act. The patient shrinks down, spine curved forward, knees bent, chin down and shoulders raised, hands pulled across the front, face contracted into a mighty squint that puckers the skin around the eyes and exposes the eyes." He explains that the reaction is designed for efficient protection. It comes involuntarily and unconsciously and in "the first fraction of a second the startle reflex puts you into a generalized safety stance" (2018, p. 6).

I see in all this exactly the body language that characterized my response while I was doing my routine, everyday work. I did jobs like these over and over, went through the stereotypical physical response repeatedly, and had it all sink into my bones. In Chapter 8, when I discuss what I call "lamination," I'll return to this phenomenon.

These passages about working in the radome are among the very first things I wrote about the war, and they really are at the beginning of my understanding of it. It wasn't until I looked back at what I'd written that I could see what was going on. For all the power and drama of some of what I did, flying in North Vietnamese waters and making daily catapult shots and arrested landings, it was the routine maintenance work that stuck out most in my mind. In the telling of it I began to sense why it stuck with me. I felt pushed to write all this by the startling realization that some of the things I was unaware of at the time were the things that had the most impact on me.

Changing a Scope on the Flight Deck

While the antenna was the scariest element of the radar system to work on, it wasn't the piece that gave us the most trouble. That distinction goes to the radar indicators, or scopes. It was rare for one of our missions to return without at least of the plane's two scopes in need of repair. The relatively primitive circuitry simply wasn't up to the incessant strain. We were continually replacing scopes, and each weighed 113 pounds (a number etched in my brain by all times I hoisted one onto my shoulder). On land, at the naval air station, two technicians could easily carry a scope together, but aboard ship, where we moved continually up and down steep, narrow staircases (or "ladders," as sailors call them) it was nearly impossible for two to efficiently carry a scope. At sea, with only a small handful of technicians in a Fudd detachment, I soon learned how to back up to the workbench, squat, heave the scope up onto my back, stand, stooping forward, and rest the weight against my shoulder and upper back. Then I would climb the ladders from the shop to the flight deck, my left hand free to pull me up. (I followed the reverse course when pulling an inoperative scope out of the plane and hauling it to the shop.)

On Yankee Station combat readiness conditions kept the carrier's flight deck in absolute darkness at night, which was my shift. Under these conditions one does not shine a light. Although neither the Viet Cong nor the North Vietnamese had submarines to threaten us with torpedoes, World War

II wasn't far in the past—there were still more than a few hands who'd served then—and we operated with the mindset that any breach of this strict discipline could expose our position and draw an attack. I can't speak for others, but I certainly never showed a light on a dark deck. Beneath the nearly perpetual overcast, no moon or stars broke through: it really was pitch black.

The seas were not particularly heavy in the Tonkin Gulf, but we were always underway, and the deck pitched and rolled. I would climb onto the flight deck somewhere aft, hunched over, scope on my back, and start forward along the deck's centerline. Bearing the scope along the flight deck of the rolling ship caused me to move pretty much like a drunkard, weaving from side to side as the weight and inertia kept me from walking straight down the deck.

The easiest way to locate a Fudd in the dark is to feel for its tall vertical tailfins, one rising up from the end of the horizontal stabilizer on either side of the plane's tail. When I reach a point on the deck's centerline that I think is parallel to the plane, I stop and face to the right, toward what I hope is the plane, but certainly toward the edge of the deck. There are no railings on the deck and the catwalks running alongside are well below its edge. I've got this massive radar scope perched on my back and I am bent beneath it. I begin to creep slowly toward the edge, my left arm stretched out ahead of me, waving back and forth, feeling for the plane's tailfin. The ship is pitching and rolling, and I'm using much of my attention just to steady myself. As I move closer toward the edge of the deck, my steps get shorter and shorter. The planes are held in place, so they won't slide off the deck in heavy seas, by "tie-down" chains that stretch out between fastening points on the planes and anchoring points recessed into the deck. I move cautiously so that if I encounter one of these tie-down chains I don't trip over it.

I can't see a thing; all I can do is feel for the tailfin. I'm drawing closer to where I know the edge of the deck looms before me. If I miss the plane and keep moving ahead, I'll come to the edge of the deck, which I won't be able to see. I won't know it's there till I've stepped off and vanished into the night and sea. (We lost men who simply disappeared while working on the flight deck in the dark.) I continue waving my left arm, trying to find the tailfin, shuffling forward, not at all sure how closely I'm approaching the edge of the deck. Finally, I conclude that I've missed the plane and am about to plunge off the side of ship and into the sea, so I stop, turn around, and walk slowly and carefully, avoiding tie-down chains, back toward the centerline. When I sense that I'm well inboard, I move a few feet forward, face right, and begin the process all over again. Slowly I head toward the edge, arm waving, body hunched under the scope, moving blindly, feeling again for the tailfin I haven't been able to find. Perhaps this time my hand will brush against it, or maybe not. If not, I start again. When I find the fin, I face left and begin to move toward the plane's hatch, to climb in, drag the scope along the floor, mount it, hook it up, and check it.

Nearly all of the aspects of work up in the womb of the radome have their equivalents out on the flight deck in the open air of night: the utter blackness, the hunching under the weight of scope, the shuffling feet, feeling for tie-down chains. Instead of focusing my concentration on the tilt gauge though, now I'm feeling for the tailfin. And instead of trying to keep out of the way of the massive, sweeping antenna that could crush me, or hurl me through the side of the radome, I'm trying to avoid stepping off the edge of the flight deck and plummeting into the sea. I cannot do the job if I focus my attention on my own safety.

As I've worked at writing this, I find myself asking, all these years later, why I didn't put the scope down or use a light. It seemed there was never enough time to get the planes repaired and ready for the next mission. We worked as fast as we could and setting a scope on the deck in the pitch dark would have led to all sorts of seemingly unconscionable delays. Under full combat readiness conditions, as I've said, one simply does not show a light on an exposed deck. I took my job and my responsibility to the ship and the rest of the crew with complete and utter seriousness; it simply never occurred to me to do either.

When I wasn't flying or working to repair and ready a plane for its next mission, I was in the avionics shop, at the radar bench, troubleshooting and repairing the black boxes we'd pulled and replaced. The replacements, of course, were the boxes we'd fixed in the shop. I shuttled from one task to the other continuously, either operating the radar, troubleshooting the system as a whole in the plane, or repairing the components in the shop. While we were on Yankee Station, I lived radar, I lived our mission, I bore the weight of protecting the fleet, the air group, and the other aircrews on my shoulders, in the same way that I carried those heavy scopes on them.

As I say, there were multiple sets of tasks entailed in maintaining the Fudd's radar. While I was at work in Benn's avionics shop, technicians from the air group's other squadrons toiled at nearby workbenches. They were guys my age, guys I was friendly with, like Fallon, Roa, and Carson, who were, like me, completing our first and only 4-year hitches. The shop, though, was the only place they worked, and they worked regular shifts, just 12 hours a day, 7 days a week. I mention them because they loved giving me a hard time for being, as they saw it, so very gung ho. At the time I didn't see myself that way: I was simply doing my job. But from their perspective I certainly seemed driven, since I never worked less than 16 hours a day, and usually much longer, sometimes without a stop for days.

We'd all joined the Navy for the same basic reasons: the training, the travel, and to avoid the draft. None of us spoke in terms of anything like patriotism or an eagerness to fight. We'd all signed up at about the same time, that is, before we realized there was going to be a war; we all thought we were joining the peacetime Navy. They were my peers—bright guys, eager to work but without prospects for attending college—yet their outlook was, I guess, very different than mine. They were content just doing their jobs, perhaps. Though we all started from roughly the same place, I soon bolted off in another direction. Out of all the guys passing through the avionics schools, nearly all of them young like me, only a handful of us actually craved action, or felt an urge to do something heroic.

There was a sort of method in my madness, though. For the harder and longer I worked, the more skillful I grew. I went from an apprentice-like status to being a fully qualified, expert technician in a short time, and as with everything else, this had multiple consequences. It meant that when I was working aboard ship, whether on the flight deck or the shop, I understood what it meant for the system to work properly, what it looked like, and how effective it was. And within my being I felt the importance of the equipment—how the radar operators, charged with a multitude of responsibilities, depended on it to work at maximum efficiency. My consciousness of every element meant there was a never a time—because I was always working—when I wasn't thinking at some level about how crucial the work was. I was always burdened, always tense, always concerned.

But it also meant that I was performing with a level of expertise that allowed me to transfer knowledge from one sphere to another. And that's when something began to shift in me. I wasn't content with simply doing my job. It became personal, a part of me. I couldn't entirely separate myself out from the job and the radar and our mission. That's when I pushed myself beyond merely doing dangerous work without reflecting on it. I became reckless and foolhardy, in the name of completing our missions.

I started doing something I now find myself almost disbelieving.

In-Flight Scope Repair

The complex radar system's many elements all merged together in the radar indicator, the scope. The Fudd carried two, one for the radar officer and one for the enlisted flight tech. Their round, green radar screens were about a foot in diameter, set in the center of the unit's face, which was about 16 by 24 inches. The entire black box, roughly 32 inches deep, slid into a deep recess directly in front of the radar operator's position. A dozen or so cables attached to the rear of the scope, which was, because of the way it slid so tightly into its casing and pressed up against the pilot's back, nearly inaccessible. When I installed or removed a scope, I had to reach my arm through a narrow slit at the rear and connect or disconnect the cables entirely by feel and memory, since it was impossible to see what my hands were doing. It was an exacting task and had to be done slowly because it was so easy to make mistakes.

When radar images failed to properly display, I had to troubleshoot the entire radar system in order to determine whether the problem lay with the scope itself or in one of the many other pieces of equipment that fed into it, but the scopes themselves were fragile and the most common source of problems. When it was clear that the scope was causing the problem, it had to be removed, repaired, and replaced. Normally, I pulled it from the aircraft after the plane had returned to the ship, hauled it to the avionics shop, and hooked it up to a work bench. As an experienced bench tech, I could sometimes diagnose simple problems just by looking at the display on the screen, but other failures might take hours to diagnose and repair.

The Fudd's APS-82 radar was designed and constructed in the mid-1950s, before transistors were available, and these scopes used vacuum tubes, technology most people alive today have never seen. A dozen or so circuit boards, each fitted with eight or ten tubes, sat on either side of the giant cathode-ray tube that was the radar screen. While capacitors, resistors, and a multitude of other components often broke down, it was the brittle glass tubes with their delicate filaments that most commonly failed—not surprisingly, considering the enormous forces the equipment was subjected to during catapult launches and arrested landings, along with ceaseless vibrations from the two powerful aircraft engines. There were so many tubes, though, and so many types of them, that even if it was likely that a problem was caused by a failed tube, it usually took much careful troubleshooting to figure out just which had to be replaced.

Several of the circuits and several types of tubes were more prone to failure than others, and I could sometimes narrow the problem to a specific circuit simply by observing the behavior of the images on the scope's screen display. Because I also worked at repairing the scopes in the avionics shop, I understood their circuitry well enough to visually diagnose the more common tube failures while we were still airborne.

As I grew increasingly familiar with the Fudd and the entirety of its radar system, I came to know which types of tubes and which circuits were most likely to fail, and what symptoms would appear on the radar display when they did. I began stuffing spare tubes into the pockets of my flight suit so I could make repairs to the scopes in-flight. Without being able to put the scope on the workbench with all its testing equipment, of course, diagnoses still had to be guessed at, and these repairs had to be done entirely on a trial-and-error basis.

Sometimes a malfunctioning scope could be fixed and put back into service fairly quickly, but more often it took several attempts to locate the tube that needed replacing. While the tube itself could be swapped once the scope was withdrawn from its narrow sleeve, it took a lot of time to disconnect the scope from all its cables, pull it out, fix it, slide it back in, and reconnect the cables. The entire process might have to be done multiple times before I located appropriate tube. But the radar was useless without the scopes, and I felt pressed to keep them in working order.

At some point during our tour, after months of constantly operating, repairing, and maintaining the radar, I assumed such a sense of responsibility for our missions that I began doing something that was especially reckless and foolhardy. No one stopped me, though, so I went ahead with it on a regular basis.

When a scope malfunctioned in flight, and I could see that it probably needed only to have one or another of its tubes replaced, I would make the repair while it was still hooked up to the system and operating. This meant pulling it part-way out of its sleeve and exposing the first circuit board or two. I would then slide my hand and arm down inside the scope, curling my fingers around the tubes most likely to have failed. Pulling a red-hot tube loose, I would slowly withdraw it from inside the scope, then thread my hand back down inside the scope and insert a replacement into the empty socket. A glance at the radar screen would tell me whether it was now working properly. If it wasn't, I repeated the process until I had either fixed the problem or run out of options. I could then slide the scope all the way down into its sleeve and put it back into service.

The problem of course was that all these circuits were live. That is, the scopes ran on high-voltage, high-amperage electricity, and had no on/off switches. They switched on along with the entire system. The radar transmitter's power had to be raised and lowered slowly and thus the system could not be readily shut off and on; I had to work on the scopes while they were fully powered. I could not see where my hand was going and I had to direct its movements entirely by my recollection of how the circuits were laid out, but if I brushed against the wrong part I would be electrocuted.

Undertaking this risky procedure was entirely voluntary on my part. It was my own idea, and I pursued it on my own. No one was ordering me to do it. In fact, if any of my superiors in the avionics division had known what I was doing they would probably have had a fit. I was so eager to save time and to keep my aircraft operating as effectively as possible, though, that I was willing to risk electrocution in order to get the radar operational as quickly as possible.

None of the situations I've been describing here were momentary episodes, rare occurrences, or responses to sudden attacks. They were *everyday tasks*—the work I did each day, sometimes several times a day—exposing me to *everyday danger*. I tried to ignore the danger, and still try, and yet at the same time, the sheer force of these physical experiences impresses itself so deeply upon me that I cannot entirely disregard it. At the time I didn't think much about it, didn't acknowledge it, yet even today it hasn't dissipated, hasn't gone away. It's here, etched more permanently into my body than any tattoo. It's part of my flesh. I can call these events, these tasks, to mind, and see them, but even now as I write them down I can barely call the fear up into consciousness, because it's as submerged and embedded now as it was then. I couldn't have done the job if I had allowed myself to be conscious of what it was doing to me, and now I seem to have no way to reclaim that which I so successfully suppressed.

I find myself likening the impact of all this to thinking about how my spleen feels or my endocrine system's working. They're there and I have every reason to believe that they're functioning, but I cannot know them firsthand, I can't feel them—my knowledge of these things is purely theoretical. And those repeated stress events, and others, seem to occupy similar places for me. I can reasonably believe they exist, but I can't call up the fear. Perhaps that's not entirely true though, because as I write these passages I can so clearly visualize the scenes, and feel my body hunching, feel my neck tautening, feel my breath shorten, feel the tension in my body, see my hands shaking. I just can't cleanly open the connections between the images I describe and the state my body is in. I know the connections are there, but I haven't been able to get access to them. The same evident strengths and hidden emotional wrangling that allowed me to hide these from myself then keep them concealed now.

THE CATAPULT LAUNCH

When it was time for me to fly, I stopped whatever else I'd been working on, pulled on my flight suit, and headed to our ready room for the briefing. I gathered up my equipment: helmet, sidearm (a .38 revolver with lots of tracer bullets), survival vest (packed with gear), Mae West (the Navy's term for flotation vests), a camera, and charts and maps. And then I donned my parachute harness. We didn't keep our parachutes strapped on while flying; they hung instead beside the escape hatch through which we'd bail out if we had to abandon the aircraft.

Making our way from the ready room up to the flight deck, we stopped in the flight deck control center and checked a mock-up of the deck that showed us where our aircraft was spotted. When it was a nighttime mission, which is what I invariably flew, we waited in the red light for a time as our eyes began adjusting to the dark. Then we stepped into the inky blackness.

Out on the open deck, we were greeted by the roar of jet engines and thumping rotors, and physically felt the shift in intensity as the choppers began to lift off. These were the plane guards or "angels" that took station, one on either side of the ship, during flight deck operations. Their job was to pick up anyone blown or knocked off the deck into the sea below, or to attempt the rescue of any survivors of crashes that might take place during the launch and recovery procedures, and as they took to the sky, they reminded us, in case we were in any need of reminding, of all that could go wrong in the next few minutes.

Heading forward into the wind that ripped across the deck, searching out my aircraft, I tugged the harness straps, trying to fit the harness as closely as possible to my waist, hips, and thighs; the walking motion pushed back against the straps and helped get the harness to sit as snugly as possible. I'd been taught that the snap and jerk of the chute's sudden opening can slice the harness deeply into one's inner thighs and groin if there's any slack in it, and been warned to wear my harness as tightly as I could bear it. In doing do so, I was engaging in a timeless ritual, well known to the ancients. I was literally girding my loins.

"Girding your loins" is a metaphor we still use when we speak of preparing for battle, but it's normally just that, a metaphor. As I advanced up the deck, I actually *was* girding my loins, and the old phrase captured both the spirit and the fact of getting ready for combat. It was one of many potent physical sensations lodging in my body (and lingering still in my nervous system today) as I moved toward my plane: the bone-shaking roar of jet engines, the wind thrusting at my body as the ship built up steam and began its turn into the wind, my steps adjusting to the rolling deck and my hands insistently tugging at the harness straps, tightening them not simply to the point where they began to hurt, but also to wrap myself in emotional armor for what lay ahead.

Growing out of all these sensations, yet in some odd way offsetting and diminishing them, making them bearable, was the sweetest, lightest touch of *swagger*. All the flowing energy of the flight deck crew scrambling around us and the hulking power of the planes, impatient to return to their element, were focused on getting my comrades and me aloft. Despite the fact that most of the other enlisted sailors thought the handful of us who served as crewmen in our birds were crazy, in that brief moment I was acting out in real life all the glorious movies I'd watched as a kid. It wasn't big or boastful, but it was there, and in some ways that hint of swagger was the point of it all. Girding my loins for battle was the foretaste of action that pulled it all together, and down through the years since then all the competing, colliding physical sensations that are the essence of the flight deck are still lodged in that simple gesture.

As our crew reached the aircraft, we returned to routine, each of us proceeding with our own portions of the preflight inspection. I clambered up on top to see that the hatch leading into the radome was fastened securely, checked that all the other hatches were secure, then double-checked the escape hatch directly over my seat, to make sure its handle was tightly locked into place (the change in pressure as the pilots closed their overhead hatches just after we became airborne could pop the seal on my hatch, yank it out into the slipstream, and then slam it into the leading edge of the wing if the handle were not properly seated; I knew this because it had happened to me). I made sure that all the black boxes—all the radar components—were securely locked into place with the twisted wires that kept them from vibrating loose (between each mission, we'd been removing and replacing the many pieces of equipment that had failed during the plane's previous mission, and in our exhausted state we couldn't always be counted on to secure things properly).

As the fleet's eyes in the Tonkin Gulf, our Fudds were the first aircraft launched during combat missions. We strapped ourselves in and the pilot turned the engines. Still in the realm of the routine, we continued checking to ensure that everything in the aircraft was ready for action, always a dubious proposition in those badly abused old crates. Switching on my radar, without powering up the transmitter, I held my breath until I could be sure everything was operational. When we'd determined that things were functioning well enough to proceed, we were towed into position, then taxied toward the catapult. The pilot twitched us forward until we reached the foot of the catapult.

The catapult harness is attached to the plane's front landing gear, while the holdback bar restrains it. At a signal from the catapult officer the pilot runs our engines up to full power. The aircraft is vibrating intensely. The pilot and copilot position their hands behind the throttles to keep them from being jarred loose by the catapult's jolt. When the pilot is sure we're at maximum power, he salutes the catapult officer, who throws his arm forward with the launch signal, and the holdback bar releases. The catapult shuttle rockets us down the deck. In the aircraft, we're slammed back against our seats and pinned motionless by the g-forces of acceleration.[2]

The carrier is heading directly into the wind, steaming at full speed as it launches its aircraft, and the combination of the catapult and the wind over the bow are, under ordinary circumstances, enough to lift the plane into the air. There is a problem, though, that haunts everyone who flies off the decks of aircraft carriers, the "cold cat shot." I'd heard about this malfunction from the moment I became a Navy flier, and I'd even seen it in films before I understood exactly what they were. Because of the tremendous beating all the equipment on a carrier receives in the course of normal operations, it frequently breaks down. When the hydraulic system that drove the catapults on the old World War II–vintage carriers like *Bennington* misfired during a catapult shot, it might fail to engage the pistons, in which case the plane goes nowhere. But if it fails as it is dragging the plane down the deck, which is when it is most likely to conk out, it simply hauls the plane forward and off the ship's bow, without sufficient airspeed for the plane to lift off. The plane drops from the bow, cannot rise, and plunges into the sea below. The carrier,

Figure 3.2.   A Fudd being catapulted off USS *Hancock*. *US Navy*

steaming at top speed, slices over the plane as it pancakes into the water just ahead. This is the cold cat shot.

Fighter planes have ejection seats that rocket the pilots high enough into the air for their parachutes to deploy. They then drop into the sea alongside or astern of the ship. But in the stodgy old E-1Bs there were no ejection seats, only overhead escape hatches. If the crew somehow survives the crash into the sea below, they have only a second or two to react. This is why pilots leave their hatches open. Sitting behind them, I would have to unstrap and open my hatch before climbing out, and then attempt to swim away from the onrushing ship and its whirling screws. The chances of accomplishing all this in the brief instant between the plane smashing into the sea and the point at which the ship steams over it are slim, and the odds of surviving a cold cat shot are not good (I think the technical term here is probably "fat chance"). Cold cat shots aren't common—we would lose too many crews and their aircraft if they were—but they're frequent enough that everyone who flies off carriers is fully aware of the likelihood that they may experience one each time they launch.

I vividly recall my first carrier launch. First, the sudden shift from the routine check lists and careful taxiing to the intense vibration of the aircraft as the pilot ran the engines to full power. Then the instantaneous and unbelievable force of being slammed against the back of my seat as the catapult engaged, gravity and inertia enveloping me with the impact of what felt like an onrushing freight train. The sense of being pinned helplessly in place, unable to move as the plane roared down the deck to the bow. And then it happened. As we left the deck, the plane dropped toward the sea below instead of leaping upward into the sky. A cold cat shot! I was sure of it. As we plummeted through the air my mind raced, running through everything I'd have to do if we survived the crash into the sea. I slid my right arm up over my head to get it as close as possible to the handle on the escape hatch. With my left hand I prepared to unlock my seat harness the moment we hit. I was going to push myself upward, hit the release handle with my right hand as I rose, shove it free, pop the hatch, and climb out all in one motion.

I remember no prayers and no regrets. Just, what is it that I can do to save myself? On that first cat shot, after what were in fact only a few seconds, but which seemed like an eternity, I began to grasp that we were no longer hurtling down toward the sea. We were in fact flying straight and level, and then gaining altitude. We were not going to crash. I was not going to die right then.

I grasped a simple fact no one had ever bothered to explain to me. In the films I could recall, high performance aircraft reached the end of the deck and either shot upward into the sky or plummeted down into the sea. I'd never seen—or at least never noticed—a lumbering old reconnaissance aircraft overloaded with technology launch from a carrier. I discovered the Fudds were so heavy that after reaching the end of flight deck, they routinely dropped off the ship's bow before gaining enough airspeed to ascend into the sky. I survived that first carrier launch, but only after being entirely sure that a carrier was about to steam over me. And in the next three years, on every carrier launch I made, I relived that first one. With the run-up of engines, the roar and vibration, the impact of the catapult, arrival at the end of the deck, and precipitous drop off the bow, I felt in my bones that we were experiencing a cold cat shot and that I was going to crash into the sea.

THE ARRESTED RECOVERY

Landing on a carrier—technically an "arrested recovery" or simply a "recovery," but better-known in the business as a "trap"—is a lot like the launch, only hairier. Much hairier. During a launch, tension builds, there's a sudden explosion of g-forces, and then relative calm. But so very much more can go wrong during a recovery that the fear is far more intense than it is during the buildup to a catapult shot. Emotionally, what naval aviators call a recovery is sort of the exact opposite of what recovery means in normal speech.

I suspect that landing on a carrier deck is the single most exacting task anyone can routinely carry out, brain surgery notwithstanding. Riding in the seat behind the pilot isn't difficult, but it involves enduring the same risks, without any sense of control over what happens. The pilot can decide to abort a landing, go around, and try again. In the backseat you can't decide anything. It gives a very different meaning to the phrase going along for the ride, and right now I'd rather be doing almost anything than imagining myself back in a plane about to make an arrested recovery.

At the end of the mission, we'd return to *Bennington* and enter the Delta-pattern, the holding pattern as the planes line up to land. I'd run the transmitter's power down, stow the antenna, and shut off all the radar systems. Occasionally, I was so exhausted that I fell asleep the moment my scope went blank and woke up only as we slammed against the arresting wire. I find it hard to believe that I could sleep through a carrier approach and landing, but that really is how bad it got at times. Every part of a carrier landing must be executed perfectly for it to be successful—that is, to avoid crashing—and it's a powerful statement to say that my exhaustion outweighed my apprehension.

As the descending planes approach, the carrier itself is steaming into the wind at high speed to achieve maximum airflow along the deck. The ship is pitching and rolling, and the tail-end of the flight deck can be heaving up and down by ten feet or more. The plane must remain relatively high or risk crashing if the ship's stern is on the upswing as the plane crosses it. But the plane must also drop down onto the deck within a very short distance in order for its tailhook to catch one of the steel arresting cables that stretch across the deck. That is, the plane must come in high but drop down almost instantaneously. The solution to this puzzle is radically simple. As the plane passes over the ship's stern, the pilot cuts power and the plane slams down onto the deck, like a slab of meat tossed onto a griddle. This is why carrier landings are known as controlled crashes.

The plane has now lost all forward thrust and is relying entirely on its tailhook and the arresting cables to stop it. But if the landing isn't perfect or if the tailhook should bounce or skip over the arresting cable or if the cable snaps or the hook rips out, the plane faces a new challenge. It keeps rolling forward at high speed along the line of the angled deck. The pilot returns his throttles to full thrust, so that as it rolls off the angled deck and begins dropping toward the sea below, it regains enough power to get airborne again.

These failed landings, when the plane touches down but is unable to stop, are called "bolters." They're pretty common. I flew with one pilot who made so many of them that he was nicknamed "Bolter." High performance jets,

Figure 3.3. E-1B making an arrested landing aboard USS *Bennington*. *US Navy photo [1] from the USS* Bennington *(CVS-20) 1968 cruise book available at Navy-site.de*

with the ability to go to the full military power of afterburners, can manage them pretty well. But propeller planes, with piston-driven engines, and especially Fudds laden with heavy steel radar components, don't respond that way when the pilot goes to full throttle. When a Fudd boltered, it rolled off the angled deck and began falling toward the sea. Outside my hatch I see the carrier's gray side rising. I listen to the roar of the engines; in fact I feel the starboard engine—just a couple of feet from my head—viscerally as it throbs. I wait, unable to do anything else, for us to gain enough airspeed to level off before we strike the water. For some reason we didn't lose any of our aircraft this way while we were on Yankee Station, but we certainly lost planes this way during training exercises (which is, of course, why we trained so intensively *before* we deployed).

Here's the essence of the dilemma that lies at the heart of every carrier landing. If the pilot's approach is just inches too low, the plane crashes into the round-down, the curved, trailing edge of the flight deck. If it's too high, the tailhook misses the wires; the pilot's cut the power and the plane rolls forward and off the angled deck, striving for enough speed to get airborne again. There's a system of lights and mirrors, the "meatball," that allow the pilot to line up precisely in this agonizingly tiny window, but with the ship heaving and the winds shifting, it's a lot like trying to thread a needle while at full gallop on horseback. Although I've made hundreds of carrier landings, and know it can be done, it still sounds impossible when I describe it.

It's intimidating, it's scary, and almost no one can do it. In fact, hardly anyone in their right mind would even consider doing it. It is something that requires not only incredible physical skill, but also a fairly bizarre mindset that thrills to turning the seemingly impossible into a routine operation. It's a glamorous job, but only a tiny percentage of those who aspire to it can qualify to bring these beasts of weaponized technology onto a carrier on a daily basis.

I sat behind my pilot trusting that he was just the right degree of crazy. I was still a teenager, and crazy enough myself to believe in him. While I can still conceive of landing on a carrier under optimal conditions on a one-time basis, the thought of doing it every day under every imaginable condition strikes me as sheer folly now. I'm no longer even able to understand how I did that night in and night out under combat conditions.

I still live with this recurring image: We're returning from a 7-hour mission on Yankee Station, descending toward our carrier, its deck ahead of us, rising and falling with the swells of the sea. Directly in front of me, the pilot grips the overhead throttles tightly in his right hand, varying the thrust ever so slightly, working to keep the landing signal light—the meatball—lined up and our plane on the proper glide slope. No matter how many times we do this successfully, my mind keeps running through images of failed approaches that bring the plane in too low, allowing it to crash into the ship's stern, rather than slamming safely down onto its heaving deck. I want desperately to have those throttles in my own grasp, to add power, to get us up higher, above the massive steel round-down that caps the tail end of the flight deck. My arm wants to reach up, to take control, to avoid imminent calamity.

ROUTINE MISSIONS

Telling of the Fudds's long, routine missions feels anticlimactic at this point. If I'm not thinking carefully about them, what stands out is how uneventful most seemed, broken up only by occasional, classic intervals of danger, excitement, and fear. Some of the excitement and fear was accidental, like springing an oil leak and having to land as an engine was beginning to fail. With just one engine, the pilot loses most of his ability to maneuver, and if the tailhook should miss the arresting wires, the plane can't possibly get airborne again; you drop off the side and crash into the sea below, a pretty sure way to get killed. We were in theory supposed to "bingo" to the big American airbase at Da Nang, on the South Vietnam coast near the demilitarized zone (the border with North Vietnam) when this happened, but operational concerns—that is, having enough aircraft available—tend to wreak havoc with protocols.

On *Bennington*'s next tour on the line, my friend and fellow flight tech Nate Terry made a landing when his Fudd's tailhook ripped out as it hit the arresting wire. The plane skidded off the side and caught on a sponson, preventing it from falling into the sea. These perils weren't routine, but they constantly threatened, and our minds and emotional networks were continually on high alert in order to prepare for them.

There were times, though, when the dangers were more calculated and deliberate.

Our normal task was to fly back and forth along a track called a barrier. Depending on the specific mission, our barriers were lengthy parallel lines (sometimes described as a racetrack pattern) running either approximately east-west across the Tonkin Gulf, creating a surveillance barrier between North Vietnam and the fleet, or roughly north-south off the coast of North Vietnam. We established a picket line between our ships and North Vietnam and were charged with keeping an eye on everything that was happening in the Gulf, to ensure that the fleet remained safe from attack. We operated with six aircraft under our control and we directed them toward the surface contacts—mostly small vessels—we tracked on our radar. At times we were responsible for "delousing" attack groups returning from bombing missions, that is, checking radar and identification (IFF) signals to spot any North Vietnamese MiGs trying unobtrusively to tuck themselves in behind our planes as a means of closely approaching and attacking the carriers. [3]

At other times, we flew along the coasts of North Vietnam, the demilitarized zone, and northernmost South Vietnam as part of Operation Sea Dragon. Then our task was coastal interdiction—locating small vessels suspected of smuggling weapons and supplies out of the North to the Viet Cong in South Vietnam—and directing aircraft under our control to overfly and inspect them. It turns out that the VC mostly captured their weapons in the field. This could mean our efforts were effective, but most historians have concluded that there really weren't many weapons being shipped in.

The routine character of these jobs often made it seem that we were doing little more than boring holes in the sky. That, of course, is the nature of war. But a lot was happening amidst all this routine. First, some of our pilots were more gung ho than others and keener on earning medals. Fudds were slow, not very maneuverable, unarmed, and unarmored. They were meant neither to attack nor to get shot at. But when we picked up surface contacts near us and no patrol aircraft were immediately available, our pilots would sometimes take it on themselves to check out the contacts, which is when we exposed ourselves to small arms fire. This not only gave us something to talk about but provided us with a reason to call attack aircraft in for a strike, blowing some otherwise harmless junk out of the water.

On our first deployment to Yankee Station we replaced USS *Kearsarge*. A pal of mine who I'd trained with, R. R. Moore, was a flight tech in

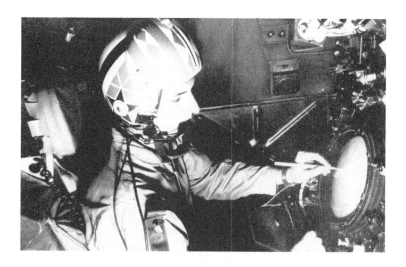

Figure 3.4. Radar intercept controller at an E-1B's radar scope. *US Navy photo [1] from the USS* **Kearsarge** *(CVS-33) 1966 cruise book available at Navysite.de*

Kearsarge's Fudd detachment and when we met briefly as our carriers swapped positions, he told me a story. One of the S-2Fs they were controlling simply disappeared during a mission; wreckage was located in the sea but no survivors were found. It was assumed they were shot down by a small craft they approached (this episode is documented in Homecoming Project 1990). The fact that we weren't an attack outfit didn't necessarily insulate us from attacks.

Bennington would occasionally shift to Dixie Station, off the South Vietnam coast. These sorties didn't count towards Air Medals unless we came within close proximity of the shoreline. That's when pilots would instruct us to locate contacts close inshore, which of course exposed us to coastal fire. If this all sounds like crazy risk-taking, it was. This was, of course, what pilots who had hoped to be flying jet fighters did as a means of offsetting their frustrations at not being in the thick of things over Hanoi, and perhaps as a means of gaining points and renown that would help them graduate into jets.[4]

There was, I suppose, an aspect of shepherding in our missions. Words and phrases like "pastoral" and "the Good Shepherd" convey our society's general attitude toward shepherds, which doesn't coincide much with traditional notions of virility. On the one hand, this called the martial character of what we were doing into question. On the other, we *were* keeping watch over the entire fleet, and at that point, still relatively early in the war, we really had no sense of whether the North would continue launching torpedo attacks on our ships. Our full attention was required, and if we worked hard at it, we

Figure 3.5.   The author being awarded the Air Medal. *Author's personal collection*

could feel we were doing something at least marginally important, even if it wasn't what we'd seen in the movies.

We also directed helicopter traffic all over the Gulf, as Benn's choppers traveled among the fleet. And we located and helped rescue the pilots who bailed out of shot-up aircraft as they returned from bombing runs up north.

Underlying everything I did was the relentless intersection of exhaustion and responsibility. Despite the commonplace notion that combat consists of long periods of intense boredom interrupted by short periods of equally intense danger, my own experience tells me there's a lot of overlap between the two conditions. Because I was doing so many different jobs, and because the planes were in need of almost constant repair, I was pushed—and more to the point, I pushed myself—to my physical and emotional limits. I had few reserves of energy and alertness left. Yet I had eagerly taken on this enormous responsibility, controlling planes in hostile airspace and maintaining a close watch over our portion of the Gulf. We flew 7-hour missions and for six of those hours I remained intensely aware of anything and everything that appeared on my radar scope. It sounds dramatic in retrospect, and it was, I suppose, but I was mostly too dazed to know it at the time. It was a struggle simply to remain alert, let alone make the decisions I faced.

Things were a bit different for our pilots, though. With the autopilot engaged, they had little to do while we were flying a long barrier leg. I recall them playing cards with one another at times or tuning in the armed forces radio broadcasts of popular music. Or even engaging in a rare bit of horse-play.

Occasionally, one or the other of the pilots would come back and sit at a radar scope, and one of us on the radar would go forward and take the controls. Once while I was in the cockpit, in the copilot's seat, the pilot wrote a note on his kneeboard, instructing me to pull my visor down, unzip the flap that kept the sunlight out of the radar compartment, go aft to the relief tube (a funnel and hose for urinating while on station), and hold on for dear life. Then over the intercom he said he was going to take a leak, and that Pete would handle the controls. Back I went and grabbed onto a stanchion. Then the pilot began whipping and flipping the plane, up and down and around (undoubtedly reprising a scene from the classic comedy, *It's a Mad, Mad, Mad World*, which had been released a couple of years earlier). The copilot, sitting in my seat, struggled desperately against the jolting as he climbed forward into the cockpit and grabbed the yoke, then turned to see the pilot laughing his head off beside him.

I'd love to say that morale-easing antics like this were common, but they weren't. We were mostly deadly solemn while we were on station and took our work seriously. Sometimes we pushed beyond what seemed prudent, but that's what carrier fliers are renowned for. I still shake my head at some of the things we did. In particular, helping with search and rescue operations called for some crazy activity, dropping flares from a Fudd.

SMOKE LIGHTS

Some part of me, writing about this 50 years later, has a lot of trouble believing it. Not the relatively straightforward action of dropping the flares we called smoke lights but imagining how I did this so unquestioningly. Part of it was simply that I was accustomed to following orders. Part of it was the notion that I might well find myself in the same straits someday and would have to rely on someone to take the same risks for me. There were probably lots of other things going on inside me, too, things I was quite unaware of. But what I see most starkly right now is the break from the tension of sitting at a scope, and the chance to do something that seemed riskier and more exciting than gazing endlessly at it. This is a relative thing, I realize. Flying off a carrier in the Tonkin Gulf seems risky enough from this distance. But I was 19. I fantasized danger and valor. This was a step closer to it. That, of course, is one of the main reasons that it's boys we send off to war, because they're prone to thinking there's glory in doing stupid stuff.

The little that's been written about carrier aviation in the Vietnam War is about the jet fighters and bombers. Surprisingly, though, a lone Fudd did make it into one of the more comprehensive accounts, J. D. Sherwood's *Afterburner,* where we hear about the career of James McBride, who flew Fudds on Yankee Station before moving on to A-4 Skyhawk bombers. This is one of the few things ever published about the exploits of either E-1Bs or their radar techs, and it only made it into print as a minor, fleeting incident in McBride's story.

After starting off piloting large transport planes, McBride says, he sought out carrier duty and made his way to an E-1B outfit. As Sherwood writes,

> The E-1, an airborne early warning plane, carried a large radar (enclosed in a dome) on its back and typically directed fighters toward enemy aircraft approaching a carrier task force. The ungainly E-1B hardly represented the pinnacle of carrier aviation; in fact, such an assignment might have been greeted by laughter from a group of fighter pilots, but for McBride it represented a vital stepping-stone into the more glamorous world of jets, or "fast-movers," as they were often called.
>
> In May 1965, McBride deployed with Detachment 62 of VAW-12 to Vietnam and experienced his first taste of the air war over Southeast Asia. Although the primary job of the E-1 was to fly ten miles off the coast of Vietnam to scan the skies for MiGs with its over-horizon radar, McBride on occasion flew "ash and trash missions" over the beach to pick up mail in Saigon or perform other errands. He even participated in an experimental night flare-dropping mission with the E-1. On that mission, McBride flew over the designated target and ordered one of his radar men to kick four flares out the hatch of the E-1. Initially, only two of the flares ignited, but another one did so as it hit the ground, touching off a secondary explosion. Using this secondary explosion as a beacon, attack planes pulverized the target. McBride received a letter of commendation from his carrier air wing commander (CAG) for the mission; however, given the difficulty of ejecting flares from the E-1, the CAG opted to cancel the experiment and return the E-1s to their original surveillance and fighter direction duties (2004, p. 20).

I've quoted this passage at length because it mentions a radar man "kicking" flares out of the E-1's hatch and then, in passing, the difficulty of doing so. I was one of the radar men who dropped the flares out of E-1s and "difficult" hardly captures the nature of the task.

Among the many responsibilities we handled during our daily missions in the Gulf was a role in search and rescue (SAR) operations for pilots downed in the Gulf's waters. A steady stream of shot-up attack aircraft headed back to their carriers from sorties over North Vietnam. Some of them didn't make it all the way, and their pilots bailed out over the sea. Along with venomous sea snakes, those waters were known for their dense fogs. At times visibility was so bad that the helicopters and destroyers engaged in searches couldn't find the downed aviators. Our Fudds, with their powerful radar, were then called in to assist. We were able to direct the rescuers to the life rafts where the fliers waited to be hoisted up out of the drink. Once they were close, the destroyers could locate survivors with their own equipment, but the choppers, up in the fog, could not always spot life rafts even with us directing them. Something more was called for.

Our Fudds' immediate predecessors had been modified versions of A-1 bombers with radar pods in their bellies, giving them an appearance that led to their being nicknamed "Guppies." They had a tube for jettisoning a "smoke light"—a heavy-duty flare that sends up fiery sparks and billowing smoke when it strikes the water. These were used for marking objects in the sea, including submarines at periscope depth. So we were still familiar with the practice of dropping flares, though the Fudds themselves weren't rigged to do this. My outfit's can-do spirit led us to install simple brackets for mounting smoke lights with us inside the aircraft, for marking downed aviators rather than targets.

At its shortest, most detailed range setting, the Fudd's radar scope displayed an image with only a two-mile radius, as opposed to its 200-mile maximum range setting. At the 2-mile range we could easily paint the radar reflection of a life raft and home in on it. We'd direct our pilots toward the raft as our aircraft approached low enough for them to make visual contact through the fog. The flight tech—me—was sent aft to the emergency escape hatch.

The E-1's entry hatch was designed to serve double duty as an emergency escape hatch through which we would leap if we needed to bail out. There was a quick-release lever beside it, which would spring the hatch door from its hinges with just a short, quick jerk. The release mechanisms on escape hatches were designed so that they would open easily under the worst of circumstances, which meant they could accidentally pop open under even the best conditions. I had the escape hatch directly over my seat accidentally pop open once just after we launched, despite the fact that I'd carefully checked it just minutes before as part of my preflight inspection of the aircraft. It sailed directly back into the leading edge of the wing and gouged it open, exposing fuel lines, hydraulic lines, and mechanical systems, and sending us immediately back for an emergency landing. So I held in my mind a very vivid understanding of just how readily the aft emergency escape hatch might break loose and fall away.

During these SAR missions my job was to open the hatch and lean against it with all the force I could muster, in order to keep it open 8 inches or so against the force of the wind in our slipstream. There was nothing I could hold onto to brace or steady myself, and I needed both hands to hold the smoke light anyway. So there I was, shoving the hatch out against the wind with all my weight and force, steadying it while holding a smoke light, knowing full well that the hatch could fall away at any moment, with me tumbling out, at an altitude much too low to make my parachute of any use.

As the pilots gained visual contact and approached the downed aviator in his life raft, I would maintain my position, with my weight full against the open hatch. Just as we were about to pass over the raft, the pilot would wave his arm as a signal for me to jettison the smoke light. The flare would drop nearly on top of the raft (I always worried that we'd hit one, and I think we once got a complaint for coming too close), and we'd peel away. Then the helicopter trailing us would home in on the flare, make visual contact with the raft, drop its cable, and haul the flier to safety.

Given the fog's density and the general difficulty of spotting a tiny raft in the open sea, especially at night, it sometimes took us several passes to locate the raft. In the meantime, though, I had to remain in position, leaning outward, using all my strength to keep the hatch open against the wind, hands gripping the flare, tensely waiting the order to hurl it out, all the while remaining fully aware that at any moment the hatch might break away, sending me to my death. In Sherwood's book the dropping of flares at first sounds quite casual—a radar man simply kicks them out of the hatch, he says. But then he goes on to note the difficulty of ejecting flares from a Fudd. That's because there was in fact no way to simply kick the flares out; it required the radar tech to literally take his life into his own hands to do the job.

Long after the war, when I was having trouble explaining to the Veterans Administration just what my duties were in the war, and tracking down documents with which to do so, I came upon a report my commanding officer had filed as we left Vietnam for home. One of his recommendations for the future was to retrofit the Fudds with tubes like the old Guppies, designed expressly to eject smoke lights. He explained that while no one doubted how valuable the practice of dropping smoke lights near downed aviators could be, the chances of losing a flight tech in the process were too great, and entirely offset the value of any rescue efforts.

Having lulled you with routine, I can now tell you a truly cinematic story, one with real drama and cinematic value: the day my Fudd wound up in Red China.

NOTES

1. I was recently able to climb up into the radome of the Fudd that sits on the deck of the USS *Intrepid* (in New York Harbor) as part of its naval aviation museum collection. It looks

exactly as I remember it. I thank Eric Boehm, the collection's curator, for allowing me to make this visit.

2. In recent years we've learned that the g-forces football players experience as they routinely smash their heads into one another can and do cause concussions, and that these impacts, endlessly repeated, have been conclusively shown to result in the brain damage known as Chronic Traumatic Encephalopathy (CTE), which often leads to early-onset dementia. The National Football League refused for years to consider the possibility that the sport was causing this characteristic injury, but conclusive evidence eventually forced it to undertake major changes in the ways the game is played, the sorts of equipment used, and medical oversight on the playing fields. More recently, CTE has been linked to other sports as well. I can think of no reason why the routine g-forces of catapult launches and arrested landings should not be studied in order to determine whether they, too, might be inflicting similar damage on Navy fliers' brains. I have thus far found no one willing to fight to have such studies undertaken.

3. I'm always fascinated by historical precedents for events and situations I've experienced. The problem of delousing is not new: the development of the IFF (Identification Friend or Foe) system (also known as a "squawk") helped solve a problem dating back at least to the time of the emperor Charlemagne. According to a contemporaneous eighth-century chronicle, as a band of Charlemagne's Frankish troops returned from a skirmish, some of the Saxons with whom they'd been battling "intermingled themselves with them as if they were their comrades and so got into the Franks' encampment," where they wreaked much damage (Nelson, 2019, p. 112).

4. The various service branches set different requirements for earning the Air Medal. In that era's Navy we were awarded an Air Medal for each twenty combat missions we flew. Sorties flown on Yankee Station were by definition combat missions. When we were operating further south, on Dixie Station, however, sorties only counted toward a medal if we flew close inshore. Each subsequent twenty combat missions earned us another medal, which entailed adding a gold star to the original medal or ribbon. I earned two gold stars to go with my original Air Medal, for having flown 70 combat missions. Later, I would have trouble convincing the Veterans Administration that I flew combat missions, because in the Army, apparently, any flight in the Vietnam theater counted toward a medal, whether it was a combat mission or not.

Chapter Four

Stress and Decompression

My war's climax came as we were returning to Yankee Station from Hong Kong, where we'd enjoyed a few days' rest and recuperation (R&R) and I was able to spend a few months' pay eating, drinking, and buying tailored suits, shirts, and shoes. The date was February 9, 1967, according to Neil Sheehan's article in the *New York Times*. *Bennington* was steaming south along the eastern and southern shores of Hainan, the vast Chinese island that borders the Tonkin Gulf. My crew launched with Dan Tootle as pilot. Not long after we were airborne the antenna, up in the radome, malfunctioned; it wouldn't tilt as it rotated, rendering our radar useless. There was no way to get at the antenna while we were airborne and there was nothing I could do to repair it. We still had our radio-relay equipment, though, and we were ordered to remain on station—to keep flying—in order to facilitate communication between the ship and the other aircraft that had launched with us. We were flying a barrier, a straight line, near the southeast corner of Hainan. The cloud cover was heavy and we flew above it at maybe 5,000 feet. We should have been traveling roughly tangent to the coast.

U.S. Says Plane Flew Over Hainan Accidentally;
Reports Unarmed Navy Craft Returned to Carrier Safely
Peking Complains of Previous Intrusions Over Island

By NEIL SHEEHAN Special to The New York Times
February 10, 1967, Friday
Page 2.

WASHINGTON, Feb. 9--An unarmed United States Navy plane accidently flew over part of Communist China's Hainan Island today, the Defense Department announced.

Figure 4.1. *New York Times* February 10, 1967, headline. *New York Times*

Lt. Tootle made a navigation error. I no longer recall just what his mistake was, but the simple fact is that our pilots ordinarily relied on the radar team to do the navigating. It wasn't that surprising, I suppose, that he miscalculated. We weren't aware of the error, of course, flying above the clouds. Then Lt. Jake Froelich, the copilot, commented that the cloud cover seemed to be breaking up ahead of us.

Suddenly, all hell broke loose. Below us, through the parting clouds, we saw a large bay and a harbor. We had already crossed the shoreline and were over what, we realized, could only be Hainan. Just as we grasped where we were, the antiaircraft fire began. The Chinese guns opened up and flak was exploding all around us. Tootle did exactly what he needed to do: he dove down into the oncoming fire. Since we had no idea where exactly we were (I later determined on our navigation charts that this was Yulin, site of a major Chinese naval base), we had no idea of what defenses were arrayed below us, but we assumed that interceptors or surface-to-air missiles (SAMs) would

Figure 4.2. Map of Yankee Station. *US Navy photo [1] from the USS* Somers *(DDG-34) 1969–1970 cruise book available at Navysite.de*

appear at any moment.[1] We weren't aware of all the details, but we had a general sense of what Naval Intelligence would later report: "During the war, Chinese fighters shot down five Navy aircraft and two Air Force planes that inadvertently strayed over the island of Hainan or southern China. Only one naval aviator returned from his mission in these cases" (Mobley and Marolda, 2015, p. 41).

SAMs don't arm themselves until they've reached a preset altitude (so that if they misfire and fall they don't kill the people firing them), and the rule of thumb is that when SAMs are fired, the appropriate defensive move is to dive immediately for low altitude. And so it was that Tootle dove down into the flak, trying to get us as low as possible as quickly as possible.

The E-1B wasn't a high-performance aircraft; with its hulking radome, it was in flight even more awkward than it looked on the ground. And ours flew slowly, agonizingly slowly under the circumstances. We were diving directly into the gunfire, which seemed not be training down very effectively—the flak continued exploding above us. We were waiting for the SAMs to appear, fully aware that the Fudd was incapable of anything remotely resembling evasive action. And with even greater apprehension we were expecting that at any moment Chinese interceptors—MiGs—would attack. We understood that they would not be signaling us to change course or to land. They would be piloted by airmen determined to rub out the insult, opening fire at us with air-to-air missiles, cannons, and machine guns the moment they were in range.

Tootle's first task had been to get us as low as we could possibly get, and it soon seemed like the waves in the bay were breaking right outside my window. Flying just a few feet above the water made the 200 or so miles an hour we had achieved seem much faster—certainly I'd never been in a Fudd moving at such speed. Then he got his bearings and headed for the open sea. As we roared along, we anticipated the explosions we were sure were coming, the missiles, direct hits from the antiaircraft flak, and the MiGs' cannon and machine-gun fire.

We knew we were sitting ducks, or at least like the mechanical ducks that swim slowly along an old-fashioned shooting gallery's conveyor belt. Despite the sense of great speed as we rushed over the water just below our wings, we felt at the same time a terrible slowness as it seemed to take forever to clear the bay and gain the open sea. We anticipated being hit, knowing that it was entirely unlikely that our unarmored Fudd, constructed of little more than sheet metal, would survive even the lightest of strikes. But we also understood that even if by some bizarre chance we were able to ditch into the sea successfully, and then manage to escape the aircraft alive, we would immediately be captured by the Chinese.

The Navy had standing orders to stay well clear of Chinese waters—the United States was at that point extremely wary of provoking China into war with us—and we knew we would not be rescued. In the unlikely event that we managed to survive a crash landing at sea, we would be spending the rest of our lives in Chinese prisons.

I cannot say how long this all took. It seemed both to go by in a flash and to last an eternity. What I do remember is that at some point we began to comprehend that we hadn't seen SAMs, that there were no interceptors, that finally there was no more flak, that the open sea lay ahead of us, and that as impossible as it seemed moments before, we might just make it out of China alive.

At some point we let the ship know what happened, and that we were headed back. We didn't know if we'd been hit or how badly, and the pilots didn't know whether we'd been damaged to an extent that would prevent the maneuvering needed to make a carrier landing.

The only remotely comic part that I can recall from this entire episode came next. *Bennington* sent a pair of helicopters out to join up with us. Circling our Fudd, the jet-powered choppers inspected us closely to make certain we were airworthy enough to land. The notion that we had just flown into and out of Red China in a plane so slow that helicopters could circle us in flight seemed thoroughly absurd at the time. It turned out that despite the flak, and Dan Tootle's desperate dive straight into it, we hadn't been damaged and we managed to land without further event.

From my seat amid all the radar, I didn't have much of a view of the flight deck. As we taxied forward from the arresting cable, though, I heard the pilots note the Marine guard standing there, in his dress uniform. We understood that it did not augur well for us. I immediately intuited that my first action should be one of self-preservation, known otherwise as covering my ass, and went into action the moment we jerked to a halt and cut the engines. I tell this detail of the story not for its own sake so much as to explain the essence of what one learns in the Navy. Before even opening the main hatch, I'd popped the overhead hatch and climbed up into the radome.

From the outset I figured I'd be held responsible for what happened. If it turned out that the radar problem was not with the antenna up in the radome, but had instead been somewhere inside the aircraft, where I might have repaired it in-flight, I assumed that as the only enlisted man on the crew, and thus its most junior and vulnerable member, I was the one who'd be saddled with responsibility for the near-fatal error. A glance inside the radome with my flashlight assured me that the antenna's dish was indeed jammed at an upward angle, rendering it useless. Reassured that I couldn't be charged with failing to carry out my duties as flight technician, I clambered back down and out onto the deck. The tight-lipped Marine ordered the three officers—the pilot, the copilot, and the radar officer—to accompany him to the admiral's quarters. There were so few enlisted men in carrier-based aircrews that it didn't even occur to the admiral, I guess, to haul me along, too.

Lt. Jake Froelich, the copilot, spoke to me later in the ready room, describing the blistering reprimand they received from the admiral, who informed them that we had created "an international incident." The admiral proceeded to ground the entire crew—this time including me—until further notice. Having made it back aboard ship in one piece, I could feel excited by all this. I sensed that I had at last been part of something of note; our missions had come to seem routine by that point, but now I had something to talk about. The admiral, however, had something else in mind; he ordered us to keep silent about what had happened.

As I reflect on it now, I begin to comprehend the consequences this silence imposed on me. I had come as close to being shot down in enemy territory as a man can come. It was without a doubt the single most terrifying event I experienced during the war. It was by far the most dramatic event that took place in our Fudd squadron and probably the most dramatic event that took place during *Bennington*'s time in Vietnam. It was the closest I would ever get to the heroics I had watched in countless movies and television shows as a kid growing up. And yet I was ordered to tell no one about what had taken place. From the moment it happened I was forced to bottle it up, to ignore it, to pretend that it hadn't occurred, to forget it—in a word, to *repress* it. It occurs to me now that if I'd been able to speak about it at the time, I might have been able to grapple better with it, to make some sense of it, to gain some understanding of what I had experienced and of how I experienced it, to make it a part of myself, and thus to gradually let go of it. Instead, I ended up with a bottle-stopper thrust into my personal history.

I realize that I don't even know if the other aircrewmen understood why I had been grounded, why I wasn't flying my daily missions. And there was the rub. *Bennington*'s routine was to launch five missions a day. Our squadron had only the five of us flight techs to man these five daily sorties, which meant, obviously, that each of us flew one a day. When I was grounded, though, it meant there were only four techs to man the five flights, and so each day one of the others had to fly a second 7-hour mission—my mission—for a total of 14 hours. And this was in addition to the grueling maintenance schedule we worked. I felt terribly guilty that someone else was being sent out in my place each day. And I'd been ordered not to explain to the others why I was grounded.

After a couple of days of this, my detachment's commander could see that the demands on the other enlisted flight techs were swiftly growing to be more than they could handle. He explained to the admiral that he had enough pilots and radar officers to take up the slack for the rest of his grounded crew. But, he said, he had only the five flight techs to man the five daily missions, and with me grounded he was sending one of his techs out on a second sortie each day; this was proving to be a near impossibility. He asked the admiral to return me to flight status. As commander of the task group, the admiral knew the Fudds were not much good to him without the techs who kept their fragile equipment operating, and that if a tech was flying twice a day, he was not likely to be much good at handling the radar. He acknowledged my skipper's request and restored me to flight status.

I was ordered out on the next mission a couple of hours before we launched, and I tried to grab a little sleep before suiting up. That's when it happened, the final piece of this episode as I experienced it. As I crawled into my bunk and shut my eyes, I found myself contemplating how close I'd come to dying. It seemed like utter, pure, dumb luck that we hadn't been shot down over Red China. And I found myself thinking that if I continued to reflect on how close I'd come to dying, I wasn't going to be able to climb back into my plane again. It was, I thought at the time, like climbing back onto a horse that had just thrown me—something I'd done as a young man. I willed myself to stop thinking about the episode, forcing it out of my mind. I managed to repress the memory. For the time being.

Among the many contradictions that characterize the US military (and probably all militaries) are the gravity-defying flows of liability. At one level, there's an official notion that a commander bears ultimate responsibility for what happens under his command, and that accountability travels upward through the web of authority known as the chain of command. On the other hand, one of the important practical truths and life lessons I learned in the Navy is that "shit rolls downhill" toward the one who's least able to dodge the repercussions. When something goes wrong, culpability and punishment pass downward through the ranks. These two notions are indeed entirely contradictory but coexist comfortably in the ordered chaos that is the military.

When we'd made it back from Hainan to Benn, and spotted the Marine waiting on the flight deck, we knew it meant only one thing: the admiral's wrath was coming down on us. And the admiral's wrath could mean only one thing: heads would roll. The only question at that point, which went quite unspoken, was who was going to be the goat in a system where culpability flowed both uphill and downhill. And that meant that I had every reason to suspect that the buck would stop with me.

That's why I'd gone up into the radome before doing anything else, eyed the antenna's tilt gauge, and proved to my own satisfaction that the parabolic reflector (the dish) was indeed jammed upward, effectively shutting down the entire radar system. I was off the hook. This was later confirmed by the avionics quality control "checker," who was sent to determine just what had caused the radar's failure.

REFLECTION: THE PIVOT POINT IN THE LONG ARC FROM BOY TO MAN

I've told this story of our incursion into China in particular detail because the episode played such a pivotal part in my experience of the war. But it also illustrates a broader issue I've been exploring here. It's not merely that I assumed I was the one who'd be held culpable for straying into China unless I could prove otherwise, but that my assumption was so entirely automatic, so thoroughly a part of how I understood both the Navy and the world. Our crew was still pretty much in shock, but every fiber of my being grasped what might happen if I didn't act quickly to exonerate myself.

In the last year or two of my boyhood, before I ran away, each time I saw my father walking down the path to our door, my mind shrieked, "What's he's going to yell at me for today? What did I do wrong this time?" I assumed that my father was going to find fault with me, no matter what I'd done. It was partly to escape this incessant fear that I ran away, and it was partly because I'd found the Navy vastly more reasonable than my father that I adapted so readily to it. But it also meant that I was primed to assume the worst. If the responsibility could be pinned on me, it would be.

What I'm saying—and this is one of the main reasons I've written this book— is that I experienced that entire episode in the way that I did at least in part because of what *I brought to it*, both from my own nature and from the circumstances of my upbringing. But I also want to make it clear that I've carried that burden with me in the wake of the war, as part of how I've perceived the world ever since.

This seems to be the way I live my life. Always, I expect to be held accountable. As more than one psychotherapist has pointed out to me, I carry the world on my shoulders. And this goes a long way toward explaining why, for instance, I insisted on working up inside the radome, where I could get killed, rather than at the controls where instead I might kill someone. I learned early that I was responsible for what went on around me, and that this has its upside and its downside. I don't like to think of myself as a victim. I prepare. I think ahead. And I'm continually blaming myself for everything that goes wrong.

Our intrusion into Red China provides the pivot point around which my sense of what happened to me in the war turns. What's especially crucial about the way I experienced it is that I was ordered not to talk about it, and I deliberately, consciously, and forcefully repressed it in order to fly my next mission. I was told that it was a very big deal, and because of that, I was told to pretend it didn't happen. The clinical term for this sort of thing, I think, is mindfuck. It's not all that uncommon, but I don't know that it's been well explored, with the major exception of *Catch-22*.

I've explained how *Catch-22* prompted me to enlist in the first place, and how it underpinned the ambivalence that characterized my entire experience of the military and Vietnam. But there's more to it than that, I now realize. Long after *Catch-22* appeared, Joseph Heller (1998) wrote about how simple the war had initially seemed to him, flying bombing runs in Italy late in the war. But then came the crucial incident that clearly traumatized him, and it changed the way he experienced the rest of war. That experience stayed with him, and as he wrote *Catch-22* that incident, when a fellow crew member was killed by antiaircraft fire, provided the axis around which his entire novel turns.

My experience over Hainan was in some ways just what I'd been hoping for, and it was then ripped away from me. I had my brief moment of drama and then had to abandon it, pretend it never happened. In many ways, my greatest recollection as I left the war was that nothing happened to me. I wasn't a rifleman in an infantry company in the rice paddies, so nothing happened, I thought. There's something very elemental in this. This episode both was and wasn't a big deal, but whatever it was, it confused the hell out of me, and kept me from gaining any understanding of all the rest of what I was doing.

And here's the deal. Having grown up with visions of martyrdom and heroics all around me, that experience seemed both validating and unremarkable. At some level, it was the point of all I aspired to, my opportunity to be somebody. And still it was yanked away from me. It wasn't the memory of being under heavy fire so much as it was having in effect to deny it. By saying I repressed it, what I mean to convey is that I managed to move the event from a place in my consciousness where it was readily available for me to describe and reflect upon, to a place where I could access nothing more than the fact that something happened to me. I'd been ordered to ignore this very big thing; in order to accomplish that, I had to hide it from myself. I could take no pleasure in having done something I aspired to do—it lost whatever meaning it held for me.

At the same time, I lost my conscious awareness of the fear. I knew it was there—it had come back quickly to haunt me—but I literally wrestled it into submission. I can honestly say that for the rest of our time in Vietnam I never consciously experienced the fear that I'd be killed. And this touched on everything I did. I can see by looking at my behavior and my body language—when I was out on the night-cloaked flight deck, for instance—that I was quite afraid. But I have no recollection of the sensation of fear except for that one critical moment. As I tell it, this sounds to me like an extraordinary thing—in the literal sense of something quite out of the ordinary—but it's exactly what you do in order to fight effectively. It's not that you're not afraid, it's that you don't allow yourself the luxury of feeling the fear. You concentrate on the task at hand. Experience tells me that not everyone can do this, but I did. I did it day in and day out as I engaged in a multitude of routinely dangerous tasks both aboard ship and in the air.

Some readers will be struck by the drama in this story, while others will dismiss it as no big deal. For me, it's both. But in order to understand what it all means to me, I have to look much further than just the incident itself. It has remained with me because it wasn't simply the overflight and dodging the antiaircraft fire and attempting to escape from SAMs and MiGs. This was no more than the surface. Beneath the surface was our knowledge that no one would rescue us if we went down in China or Chinese waters and that if we should somehow manage to survive a hit and ditching in the sea, we'd wind up in a Chinese prison for a very long time, maybe until we died.

More than that though, was the residue of the time we'd spent in the Navy's mock POW camp and the torture we'd undergone there. Within the brief moment that this incident unfolded, our training and indoctrination shaped what we expected to happen to us. We're probably going to die, we're thinking, but if we survive, we may well be facing something worse than death.

That intense POW training in the SERE camp wasn't simply preparation for capture. It was also a process of indoctrination, an indirect form of brainwashing. We were being imbued with a sense of how evil the enemy was. This in turn reminded us of how noble our side was. Without ever really mentioning it, the instructors were teaching us about good and evil. The logical conclusion for me, even if I wasn't consciously aware of it, was that I was putting my life on the line to fight evil. It helped me believe that I was engaged in something heroic. Mine wasn't a merely technical job. I was playing my part in the long blue line of naval aviation and the tradition of America saving the world. I was fulfilling a charge the nuns had given me in second grade.

TRYING TO BOMB THE *PHOENIX*

One more episode, deceptively inconspicuous, lingers as possibly my most disturbing memory from the war and Yankee Station. I attempted to call in a strike on a small, unarmed sailing vessel, the *Phoenix*. A group of Quakers had been working without success to get medical supplies to civilians injured by the US bombing in North Vietnam. They joined with a peace activist anthropologist, Earle Reynolds, who had sailed the *Phoenix* on a number of protest voyages after having studied radiation casualties in Hiroshima. The group made no secret of what they were doing—it was a deliberate act of civil disobedience—and the United States threatened them with 10 years in prison for violating a 1917 Trading with the Enemy Act. They traveled with a ton of supplies from Hong Kong in March 1967 and transited the Tonkin Gulf. I tracked them as they crossed.

As I understood it at the time, the *Phoenix* was bringing medical supplies to North Vietnamese soldiers who were killing American troops, and I saw red. I radioed the ship's coordinates and directed one of our patrol aircraft to it. I was hoping to provoke some sort of confrontation that would allow us to attack the ship, but wiser heads prevailed and nothing came of the incident.

According to an online article about Reynolds and the *Phoenix* by Nicole Pasulka (2016), one of the voyage's organizers told her "hearts were in people's mouths" as they made their way through the massed forces of the Seventh Fleet. "Oh my God," he thought, "these people are going to die." Tension among the crew was palpable, but they made it safely to Haiphong Harbor and delivered their cargo, despite my feeble efforts to stop them.

I remember this episode as the high-water mark of my aggressiveness. That I was eager to sink a Quaker ship hauling medical supplies is almost beyond my comprehension now. But it stands for me as my own personal experience of being turned into a monster by fighting with monsters.[2] I don't think the North Vietnamese, or the VC or anyone else for that matter, were monsters, but that's how I perceived them at the time, as a direct result of all that I'd learned growing up in the days when we believed that world communism was plotting to kill us and our families in our beds. If we didn't meet them on the battlefield in Vietnam, we'd been taught, it would be too late for us. And if I didn't strike at people who were abetting them, I would be failing in my duty.

I don't want to blow this out of proportion. Within the sweep of what the task group or even my squadron was doing, this was nearly meaningless. And yet it wasn't small potatoes for me: over the years it has always represented the extreme to which I had moved. I want to say "been pushed" rather than "moved," but in fact others exercised far better judgment than I. It was something I tried to do in response to the classic frustration that overtakes men in combat, when they lose a sense of proportion and act even more irrationally than they ordinarily do. No one knows this event happened, and I could certainly keep it hidden in the recesses of my own conscience. But that's just the point. My conscience refuses to let it be. If it was the high-water mark of my battle cry, it also demonstrates just how badly my moral compass was thrown out of whack. There was no atrocity, but I understand full well how they can take place.

ROUTINE MAINTENANCE

Routine, by definition, isn't nearly as interesting or exciting as an event like that accidental flight into Red China or my attempt to blow the *Phoenix* out of the water. But that doesn't mean that it's any less dangerous. As I write about routine, I realize that I'm dealing with things I can't see sharply. Their everydayness means that they don't stand out brightly after all these years. I have to guess at what they are by recalling what's around them. I've told you about some of the more memorable things I did and tried to explain the context of what I was doing aboard ship in terms of what I was doing in the air. Now I want to show you how routine work—the day-in and day-out, everyday work—on the Fudds's radar, which seemed so ordinary, masked a high level of stress and played an outsized role in my experience of trauma.

When wasn't I stressed? There were clearly moments when it peaked, and I've described some of these. But my experience of the war wasn't an alternation between peaks and valleys. It was long, intense plateaus of strain, from which there was little respite, interrupted only by peaks of particular stress and danger. And I use the word danger, rather than terror here for a reason. *I couldn't do the damn job if I allowed myself to be conscious of my fears.*

I can look back at my body language and my descriptions of how carefully I was cordoning off the fears and see that some unconscious part of me was aware of just how dangerous it all was. But I emphasize the "some unconscious part of me." In order to do it, I couldn't allow myself to be really in touch with that part of me. There was a divide between what was going on somewhere inside me and what I was conscious of. And this extraordinary division of myself just went on and on.

What I think about now is the degree to which the stress, that is, the production of biochemicals—of hormones like adrenaline, cortisol, and serotonin—that saturated my brain, and all the other physiological processes in my body, was a constant. And the degree to which my brain and body, and all the rest of me, were permanently affected by this.[3] I ignored the threats to my physical and emotional integrity. I couldn't have done what I did as well as I did if I'd been thinking about the danger. And here's the dilemma, then. I was intelligent enough to have a sense of how dangerous it all was and driven enough to mask it all from myself in order to be effective.

I've come to believe that these sorts of nearly invisible, seemingly lowkey strains played—at least in my case—a much larger part than is usually recognized in producing traumatic stress and in particular complex and late onset PTSD, topics I'll come back to in later chapters.

The daily missions I flew and my maintenance responsibilities overlapped almost seamlessly. After we'd landed, I'd change out of my flight suit, get some hot chow (and I sometimes fell asleep standing in the chow line), then head back to the plane I'd just been flying in. I'd begin troubleshooting whatever radar problems had developed during the mission or as we made our arrested landing. It was better if I was the one who did this, because I'd just seen all the indications.

As I've said, the multiple interconnections among all the radar's components meant it was rarely obvious where a problem originated, but I would have been trying to isolate it while we were still in the air; this left me in the best position to solve the problem back aboard ship. It took a series of electronic readings, some trial-and-error work, and a measure of intuition, luck, and "swag" (scientific wild-ass guessing) to get a handle on what needed to be done. Sometimes the problem was in the plane's wiring and connections, in the waveguides that channeled the radar signals, or up in the radome, but more often than not I'd need to replace one or more of the black boxes.

After locating the problem's likely source and pulling the boxes, I'd take them to the avionics shop, mount them on the workbench, and begin troubleshooting the internal circuitry. This could take minutes or it could take hours. It was usually a matter of figuring out which tubes had failed, since it was a rare mission when at least a few tubes didn't break down. The circuits were made up of individual bits and pieces—resistors, capacitors, and a dozen more devices—that easily failed under the demanding conditions of carrier aviation in the tropical heat and humidity. Working with an array of testing equipment, I puzzled out which circuit was causing the problem, and then which component. With my soldering iron and a boxful of tools, I'd replace parts, often multiple parts, do more testing, and eventually get the whole thing working properly again. Then like as not I'd have to recalibrate it.

After returning a black box back to the plane, I'd have to run the whole system up to check that everything was operating correctly. Given the Fudds's brittleness and temperament, it was rare that everything worked properly on the first try. Eventually, though, everything would check out and the plane—or at least its radar—would be ready for its next mission. While I was working on circuits in the shop someone else might be installing a replacement box in the plane and continuing with the troubleshooting, but we were chronically short of both spare boxes and spare parts, and if a piece wasn't repaired as quickly as possible, there'd be nothing available to install in the next plane, which would be returning just about then.

Then I'd begin the process all over again, readying that plane's systems for *its* next sortie, repeating everything I'd just done. And on and on I'd go until it was time for me to fly my next mission.

Reflecting on how short-handed we were, I now see why my own drive undid me. I'd insisted on learning to do—and doing—everything, which meant, perversely, that I then *had* to do everything. Some of the other flight techs didn't have to sweat getting the planes ready; most of the ground techs didn't have to sweat the possibility of flying a mission with a system that wasn't working properly. My sense even today that everything depends on me is in some measure based in the reality of that experience.

We carried four Fudds in our outfit, though five were considered optimal for the antisubmarine warfare (ASW) operations that were a key part of our responsibilities. In theory, four should have been enough for us to keep a bird in the air at all times. But we'd lost one early on, our "hangar bay queen" sitting idly throughout the cruise. That meant only three planes were available to fly our five daily missions. There was an hour overlap, when there were two aircraft in the air, at the beginning and end of each mission. Some of the time, then, there was only one bird aboard ship where we could work on it. Looking back, I have no idea how we managed it.

Somewhere in all of this I tried to find a few hours of sleep. Forty of us occupied a berthing compartment about the size of an American living room, sleeping on strips of canvas hung from chains, four in a tier, no more than 2 feet apart. Fumes from the ship's fuel oil, in tanks just beneath us, often filled the space.

What I'm hoping to convey here is the intensity with which we worked. I've described the harrowing character of much of what I did, and I want to emphasize that I worked full-bore all the time, trying to keep our planes in the air. I was exhausted all the time, I was doing life-threatening work all the time, I was flying my missions, and when I wasn't actually flying them, I was trying to get the planes back into the air so that we could continue carrying out them out. I was half-asleep most of the time and I recall dozing off once in the middle of troubleshooting a plane with Bates. He slapped me, to wake me up—and to protect both of us.

SPARE PARTS

I shouldered so much responsibility during these missions that I was driven to repair the radar as quickly as possible. At times, though, this was nearly impossible.

The Fudd was a very limited-edition aircraft; the Grumman company manufactured fewer than a hundred of them in total. By the mid-'60s it hardly seemed worthwhile manufacturing a lot of spare parts for a radar system that was supposed to have already been phased out as the much more sophisticated E-2 was introduced to the fleet. But these new Hawkeyes ran into major radar and avionics problems and our old jalopies were kept operating for a lot longer than planned. The intensity of our operations generated constant demand for spare parts but getting hold of them at the end of a very long supply chain, especially on station out in the Tonkin Gulf, was something we couldn't take for granted.

I've taken pains to describe just how concerned we were to keep our birds in the air, fully operational. But these efforts, and all the round-the-clock shifts we worked, were worthless if we lacked the parts needed to keep the equipment running. I've also described how cantankerous the Fudd's radar was; given the catapult launches and arrested landings and the pounding vibrations in-flight, it was a rare mission that returned with all the gear intact. We were in constant need of replacement parts in a situation characterized by a chronic shortage of them. Problematic supply chains, of course, have long been characteristic of warfare.

I soon learned how to deal with this problem: When a part fails, you order at least two of them, one as a replacement and the other to keep on hand, hidden out of sight. Gradually you build up an informal stock of most items that you need on a day-to-day basis. This was especially true with the vacuum tubes, whose life spans weren't much longer than a mayfly's, but it applied to almost everything. This was during Robert McNamara's reign, when his Defense Department had moved its maintenance and procurement accounting systems into high gear, and everything we did and every piece of materiel we used required us to fill out multiple copies of multiple forms. As any competent gang of workers figures out, of course, we worked our way around the formal policies; we got the job done first and dealt with the paperwork later.

As a gung ho flight tech willing to undertake inflight repairs to individual circuits, I also accumulated a store of spare parts, mostly tubes, stashed in my flight suit and helmet bag. I've described changing tubes on the radar scopes while the system was still powered up. I mention this story again simply to convey the depth of my concerns about keeping the radar operational, and the intensity of my dedication to doing whatever was necessary to get the job done. Along with this, though, came something more.

Having this store of spare parts was fundamental to our ability to keep the equipment running. I felt this acutely because I was the one operating the radar on station, but everyone in our outfit experienced it to one degree or another. To reach for replacement parts and find there were none was distressing, even if it wasn't all that unusual. It meant that a part would have to be ordered, and we had no idea when it would arrive. A faulty—"down," we called it—piece of equipment then sat in the shop until we had what we needed to repair it, and if more than one or two black boxes piled up in the shop awaiting parts, we had no replacements to put into the aircraft. Then we had to start cannibalizing, stealing parts from one box to use in another. We wound up doing this a lot, but whatever problems this stopgap temporarily solved for us, it also amplified the longer-term complications we faced, and we tried hard to avoid it.

I'd be in the avionics shop, troubleshooting a scope that failed during a mission earlier in the day. Using bench-mounted testing equipment to generate signals and a multimeter to make voltage readings, I narrow the problem down to a malfunctioning circuit. A visual inspection tells me there are no obviously blown components, ruptured connections, or failed solder joints. I start pulling tubes and inserting them into the tube tester. It tells me one of them has broken down. I slide open a drawer and rummage around for, say, a 6AQ6. There are none. I dash from the shop into the hangar bay and climb up into the tiny space where we enlisted crewmen hang our gear, where I dig through the pockets of my flight suit and the recesses of my helmet bag. Lots of tubes and miscellaneous other parts, but no 6AQ6. Back in the shop, I dig through drawers and cabinets to no avail. Oh, well, I'll just have to order some tubes and set the unit aside until they arrive, in a few days if we're lucky, a few weeks if not. And then I try to locate another scope to replace the one I'd pulled from 760. There are none. All the spare units are awaiting parts.

In a couple of hours, 760 is slated for the next mission. It's got to have another scope installed before it can launch. I'm going to be flying that mission, and I've got to have a fully operational radar system. Without it, we'll be leaving the task group exposed. This isn't exactly my thought process, mind you, but underlying all my anxieties about solving the problem efficiently lies the issue of exposing us to attack. I'm feeling the weight of failing to get my job done, and I'll do whatever it takes to avoid this.

So I open up another scope, one that's been sitting in the corner awaiting parts, and slip a 6AQ6 out of it. After testing the tube, I slide it into the scope I've been working on. I check the unit out, then lug it to the flight deck, hook it up in 760, turn the system on, check it out, and start readying myself for my next mission. (We called 760, by the way, "Zero the Hero" because it always seemed ready to fly; if 762 was our hangar bay queen, 760 was queen of the skies.)

This is a workable expedient, for the moment, but when whatever part that unit in the corner was waiting for, the scope I just cannibalized, comes in, it still won't be ready to go, because now it's missing a 6AQ6 and we haven't got any. What follows is a cascading series of missing parts. We've run out of spares, and those waiting for parts are rapidly becoming more and more inoperable, because of all the parts we've stripped from them. At some point very soon, we'll be dragging boxes out of one plane and sticking them into another right on the spot, in order to turn the plane around for its next mission. Inexorably, the entire process speeds up, into a frantic game of musical chairs.

And it's not just parts and boxes. It's the missions themselves. I fly them, I use the equipment, I need it to do my job. I need it to protect the task group. I need it to vector the S-2s in the coastal interdiction operations. I need it to locate downed pilots and direct the choppers to them. Standing at the bench in the avionics shop, pulling a tube from a circuit board, seems like one of the most mundane things one could be doing, I know. But for me, it's freighted with anxiety, because for me the missing part lies directly within the larger process of getting my plane back up into the air. It's not merely a generic piece of equipment for me. It's more than my job; it's my duty. I risk my life every day in order to do my job because I think it's important. There's no piece of it that isn't of immediate importance to me. I believe that implicitly and explicitly.

And so I pause here for a moment to stress that *this* is why questions of what is "combat" versus "combat support" are so problematic for me, at least when it comes to the question of stress. I'm stressed out standing in the shop because the missing tube is as crucial as every other link in the chain. And as I write, it comes to me:

> For want of a nail the shoe was lost;
> For want of a shoe, the horse was lost;
> For want of a horse, the battle was lost;
> For the failure of battle the kingdom was lost.

It's an ancient theme, but it has persisted for 1,000 years or so because it captures the essence of how complicated war actually is. Or as Shakespeare's King Richard cries out after he's been unhorsed at Bosworth Field: "A horse, a horse! My kingdom for a horse!" (*Richard III*, 5.4.7–10).

Along with this pervasive fixation on parts and supplies and on ensuring ready access to them, came a heightened awareness that others were working on the same aircraft and on the same workbenches, and that they faced similar pressures to get the job done well and quickly. My need to grasp hold of a tube or a meter lead simply by reaching out for it was paralleled by my awareness that the guys working on the next shift experienced the same demands. We simply couldn't work efficiently if we had to stop and search out the equipment we needed, and I developed a deeply rooted habit of placing things back exactly where I found them.

This hardly sounds like a big deal, but the momentary shock of not finding something you need when you reach for it is disruptive, and the shock can embed itself in you. When a specially designed pair of pliers can't be found, for example, preventing you from efficiently replacing a failed part located in a nearly impossible-to-reach spot, it can be as stressful as more obviously dangerous experiences.

Some part of me was so thoroughly impacted by the urgency of all this that I've never really gotten over it. To this day, if I reach for something I need and it's not there, I get upset. This applies particularly to domestic supplies, but also to tools and utensils and anything else I might rely on. If I reach for something I need and I don't find it, synapses in my nerve system start barking.

SHIPMATES, SHORE LEAVE, AND DECOMPRESSING

I'd love to tell you tales about how close the guys in my aircrew were. But I have so very few. While I flew my daily sortie at the same time each night, there was a lot of rotation among the pilots and the radar officers, and we rarely flew together often enough to forge any relationships. And of course I was the only enlisted man on the crew, so I spent no time in the others' company when we weren't airborne. Although ships, even aircraft carriers, push their crews into tight quarters, the distance between what's called officers' country and the enlisted men's spaces is nearly unbridgeable. There are classic tales of World War II bomber crews and the tight bonds they formed, like Louis Falstein's (1950) *Face of a Hero* and John Steinbeck's (1942) *Bombs Away*, and the film *Memphis Belle*, but it was nothing at all like that for Fudd crews.

I knew the officers I flew with, and they knew me, but unlike an idealized World War II bomber crew, which spent only a brief, intense portion of a long mission over a target and could engage in bantering conversation for at least some of the time and then recuperate together as they waited to fly their next mission, we were hard at work, deep in concentration and engaged in directing the other aircraft throughout the entire mission. There were those occasional light moments on the long leg of a barrier, but there weren't many. We really didn't talk that much with one another.

When I wasn't flying or trying to grab a little sleep, I was working on one of the aircraft or in the avionics shop. The work was mostly solitary. At times a couple of technicians worked together, dealing with an erratic antenna or trying to troubleshoot the wiring and microwave channels, but even then we weren't likely to be side by side and were entirely focused on solving the problem and making the necessary repairs. There was little chatter. Aboard ship, and especially on Yankee Station, I spent very little time talking to anyone. I overheard conversations in the squadron maintenance shack, in the avionics shop, and in our berthing space as I was falling asleep, so I was aware of what the other guys were talking about, but I rarely heard anything significant or memorable from them.

What guys mostly talked about was where to drink and party and to otherwise entertain ourselves during our occasional port calls. I heard many conversations weighing the merits of the stereo equipment we were buying in Japan. Some of the younger guys talked about missing their girlfriends (but I don't recall hearing any of the older guys speak about missing their families). What I particularly *don't* recall is anyone talking about the war itself.[4] My recollections are that our primary concern about what we were doing aboard ship had to do with doing it right, that is, in keeping our planes in the air. We spoke, and probably thought, of the work we did as just that, in terms of the job to be done.

It troubles me to use the phrase "only following orders" in the context of our war, but what we were doing, and how we did it, really wasn't that far from what's known as the Nuremberg Defense. We knew we were part of a war, but out there in the Tonkin Gulf, fixing aircraft and launching them into the air, we rarely—if ever—spoke about the countries we were bombing, or the people we were bombing, or why we were bombing them. It might be an exaggeration—I'm not sure—to say that where the bombs were coming down was the farthest thing from our minds, but it was nowhere near the main thing on our minds. We wanted to do our jobs well, we wanted not to get killed or injured while doing them, and we wanted to get home as soon as we could. We certainly had no Tojo or Hitler to focus our energies on.

DECOMPRESSION

My tour in Vietnam wasn't only about fighting the war, of course. Though I had no free time when we were at sea, we did make a few calls in East Asian ports, and I spent most of my time ashore with two older guys who taught me a lot about life.

When vets recall our time in the military, we tend to talk a lot about the buddies we served with. We think about those days in many different ways, of course, but whether we actually formed deep friendships or not, we like to dwell on them. At different points during my years in the Navy, engaged in different sorts of duties in different places, I had my share of buddies; we were all part of a rotating cast as we moved from one base or ship or squadron or barracks to another. I had no idea back in those days that friendships were things one could deliberately cultivate or pursue; to me they simply happened. And so it is that I have no recollection at all of exactly how I started spending my time with Terry and Vega, the guys I pulled liberty—went ashore—with overseas. Unlike most others I knew, though, these two had a significant influence on me.

I didn't understand just what or how much I learned from them until I started writing about our time together. I sometimes wondered what they'd seen in me, or what drew me to them, but it wasn't a line of thought I indulged much. Now, though, I can see a lot of what we had in common, and what I learned from them. They weren't guys I worked beside, whose company I was simply thrown into by proximity. We sought out one another when we spent time ashore, decompressing from the demands we faced at sea, and the time I spent with them really did allow me to rejuvenate my spirits. I had good times. Because of who they were and how they treated me, they exposed me to some new ways of seeing things. When I look back, I realize that nearly everything I recall about what happened to me overseas is in some sense colored by my time with the two of them.

Our opportunities for companionship and conversation came when we pulled into port for a few days of liberty in Japan, the Philippines, Hong Kong, and Australia. I'm not sure how it happened, but I was soon spending most of my time ashore with Terry and Vega. When I reflect on it, though, I realize that I saw little if anything of them once we'd returned to the States, and I also see that I have absolutely no idea why that is. It could well have been that when we were back in San Diego they had their own friends and communities; overseas, we were in some sense fish out of water, with few other birds of a feather to flock together with. We gravitated to one another, or at least I gravitated to the two of them.

Nathan Terry was an Air Force vet. He'd left the service, decided it hadn't been as bad as he'd thought, compared with what he had to deal with as a black man in Chicago in the 1960s, and then joined the Navy. He worked as a radio repairman and was one of two radio technicians who flew as flight techs. He was in his mid-twenties. Terry was cool, listened to jazz, bought elegant clothes in Hong Kong, knew some things about cameras, and drank good scotch. We didn't have all that much in common, but he was smart and aware, was deeply skeptical about everything, practiced a high level of irony, and tolerated me. He was great example of a career man who saw the military for what it was, decided it was worth sticking out, but never, as we now say, drank the Kool-Aid. I enjoyed my time with him immensely.

John Vega was a lot like Terry. He was in his mid-20s and had already been in the Navy for a while. He was our detachment's yeoman, or clerk. A Puerto Rican from New York City's Spanish Harlem, Vega found the military providing him opportunities he might not have had at home. He was intelligent, thoughtful, and funny. He loved the music that would come to be called salsa and knew how to dress in style. He was successful with the ladies. He talked to me a lot about music, especially the Cuban peasant style known as "Guajira," Willie Bobo and "Spanish Grease," and Joe Cuba's band from his own New York City barrio and a song of theirs, "El Pito," with its chorus, "I'll Never Go Back to Georgia." We often sang snatches of it and during one of our port stops I had a baseball cap embroidered with our squadron insignia—a rooster nobly crowing an early warning—on the front and "I'll Never Go Back" in Japanese characters on the back. It was the Tonkin Gulf, of course, that I'd never go back to; by that time, I'd had more than enough of it, even though we still had plenty of missions left to fly.

Like Terry, Vega's attitude was entirely skeptical, but he did his job well and got promoted. Both he and Terry were third-class petty officers. And like Terry, Vega tolerated me.

The two of them were drawn together by their urban sensibilities, their intelligence, and their outsider backgrounds in a unit that was mostly made up of white southerners. I really don't know why they accepted my company, but they did. They considered me weird—that was their word for it—though

I'm not entirely sure why, except that I wanted to hang out with them. I had a habit in those days of responding to questions by saying, "Well, to be frank about it," and soon they were calling me "Weird Frank," a nickname that stuck with me.

I've been telling you how serious I was, but however serious I was, I was also full of life and spirit, wanting to experience and learn a whole lot more than just my job. I was too young to drink in the States, but I drank everywhere we went overseas. I'm not going to spend time telling you about the exciting times I had as a drunken sailor on liberty, but I had them. I will say that because we were at sea so much of the time, with no place to spend our money, we spent like sailors during our brief stints in port. I'm pleased to say that because I was usually three sheets to the wind, I don't remember too much about those adventures, but I do recall that I had great fun.

In the port towns where our carrier group headed for R&R it was common for the black troops to find bars and night clubs where they could hang together. This segregation was informal and it certainly wasn't rigid, and I suspect that a lot of the white guys had no idea it was happening. But by hanging with Terry and Vega, those were the clubs where I spent my time. I bopped to Motown music and learned to dance a variation on the twist known as the "skate." I awakened to as much about life in the real world in those places as I did in combat. This wasn't about acquiring skills that might land me a job later on; it was about paying attention to how I carried myself, how to be present without making a fool of myself, and about what Curtis Mayfield and the Impressions meant when they sang, "It's Alright to Have a Good Time."

I drank heavily, as a quick and dirty way of recovering from the stress, among other things, and it soon became a bad habit. But because I was so well-lubricated, I was also able to take much of the edge off my natural self-consciousness. I could relax and have a good time without thinking about how much I stuck out like a sore thumb in those joints. It was kind, if nothing else, of my pals to show their faces with me tagging along.

I learned a few other things from them as well. In Hong Kong we made our way to a shop with the slightly misleading name "David Naval Tailor," which specialized in swiftly crafting custom-made civilian dress-clothing for sailors who were in port for just a few days. Terry and Vega helped me order a range of handmade suits, sport jackets, slacks, shirts, and even a pair of wingtip shoes (cordovan, of course; I've avoided regulation black ever since navy days). When we visited Nagasaki later on, we were dressed to the nines.

This sort of thing seemed quite ordinary to me at the time, because I was doing it with my friends. But I saw no one else from our squadron come back with a wardrobe remotely like ours. I suspect that without the two of them I would have spent my money and my time doing little more than drinking and whoring. We did quite a bit of that, too, but it was hardly the sole focus of

Figure 4.3.   From left, John Vega YN3, the author, and Nathan Terry ATN3 in Hong Kong. *The author's personal collection*

our time ashore; we saw quite a few of Hong Kong's sights and ate in some of its better restaurants.[5]

Later on during that WestPac cruise, Benn's aging flight deck began crumbling under the beating of our round the clock operations. We steamed north to Kyushu, Japan's southernmost island, and tied up in the shipyard at Sasebo for repairs. Terry, Vega, and I dressed in our nattiest new clothes from Hong Kong and took the train to Nagasaki.

In the mid-1960s, Nagasaki was a small city by Japanese standards. It was provincial in almost every sense of the term, and in the few days we were there I don't believe we saw any other westerners. Virtually no one spoke English and we found a place to stay because we were handed a card for a guesthouse as we exited the train station. After a taxi brought us to the address on the card, we managed to arrange a room only when the desk clerk telephoned an interpreter service. We ordered meals by pointing to plates of plastic food in the restaurants' windows. One of my sharpest memories is of Vega looking down at a dish of large prawns set before him, with their heads still on. He said, "Guys, I can't eat these suckers. They're staring at me." And he meant it. By that point he'd become agitated by the stares we'd been attracting all over the city. Everywhere we went, people stopped to gaze at us, and he said in a disturbed voice, "They're staring at me" several more times.

I mention Nagasaki not so much because of the oddness of three sailors in bespoke suits wandering blindly around a strange city, but because of the fact that we chose it at all. Why did we go? Fifty years on, I can't say for sure, but I've got an idea, now that I've started thinking about it. I feel the sense of it rising in me, drifting over my head like a cloud.

I feel awkward imputing states of mind to Terry and Vega, but what comes to me now, with a surprising degree of certainty, is the notion that these two guys, who in growing up had been shouldered aside by almost every feature of American society, but who found they could command a measure of respect in the US military, were drawn inexorably to the contradictions implicit in Nagasaki's history.

Sometimes when we were simply talking, and not dancing and carousing, Terry spoke about growing up poor in Chicago, of not having enough to eat, and pointed out to me that this was an experience I would never know. And Vega spoke of the streets of Spanish Harlem and especially of the omnipresence of the police. We laughed and joked almost continually, it seems, but all that hilarity covered over the life histories that had shaped them.

Nagasaki, for readers who may have forgotten, was the second city that the US Army Air Force dropped an atom bomb on, three days after Hiroshima. Estimates of those killed by the bombing and subsequent radiation range from 60,000 to 80,000.

To me, at the time, it simply seemed like an interesting place to visit. But nobody else went, just the three of us. And it was their idea, not mine.

Now I think I understand what Vega was trying to communicate when he said, "They're staring at me." I feel uncomfortable suggesting that there was more to what he was saying than the words he used, but I know very well that most of us aren't ever entirely sure of what we're saying when we speak. There we were, three American servicemen, just 20 years after we'd reduced the city to rubble with a weapon that shocked the world, wandering through their city. And Terry and Vega knew viscerally what it was like to be on the short end of the stick, to be stigmatized and to suffer because of their race. I could, I suppose, write a novel or a short story that would ascribe thoughts and feelings to them, but I'm not that kind of writer. I think Terry and Vega were drawn there, to some unspoken degree, by the screaming ambivalence of making their livings in the prosecution of a similarly destructive war on the Vietnamese. And when Vega said, "They're staring at me," what he was talking about was all the citizens of Nagasaki looking at him, asking wordlessly, "What in the hell are you doing here, man? Why are you guys doing this again? Is it really worth it to you?"

I can still hear Vega and Terry joking, shouting "Woxtry, Woxtry," a twist on the newsboy's "Extra, Extra, read all about it" call that appeared in a series of the Popeye cartoons running in *Stars & Stripes*, the military newspaper and our only source of news at the time. Or Vega channeling The Little Rascals' character Stymie: "I ain't giving my apples to nobody." These are random recollections, but they reflect aspects of our constant commentary on cultural life around us. Terry could bounce from the merits of Black & White scotch, to Pharaoh Sanders' and Sun Ra's vanguard jazz and Les McCann's luminous "A Bag of Gold" album, to professional-grade cameras (he was the first person I ever knew with a single-lens reflex, a Pentax Spotmatic), to a black-on-black monogram on his tailor-made blazer, to Popeye and Wimpy. He explained to me what Muddy Waters was singing about in "I Got My Mojo Working." Vega leapt from Joe Cuba and Tito Puente to stickball to the Little Rascals. He taught me the proper protocol for drinking beer on New York streets long before I moved to the city and needed to know it. They had both an acute sense of power and a powerful sense of the absurd.

As I summon up my memories of the time I spent ashore with them, and especially of my keen desire to spend it with them, I can see and feel in what I experienced the essence of one part of what I recall about myself at the time. Serious, dedicated, hard-working. Ironic and cynical. Laugh at everything, doubt everything. Do the job as well as can be done, but let it have little effect on the way I see the world. I encountered something like this everywhere in the Navy—it's central to nearly every aspect of military life—but it crystalized in my consciousness and became a permanent part of everything I am, I think, in the intense times I spent ashore with Terry and Vega.[6]

COUNTER CURRENTS

Tugging at me constantly as I drag the war back into my consciousness, and try to view it more clearly, have been a stream of recollections about things running contrary to the main story and sometimes subverting it. As I recount the sorts of changes I made following the war, I'll point to ways in which I was unwittingly undermining everything I'd done *during* the war, inverting steps I'd taken to shape myself into a fighting man. In retrospect, I see that many of these postwar changes came surprisingly easily, and the speed with which I evolved had a lot to do with contradictory parts of me that were fermenting just beneath the surface even as I focused on becoming a warrior.

Music has served as a driving engine throughout the course of my life, first of all folk, but also a crazy quilt of rock, country, blues, jazz, and American standard tunes. There are ways in which the catalyst for the fractures in my life came at the intersection of Bob Dylan's tunes and rock music, with the almost revolutionary blossoming of what came to be called folk rock.

Though there were only three television channels in those days, it was nearly impossible to find programs that guys in the barracks would all agree to watch on TV, with one major exception, the shows Shindig, Hullabaloo, and Shivaree, all of which presented the same rotating casts of popular singers and bands, accompanied by go-go dancers. But in the barracks common spaces guys with guitars had also begun singing some of the bedrock protest songs, like Dylan's "The Times They Are a-Changin'," in 1964, and by the summer of '65 some of us were singing lines from "It's All Over Now, Baby Blue": "All your seasick sailors, they are rowing home." *We* were the seasick sailors, and if we weren't necessarily going home, we certainly wanted to get the hell away from the Naval Air Technical Training Center. But I also recall a barracks trio harmonizing with impossible sweetness on the Beatles' "I'll Follow the Sun." We were young in the sixties, and even if we were in the Navy, the music pulsed through us.

Dylan turned to blues and rock in the summer of 1965, while I was still there in Memphis, and a divide was crossed. "Like a Rolling Stone" hit like an electrical storm, rocking the boat we were rowing. By the time I reached San Diego, it was near the top of the charts. The Byrds's version of Dylan's "Mr. Tambourine Man" was on the air constantly, with Roger McGuinn's jingle-jangle 12-string guitar echoing through the barracks. As the Vietnam War began ramping up in '65, Barry Maguire recorded "Eve of Destruction." It was hardly the first protest or antiwar song, but it was one of the very first to get played on popular radio. And then the Byrds followed up with what I recall as the song that turned popular music, popular rock, really, into the music of the sixties as we remember it. It was their version of Pete Seeger's "Turn, Turn, Turn" and it became synonymous with protest and opposition to war. It was on the radio in the late fall of 1965 and with its refrain, "To everything there is a season," I thought at first that it was a Christmas carol. Only when I listened closely did I realize what its message was . . . "A time for peace, I swear it's not too late."

The music I listened to most attentively, always, was folk, a genre that cast a wide net, including topical and protest songs. Tom Paxton and Phil Ochs had been writing about the military, the draft, and war for a while, and though they rarely made it on pop radio, some of their songs, covered by others, did. Along with going to see Dylan and Joan Baez and others in the city's main concert hall, I haunted San Diego's folk clubs, and heard not just antiwar music, but all sorts of songs devoted to what we now call social justice, to civil rights, labor, and other movements. In some of those tiny spaces, and the folk clubs in a Navy town like San Diego were always in tiny spaces, I sat no more than a few feet away from extraordinary blues performers with explicit messages, like Nina Simone and Sonny Terry and Brownie

McGee. The guys I hung out with were young and intelligent, and even if we were cut off from the college culture of our peers, rays of light filtered in. We heard the music, and were aware of the temper of the times, even if we were well outside the flow of it all.

I saw *Zorba the Greek*, a film based on Nikos Kazantzakis's novel with an extraordinarily stirring performance by Anthony Quinn, in 1965. In much the same way that I'd found myself wanting to be like Yossarian after I read *Catch-22*, I wanted to be like Zorba, a natural philosopher and jack of all trades. In some ways, I suppose, the feeling has never left me. At a very basic level, what most appealed to me about Zorba was his sense of reckless abandon, of living life as it came and to the fullest, and his freedom from social constraint. Zorba was, more than anything else, his own man. He was, in the same way that I've come to think of Yossarian, an existential hero. His wildness made sense to me, and I wanted to cultivate it in myself. If there's a point at which the free spirit and the warrior in me intersected, this must be it. I wanted to be wild and crazy, as we put it, and that was of a piece with the risks I ran in the war.

Given the intensity of my search for meaning, and my commitment to creating a persona for myself, it's not surprising that I took paths with twists and turns. In my intellectual and emotional ferment, I went through a period when I revolted against the freedom I cherished and sought existential hero-ism elsewhere. For a time I latched onto Ayn Rand's ideology. I took courses in Objectivism, her "philosophy," while I was in San Diego, and it pained me greatly to set aside, for a time, my attachment to Zorba. The leap from one outlook to the other strikes some people as odd, but to me it represents the degree to which I was willing to search for something larger, beyond myself, a different way of looking at and thinking about the world. More importantly, though, and this is something I've only recently come to understand, Rand's attacks on what she called collectivism, as the evil antithesis of the unbridled spirit of capitalism that she celebrated in her writings, provided me with the rationale I needed to fight in Vietnam.[7]

I'd joined the Navy for a host of reasons, and while patriotism and a desire to engage in heroics were among them, they were hardly at the fore-front of what motivated me. Looking back, I see that my political and cultu-ral outlooks were more in tune with the ideas and forces that shaped what would soon become the antiwar movement, and yet I was on my way to fight in the war. What I see now is that I needed some way to explain to myself why I was about to risk my life for a cause I wasn't all that clear about.[8] I seized on Rand's ideas as a way of rationalizing what I was doing. I can make little sense of the contrary paths I was exploring in those days, but I was young and was casting about a bit wildly for materials with which to create my persona. Rand's austere vision helped me explain to myself the fierce dedication I felt toward my duties in the war; I managed to provide myself with a strain of anti-communism that would fuel whatever heroics I was able to engage in. Fighting in the war was clearly the dominant strain, but a hodge-podge of ideas and outlooks and aspirations streamed just beneath the surface, some of them features lingering from my Catholic school training.

And then I stumbled across yet another existential hero, Jack Kerouac. For those of my generation who *were* in college, the early stirrings of the Beats (better known in those days as beatniks) and the counterculture were simply a part of the milieu they lived in. That's not what it was like in the Navy, and I had to discover those things by myself. I started with Kerouac because a copy of his book *Big Sur* was sitting on the counter of a bookstore I'd wandered into. My family camped in the woods at Big Sur when I was a boy and it was possibly my favorite spot in the world; I bought the book simply on the strength of that association, and that led to all the rest.

I quickly moved along to *On the Road*. I don't think we were using the phrase quite yet, but it definitely blew my mind, and I was soon reading read a series of Kerouac's other books. Kerouac's work was about rebellion and running free and being crazy, as we called it, even as it drew upon classical traditions. Its beat-hip bohemianism helped set the stage for the late '60s counterculture. In some perplexing way that I don't entirely understand, Kerouac, more than anyone else, pointed a way toward hard work *and* craziness, intelligence and an intense skepticism about nearly everything.[9]

When we weren't at sea, I'd work the day shift, in the shop or on the flight line, come back to the barracks, shower, and head off to night classes at the community college. By the time I returned to the base, intent on settling down to study, the guys working the night shift would be back and raring to go. I had the only car, and they'd plead with me, cajole me, and ultimately convince me to drive them to Tijuana. I've got to study guys, I'd insist. Around and around they go, till they wore me down. We'd roar down the Silver Strand and be drinking in TJ in less than half an hour.

We'd drink and carouse till dawn at the semi-tawdry El Rancho Café, at which point my companions could return to the barracks and sleep till afternoon. But I had to report at 7:30 or so, with little chance to sleep. I dealt with this problem by using "bennies," the Benzedrine tablets that were a mild amphetamine guys bought in TJ. I took them so I could go to work. I'd be a hard-charging tiger until 10:00 or 11:00 a.m., and then start to peter out. My only drug use while I was in military was, contrary to common mythology, to allow me to do my job effectively after I'd been out carousing, in order to recover from the stress of working.

All my inner contradictions are wrapped up in this pattern of work, study, and booze. I went full-tilt at everything, and set the stage for what followed when I returned from the war.

MY INTELLECTUAL PATH

It's clear that I'd already set my life along a new path by the time I got to Santa Barbara. I could devote my energies to raising myself, rather than burning them up in mismatched struggle to survive under my father's roof. In some ways, the Navy took on his role. The parts of me that have such contradictory relations with authority—both identifying with and resisting it simultaneously—took off on a different heading. Before I got to Santa Barbara, I'd wanted to follow in my father's footsteps by becoming a naturalist or ranger. I know I lost interest in pursuing a career in the woods just about then, but I don't think I've ever really asked why.

I'd chosen not to kill my father. By seizing the alternative, and running away, I freed myself from much of his influence (though hardly all of it). Among the many things that happened in that brief period when I was in Santa Barbara are two that had particular impact on the way I experienced the Navy. First, I'd set out to get training that would allow me to advance quickly in my newly chosen occupation at the phone company. Second, and this I find the more interesting one, I began to envision myself as an intellectual.

These two paths don't seem much related at first glance, but they drew upon one another. At the outset, my main concern had been with surviving. I understood perfectly well that I needed a skill. The phone company promised me a spot to ply my trade after I returned with the necessary training. Gaining a set of technical skills made absolute sense to the pragmatic part of me. But I wasn't rebellious merely because I had a father I needed to rebel against. I also wanted to separate myself out from the masses and go my own way.

My spirit—my *thumos*—and ambition weren't limited to my military duties, and expanding my horizons seemed like a crucial part of surviving. Having liberated myself from my father's immediate sway, I might have learned simply to ignore his influence, but instead I decided to surpass him in an even more daring way. My father was a smart but only marginally educated man. He was unsure of his own knowledge and intelligence. I was intent on becoming not just educated, but sophisticated, a man of the world.

With my pal Don in Santa Barbara, I'd started listening to classical music (Bach's "The Well-Tempered Clavier" and "The Art of the Fugue" come to mind) and LP records of avant-garde plays (I still recall listening to Samuel Beckett's *Waiting for Godot*), reading poetry (Dylan Thomas), and wandering the art museum. When I got to San Diego, I introduced myself to the ballet, the symphony, the opera, and most of all, the Old Globe Theater in Balboa Park, where I watched Shakespeare in continual repertory. I saw my first, but hardly last, performance of "Godot." I spent time at all the city's museums. Looking at me from atop my computer as I write is a soaring hawk, carved from soapstone by an American Indian, that I bought during a visit to San Diego's Museum of Man about 20 years ago. It's there to remind me of how ardently I worked at creating a persona—that is, that I was deliberately working at making myself into an intellectual—in those Navy days.

I was getting valuable training in electronics, and I knew both that it could land me a well-paying job when I finished my hitch and that, as I thought of it even in those days, I was unwilling to envision myself spending 8 hours a day working on machinery. I had a sense that I'd go on to something quite different when I finished up, and as early as the year I spent in Tennessee, grinding away in technical schools, it was in the books I was reading in the evenings and on weekends that I found what most appealed to me, not the life of a technician.

It would be wrong, though, to imply that I was conscious of tension between seeking a life as an intellectual and performing my military duties as well as I could. At the time, in fact, I don't think I even noticed that there was a strain. I was having a blast doing all these things in ways that I'd been unable to when I'd been under my father's thumb. And then there was a third stream, one that flowed somewhere among, or maybe even outside the realm the other two occupied. It was the piece of me that was fundamentally a rebel, not just against my father, but against mainstream society and authority in general.

And that's what I'd turned to Kerouac and Beckett for. This need to doubt—to argue with—the status quo had been flowing through me even as a kid studying *Mad Magazine*, and it took a sharp turn as I started reading a strange newspaper I stumbled on at a San Diego newsstand, Paul Krassner's *The Realist*, which has been aptly described as "Mad Magazine for adults." It was punching ragged holes in everyday American life. This was just a few blocks up Broadway from where the ferry docked when it carried us across the bay from the Navy base, and I stood there pretty much the same way I did as a kid reading comic books in the drugstore. I'm struck now by how available the counterculture was, no more than steps outside the base.

And though the Beatles may seem as mainstream as one could get at the time, the fact is that their films *A Hard Day's Night* and *Help* were, like the Marx Brothers early films, hymns to the absurd. They occupy in my mind some of the same space as *Waiting for Godot, Zorba the Greek*, Bob Dylan's lyrics from his 1965 albums, "Bringing It All Back Home" and "Highway 61 Revisited," and Kerouac's *On the Road*. And Dylan was of course channeling Dylan Thomas and Kerouac, among a host of others.

These are no more than the most visible faces of the ferment going on just below the surface of my warrior persona. At some level, they all represent artists' deliberate efforts to push back against high art and culture, to use art against itself. As Zorba asks his boss, when he can't satisfactorily answer Zorba's questions about why men die, "What the hell's the use of all your damn books if they can't answer that?" I was arming myself not only with the practical skills required to survive in a war, and with the highbrow knowledge I'd need to become an intellectual, but also with a sardonic stance toward everything I was trying to learn or become. I intuitively grasped that my salvation was going to lie in irony.

I was all of these at once. I was a stalwart flight tech flying my missions. I was an intellectual aborning, haphazardly fashioning myself into a cultured man. While these managed to coexist most of the time, at times they collided. I'd heard about LSD and wanted to try it early on, but I'd also heard of delayed reactions, called acid flashes, brought on by unexpected stimuli; they could prove fatally disorienting. I was flying nearly every day, surrounded by all sorts of odd visual effects, exactly the sort of thing said to set these flashes off, and I was concerned about the possibility of having one while I was in the air. It could have been catastrophic, and I wasn't scattered-brained enough to take the risk. As I went to sea for the last time, during a set of training exercises just prior to redeploying to Vietnam, a few weeks before my discharge, I was agitated enough to paint Day-Glo flowers on my sea bag. Fortunately, in the chaos of loading the squadron's gear as we embarked, no one noticed.

I'd come back from the war as a warrior, but that's hardly all I was. I wasn't just one thing or two things, I was many things. It wasn't inevitable that I'd head in any particular direction, but I can see now that as I turned away from the war, I was certainly destined to follow a twisting path, full of contradictions and challenges.

I suspect that this is when my tendency to think about things and then to immediately think the opposite about them crystalized. I was a man of action and utterly serious about what I did. Part of my psyche was organized around doing whatever it took to get the job done. At the same time, I doubted the meaning of nearly everything and looked with intense irony at the world around me. I can't quite fathom how this was possible at that age, and in that crucible, but it helped me survive. Not surprisingly, though, the adaptation I made to the war, doing what was necessary and doubting it at the same time, which seemed to serve me well, has burdened me ever since. It's possible for me to see things simply, or at least in a single vein, but it's rare. I doubt everything, I see alternative ways of understanding everything. It's another thing Zorba put his finger on: "You think too much," he says to his boss. "That is your trouble. Clever people and grocers, they weigh everything." And it's for this reason that I heeded yet another of Zorba's exhortations:

"Damn it, boss, I like you too much not to say it. You've got everything except one thing: madness! A man needs a little madness, or else . . ."

"Or else?"

"He never dares cut the rope and be free."

I understood this intuitively, perhaps, and it's why I listened to Zorba. I'd cut the rope when I left home, and again when I'd walked away from a stable job and joined the Navy. Coming back from Vietnam, the question for me was whether I could do it again. Everything I'd become by then was, I now see, aimed in that direction.

NOTES

1. In April 2001 a Navy EP-3 electronics reconnaissance plane collided with a Chinese fighter aircraft off the coast of Hainan and made an emergency landing at the Yulin airbase. It was then that I learned that the vast bay there serves as a major naval installation, the homeport for Chinese operations in the South China Sea. Shane Osborn (2001), the US pilot, tells the story in *Born to Fly*.

2. "He who fights with monsters should look to it that he himself does not become a monster" is a line from Friedrich Nietzsche's (1886) *Beyond Good and Evil*.

3. I discuss the neurobiology of stress, trauma, and post-traumatic stress disorder below in Chapter 8.

4. As I thought my way through this section, I found myself returning to things I'd been only vaguely conscious of during the war, and I began digging more deeply into them. I'm speaking specifically of my recollections of what we talked about—and more to the point, didn't talk about—aboard ship. Why was it, I wondered, that I can remember no conversations about the war, about either why or how we were fighting it? It all seemed quite bloodless. It turns out that this wasn't random. It was, rather, a deliberate decision made by the US government. The US military began its buildup in Vietnam at a time when a notion of "limited war" was the prevailing theory of warfare. Fears of all-out nuclear war led strategic thinkers to argue that nuclear powers should engage in armed conflict in small, incremental steps, with the hope that larger, more widespread conflict could be avoided. As an element of this strategy, the Johnson administration expressly pursued a policy of remaining "cold-blooded." It feared, that is, that if there were too much jingoistic rhetoric, working the population up into a war mentality, there would be too much popular pressure for the war to be ramped up to high intensity. Cold-blooded was, then, the way to approach what was initially intended to be a low-intensity conflict. As George Herring spells this out, the United States went to war "in a manner uniquely quiet and underplayed." Specifically, President Johnson said, "I think we can get our people to support us without having to be provocative" (Herring, 1994, p. 31). Even more to the point, Secretary of State Rusk said, "We never made any effort to create a war psychology in the United States during the Vietnam affair. . . . We felt that in a nuclear world it is just too dangerous for an entire people to get too angry and we deliberately played this down. We tried to do in cold blood perhaps what can only be done in hot blood" (Charlton and Moncrieff, 1978, p. 115).

5. Over the years I've gradually grown aware of a sort of mythology about servicemen and prostitutes that I'd like to draw attention to. When I first reported for my technical training in Memphis, a new group of fellow trainees had just arrived as well. These sailors had in the wake of boot camp spent six months at a set of naval air stations along the Texas-Mexico border, where the mild climate allows year-round training for pilots. They were stationed in places like Beeville, Kingsville, and Corpus Christi, and they regularly made trips to Mexican border towns like Nuevo Laredo, "Boys' Town" in Villa Acuña (now Ciudad Acuña), and Matamoros. They regaled those of us who hadn't yet had a chance to serve in what's loosely known as "the fleet" with stories about their exploits in those towns' fleshpots. I mention this because they told an almost standardized set of stories about the activities of the prostitutes working there and how the sailors treated them. I assumed their stories were true. Later, however, I read about what were essentially identical activities in Olongapo, in the Philippines, in Missy Cumming's book *Hornet's Nest*. And then I read about some of the same activities in the short story "In Vietnam They Had Whores" in Phil Klay's *Redeployment*. Speaking now as an anthropologist

who's written a lot about using mythology to study history (Petersen, 1990), the repetitive character of this pattern leaps out at me. There are just too many close similarities, which is a common aspect of myth (sometimes known as urban legend), as opposed to real history. Now, it's possible that I am mistaken about this, but in fact I spent a good deal of my time in Mexican border town fleshpots when I was a young sailor. And I spent a fair amount of time in Olongapo's bars and clubs, both as a drunken sailor and on Shore Patrol, when I was stone-cold sober. I never observed any of these particular debaucheries firsthand, and I'm inclined to think that most of these accounts are not of firsthand experiences but are instead sea stories that sailors and others have passed along for generations.

6. I tracked Terry down 50 years after last seeing him and showed him these passages; he says they ring true to him.

7. The quintessential account of Rand's ideas appears in her *The Virtue of Selfishness*, published in 1964—just as I was joining the Navy. Her fame (or perhaps notoriety) was peaking while I was at my most open.

8. In *Lies My Teacher Told Me* James Loewen (1995, p. 300) describes this change in outlook among those going to war in some detail.

9. Kerouac, on Steve Allen's TV show in 1959, read from *On the Road* to a jazz accompaniment. In response to Allen's question about how he would define "beat," he said "sympathetic." https://www.youtube.com/watch?v=3LLpNKo09Xk. Theodore Roszak's (1969, p. 63) *The Making of a Counter Culture* explores the evolution of this beat-hip bohemianism and Kerouac's place in it. Roszak was on Cal State Hayward's faculty while I was an undergrad there, but I have no sense that we ever crossed paths or that he had any influence on me at the time.

Chapter Five

Thinking I've Left the War

On the face of it, we'd left the war. Benn was steaming southeast toward Sydney, Australia, making its way through the scatterings of South Pacific islands. Captain Graffy ran a taut ship and while we were thinking this would be our chance to unwind, he was having none of it. He knew that a warship at sea remains a dangerous place, whether it's engaged in combat operations or not, and was determined to keep us fully alert to the hazards around us. He kept us in fighting trim as long as we were at sea, flying sorties and engaged in all the many operations that get planes into the air.

The skipper worried that his crew, no longer galvanized by round the clock operations, would lower its guard, and he arranged a subterfuge that still astonishes me each time I recall it. He had the boatswain fashion a dummy, loaded with ketchup or tomato sauce, then toss it into a turning propeller on the flight deck. It seemed entirely real in the moment it happened, and it kept us aware of how easy it is for the smallest misstep or moment of inattention to reap instant death. It did the trick, but it also sharpened my lasting sense of just how perilous work on the flight deck is.

We launched a Fudd each day to help the ship with its bearings and to ensure that the planes remained fully operational. The other flight techs had no interest in flying by that time (especially since these sorties didn't count towards the Air Medals we'd earned in Vietnam), while I, still curious despite my weariness, remained eager to fly as often as I could. Each day one of our planes went exploring, in a sort of glorified version of joyriding, and as we traversed the South Pacific we soared over island after island, each more beautiful, more exotic, and more seductive than the last.

The coral atolls especially enchanted me. We swept in low over deep blue lagoons, dazzling white beaches with outrigger canoes drawn up, thatched huts, and islanders waving madly at us. It's no exaggeration to say that I'd come from hell and sensed with every fiber of my being that I was gazing at paradise. I heard Sirens calling to me, just like those who sang to Odysseus on his voyage home from Troy.

That leg of our voyage home shook something loose in my soul. For what was perhaps the first time, but certainly not the last, the contradictory, clashing vectors of peace and war disordered whatever sense I had of up and down, of in and out, of right and wrong. We'd been dispatched on one last mission, and as we made our way through the islands, we were playing one more small role in the political drama of the war.

Australia had deployed an infantry battalion to South Vietnam in 1965, and the question of continuing participation in the war had been a major political issue in the country's 1966 national elections. Given that most of our major allies opposed American intervention in Vietnam, President Lyndon Johnson was working hard at convincing other countries to supply troops as a means of demonstrating international support for the US campaign. Our port call in Australia was a diplomatic gesture, not a pleasure cruise (McQueen, 1991).

In the years following World War II, the United States had pushed to make the anniversary of the Battle of the Coral Sea a key event celebrating Australian-American relations.[1] A visit by a group of US warships to mark the 25th anniversary of the battle in May 1967 was thus an artful means of reminding Aussies of their continuing debt to the United States for its sacrifices in the naval battle that halted Japan's advance toward their homeland. We were sent home via Sydney in order to show the American flag during Coral Sea Week.

And so we charted a course from Yankee Station to Luzon in the Philippines, through the Central and South Pacific, and across the Coral Sea to a berth alongside Sydney Harbor's Garden Island. We spent nearly a week indulging in the sweetest liberty a young sailor could imagine. It was nearly impossible for us to buy a drink, so eager were folks there to host us. Then we weighed anchor and headed northeast for Pearl Harbor and for our home-port on the West Coast. In the course of this sweeping trans-Pacific crossing we traversed the great swath of islands collectively thought of as the South Pacific, spots long enshrined in nearly every vision of paradise.

DISCOVERING ANTHROPOLOGY

I was still in the midst of war, and not only the one I'd been fighting in the Tonkin Gulf; now I found myself entwined in the one I'd grown up with as well. World War II and Vietnam became nearly indistinguishable in my mind.

Soaring above the islands, I gazed at places where it appeared that everything was quite the opposite of what I'd just been through. "I'm looking at paradise," I thought. "I've got to find a way to get onto one of these islands." This was more than an idle fantasy: I felt a real compulsion to bail out, to parachute down onto one of them. Having managed to survive a war partly because of my cool head, of course, I was also practical enough to know that the skipper would simply dispatch a helicopter, haul me back aboard, and court-martial me for desertion.

I'm not sure whether it was a matter of minutes or hours before I worked out the solution to my dilemma, but I do see that I spontaneously arrived at a decision that would play as huge a role in shaping my life as those I made when I ran away from home and when I joined the Navy. I knew that what I wanted wasn't just a brief visit to one of these islands—no, I yearned to live on one, to learn what it was like to really *be* there, and to let an island and its people help mend some of the damage I'd done to myself during the war.

A movie I'd seen when I was small, *Return to Paradise*, starring Gary Cooper, was based on a story in James Michener's book of the same name. It was a romantic tale of a World War One veteran who'd retreated to a remote Polynesian atoll to escape civilization following the war. In the same way that movies got me headed toward the war, this one in time helped me get away from it.

I've already made it clear that when I was young, my life was repeatedly and radically influenced by books. *Huckleberry Finn*, *The Catcher in the Rye*, and *Catch-22* each had a startling impact on me; they did more than seize my imagination, they catapulted me into action. When I was attending technical schools in the Tennessee countryside with little to do in my free time but play cards and study, I often grabbed a pile of books from the post library and read my way through the weekend. One of the volumes I picked up by chance—it was sitting out on the new acquisitions table—was Oliver La Farge's *The Door in the Wall*.

La Farge, an anthropologist as well as a writer of highly-regarded fiction, wrote a series of short stories about anthropologists and archaeologists at work, most of them published in *The New Yorker* magazine in the late 1950s and early '60s. Following his death, they were gathered up and published in 1965 as *The Door in the Wall*. La Farge was best known for his incisive accounts of Native Americans, especially his novel *Laughing Boy*, which earned him the 1930 Pulitzer Prize, but in these stories he turned his attention to the sorts of issues that scientists confront while doing ethnographic fieldwork.

As I was pondering how I might find a way to live on one of these Pacific islands below me, La Farge's stories came to mind. Anthropologists spend time in exotic places, I recalled, and I quickly imagined myself as an anthropologist, not merely visiting one of these spots, but earning my living by settling down on one of them for a spell. The central character in some of the stories, Wally Caswell, was a young grad student in anthropology. I could identify with him, and imagine myself in his shoes.

I like to say I was so ignorant about all that was entailed in becoming an anthropologist that I failed to realize I'd never be able to do it. But that's not entirely true. I was so seized in that moment with a sense of what I had just accomplished in the war that I sensed I could achieve anything I set my mind to.

Fortunately, I understood at some not entirely conscious level that I had good reason to trust my impulses, and that my decisions ultimately paid off. Leaving home had saved my life. And although I'd come close to losing it by going to war, I had also transformed myself from an uneducated kid working on an assembly line into a competent and confident warrior, a man who could handle whatever challenges he sought out. But I also had an intuition about the damage I'd incurred. That's why I knew I had to get as far from the war as I could, in order to do some healing.

It was in the context of believing I could achieve whatever I set out to do—and that I needed to do something radical—that I made this seemingly bizarre decision to become an anthropologist. All I really knew about anthropologists was that they earned a living by living in exotic places. If I became an anthropologist, I'd have an occupation that would enable *me* to do so, too.

That was in 1967. I began studying anthropology in 1968, and by 1972 I was teaching it. I did my earliest field research in 1969, began working in the Pacific islands in 1970, and have worked as an ethnographer in the islands ever since. It was clear to me from very early on, and has only gotten clearer as the years roll by, that there's nothing I'm better suited for than being an anthropologist. Yes, I would have liked to play second base on a pro ball club, or guitar in a rock band, but given who I am and my actual abilities, I'm sure these couldn't have proved nearly as satisfying to me as anthropology. And it's not just that I'm suited to be an anthropologist and that I enjoy it so much, it's that anthropology so satisfies my soul.

I don't think I could have made a radical decision like that if I hadn't had an intuitive grasp of who I was and of what my capabilities were. It's not just that I said, "Oh, I want to be an anthropologist." It's that I both fixed on exactly the right thing and then poured all that I'd become during the war into it, directing every bit of my focus and drive and fearlessness at it. It wasn't easy. I nearly derailed quite a few times, and often doubted whether I was still on the right track. But the guy who climbed back into his plane and flew his next mission after that China incursion kept on going.

PREPARING TO DEPLOY AGAIN

While we saw some respite when we got back from Vietnam, there wasn't nearly as much as you might think. Even as we returned to homeport we'd begun readying for our next deployment. During wartime, a carrier and its air group, like an infantry unit, are either in combat or preparing for it. We were continually training, and the brutal fact is that during preparations for war, when the training is at its most intensive, new flyers and crews are acquiring crucial skills. Precisely because the stakes seem a little lower, and not everyone is at their wariest, the likelihood of fatal errors can be greater than in actual combat. While we were in the mid-Pacific a few months after our return, recovering one of the early Apollo space capsules in the lead-up to the moon shots, a flightdeck hand was run over and killed by an aircraft he was moving.

In the course of the next few months of training operations we had more major accidents aboard *Bennington*. Two of the Hawkeyes, the planes that were gradually replacing our Fudds, snapped arresting wires as they landed, hurtled off the angled deck, and crashed into the sea below. An A-4 bomber hit the tail end of the flight deck and exploded as it went over the side. And one of our helicopters fell into the sea just short of the ship.

There's a romantic notion about coming home from war, poetic lines that speak of safe return: "Home is the sailor, home from the sea." But our transition back from the war held for us nothing more than a minor drop in the intensity of what we did; the hours weren't quite as long and the fears about what might befall us if we did something wrong diminished a little. I wasn't worrying about shielding the fleet, but the signs of all that could go wrong on the flight deck or in the air were everywhere around me. I fell into what would become my pattern for the next few decades. I worked hard at my job. I enrolled in a night class at community college (which I had to drop because of all the time we spent out in the Pacific waiting for that Apollo shot to launch). And I drank every day, usually a lot.

Twice in the months after we returned from overseas, I drank heavily enough to oversleep and made it into work an hour or so late. I'd been sent to a central repair shop on the far side of the base, where they'd relocated the radar benches to free up space in the squadron shops as our Fudds were phasing out. If I'd been with my own unit, nothing much would have happened, but the people running things where I was working didn't know me; they announced that they were going to take a stripe from me—bust me—for being an hour late *twice*.

I spoke with my pilots about it during a training flight. My detachment immediately transferred me back, convened a disciplinary hearing, admonished me, then sent me back to the central avionics shop. Since I'd already been disciplined, there was nothing they could do to me there. Though this episode seems trivial, it had a lasting impact on me. I understand that life is not fair, but I also know that if you have the good fortune to be in a reasonable environment, and that if you work hard, the odds run a little better in your favor. I'd given my squadron everything I had and they took care of me in turn. The leaders in the shop where I'd been transferred, on the other hand, demonstrated the sort of chickenshit the military is famous for—they hadn't even bothered to confer with my own outfit. And we can see how entirely oblivious they were to the stresses and strains facing troops just back from the war.

This episode played a part in the oddly contradictory way I've learned to think about the world. I'm aware that I've got roughly equal measures of trust and distrust in me (or in other terms, I'm both optimistic and pessimistic). I'd already come to understand that flying in combat meant I had to trust that everyone involved was doing their job, while still fully expecting that anything could go wrong at any moment because someone had failed at their job. This sounds impossible on paper—to trust and distrust at one and the same time—but that's precisely how I experienced combat. And the simple fact is that that's how I've come to experience everything: deep trust and distrust simultaneously.

But I also see another pattern forming, one that's persisted over the years. Although the Fudds were phasing out and few experienced radar technicians were being assigned into the E-1 detachments, the older, smaller Essex class carriers couldn't handle a full detachment of the significantly larger E-2s and the arduous pace of operations on Yankee Station meant that Fudd detachments were still deploying. The squadron's E-1B radar shop was still in full swing. Though I was only twenty, and still the youngest guy there, at times I was the ranking petty officer in the newly centralized radar repair facility, which meant that I ran the shop.

In those days the Navy was focused overwhelmingly on technical proficiency and did little to train its technical crews in leadership skills. To put it mildly, I knew next to nothing about running a shop and I had no sense of how to order people about. My leadership style evolved on the spot, one that I still characterizes me: I lead by example. When our shift began each day, I'd point out all the equipment that needed repair, specify the pieces I was going to go to work on, and tell everyone else to turn to. It worked. As long as they could see their boss hard at work, the others pitched right in.

I haven't changed much over the years. I still feel that setting an example lies at the root of leading people, I resist issuing orders, and nothing's happened to change my mind. Yet I still find that it works.

I didn't always escape so easily from the consequences of my drinking. I drank far too much at my detachment's Christmas party that December. But by age 20, I was already skilled at hiding it. No one stopped me as I got into my car to leave the Navy Amphibious base in Coronado and headed down the Strand, the long stretch of sand that forms the western side of San Diego Bay, toward the apartment I was renting in nearby Chula Vista. I hadn't gone more than mile when I passed out and ran off the road. My car rolled over and crashed. I recall nothing of this, till I woke up the following morning in a Coronado jail cell, that is. It was the first time I totaled out a car, but it was by no means the last.

The contradictions that characterized my postwar life were already surfacing. I was drinking heavily and making big mistakes, but I was good at what I did, and what I did was important in the eyes of those around me. How could I have been affected by the war? I was, for example, flight tech in the aircraft that was backing up the command plane when we recovered the Apollo 4 shot.[2] Equipment problems flared up just as we were about to launch (which is why we always had a backup ready to go) and the admiral leapt out of his plane, climbed into ours, glanced around, and tossed the radar officer out. He wanted to maintain charge of the recovery, but he couldn't do it unless I was there to keep the equipment running. And when the Pentagon announced a budget shortage at the start of 1968 and ordered that all hands who were about to be discharged should be released two months early, as a money-saving tactic, our squadron's commander decided it didn't apply to me.

My discharge was scheduled for April 12, the day before my 21st birthday and days before we were redeploying to the Tonkin Gulf. The squadron cabled Washington that they had no one to replace me and that they wouldn't be letting me go until they absolutely had to. I was officially irreplaceable. The Pentagon bureaucracy failed to respond to this message until mid-February, and so I learned on the 10th that I was to be discharged on the 12th. As I was racing through the maze of administrative offices with my paperwork, I was sent in to speak with our personnel officer. I'd flown many missions with Brent Jacobs (the pilot nicknamed "Bolter" because he'd blown so many carrier landings) and he knew me better than most officers knew the men in our squadron.

"Sit down, Pete. I'm supposed to give you a reenlistment pitch.

"Look, we've just seen how indispensable you are to us. The Navy will give you a lot to ship over. You'll get some really great reenlistment bonuses and benefits. Let's talk about your future."

"Yes, sir."

"Do you know what you're going to do when you get out?"

"I've been accepted into college, sir. I'll be starting soon."

He smiled a wry grin. "That's great. It was good flying with you, Pete. I wish you luck," he said as he shook my hand. Placing his arm around my shoulder, he walked me out of the office telling me a story about his own college days.[3]

Then I was out. A civilian. And even if I was no longer at war, or even engaged in the grueling operations that followed it, it seems that I missed barely a beat before I found my way back into a nearly identical groove. It was no more than a day or two after my discharge before I was in a temporary employment agency, Manpower Inc., applying for work. When I proved myself on a few one-day jobs they handed me a longer-term job with a building contractor who kept me working till my classes started. While we were installing industrial shelving, working side-by-side, he explained to me that he was billing the warehouse 8 dollars an hour for my labor and paying the temp agency 3 dollars an hour for it. The temp agency was in turn paying me little more than a dollar an hour. It took only days for me to realize how much civilian life mirrored the military. I'd done three jobs to the radar officers' one and got paid less than half of what they made; now I was getting about fifteen percent of the money spent to pay for the work I was doing.

And in those few days between my discharge and beginning classes, my ways of thinking took another hit. My old newspaper, the *Tribune*, ran a short piece about a boyhood friend of mine, Benji Yamane, an infantry sergeant, who had just been killed in battle. Benji's death struck me with particular force, not simply because he'd been a beautiful guy, but because Benji had been born shortly after his family was released from one of the internment camps where the United States imprisoned Japanese Americans during World War II. We were born a few days apart and lived a few doors apart and played together as small boys in the immediate shadow of that experience, though I knew nothing of it at the time. But when he died, the irony kicked me in the gut. He'd been killed fighting an American war against Asians.[4]

The GI Bill paid a flat ninety dollars a month in those days, not remotely enough to live on, so I'd applied to Safeway, the supermarket chain, and started working three 8-hour shifts a week in one of their stores just as my classes began. The boss had me pushing grocery carts around the parking lot and refused to make me a clerk, as I'd been promised, but I wangled a meeting with the district manager and after explaining to him that I'd just come back from flying combat missions in multimillion dollar aircraft over Vietnam, he moved me into a better job on the spot. Again, I saw parallels between civilian and military realms: sometimes hard work and advocating for yourself pay off.

That first term in college, in a basic psychology course, I learned something that gave me a startling new understanding of what I'd been through, though I was hardly prepared to make much of it at the time. We watched a film about research on attention spans. It included a sequence demonstrating that the optimal time a radar operator could focus on a scope was little more than 30 minutes, and that 2 hours was the longest anyone could be expected to be effective on one. In the Tonkin Gulf, with all our aircraft under my control and the fleet's security at stake, I sat the scope for 6 hours without a break. I was now confronting the fact that just because the military engages in applied research doesn't mean they apply it.

I've been pondering this ever since, trying to come to terms with it. I suppose it makes sense, from the Navy's point of view, not to inform the crewmen charged with these sorts of duties that research shows they're impossible to carry out. If we were told this, perhaps, we might use the knowledge to excuse the lapses we were bound to make. But if we were kept in the dark, then we'd strive to the utmost to fulfill our duties. At some level, that is, the guilt is intentionally built in. The higher-ups want us to be scared to death, as a means of focusing our attention, but in extracting enhanced performance from us they also leave us feeling personally responsible for mistakes inherent in the system. One of the many ironic lines I recall hearing back in those days was that we do the difficult immediately; the impossible takes a little longer. We said it as a joke, but that's exactly what they expected of us.

Given my hard-charging approach to everything in those days, college went by in a blur. I'd earned a GED equivalency diploma and managed to get a couple of night-school community college courses under my belt while I was in the service, so having had only 1 year of high school didn't really hamper me as I began studying at what was then California State College, Hayward (and is now California State University, East Bay), in March of 1968. I saddled myself with a heavy load of classes, plus a full load in the summers, and graduated in 2 years while earning nearly straight A's, even as I was working at Safeway three full shifts a week. In the same way that I'd gotten a measure of self-regard from my radar skills, I was pleased to see that even though I'd been away from school for 5 years, I graduated only a year later than any high school classmates who'd managed to complete college in 4 years.

When I look back at myself though, I see a barely civilized barbarian of the sort I've heard described as a living-room baboon. I had no idea how to talk to other students, especially women. During my first year at Hayward I went to classes in the mornings, worked at the supermarket till 10:00 or 11:00 at night, then drank beer in a local tavern until I could fall asleep. I spoke with virtually no one.

At end of my first year, though, I heard about an all-day Saturday field archaeology course, and enrolled partly because it was okay with Clarence Smith, the old-timer who was our professor, to bring along a cooler of beer.[5] That's where I discovered how well alcohol could lubricate my path through professional life (and not just knock me out at night). After a few beers, I could begin to talk a little, and I soon wound up stopping for beer and pizza with some of the others after each day's work on the dig. *That's* when I was able to free up my limited interpersonal skills. It wasn't long before I was heading off with a group from the field class to parties in the evening after the pizza stop, and as long as I was drinking beer or Red Mountain burgundy from dollar jugs, I seemed to function fine.

It was on that dig that I met my first girlfriend, but I was still so out of synch with college life that Robin had to take matters into her own hands in order to catch me. It's not that I wasn't interested in her, but that I'd been away from the company of women for so long that I had no idea of how to interact with them. The two of us were assigned to work together in the same square of the field site—we were pit partners. Although I was madly attracted to her, I was utterly incapable of imagining that she might be interested in me, and that stood in our way for a long time, until at one of those Saturday evening parties she finally threatened to assault me physically if I didn't kiss her. It was the sort of contradiction that's shaped my relations with women (along with other things) throughout my life: the more I'm interested in something, or desire it, the more certain I become that it's not available to me.

My hunch about anthropology had hit the mark. I took to it like I'd taken to the air. In the same way that I'd pushed myself to my limits to master every aspect of the Fudd's radar, and to shoulder responsibility for every task, I sought to soak up as much anthropology as possible. In addition to going on digs, I worked in the lab analyzing the artifacts we dug up. I studied human evolution and linguistics, map and photo interpretation, and geology. And I began learning the craft of field ethnography—the essence of what it means to be a cultural anthropologist—as I conducted elementary research projects on several different California Indian reservations. In time, my sense of who I am in the world would come to be defined by this work: I know myself as an ethnographer as much as anything else.

Those remarkable short stories by La Farge, the ones that first offered me a vision of anthropology as a grail to pursue in the wake of the war, gave me something more as well, a moral compass for my life's work.[6] A couple of them, about young or aspiring anthropologists working with Pueblo Indian communities in the southwest, had at their core some of the basic ethical problems ethnographers confront. Fieldworkers always face competing responsibilities: to the people they study, to the furthering of scientific knowledge, and to their own professional ambitions. Without being in any way didactic, La Farge made it clear that in his view it's the people and the community being studied that have first claim on the ethnographer's loyalties. I wasn't really conscious of how vital this perspective was when I first read his stories, but I took in that sense of moral obligation along with the romance of the fieldwork.

I substituted anthropology for all that had gone before, pouring myself into it, body and soul. My job in the war had been big enough to absorb all the force of the *thumos* I'd brought to it. Now I was trying to do more than just be some sort of hero. I was also working as hard as I possibly could to keep myself from understanding what had happened to me in the war, from grasping the scope of the war's impact on my soul. As long as I could continue running as fast and as hard as I had in Vietnam, I could keep the war at bay. And coupled with my drive, my native intelligence, and my ability to pay attention to what was going on *outside* me, an element of luck enabled me to continue galloping full tilt. The force of my drive and spirit could easily have killed me, or thrown me into lifelong depression, if I hadn't stumbled in through a brief historical window when there was ample money to fund graduate studies, even for crazies like me, and even more amazing, when a few good academic jobs remained.

And I did come very close to killing myself in those days. Besides the car I crashed weeks before I was discharged, I totaled out two more cars while I was in college. All these wrecks took place while I was drinking. For the life of me, I cannot understand how I failed to see that I had a problem, but then no one else seemed to notice it either, certainly not my family and friends.

Decades later, after I'd gained some perspective on those first years following the war, a conversation with my brother confirmed all this. It was the Fourth of July, about 2006. My brother was holding an Independence Day barbecue at his house on the Severn River. I sat at a table overlooking the water, a couple of miles upstream from the Naval Academy at Annapolis, with my brother Steve and the father of one of Steve's sons' friends, a young Marine recently back from Iraq. He asked what it was like for me when I returned from Vietnam and expressed concern about his son's state of mind. I was nearly overwhelmed right then with agitation stoked by the wars in Afghanistan and Iraq, and I wanted to contrast how I was feeling with what I'd been like when I returned from Vietnam. I tried to explain that I could now see the troubles I'd had when I came back from the war, though I'd been pretty much oblivious to them at the time. My brother objected.

"I was around then," he said. "You didn't seem to have any particular problems."

"I did total out three cars in the span of two years after I came back from the war," I pointed out. "I think that's evidence that *something* was going on with me."

He shrugged and we wordlessly agreed to disagree about the matter, returning instead to the young Marine and what he'd experienced in Iraq.

The responses of those around me can be seen even more strikingly in a conversation with my mother. In about 1989 my parents had traveled cross-country to New Jersey to see their granddaughter, who was growing from infancy into toddlerhood. I was participating in a Vietnam vets combat rap group at the storefront Vet Center in Trenton and had begun to wonder if maybe something *had* happened to me during the war. My sense of what I'd undergone was still vague, but I was starting to think that if I could find a way to talk about what had happened, I might gain some insight into what was going on with me.

My parents and I are sitting in the living room. I'm telling them that I've been in these conversations with other vets, and that I'm getting some dim sense of what I actually experienced during the war; not just of what I did, but of how it affected me. I'm starting to see that it was problematic, I say, and that I'd been through a lot more than I'd realized.

"I don't want to hear about it," my mom says abruptly. "It's too upsetting." End of conversation.

So it seemed that no one noticed this reckless pattern of working nonstop, drinking heavily, and crashing cars, and I would have undoubtedly kept it up until I killed myself or someone else if I hadn't moved to Manhattan for graduate school—I didn't need to own a car, and that saved my life.

I'd gone to Hayward thinking it would serve as a good transition from the military to the University of California. Cal was the big leagues, which were what I aspired to, but I was conscious of all the years I'd been away from school and not at all sure how I'd fare there. I soon changed my mind, though, and decided to stay on at Hayward, mainly because I could see that as an undergrad at Berkeley I would have gotten lost among the multitudes, while it was clear that I was thriving as a big fish in a small pond at the state college. But there was something more: the thoroughly working-class character and ethnic makeup of Hayward's student body.

The San Francisco Bay Area was at the epicenter of the country's antiwar movement in those days. The Free Speech Movement of 1964 on the Berkeley campus (a few miles north of Hayward) had heralded the tectonic shift in the baby boomers' sensibilities and marked the beginnings of what most think of as '60s rebellion. Cal Berkeley, San Francisco State College, and Stanford were engaged in a bizarre version of a sports rivalry as their students led efforts to protest the war in Vietnam and the draft, and to push for a host of other causes, including the fight for civil rights and resistance to authority in general. Oakland, where I was living, was the major embarkation point for war materiel and many of the troops heading overseas, and its Army Terminal was a continuing focus for off-campus demonstrations. Opposition to the war, most of it loud and some of it violent, was everywhere around me.

By comparison, though, Hayward was a haven. It's not that the campus saw no antiwar demonstrations or student strikes, but that they were small and peripheral. I'd always held deeply contradictory views about war in general, but in the course of my tour in Vietnam, as I've explained, I convinced myself that what we were doing there was an essential part of saving the world from communism. I can't imagine how I could have climbed into my plane each day and flown those missions if I hadn't believed fervently in what we were doing. My politics were pro-war when I started college, but I wasn't keen on confrontation, and my well-honed adaptive skills told me to lay low and scout out the land. I didn't hide the fact that I'd been in the war, but I certainly wasn't broadcasting it loudly.

There are many different sorts of stories—some quite contradictory—about what the United States was like for returning veterans in those days. [7] All I can do is tell you what I saw and experienced there, near the epicenter of antiwar activity while it was at its peak, but I've always been a careful observer and I believe I saw things clearly. The simple fact is that in most contexts it was next to impossible to know that someone had come back from the war. I've heard so many accounts of vets saying they were spat on or called "baby-killers" when they returned, but I've never understood just where and under what circumstances this was supposed to have happened. How would people know you were just back, or that you'd fought there at all? And there was the draft—how many in the Army went willingly to Vietnam? While protesters did assail the bayonet-brandishing troops at the Army Terminal while they were trying to shut it down (and of course there were fatal blunders when the National Guard was called onto campuses, as at Kent State), those were soldiers on active duty engaged in crowd control, not vets innocently passing by. I have no reason to think that vets weren't occasionally harassed, but it's hard for me to believe it happened often.

I do know that when I'd wanted to travel from San Diego to the Bay Area quickly and cheaply, hitchhiking in my uniform was amazingly effective. I rarely had to wait more than a minute or two between rides, and I could make the 500-mile trip as swiftly by hitching a ride as by driving myself, without having to fight off sleep or pay for gas. The folks who gave me lifts were invariably friendly. I don't think I ever encountered hostility when I was in uniform, or when the fact that I was recently back from the war came up.

But that may not be the real issue. Though it had to have been different in different parts of the country, anyone attending college in the Bay Area at the time knew just what they were getting into. There was a continuum of sentiments and outlooks, and in many ways popular music traced its contours. Troops were listening to the same music as the kids who opposed the war, and the airwaves were full of protest songs. Many—in some cases, most—of the kids we GIs had grown up with were finding ways to avoid going to war. Vets were returning to a society that didn't especially value what we'd just done, but because so many were terrified of the draft, the young men who'd been caught by it, or who had enlisted in a service branch other than the Army in order to circumvent it, were looked upon as unfortunate rather than bloodthirsty. I suppose my ambivalence about the war was typical. I believed in it, but that didn't mean that I didn't have lots of doubts about it, and I understood why people opposed it, even if I thought they were wrong.

I can't really say with any certainty how I felt about people who avoided the draft. It was one thing to be willing to go to prison for a couple of years for your beliefs, or even to give everything up and leave the country for

Canada, actions I admired, but I thought it was something else to avoid the draft with a deferment or trumped up medical problems. I can say that very few of the guys I knew from childhood went to Vietnam, and I just don't recall feeling hostility toward those who didn't go. I might have felt differently if I'd been drafted, I suppose, but having gone in on my own accord, for my own reasons, this wasn't something that upset me.

However much I had in common with the young people pushing back against the war, at first I was distanced from them. But the music we shared soon transformed my outlook.

FM radio was taking off, moving on from its early classical and jazz niches to popular music. And popular music itself was exploding in the wake of psychedelia and 1967's summer of love and the San Francisco sound. The air was exploding with strangeness that spoke to my sense of the absurd. The first songs I remember hearing when *Bennington* returned from overseas were psychedelic, the Doors' "People Are Strange" and Jefferson Airplane's "White Rabbit." This music, the music I wanted to hear, with Lennon and the Beatles and Dylan at the center of it all for me, was best heard on the new free-form, underground FM stations in the Bay Area. KSAN had just started broadcasting this format as I moved back, and in order to listen to it, I installed a used FM receiver in my VW, so big and clunky that I had to mount it on top of the dashboard.

I drove to my Hayward classes listening to KSAN's morning show, hosted by a couple of guys known as The Congress of Wonders, who mixed the music with theater of the absurd in the sardonic vein of *Mad Magazine*, Firesign Theater, and *National Lampoon*. It was relentlessly political as well, and I heard a massive cross-section of the antiwar mentality delivered in a whimsical mode that grabbed me by the lapels (I actually wore coat and tie— my Hong Kong treasures—when I started college), refusing to let my attention wander. As much as anything else, it was this influence that upended my thinking.

Timothy Leary, the LSD guru, had urged our generation to "Turn on, tune in, and drop out." I'd avoided drugs but turning my radio on and tuning it in had much the same effect on me. I did not drop out, though; I worked even harder, but the music fed me. And as always, the folk scene. I sang a line from Dylan, "I ain't gonna work on Maggie's farm no more" while thinking about the Navy. It was only a minor shift from Joe Cuba's "I'll never go back," the song I'd been singing not long before.

My attitude toward the draft changed first. Without really thinking it through or making any deliberate decision, I concluded that the United States should do away with it. But I continued believing in the Vietnam war itself for a while. I know this because I can recall from this same time the only direct interaction with antiwar protest I had in those days. This would have been at the time that Bobby Kennedy entered the race for the Democratic presidential nomination, that is, in the spring of 1968, not long after I started school.

I somehow found myself arguing with a student my age who was campaigning for Kennedy and for Bobby's antiwar position. I'm not sure what I said to him, but I know I was defending the war, insisting it was imperative that we continue to fight in Vietnam. He asked, if I believed so strongly in the cause, why wasn't I over there fighting? I replied that I'd just come back. His entire attitude abruptly shifted as he said, very respectfully, "Well, then I have no quarrel with you, man. If you were willing to fight over there, then you're entitled to believe in it." I can't say how representative he was of all those who opposed the war, of course, but there was no spitting, no "baby killer," not even hostility. Just respect and a willingness for us to hold opposing views without enmity.

By the time I'd finished up as an undergraduate, in those days of extraordinary turmoil, I was aware of how impossibly old I seemed compared to my contemporaries. I felt like I was fifty or so when I got out of the service, and as I came to grasp this I set out to strip off the years. What I was able to see was no more than the tip of the iceberg, but it told me that I needed to do *something* to reverse the aging process. I'd been fanning the embers of anarchy and rebellion beneath the surface all along, listening to the voices of Holden Caulfield, Yossarian, Kerouac, and Zorba. To this day, a line from Dylan's "My Back Pages" immediately transports me back to how I felt in those days: "Ah, but I was so much older then. I'm younger than that now."

Challenging authority, the same authority I'd embraced during the war, was in order and I began by embracing political radicalism. But all that did was change the direction of my headlong charge. I redirected my intensity and kept it fully aflame. By keeping myself occupied and preoccupied I continued to hold the war at bay. It wasn't that I was entirely oblivious, it was that I insisted in looking in all the wrong directions to discover what was ailing me, and with good reason, because when I finally did figure it out I found myself in a terrible jam.

When I left Hayward and headed for New York City to start graduate school in anthropology I was not the same man I'd been when I left the Navy two years earlier, but it was obvious that my ability to focus so tightly on my work and to pour most of my being into it was paying off. I'd earned a full fellowship to pursue my PhD at Columbia University, making the transition from high school dropout to the Ivy League in a little more than two years.

GRAD SCHOOL CRAZINESS

Knowing my interest in the Pacific islands, Columbia's anthropology department sent me off to a field school in Hawai'i the day after I graduated from

Hayward. I lived for a couple of months among some aged, old-time farmers in the depths of Waipi'o Valley, in the most isolated part of the island of Hawai'i. My experience in those exhilarating surroundings made me sure, in the most emphatic way possible, that that impulsive decision to make my living by spending time on beautiful Pacific islands had sprung from the most deeply observant and nurturing part of myself. With similar good fortune, I travelled through Central America the following year on a research project sponsored by the National Science Foundation, and my fascination with farmers and small-scale tropical farming continued to flower.

By the time I arrived in New York City, fresh out of Waipi'o, my appearance had changed radically. My shoulder-length hair and full beard reflected the changes that had been building up inside me. I swapped the prematurely aged, clean-cut GI for a much hipper young radical. Perched on Manhattan's Morningside Heights, Columbia University had been the scene of massive protests and police actions in 1968 and its anthropology department had involved itself in the ferment. It was just what I was seeking.

One of the many reasons I'd chosen Columbia (and living in New York City wasn't among them) was my desire to study with Marvin Harris (1968), who had just published a landmark book on the history of anthropology, the work that first introduced me to Karl Marx's social theory, and I understood when I arrived that I was entering into a hotbed of confrontational thought. It seems a bit absurd to say this now, but by the time I arrived there I had already begun thinking of myself as a Marxist—that's how quick the transition was. Soon I was listening to the nightly "War Report" on WBAI radio, a news program that challenged virtually everything the US government had to say about what was transpiring in Southeast Asia.

One of the most striking images I can summon up from that time is a montage I mounted on the wall over my desk. Under a photo of one of the Fudds I'd flown in during the war I placed a newspaper picture of the Pentagon, and between them I stuck a drawing of a large bomb. The Fudd bombing our own military captured my rapidly changing mindset. I also found my way to rallies and protest marches against the war and attended meetings of the Committee of Concerned Asian Scholars, a group of professors and students who combined their academic skills with a commitment to resisting the war in Southeast Asia.

And then the puzzle pieces of my intellect began reassembling themselves. While I was in Harris's year-long course on the history of anthropology I began formulating a topic for the required research paper. On the face of it, an essay for a first-year grad school course doesn't seem like much of a place to discover the precise focus of your life's work. Though I knew I wanted to live on a Pacific island, I hadn't narrowed down just what I would do once I'd made my way to one, nor just where in the Pacific I wanted to go. Hoping to get Harris's attention and understanding that he was a man of strong dislikes, I found myself researching the intersection of pieces of anthropological history I could weave together with political activism and the Pacific islands.

I chose to write about a very minor theoretical controversy set in Micronesia; it was set on islands the United States had seized from Japan after World War II and involved an anthropologist whose work Harris detested.

Harris was also engaged with decolonization politics in Portugal's African colonies and I sensed that an anticolonial slant would further attract his interest. The Micronesian research I was writing about had taken place in the immediate wake of the Navy's colonial occupation of Micronesia at the end of World War II and the creation of a United Nations–chartered trusteeship over the islands. There was a brief period when anthropologists played a role in implementing American rule over the far-flung territory.

Traveling to the National Archives in Washington, DC, I dug up enough material concerning conditions in Micronesia shortly after the war to cast doubt on the ethnography in question and to criticize the anthropologists who'd worked with the American colonial administration there. [8] I impressed Harris, but more importantly, I also wound up making the fateful decision to do my own field research in the Micronesian Trust Territory. I wanted to grapple directly with issues of American colonial rule in the region and began writing grant proposals for the funding I'd need to live on a Micronesian island.

Although I'd been most eager to study with Harris (an irascible fellow who took pleasure in being an iconoclast and who taught me that it's "impossible to say anything important without offending someone"), over the long haul of my career it was another of the department's professors, Robert Murphy, who most influenced me. Murphy, a Queens-born Irishman whose gift of blarney was widely celebrated, headed Columbia's anthropology department when I got there. Bob was a World War II vet, a sailor who'd served as radioman on a destroyer in the battle at Okinawa, among other spots in the Pacific, and knew firsthand the alternating rhythm of long days of boredom punctuated by the moments of terror during the Japanese kamikaze bomber attacks. I think he saw a lot of himself in me, and he was a kind and brilliant mentor. I've never forgotten his response when I told him that after I'd read his book *The Dialectics of Social Life* (1971), published during my first year there, I couldn't think straight for a week. "Thanks," he said. "That may be the highest praise I've gotten for it."

Bob endowed me with a perspective that's shaped my way of seeing the world as much as anything else I've learned throughout my career. He got me to pay close attention to the infinitely complex webs of connections among what people think, what they say, and what they do. Until then I'd thought that there were simple and straightforward relationships among these. Now I assume that there's no necessary relationship among them at all. The gap between what we say and what we do, I've taught generations of students, is always a question for empirical observation. And this way of looking at social life underlies everything I write here. Nothing is simple, nothing is straightforward, and people commonly say things that have very little relationship to what they think or what they do. Always, the task is to figure these connections out.

As I pursued my studies, my agitation about the war in Vietnam continued to build steam. There were no large-scale protests at Columbia in the spring of my first year, but together with a group of more advanced grad students, I headed to Washington, to participate in days of anti-war protests and attempts to paralyze the city. The police were far better organized than we were, of course, and though we gave it our best, we failed to shut the capital down. While I was there, though, I joined with other anti-war vets in a series of actions called "Operation Dewey Canyon III," during which we tossed away our Vietnam medals as an act of opposition to the war, even as I was keeping up my research at the National Archives.

Because it reflects just how confused I was at the time, I'm going to dwell on this episode a moment longer. I was attuned enough to academic life to figure out what would impress the professor I most wanted to impress. I was clever enough and dedicated enough to make the trip to the archives to search out relevant material. I was allying myself with grad students who were a few years ahead of me, forging networks that helped me learn how to navigate the university system and how one went about finding jobs. But I was also taking considerable risks in venting my rage in a very volatile arena. My newly acquired scholarly chops masked the chaos inside me. I had no sense of how contradictory my aspirations were: I wanted to succeed and I wanted to rebel, and I failed to see that doing both at the same time was going to cost me dearly.

I wasn't alone, of course. That act of hurling our medals back at the government shines a spotlight on the confusion rattling many vets. In *Stolen Valor*, a book excoriating men who make phony claims about their service in Vietnam, B. J. Burkett (1998) tells of a reporter querying Senator John Kerry, who'd been one of the organizers of that Dewey Canyon event years earlier, about the service medals displayed on his office wall. Kerry readily acknowledged that the medals he'd ostentatiously thrown away were not his. Burkett wonders, indignantly, how many of the other participants in Dewey Canyon threw away props?

As one who threw away his medals, I have to reply, "Well, it depends on what you mean by props, I guess." And this isn't just a semantic quibble—it reflects a dilemma at the very heart of what I'm writing about. Though I say tossed back my medals, because that's what they're ordinarily called, the fact is that what I actually threw were my ribbons, not my medals. They are equivalents: the ribbons are smaller versions meant for ordinary occasions when one wears a dress uniform, while the medals are much larger; they're for parades and special events. I was torn about what I was doing and wasn't prepared, I confess, to part with my medals.

As furious as I was at the war, and as thoroughly engaged in protesting it as I was, there remained some piece of me that wasn't truly ready to let them go. But I *was* able to brandish my ribbons. What may appear to many readers as a trivial difference in fact represents the striking degree to which many of us were of two minds. We were struggling to figure out how we could channel all that had made us willing to fight in the first place into effective opposition to a war we'd come to abhor. The same courage and honor that had won us those medals drove us to actively resist the war, and if we were a bit confused in the process of it, I see this as a powerful sign of our honesty, not of duplicity.

As the end of my second year in grad school approached, the contradictions building up within me reached a crisis point and began to erupt. I had just started on my series of three 4-hour long PhD qualifying exams in April 1972 when President Nixon ordered renewed bombing of Hanoi and of Haiphong harbor, and then the mining of the harbor. Students at Columbia, and throughout the country, launched protests. A student strike was called after I'd sat for two of the exams, and I pushed the last one ahead by a day in order to join the strike, which began while I was still inside Schermerhorn Hall, writing that third set of essays. I literally walked out of the exam and onto a picket line in front of my own department's offices. It's hardly a surprise that in my agitation I flunked the exams, but I wasn't especially concerned about my performance because I was throwing myself completely into the efforts to shut the campus down. I stationed myself in front of one of the buildings and tried to persuade people from entering, and at several points looped chains and padlocks around door handles and squeezed glue into locks in order to seal off entryways entirely.

After several days of the same turmoil Columbia had experienced in 1968 and again in 1970, the NYC police ascended Morningside Heights and marched onto the edge of campus. I was part of a demonstration in front of Hamilton Hall when plain-clothes officers waded into the crowd and seized a half-dozen protesters, including me. This led to an extraordinary ballet performance as one of the cops took hold of my left arm, told me I was under arrest, and began dragging me out of the crowd. I was exultant, thinking that I was about to realize a dream. I'd imagined that by getting arrested for opposing the war I would rid myself of the guilt I was increasingly feeling about having fought in Vietnam, and that I would achieve some sort of redemption.

But people in the crowd around me clutched my free arm, trying to pull me back out of the policeman's grasp, and a brief moment of comic relief unfolded. Though I wanted desperately to be arrested, I thought it would be totally out of keeping with the general mood of resisting authority to look like I did. I struggled unobtrusively to shake free from the folks trying to protect me, while hoping it looked like I wasn't. I wanted it to seem as though the officer himself was hauling me out of the crowd, though I was eager to be seized, and this required an award-worthy physical performance on my part: I was shrugging off those trying to keep me from being apprehended, while simultaneously leaning into the grasp of the cop I was supposed to be resisting.

Together, the two of us pried me free of the crowd and stepped out into the open space in front of the crowd. Thrusting me spread-eagled up against the wall in front of us, he frisked me as he genially explained that I was being arrested for nothing more than violating a temporary restraining order, entirely belying his rough demeanor.

"It's a civil violation," he said. "It's only a misdemeanor. No big thing. Try to break away from me, though, and you're resisting arrest. That's a much bigger deal."

He handcuffed me, grabbed my collar, and marched me toward Hamilton Hall's massive doors just as the riot gear-laden police who'd massed near the head of the quad erupted in a fury, charging the crowd with nightsticks swinging, clubbing everyone in their path. People were trying to retreat, but many were stumbling into one another and falling. It was a police riot and it was terrifying to see. The irony, of course, was that I was already tucked safely into police custody. I could hardly bear being in my secure position, though, as I watched my comrades being beaten.

I'd focused my attention on the battleground and was striving to commune with my comrades, who moments ago had been trying to save my neck. My policeman, still gripping my collar, was intent on getting me out of the melee and into the building. He pushed me through the doors into the foyer. "Solidarity forever, revolution makes us strong," I was chanting. Then I looked around and slammed my mouth shut as I realized that there was not a soul in that space who wasn't a policeman. I stumbled forward, with every eye in the place on me. And I knew that in just the same way that all *my* sentiments were with the students outside, the ties of everyone else in that space were to the police outside, and that in the same way that I felt solidarity with my comrades being beaten outside, all these cops' solidarity was with those doing the beating.

I waited for them to begin whaling on me. There was no one in sight to stop them, I thought. They're glaring at me. I stand for everything they hate. They have a perfect opportunity to beat me into oblivion; they'll say it happened outside in the riot, while I was resisting arrest. And it pained me to keep quiet—I was conscious of how my own solidarity had been compromised when I shut my mouth the instant I saw just what my situation was, even as I understood that my only chance to avoid a terrible beating was to keep quiet. (My old POW camp training was kicking in.) And then I was being frisked again, and shoved a bit, and hearing questions shouted at me. But my plain-clothes officer kept his hand on my collar and seemed to acknowledge that he and I had struck an implicit pact. I wouldn't resist and he would stand by me. I was tucked into a corner, out of the way, for a time. And then I was pulled down through the dim tunnels that run beneath the campus, still expecting the worst. Stumbling up into daylight on Amsterdam Avenue, outside the campus, I was hoisted into a paddy wagon. The doors slammed behind me, and I was, for the moment, miraculously, and entirely unexpectedly, safe.

Along with a half-dozen other students—I was the only grad student among us—I was hauled downtown, booked and arraigned, then released into our lawyer's custody. It did not escape me that we Columbia students had a cadre of lawyers already waiting in the courtroom by the time we arrived. I rushed back to campus and joined a group that had occupied Kent Hall, home of Columbia's East Asian Institute, following the police charge. We spent the evening on the top floor, in the East Asia Library. We (and I assume there must have been at least one police informer among us) talked at length about the war, opposition to the war, political strategy in general, and in particular, about our plans for responding to the police should they attempt to remove us from the building.

A maze of tunnels winds beneath Columbia University's Morningside campus, the same tunnels through which I had been hustled to the waiting paddy wagon when I was arrested. Heavy doors open from Kent's basement into the tunnels, and we had to decide what we'd do if we were invaded from underground. We eventually agreed, following a lengthy and self-consciously democratic process, that we'd charge to the basement and attempt to fend off the assault with the fire hose. In retrospect, a single hose against a heavily armed troop of police itching to pound on some punks doesn't sound like very good odds, but it seemed reasonable enough to us at the time (there was probably marijuana floating around, though I wouldn't have smoked it—I wanted to be in full possession of my senses). Most of us eventually went to sleep on the library's richly carpeted floor.

Somewhere in the deepest part of the night, well before dawn, the police quietly opened the tunnel doors. We had of course erected barricades of bulky office furniture in front of the entryway, but the doors themselves inconveniently swung *into* the tunnel, so there was nothing we could do to keep them shut. Now a riot squad was massing beyond our barricade. Our lookout heard them, though, and tore into the library, rousing us.

"The pigs have opened the basement doors. They're getting ready to charge us."

"Let's go, let's go. Down to the basement," we shouted, racing down the flights of stairs toward our agreed-upon positions below, ready to face the assault. I was in the lead, probably a residual habit from my experiences responding to general quarters aboard ship ("All hands man your battle stations") when I'd had to dash at top speed to the squadron ready room before the water-tight hatches were all slammed and dogged. I sprinted full-tilt from the top floor to the ground floor, ran to the stairway leading to the basement, and headed down. Turning the corner, I could see in the dim light that the tunnel doors were open. There, behind our makeshift barricade of battered old file cabinets and massive oak desks, was the tactical squad, impatiently checking gear, speaking softly into radios, and jockeying for position.

I stopped moving for a moment, gazing back and forth between the opened doors and the fire hose, anticipating my comrades' immanent arrival. Before anyone else had even appeared, though, I had already grabbed the nozzle and begun uncoiling the hose. I'd learned to fight shipboard fires in basic training and knew something about handling hose. I opened the valve and watched the canvas expand as it shot full of water. Hands gripping the nozzle, I looked back again toward the stairs. Still no one there.

I dragged the now-unwieldy hose toward the tunnel doors. I fiddled a bit with the nozzle. I had no idea how much water pressure I was going to have to contend with, and wanted a couple of others trailing behind me, to help me keep the hose in check when I opened up the spray, knowing that if there was too much pressure I could get whipped about like a hapless sailor in the jaws of an angry sea serpent. The puzzled faces of the police opposite me stared into the dim recesses of the basement. "What the hell is this guy doing?" they must have been asking themselves. It would not have occurred to them that this long-haired hippie punk would be grappling with some of the same issues of duty and honor that concerned them.

I waited for what seemed like an agonizingly long time, but probably lasted only seconds. And then it dawned on me what had happened. When we reached the bottom of the stairs on the ground floor, and I raced to the basement staircase, everyone else headed for the windows and jumped out onto the campus, fleeing the scene. Rats, one might say, deserting the proverbial sinking ship (though I've always wondered why any rational creature *wouldn't* leave a sinking ship). In my haste to get to the action, I hadn't noticed that I was the only one who continued on down to the basement.

So there I was, alone, aiming a fire hose at a riot squad. Pathetic. Simple reason mandated that I drop the hose, run up the stairs, jump out the window, and retreat along the same path my erstwhile comrades had taken. But in battle, simple reason gets clouded by storms of emotions, and especially by what I think of as testosterone poisoning. It's also countermanded by the endless training that prepares warriors to hold their positions tenaciously under the fiercest assaults. It wasn't that long since I'd come back from

Vietnam and was I still in the mindset I'd been trained for. Despite the absurdity of the situation, and the utter disparity of the odds, I held my position. Maybe, I thought, if I stay down here long enough, some of the others will show up. Crazy and naïve, I suppose, but that's how battles get fought. And as I write I think, too, about my abiding interest in the relationships between what people say and what they do.

I remained steadfast. At that point in my life, I really wasn't capable of anything else. I opened the nozzle very cautiously, experimenting with just how much pressure I could manage to control. I flicked a stream of water quickly towards the tunnel, to make sure they could tell what I was up to, then directed it into the corner.

They must have been under strict orders not to act if they couldn't take us by surprise. The university did not want a battle fought among the priceless collections in the East Asia Library. Once the police saw the spray, a few orders were barked, and they backed away. The doors were slammed shut. I suspect that they couldn't imagine anyone crazy enough to confront their entire squad single-handed and assumed that there were others in the dark behind me. Clearly, they had lost the element of surprise, and figured that a fracas was about to ensue.

The doors closed. I shut off the water and collapsed to the floor, my back against a wall, guarding the space for the next couple of hours, making sure the cops didn't return. Sitting there alone, mulling over what had just happened, I experienced one of the more profound political epiphanies of my life. My comrades had deserted me. I'd been prepared to give up my life there, or at least have my life nearly beaten out of me, but everyone else had simply run away. A wise decision on their part perhaps, but the night before we'd agreed on what our plan of action would be. My newly acquired revolutionary fervor and my willingness to fight as fiercely against the Vietnam war as I had fought in it began to subside in those hours sitting on the basement floor in Kent Hall. I would have to begin charting a new course for myself.

I see now how close the agitation was to the surface. I feel a bit of vertigo even as I write. In the war, I like to say, I was used to living with the sense that anything could go wrong at any time, that you couldn't fully rely on or trust anything or anybody, but equally that you couldn't do the job, face the danger, unless you felt you could trust your comrades completely. This is a very fundamental contradiction, and in some ways it runs against the grain of what is often said about the high degree of trust within combat units. But I'm sure that others will know just what I'm talking about.

In that basement scene, with all the madness flowing around and through me, I found that those who I'd placed my trust in had failed me, abandoned me. I doubt that any of them—and I never saw a one of them again (maybe they were all provocateurs, for all I know)—realized that one of us—me—

was down in that basement alone, trying to stave off the police. In that moment, I was abandoned not only by everyone with me, but by all that I'd been in the process of giving myself over to. My moorings were ripped out. The fuckers betrayed me—and I don't think I've ever felt the rage quite like I do writing about it now.

Later that morning I climbed out a window and wandered across the campus in a daze. Another anthropology student, my friend Ann Stoler, found me there. I must have looked as bad as I felt, like I was dragging myself back from a horrible defeat. She asked what had happened and I tried to explain. I don't know exactly what I conveyed to Annie, but she saw something in my face that worried her. Taking me by the arm, she led me to her parents' home, where she grabbed the keys to a car and the family's ski house in Vermont. We drove north and for the next four or five days I tried to recuperate and clear my senses, hidden far away from the battlefield on Morningside Heights.

On Annie's part it was an act not only of compassion but of extraordinary perception; she sensed that my soul had been slashed open and she knew that if I'd stayed on the campus I would have been entirely too muddled to protect myself from being drawn back into further conflict. Or that in my destabilized, disillusioned state I might well have done something even more stupid. Annie saved my life in that seemingly random moment, not simply by intuiting my state but in taking quick and effective action to stanch my spiritual bleeding.

In the same way that I look back at the war with a disorienting mix of clarity and hazy confusion, when I revisit this episode at Columbia I'm genuinely puzzled. That scene in the bowels of Kent Hall seems almost primal: I'm standing alone there with nothing more than a fire hose, facing down the police in the gloom across a hastily erected barricade. Certainly, there were echoes from adolescence, when I fled my father's wrath; this time, though, I stayed rooted in place, refusing to give into far greater force. And though I prevailed, I was shattered and had to shamble away, then retreat to a mountain fastness, as it were, to lick my wounds.

ON TRIAL

When I returned to campus, I learned that I'd failed my doctoral exams. Small wonder, since I'd barely been able to sit through them in my eagerness to join the rebellion roiling right outside the windows.

Something changed in me during those moments in the Kent Hall basement. The experience demoralized and disenchanted me, and I lost interest in the prospects of violent political action. I felt, I suppose, that I'd seen enough of combat. Although my overall views about right and wrong didn't shift much then—and haven't in the decades since—my sense of how to go about changing the world certainly did.

I struggled through the following year not at all sure what I was doing. I'd been thinking seriously about abandoning my PhD studies for law school, with the idea that I could have a greater impact on the world around me if I were a lawyer. Or simply leaving grad school and finding some more satisfying means of opposing the war. In one of those odd strokes of misfortune that teaches us more than any triumph, though, my experiences with the New York City and Columbia University legal systems showed me that achieving success in what we call our justice system requires far more patience and willingness to hew closely to established forms than I was ready to give.

The New York City judge we appeared before was obliged to dismiss the case Columbia brought against the handful of us who'd been arrested. The university's general counsel appeared at our hearing brandishing photographs of damages done inside several Columbia buildings. As our lawyers pointed out, of course, we could hardly be held responsible since we were in police custody when the damage was inflicted. Undaunted, the university's counsel insisted that someone had to be held liable and since we were the ones who'd been apprehended, we were the ones who should be made to suffer. With regret, the judge released us, but did so with the proviso that we turn ourselves in to Columbia's internal judicial system.

Ironically (though not entirely unexpectedly), I sat as a student member of the oversight committee charged with running that system, and I felt obligated to turn myself in (and it may not surprise you to learn that I was the only one of us who did so). With a student from Columbia's law school at my side, I appeared before a disciplinary panel, expecting a relatively informal hearing. To my shock and dismay, the general counsel was there to prosecute the university's case and, still splenetic about his defeat in court, he was urging them to expel me. Despite my stunned confusion, I had enough of my wits about me to ask for a recess until I could get an attorney to defend me. The National Lawyers Guild, which had represented us in city court, offered to find a lawyer to aid me at Columbia. A few days later they let me know me the problem had been resolved.

William Kunstler, possibly the most renowned civil liberties lawyer of the era and lead counsel in the epic trial of the Chicago Seven, following the chaos at the 1968 Democratic Party convention in Chicago, a trial that filled the airwaves and newspapers for months, had taken on my case. He called the university and explained to them that he was going to provide me with a defense that would become a national showcase. Columbia dropped the charges on the spot.

The following year, as I was preparing to take my doctoral exams for the second time, I heard from the FBI. They wanted to interrogate me about the Columbia uprising.

I knew two things. First, that I was reluctant to speak with the FBI, and second, that I was afraid of what the consequences might be for my ability to travel abroad to do my research, and to acquire funding to do it, if I refused to speak with them. Once again, I had a random stroke of fortune: someone sent me to Marshall Perlin, who'd been Ethel and Julius Rosenberg's lawyer during their celebrated espionage trial (though I didn't learn this till many years later), and he solved my dilemma. He asked if I wanted to talk to the FBI, and when I said no, he asked if I refused to speak with them; I wasn't sure. Hearing my ambivalence, he suggested that he call the FBI and explain that I would speak with them only if I had my attorney—him—present. He called, they declined, and I was off the hook.

Then I retook my doctoral exams. Given my agitation and my inability to focus my mind, it's not surprising that I wrote gobbledygook, and that probably explains why I flunked again as well as any other reason. Failing the exams the second time around should have marked the end of my studies at Columbia, and the fact that it didn't says a lot.

The anthropology faculty flunked me, but they allowed me to stay on. It was an unprecedented move on their part, and there is in all this something that remains hard for me to fully comprehend. They recognized that I was flailing, as well as failing, and engaging in some pretty self-destructive behavior.

Remember that in the first two years after the war, before I got to New York, I'd totaled out three cars. In Manhattan I didn't have a car, and so I turned my self-destructive energies elsewhere. In the same way that I'd poured my heart and soul into my undergraduate schooling and done 4 years of college in two, in graduate school I had been impressing my teachers with my seriousness, commitment, and intelligence, while at the same time digging myself into bigger and deeper holes with the law, the university administration, and the formal structures of the anthropology PhD program.

I was tearing myself in two. I was overwhelmed by my need to protest, to resist, and to oppose, but I doubted whether I could do this within academia. At the same time, though, I'd come to see that my generation of anthropologists strongly opposed accommodation with the long reach of colonial rule.[9] This assurance, along with knowledge that my perspective was shared by my own professors, some of whom had put together a volume of essays highly critical of the Southeast Asian wars and of war as a solution to anything (Fried, Harris, and Murphy 1968), convinced me that anthropology remained compatible with my evolving political outlook.

My sense was that Columbia's anthropology faculty would readily support my efforts to study the effects of colonialism in the Micronesian islands, which is why I never suspected them of undermining me even as they flunked me twice. I felt at the time, and still do, that the problem was with my work, not with those judging it. Today, though, I understand why I wrote so badly—I was pretty much out of my mind at the time. The contradictions between the pulls of the counterculture and rebellion, on the one hand, and my Ivy League PhD program, on the other, were profoundly confusing.

In retrospect, the truly amazing things about all this are that my department allowed me to stay, and that I mustered the determination to stick with it, in spite of so very nearly falling apart. It undoubtedly helped that Margaret Mead, whose criticisms of the draft had first helped change my mind about it, was on my doctoral committee; I was never close to her, but she personified anthropology's willingness to challenge orthodoxy and was at times a beacon of light in what I was experiencing as a darkening world.

In the course of all this turmoil, two more small acts of friendship and decency saved me as I teetered on the edge of falling apart. I'd received a grant to fund my field research in the islands, but I was about to lose it because I'd failed my exams. The department chair was going to decertify my status as a doctoral student. Two department members went to him, two people who knew me well, and pleaded with him to hold off. He did.

By this time, my funding was running short and I'd used the last of my GI Bill. I was driving a taxicab and teaching part-time at the City University of New York. Just before I was about to start class one day, I got the news that I'd flunked my exams for the second time. I was crushed, and I recall thinking about simply running off into the streets outside and disappearing. But a roomful of students was awaiting me. Steeling myself, I walked into class feeling I was an abject failure and taught. When I left an hour later, I knew that it had been a good class, and it was that act of teaching—of doing my job—that held me together through the first impact of defeat. And then another friend, another Annie, actually, gave me exactly the grounding I needed. "Glenn," Anne Farber said, "you were a good anthropologist before you took that exam. You're still a good anthropologist. Don't let those exams define who you are."

Banding together, my professors assigned me a master's thesis, in a department that didn't offer a master's degree. My willingness to sit and write two hundred pages convinced them that I was as serious as they thought I was; they waived the exams for me and I used the grant they'd preserved for me to do my first fieldwork in Micronesia, and then write my dissertation. In the immortal words of Mark Twain's Huckleberry Finn, I was going to light out for the territory.

POHNPEI AND MICRONESIA

At last! At the beginning of 1974 I made my way out to the Central Pacific Ocean, where for eighteen months I lived in a village on a small island in Micronesia, and for many decades afterwards I spent summers doing research there. After three years of grad school and my close brushes with expulsion, I finally escaped to Pohnpei (spelled Ponape in those days) in the Eastern Caroline Islands. The island is now capital of the Federated States of Micronesia, but in colonial days it was simply Ponape District in the United States Trust Territory of the Pacific Islands. The Trust Territory comprised a vast expanse of ocean (nearly as vast as the continental United States) dotted with the scores of small islands and atolls the United States had wrested from Japan at the close of World War II and then arranged for the United Nations Trusteeship Council to assign to it as a de facto, rather than an outright, colony. Pohnpei lies nearly on the Equator, about halfway between Hawai'i and the Philippines—it is a long way from anywhere, it is small and isolated, and remains, along with the rest of Micronesia, almost entirely unknown to most of the world.

I've always lived there with the same large Pohnpeian family in the tiny, remote village of Awak. I slept on a woven palm-leaf mat on the floor of Damian and Iulihda Primo's home. There was no electricity and the only

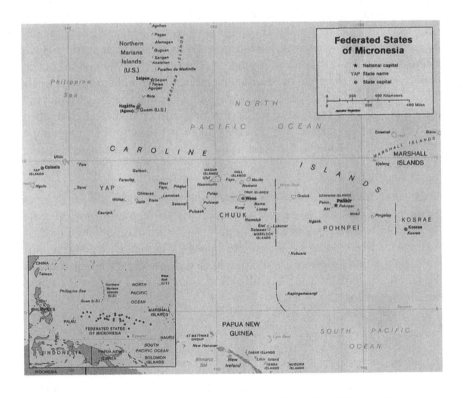

Figure 5.1.   The Federated States of Micronesia. *Central Intelligence Agency (CIA)*

running water was in the small streams flowing on either side of the house, which sits at the edge of the lagoon. Dodging the sacred eels, I bathed in the stream, I ate the local foods they cooked in earth ovens, learned to speak their language, Lokaiahn Pohnpei, and did the best I could to fit into the community.

I was intending, or at least hoping, to do several things on Pohnpei. I wanted to experience living in a tropical paradise, and I did. I wanted to pursue my interest in tropical farming and study their traditional economy and ecological relations with the island environment, and I did. I wanted to work alongside people trying to throw off American colonial rule, and to aid them, if I could, in their quest for autonomy and self-government, and I did. And I wanted to earn my spurs as an anthropologist and ethnographer by absorbing enough, while living with people in a very different sort of setting, to be able to write cogently about them and their lives, and I did. I've always had doubts about what I've achieved during my years of work on Pohnpei but looking back now I can see that during that first trip I accomplished nearly everything I set out to do, with one crucial exception. What I'd also wanted to do was to heal my soul, to redeem myself, to atone for having fought in a colonial war, to find some sort of resolution to the dilemma that continued to haunt me.

I'd imagined that by getting arrested for protesting the war I would redeem myself, but clearly I hadn't. So now I was hauling my aching soul all the way back to the mid-Pacific with the hope that by doing something worthwhile there I could absolve myself of the guilt that beset me. I was using the long-suffering Micronesian people for my own purposes, and in doing so I was to some extent exploiting them. This is a harsh judgment, one that I'm not wholly sure is correct, but it is what I fear when I look deeply within myself.[10]

Anthropologists pursue their research for a great many reasons. Most claim they are engaged in a scientific enterprise. In earlier times, anthropology was often linked with the efficient administration of colonial territories, and a good many anthropologists have also been missionaries bent on bringing change to peoples they think benighted. In recent years, though, anthropologists have tended to see themselves as resisting the imposition of Western ways on indigenous peoples, on minorities, and on exploited groups and classes. Although their motives have shifted, anthropologists' minds are still set on doing good. This is not an indictment or complaint; I believe it's better to do good than evil. I merely observe that few of us do our work with nothing more than pure science in mind.

The Pohnpeians weren't in need of my help, of course. They'd been dealing with colonial rulers for a long time—Spanish, German, and Japanese regimes had governed them before the United States took over—and in 1910 the Sokehs chiefdom in the western part of the island rose up in violent rebellion before being brutally vanquished. Though it's a source of some embarrassment for me, I have to admit in this context that when I was younger I had fantasies of joining with imagined Pohnpeian rebels in the mountain jungles as we swept down in armed raids against the aptly named administrative center, Kolonia. These daydreams reflect the warrior that still lived within me, and in my mind's eye merged with the part of my being that had come to resolutely oppose America's colonial war in Vietnam.

Indeed, one of the more relevant things I encountered there was the Pohnpeians' shock and dismay when they heard how young I'd been when I fought in Vietnam. In the early 1970s, World War II still loomed huge in their experience. Many of the war's major battles had been fought in Micronesia, including the cataclysmic amphibious landings at Tarawa, Kwajalein, Peleliu, and Saipan and the destruction of the Japanese fleet in Chuuk Lagoon, and the islands had been cut off from almost all supplies for several years. Bombardment, invasion, deprivation, harsh discipline, starvation, and constant fear had been their lot (Poyer et al., 2001). When people first heard that I'd fought in a war, they tended to assume that it had been *nan Daidow-ao*, in the big war, their war, and reacted with a bit of awe. (Pohnpeians believe that humans continue growing in physical stature throughout their lives, and because I am a lot taller than most of them they had difficulty judging my age.)

The Vietnam War held much less meaning for them, but Micronesians have strong warrior traditions—there are important aspects of male bravado woven into Micronesian cultural life (Petersen, 2014)—and they wanted to talk with me about my experiences. When they learned how young I'd been when I'd fought, though, people would cry out, "Nineteen! You were a baby! What kind of people send their babies to war?" For Pohnpeians, a warrior is a full-grown man, someone well into his thirties or forties, while a teenager is still a young child (they call males in their thirties "boys"). The notion that Americans would send children into war shocked them in the same way that Americans respond to reports of "child soldiers" in Africa. I still recall one elderly man, Koronel Cantero, saying sardonically that I'd been "*Kanen kasik lapalap mwenge.*" This translates quite literally as the "food of big guns," or "Cannon fodder."

As I look back on these conversations, I hear a certain Pohnpeian ambivalence echoing my own, and I realize that many of my perspectives have grown out of listening to them. Although they admire warriors and the warrior spirit—something akin to the ancient Greeks' *thumos* that I've spoken of—they are also profoundly kind and compassionate people, and they have difficulty imagining a society in which children are expected to fight wars that are properly the province of fully mature men.

It's always been difficult for me to think of myself as a child when I went to war—as I've said, I felt I was about 50 when I came home. Much of my confusion about how the war continues to affect me, and how I think and feel about it, flows from this conundrum: I was simultaneously very old and very young when I fought. I have no answer to this puzzle, but the fact that people who I hold in such high regard are struck by the contradiction tells me it is not something I can slough off lightly. They taught me to pay attention to it in ways that I might not otherwise have grasped.

Micronesians also introduced me to a new political style—something quite different from the one I'd adopted following the war. Before I lived with Pohnpeians I'd tried to exorcise the demons haunting me by pushing back against the war with the same intensity with which I'd fought in it. My sense of radical politics meant a loud, angry, in-your-face political style, characterized by my arrest on the Columbia campus, where I was hollering out my support for my comrades even as I was being dragged off by the police. I'd hurled myself into police lines at demonstrations and engaged in other confrontations with them. In Micronesia, though, I discovered that the way to be heard is to speak quietly and calmly. Understatement is expected. Humility and modesty and concern for others are the main currency of the islanders' political speech. And because I found Micronesians to be deeply conscious of how they faced the central dilemma in their political lives, that is, the Americans' colonial rule over them, and seemed to grapple so effectively with it, I paid attention.

The US government—especially the military—was determined to establish permanent rule over the region. Micronesians, on the other hand, plainly understood that it was the Japanese presence in their islands that had brought World War II to them and were determined not to become a permanent US possession. Micronesia's population is tiny and scattered and had, it certainly seemed, no chance at all of resisting America's plan to annex them. The Micronesians were surely in no position to resist the United States via force of arms. They spoke instead in a quiet, dignified manner about their rights, and by leveraging United Nations' oversight they eventually prevailed.[11]

FATHERS AND SONS

One more thing about my experiences on Pohnpei looms especially large for me. In writing this book I've increasingly come to understand just how deeply my conflicts with my father and with authority in general had been woven into my experiences in the war and in my life following it. I ran away from home to escape my struggles with my father, a battle so intense that it now seems to me to have been on the edge of kill or be killed. My father wasn't a physically violent man, but he was physically powerful and powerfully angry and he terrified not only me but my cousins and friends. In some ways the single most important decision I've ever made was to run away, a move that enabled me to pour my energies into raising myself rather than into resisting my father.

I admire much about my father, I learned a great deal from him, and I see much of him in me. But my bitterness makes it hard for me to see this clearly or comfortably. I know it is there, but I cannot look at it directly—to do so would be like gazing into a black hole. In the context of this story I'm telling, I can see that my relationship with the war is essentially the same thing—not just something similar, but the same thing—as my relationship with my father. I had to break away from him to survive, and the costs of doing that were so great that I've never been able to see him outside of the relationship that both bound us together and ripped us apart. And so it is with the war. Whatever I got from it will always be clouded by my anger, by my sense of betrayal, and by the effort I've had to put into separating myself from it.

Pohnpei changed some of that. I would not say that I became a member of Damian and Iulihda's family, but Damian was in many ways a surrogate father to me. I don't consciously think of Damian as a father, but I do know that I try to model myself on him. I also know that our relationship, though it was complex, never had to bear the sort of weight that my relationship with my father holds for me. I'm aware that I look to Damian, who died in his 80s a few years ago, as my ideal of what a man in full should be. He was held in the highest regard by the people of his community. He was quiet and low-key. I also know that he was feared as a man who wielded an array of supernatural powers. He was respected as one of the most accomplished farmers in a community that values agricultural production as possibly the greatest test of a man's skills. And he was deeply steeped in his community's history and lore.

He worked under both the Japanese and American colonial administrations and not only developed administrative skills but came to have an unusually deep understanding of cultural differences. He served as a leader in the institutions of local government the Americans had introduced, he participated as a leader in nearly every aspect of his community's life and was a competent businessman. He was a chief, and in a society where generosity is the highest value people expect to see in their leaders, his generosity was legendary. He was politically astute and clever, and famed for his ability to appear to be doing very little while accomplishing a great deal, as a way of stealing a march on his opponents in a highly competitive social environment.

But most important for me was what I always saw as Damian's absolute commitment, despite his own drive and aspirations, to placing the vitality of his community's social system ahead of his own ambitions. He wanted to succeed, but he wanted to do so within the rules of the game, as it were, not simply by pushing others out of the way or trampling on them.

Figure 5.2.   Damian Primo. *Author's personal collection; photo by the author*

Apart from his supernatural powers, everything I say about Damian here in some way applies to me—to what I've wished to be, how I want to be thought of, how I see myself. I'm not sure how much of what I see in Damian is simply my projecting my own aspirations onto him, or how much of it is my identification with him, but he was, as I say, my ideal of what a man should be. And my father was not.

Though he spoke fluent Japanese, Damian never learned English. The only time I ever heard him say anything at all in English was to pay me a compliment, one that would have been difficult to phrase in Pohnpeian, a language which emphasizes humility and shuns boastfulness. Although there is a Pohnpeian word for something like pride, I don't recall ever hearing it (and none appears in the Pohnpeian-English dictionary I learned from).

I was once asked to explain the concept of federalism—as in the Federated States of Micronesia's system of government—to a group of Pohnpeian chiefs. I did so almost entirely in terms of traditional Pohnpeian political history and organization, trying to demonstrate that their own political traditions provided them with entirely adequate precedents for understanding and managing a concept that had been imposed on them by colonial rulers. I cited many of the complex precedents and processes I had learned over the course of my years of listening closely to Pohnpeian political discussions (Petersen, 2009).

Though Damian's chiefly status was high enough for him to have been present, he said was occupied elsewhere and didn't attend. When I saw him shortly after I had finished, though, he'd already heard what I'd explained to the other chiefs and he said to me, in English, "I am proud." It's something I don't recall ever hearing my father say. To the assembled chiefs I was in effect Damian's white man, and in their eyes my knowledge of Pohnpei and my ability to understand how it could be mapped onto a concept like federalism were to a large extent based on the tutelage he had given me. Knowing I'd done Damian proud doubly affected me, in terms both of my personal relationship with him and my sense of myself as an anthropologist who had learned his lessons well.

My work in Micronesia allowed me to channel my drive to atone for the war into something productive, at least for me. My desire to support Micronesians' strivings for self-government paralleled my desire to understand their sense of what a proper political life looks like. By participating in their struggle, working alongside them at times, and writing about what it is they want and why they want it, I found a way to weave together my drive, my empathy, and my intelligence.

When I returned from my first long stay in Micronesia I continued lobbying at the United Nations and the US Congress, insisting that America's

Figure 5.3.   The author at work on Pohnpei. *Author's personal collection*

trusteeship in the islands be brought to an end. I returned again and again to Micronesia to observe and write about the long series of plebiscites and constitutional conventions there. Shortly after the Micronesians became self-governing and joined the United Nations, their leaders asked me to help represent them there.

When I was appointed as a member of the Federated States of Micronesia's Permanent Mission to the UN, I thought I would finally find redemption for having fought in Vietnam—that I had at last atoned. Much to my surprise, that's not what happened. A couple of years after I started representing the FSM at the UN, the United States government asked the Micronesians to cast their vote in the General Assembly in favor of the invasion of Iraq and understanding that the Micronesian government's financial dependence on the United States would require it to comply, I resigned from my position.

BECOMING A PROFESSIONAL

When I returned from Micronesia after that first long trip in 1974 and 1975, ready to write my PhD dissertation, I was painfully aware of how close I'd come to getting kicked out of grad school before I left for the islands, and I focused narrowly on finishing my degree. By then, however, the long decline in fulltime academic jobs was well underway. I applied for perhaps 150 jobs in the next two years, while I taught part-time and drove a truck.

Late in the summer of 1977, not long before a new academic year would begin, a series of extraordinarily lucky coincidences helped me land a job as assistant professor of anthropology at the City University of New York's Bernard Baruch campus. In the same way that I've never forgotten the underpaid part-time teaching and manual labor I did, I've never lost sight of how much good fortune was involved in getting the job I've held ever since. It's not that I wasn't qualified for the job, or that I hadn't paid my dues, but that the fact that you've earned something doesn't have a lot of bearing on whether you're likely to get it or not.

After a year or two of teaching Baruch's incredibly diverse working-class, mostly immigrant students, I knew there was no place I'd rather be. I don't think there's anything more socially useful I can do than teach business students basic anthropological ways of looking at things. That feeling has only grown stronger in my four-plus decades there. After the requisite 5 years, I snatched the gold ring of academic life: tenure and promotion. I continued working incredibly hard; for much of my life, my work has been most of my life. And in the same way that I strove to master the three main facets of my squadron's radar—operating it during missions, maintaining the system within the aircraft, and repairing the individual components in the shop— I sought to master what we call the three-legged stool of a professor's life: research, teaching, and service to the institution (and to teaching in three disciplines, anthropology, international affairs, and geography). And that's never changed; I've always pushed myself to excel at all three.

In much the same way that I'd been in sync with the Navy, I've found out that my university department's needs and my own ambitions harmonize. I used my skills to figure out what they expected of me, and then worked not merely to perform at that level, but to surpass it whenever I could. From the outset, I was thinking about what I'd need to do in order to someday become head of the department. The year after I earned tenure my colleagues unanimously elected me department chairman. I hadn't really noticed that no one else was interested in the job. All I knew was that I wanted to advance.

Following the Soviet Union's 1979 invasion of Afghanistan, President Jimmy Carter reinstituted universal draft registration for American men. I felt sure this would lead inevitably to re-instituting the draft, and that if the military's ranks swelled with men, our generals would lose little time finding a war to fight. My students needed to know something about what lay in store for them, I thought, and so I added Ron Kovic's (1976/2016) *Born on the Fourth of July* to the required readings in my anthropology classes. Kovic's story is for me the most compelling first-person account to come out of Vietnam War (at least from the American side), and I still use it as an ethnographic account of American society; it illustrates perfectly why so many in my generation marched off so readily to the war. Everything I've written here has in one way or another been influenced by years of teaching his book.[12]

On similar grounds—believing that a draft wasn't far away—a group of Quakers offered a course on draft counseling at the Friends Meeting House on Stuyvesant Square, just a few blocks from me. Knowing that I'd want to be able to provide this advice to our students, I signed up. In the course of a role-playing lesson, I had to plead my case as a conscientious objector. As I prepared, I began to understand that despite my opposition to recent US wars, I was not a pacifist; I was ready to fight for what I believed in. When I was grilled about whether I opposed all war or only wars I disagreed with, my performance lacked conviction, and they denied me C.O. status. I've been known to say that I flunked pacifism.

Something else happened in that class, something that stuck in my mind over the years and now takes on meaning. I found myself disagreeing with several of the Quakers over their claims that the military provided no useful vocational training. Their point was that military training in most fields was far too cursory to provide skills that recruits could readily transfer to civilian life. I understood the point they were trying to make, but this was not at all my own experience and I insisted that for young people with few marketable skills and no work experience, a stint in the military could still provide training they might easily transfer to civilian jobs. Learning to work as part of a team, learning to follow directives, learning how to work with tools, learning to set goals: these were all important lessons they might not gain elsewhere. Even if the recruiters' claims were exaggerated, I said, it made sense for at least some people to see the military providing them something of value. In hindsight, it's obvious that even if I wasn't in favor of war in general, or American wars abroad, I could still look at the larger role the military plays within our society and understand why thoughtful young men might see it as a viable path.

You may have noticed that amid all this talk about my work and my career, I haven't said much about my personal life. There's not a lot to say about the love life of a guy as driven as I was during those years, but it did exist, marked by the same need to prove myself that's characterized most of my life. Almost as soon as I got a woman interested in me I lost interest in her; having proved that I could attain something, it no longer seemed all that attractive. Something about achieving tenure, though, had an impact on me. I wound up marrying the first woman I began dating after I was tenured.

It was not an easy marriage for either of us. My tendency, always, was to work, to hide in my work, to retreat into my work, to lose myself in my work, to bury myself in my work. I had little interest in entertainment or vacations or socializing.[13] And for all my attempts to develop my emotional life, I see in retrospect how sadly lacking I was in simple tenderness. And then my daughter came along . . . and everything changed.

NOTES

1. The Coral Sea is a part of the Pacific Ocean, bounded by northeast Australia, southeastern New Guinea, and the Solomon Islands; the Great Barrier Reef lies within it. In May 1942 US and Japanese fleets engaged there as Japan sought to occupy parts of the Australian colony in New Guinea and to shore up its positions in the British Solomon Islands colony. For the first time in naval history, all the fighting was done by carrier aircraft. Although the outcome was technically a draw, it also marked the first time that a Japanese advance had been halted, allowing Allied forces time to land troops in the Solomon Islands. The ground and naval battles at Guadalcanal are among the most famous of the Pacific campaign in World War II. Although Japan was not immediately threatening Australia at the time, had their move been successful they would have been in position to invade at any time, while most Australian forces were deployed abroad in support of Britain.

2. Apollo 4 launched on November 9, 1967. It was the first Saturn V space vehicle launched from the Kennedy Space Center. *Bennington* recovered it in the mid-Pacific, near Midway Atoll.

3. I've told this story in more detail and explored the ways in which it continues to have an impact on me in "The Abyss Stares Back" (Petersen, 2018).

4. Toshio Whelchel's (1999) *From Pearl Harbor to Saigon: Japanese American Soldiers and the Vietnam War* includes many first-person accounts dealing with young Japanese American males' painful ambivalence about serving in Vietnam.

5. A clear sign of my seriousness and ambition, though, is that within a year I was presenting my first scholarly paper, "Excavations at 4-CCO-312," based on my analysis of materials we excavated from that site, at the annual meetings of the Society for California Archaeology.

6. I tell this story at length in "Finding a Moral Compass for an Anthropological Career" (Petersen, 2012).

7. The notion that Vietnam vets were spat on is now widespread, but it didn't really arise until the time of the 1990 Gulf War. Jerry Lembke (2000) in *The Spitting Image* does a careful examination of contemporary accounts and concludes that there's almost no evidence from the time that if this did happen it was anything more than a rare and isolated occurrence.

8. After I'd spent decades researching in Micronesia my perspectives on those first American anthropologists who worked in administration changed strikingly. In a piece I wrote on the anthropology of politics in the Trust Territory I argued that they had served in administrative posts only briefly, precisely because of their predilection for siding with the Micronesians against the US government (Petersen, 1999a).

9. I've written at length about the 1971 annual meetings of the American Anthropological Association, when the issue of whether the profession would countenance anthropologists doing covert research for the military or intelligence agencies in Southeast Asia became a flashpoint (Petersen, 2015).

10. I launch an in-depth exploration of this dilemma in an essay that describes how I've come to think of my ethnographic work on Pohnpei as the product of a "disordered soul" (Petersen, 2019).

11. I sometimes feel that I've written endlessly about the politics of colonialism and decolonization in Micronesia and especially about the Micronesians' independence struggles. I approach these events from the perspective of international relations and political geography in my essay on the islands' strategic location (Petersen, 1999b) and the perspective of the lessons Micronesia's leaders learned from the history of Americans' dealings with Native Americans and other minorities (Petersen, 2004).

12. I've studied many top 10 lists of American fiction and memoirs from the Vietnam War, and *Born on the Fourth of July* rarely appears on them. This puzzles me, because I think of it as among the very best books about the war. Perhaps it's because so much of it is about why Kovic, as a boy, was so eager to join the Marines or that so much of it is about his experiences as a paraplegic after he was badly wounded in the war, rather than about the war itself. But I don't think so. Speaking as one who cannot help but see things an anthropologist, I find Kovic's book unsurpassed as an account of the war's place in American society.

13. My first wife, V, commented on this in an article we wrote together about our time on Pohnpei. It appears in a collection of anthropologists' accounts of the sorts of impacts ethnographic work has on family life (Petersen, Garcia, and Petersen, 1998, p. 91).

Chapter Six

Daddy, Daddy, Daddy!

Grace was born a few weeks after I was promoted to full professor, the top of the ladder for scholars, and a few weeks before I turned 40, and then, Wham! Everything began to change. I see now that this marked the beginning of the end of what I think of as the "hiatus," the decades when I was unconsciously wrestling with the war. Despite its impact on me, there was nothing abrupt about this transformation, and I certainly had no sense that it was happening at the time. Looking back, though, I see how neatly all the pieces fit together.

Grace's birth was complicated, and V wasn't in good shape following the delivery. In those days I fell back asleep quickly when awakened in the night, and it made sense for me to rise for late and middle of the night feedings. I understood that if I drank as much as I was accustomed to—or wanted to— I'd have trouble hearing the baby, so I drank much less than usual. I sat in the night with Gracie in my lap, nursing her. At the time I had no sense that something was changing in me, but, oh, do I see it now. I was bonding with her. It's been observed that "father's brains are being sculpted and shaped by their experience of their children"; what's more, "the areas that increased in activity seemed to be associated with father's motivations and moods, and their involvement with their babies" (Raeburn, 2014, p. 132). As a result, "The father-child relationship is a two-way process, and children influence their fathers just as fathers alter their children's development" (Parke, 1981, p. 9). To my surprise, I've learned that there's quite a bit of science about this.[1] The combination of remaining sober and caring for my baby daughter seems to have worked neural and chemical changes in my brain. There was nothing obvious about this as it was happening, but some things come to mind when I reflect back on those early days.

First, I can see how comfortable I was with my baby. I felt entirely able to care for her, to carry her, to comfort her, to respond to her, to soothe her, to

171

engage her. I'm struck by this because I hadn't been looking forward to having a child; given my own childhood relations with my parents, I'd been dubious about the prospect of becoming a parent myself. But on Pohnpei I'd been surrounded at all times by the rotating cast of a dozen or so children in the extended family in Damian and Iuli's home and I learned something from them, it appears.

I simply took to Gracie, and she took to me. Because both her mother and I were working, Grace started day-care when she was only nine months old. What I recall most vividly from those early days was picking her up in the afternoons. I'd enter the room and wait near the door, unobtrusively watching her play. She always seemed busy and happy, never waiting fretfully or expectantly for a parent to arrive. When she did notice me standing there, though, she'd charge across the room, squealing with delight, "Daddy, Daddy, Daddy!" Even in elementary school, filing out of the building with her classmates at the end of the day, when she spotted me waiting she'd race across the playground with those same cries of delight.

And the delight was mutual. Having that little girl leap into my arms and then swinging her around wildly still seems like one of the grandest, most consistent rewards I've reaped in my life. Not many things compare to it, and it was something that happened over and over again. I think, too, of all the times, until she was at least ten or so, when she would hold out her arms, say "Up, Daddy" and have me reach down, pick her up, and set her on my hip. As she grew older she would sometimes speak of how unthinking she was about climbing on me, and on how much she simply took my presence and compliance for granted. I remember, too, the adolescent Pohnpeian girls—who always had a younger sibling resting on their hips—complementing me on how effortlessly I carried Grace in their own island style.

We moved to a small town, Lawrenceville, when V took a job in the New Jersey state government. It meant a 2-hour commute in each direction for me, but it was a commitment I was willing to make for the sake of my family. We bought a small place in a townhouse complex with a children's playground just steps from the door. Grace was only two and a half when we moved in, but I distinctly recall looking around for her on that first day and finding her outside, at the play yard. There was a low wooden-rail enclosure for the kids to climb on and play in, and she had climbed up onto the top rail. She sat there surveying her new domain, almost regally, and I saw in her a wonderful confidence—she felt comfortable in her world and ready to explore and engage with it. There are many facets to Grace's development, but I'm quite sure I'm not fooling myself when I think that the closeness of the ties between us played—and continues to play—a key role in her growth as a young woman who is profoundly comfortable navigating the world around her, and in Grace's case that has come to mean literally the entire world.

In second grade Grace drew a picture of our home for a class assignment and wrote a caption: "Our house has six rooms and a basement. It is dark and cold in the basement. My daddy works down there." This says a lot about both me and our relationship. It's true—I was down in my basement office much of the time. Even after Grace was born, work was my salvation. But she was conscious of it—it was clearly on her mind. I was struck by the pleasure I found in seeing that she mentioned me, but also that she found it important to say that I worked in the cold and dark, and that she highlighted her sense of separation from me.

The impact Grace had on me—and continues to have—was a product of a lot more than the neurological changes that came with nursing her. It was also that I became a father and had to start dealing in novel ways with the father—my own father—still lodged in my head, as I learned to respond to Grace. That's what broke everything open.

It was when Grace was born that I began to sense that in the same way that our government could have done things differently in Vietnam, my father could have done things differently with me. It should be clear by now that I can't separate my experience of and feelings about the war from my relationship with my father and following Grace's birth I became my father in new ways.

That's when I started hearing my dad's voice in my head, shouting angrily at her. I said to myself, no, I will not give him voice. I was holding myself to a higher standard. And if he and I are as much the same as I think we are, and if I feel that I got the good parts of me from him, which is what I said at his memorial service, then I feel like I have the right, even the duty, to be critical of him, to say that he could have done better. And that's also how I feel about the way our government got us into Vietnam. That's a big part of why Grace's birth had so much impact on me. It wasn't just the changes in my emotions and neurobiology, but also in my place in the world. I was now a father striving to do the right thing by paying infinitely close attention to who my daughter was.

I was growing in other ways, too. Not long after Grace's birth and our move to Lawrenceville, I found my way into the storefront Vet Center a few miles away in downtown Trenton. It surprises me to realize now that I don't recall why I first went there. I'd steadily avoided anything to do with the military or veterans for 20 years. But there I was, attending a combat vets' "rap group" once a week.[2] These guys were all Vietnam vets, my age. Trenton's population was pretty mixed and all sorts of guys were there. Most of them were marginally employed, or had criminal records or substance abuse issues, but all of them were trying to talk about what was on their minds, to make sense of what had happened to them.

I learned lot, but a couple of things that particularly impressed me have stuck in my mind. First was their anger against the REMFs, the "rear echelon mother fuckers," that is, those who'd been in Vietnam but were farther from harm's way on bases behind the lines—to the extent there were any lines in Vietnam.[3] These guys were angry at those who hadn't had it as bad as they had, who hadn't experienced the hardships, dangers, and fears they'd faced.

And then there was their oddly contrary reluctance to complain too much, their sense that there was always someone who'd had it worse than them. They were angry at those who hadn't had it bad and at the same time hesitated to talk about how bad they'd had it themselves, because they knew others had suffered more. I clearly recall the night the second part of this equation first leapt out at me. A Marine was talking of how much it bothered him that he hadn't had it as bad as others in his unit. He'd only been in Vietnam for eight months, he said, instead of the full tour that others served. This was a man with a prosthetic leg, and he'd left Vietnam early only because he'd been medically evacuated back to the States when his leg was blown off in action. At that moment I understood that it wasn't just me who felt that others had had it worse. If *this* guy shared that sense, I thought, then so did virtually everyone who'd been there.

It's one of the most profoundly ironic things I've come to understand about the war. Many of the guys who fought it are simultaneously angry at those who didn't suffer the way they did and uncomfortable speaking about what happened to *them* out of a sense that they got off easy.[4] This makes little sense in purely rational terms, but it captures an aspect of the scarring war does to many of us. If what troubles us can be dealt with rationally, it may lend itself to cognitive treatment approaches, the attempts to show vets another, better, healthier way of thinking about the war. But if what ails us is rooted in a contradiction, then it may be that there's no way out.

I participated in that Vet Center group for a year or so in the late 1980s and early 1990s, hoping to get some sort of emotional support that in the end it couldn't provide me. The people working there were well-meaning, but they just didn't have what I needed, or perhaps it was that I didn't know what I needed and couldn't tell them what I wanted, or maybe that too many of us couldn't figure out what we were in search of. But by then the Vietnam war had begun erupting within me, forcing its way out of the interior spaces where it was hiding and out into the light of day. I sensed that something was bothering me, eating away at me, allowing me no peace. In the time I spent there with the other vets, sharing parts of my story and listening as they spoke of the things they were carrying in the wake of the war, a host of things buried deep within me began clawing their way back to the surface.

The war didn't start coming back to me all at once or in shatteringly big pieces, of course. I just gradually became aware of things that had been there for a while. Nightmares about being attacked. Daytime fears about things going wrong in the house or while I was driving, things that were occupying more and more of my thoughts. Images of flying on Yankee Station, getting shot at, the catapult launches and landings aboard the carrier, working on the flight deck or on the aircraft. In some sense, they'd always been there—I'd never really left the war behind—but I'd never paid much attention to them; all these things were simply background noise that I'd adjusted to. Now, though, they were growing louder, and I was spending more time managing them.

My emotional budget was thrown out of whack. Psychic energy I'd long devoted to keeping the war hidden away was now directed toward navigating domestic life, and I was no longer able to overlook things I'd been ignoring for years. Being a husband and father demanded a lot more of me than I'd been prepared for.

A turning point came when I was offered a 2-year research position at the Australian National University. At the time, V held a political slot in the state government. A new governor would be taking office in the coming year and she felt that she needed to be in Trenton, the state capital, when the jockeying for jobs under the new administration began. It turned out that in New Jersey, civil-service job applicants who pass an exam and are also disabled veterans receive preference (they go to the top of the list), and that if a disabled vet isn't using this preference for himself, his spouse can claim it. If I were to prove that I had a service-related disability from the war, that is, she'd be able to use my rating to get a civil service-protected job from the state.

I'd begun to sense that I was lugging around baggage from the war, and by the end of the 1980s post-traumatic stress disorder (PTSD) was becoming known as a condition that afflicted many Vietnam vets. Reluctantly, I applied to the Veterans Administration for service-connected disability; that's when the pieces started falling together, and when I started falling apart. I would never have applied otherwise, and I suppose my story would have turned out much differently if I hadn't.

The process took so long that I had to forgo the Australia trip. Ironically, the frustration and anger I experienced during the 4 years I battled the VA dislodged the war from its hiding place deep inside me. It came kicking and screaming out into the bright daylight of my consciousness. I'm sure that many vets have experienced the same thing: the process of trying to get help merely sharpens the pain.

Abandoning the Australia trip was a small thing in the larger sweep of events, but it was an indication that something was happening to me. I passed up a significant career step and began paying more attention to the war and to how it had affected me. To compensate for the lost opportunity, I began the process of applying for a job as dean at another of the City University's campuses. I had a good relationship with the college president there, who'd previously been at my own campus. And I met with Martin Stevens, who'd been my first dean at Baruch. I held Marty in high esteem and I asked his advice on how to proceed. He gave it to me, but he also said some things that stopped me in my tracks.

He asked me, right off the bat, why I wanted to be a dean. What a question! Why do I want to move up to the next step on the academic career ladder? "Because it's the next step," I thought to myself. I'm sure I offered him a more cogent answer, but I have no recollection of what it was. What I do recall clearly is my complete surprise, not only with the question, but with my sudden recognition that I had no reason other than simply advancing. I had no ideas about what I would do as a dean, no programs I hoped to implement, not even any particular desire for more authority. It was just the next step in what seemed obvious to me, my ascent up the ladder, always higher and higher. I had no goal, really, beyond acting on the ambition that had always driven me. I don't think I'm exaggerating when I say that I shocked myself when I acknowledged this.

And then the coup de grâce. "You've got a young family," Marty said. "If you take on a job in higher administration, you're going to have a lot of demands on your time, often in the evenings, and you won't be able to spend much time with them." That's all he said about this, just a sentence or two. But I was stunned.

I spent the train ride back to New Jersey turning his remarks over in my mind. I'd been thinking of nothing more than taking the next steps my ambition dictated, and suddenly realized that if I took them, I'd be shifting a big chunk of my time and attention away from Grace. By the time I got home, I was no longer interested in pursuing the dean's job.

I'm telling you a larger story about choices and consequences, and about how the consequences of each decision I made influenced the way I approached the next fork in the road. In this case, the significance of the decision lay not merely in staying where I was, rather than climbing to the next rung. Its greater meaning lay in my sudden recognition that I'd been spending my life ascending a ladder purely out of habit, always with an eye on the next rung and how to step up onto it. But even more than that, I had the startling insight that being with Grace—or more specifically, my relationship with her and the time that we spent with each other—was the most important thing in my life, quite outstripping the vaulting ambition that had characterized nearly everything I'd done with my life until then. I got my first inkling, however vague it might have been, that I was re-orienting the direction my *thumos* had been driving me in. I seem not to have been alone: "Probably, all good fathers must reframe their career goals and, in some cases, become less ambitious" (Snarey, 1993, p. 115).

Something in me was changing.

CONFRONTING POST-TRAUMATIC STRESS DISORDER

In drafting my PTSD claim I'd faced two challenges. First, I had to make sense of the experiences I'd been through and their effects on me. Second, I had to weigh the Veterans Administration's outlook against my own. My personal sense of what had happened to me didn't seem to fit very well with what the VA was looking for. At the time (that is, in the late 1980s to early '90s), the VA's model for PTSD was, and I'm talking here about the branch of the VA that assigns disability ratings, not the staff that treats disabilities at the Medical Centers, that PTSD is primarily a reaction to a very specific event.[5]

There is what they call "a stressor," an exceptionally dire experience one undergoes in combat. That stressor produces trauma. The guidelines for what are considered stressors are well defined, and while there are exceptions, the VA's assessors largely focus on the experiences of combat infantrymen in the field. This is not an unreasonable assumption if we think purely in terms of numbers; my experience with nearly every component of the VA over the past 30 years or so has been that no one there thinks in terms of sailors or airmen experiencing trauma. The problems start to arise when it comes to documenting events that might have served as stressors and to the simple fact that all sorts of other experiences can produce stress and lead to trauma, something quite well known to many people who study the issue, as opposed to those who administer a bureaucracy charged with managing the consequences of trauma. That and the fact, that is, that documenting traumatic experiences in the fog of war isn't necessarily simple or even possible.

In the time I'd spent at the Trenton Vet Center hanging out with former infantrymen, I gained a fairly good idea of what standard-issue PTSD looked like; as a Navy flier I knew that my own experiences with stressors were very different from what ailed those guys. What I was carrying with me from the war wasn't simply the dramatic episode of flying into Red China, or even the day-in and day-out stress of catapult launches and arrested landings and the missions themselves. It was also the steady mounting up of my daily work on the aircraft, up in the radome and out on the pitch-black flight deck or repairing my radar in-flight while it was still running, or heaving myself against the open escape hatch in flight to toss flares out over downed pilots in the Gulf. What I could see was that all the death-defying things I did every day, things that became so routine to me that I didn't imagine them as life-threatening aspects of combat, had become a part of me. And then there was the invisible weight of responsibility I bore while still a teenager for all our aircraft during those combat missions and for the fleet as a whole. I can hear my inner voice discounting this latter piece—no big deal it says—but that's simply not true.

I'd learned to manage it all so well that I was barely aware of it, and yet for just that reason I continue to bear it with me all the time, everywhere. The war had so thoroughly imprinted itself on me that it had become pretty much like breathing, something I do constantly but not consciously. It was the very routineness of all this that made it such a part of me, and at the same time disqualified it from being the dramatic sort of stressor the VA would consider in deciding whether I had PTSD.

There's a fundamental contradiction here, one worth reflecting on. To work effectively in these life-threatening situations, you must be able to manage your consciousness of them, set aside your acute awareness of them. I could do that. I could deal each day with a host of things that might easily have killed me or my comrades because I simply didn't allow myself to experience them that way. So how could they have been stressful if I didn't experience them as stressful? This is a sort of reverse catch-22. If you're going to deal with things that threaten your life, you try madly to avoid thinking of them as life-threatening. And if you don't acknowledge the threat, then how can they be stressors—how can they cause trauma if you don't consciously experience them this way?[6] There's the rub.

If I was going to convince the VA on *their* terms, though, I was going to have to focus on something that would count as a stressor in their calculus, and I understood that the Red China overflight would be much more to likely convince them than the things I sensed were the bigger problems. Even now as I write, I find myself worrying that the VA is going to read what I say here and decide that I misrepresented my experiences in my claim and deprive me of my disability rating. So I stress that everything I wrote in my claim really did happen. There was no lying, concealing, misrepresenting. I simply emphasized things the VA was likely to pay more attention to. But this only added to my problems with PTSD: I felt I was in some ways being unfaithful to my own experiences, and this continues to pain me.

Inevitably, doing it the VA's way created new problems for me. I placed the China overflight at the center of the claim, but it wasn't easy to prove either that it happened or that it happened to me. In none of the official records or ship's logs I located is there any documentation of that flight into China. In fact, that day is missing from the ship's official log (I know this sounds paranoid, but I've seen a photocopy of the log and that day doesn't appear). Much to my amazement, though, I found in the microfilm that the incident had been reported in the *New York Times*, in a page 2 article by its esteemed war correspondent Neil Sheehan.

The problem was that he merely mentioned China's complaint and the US government's acknowledgement that "An unarmed United States Navy plane accidently flew over part of Communist China's Hainan Island." That was hardly enough detail to convince the VA that it had been one of our planes, or that I'd been the crewman on the incursion, or that we'd come under concentrated fire and barely escaped.

My claim was denied and for the next few years I wound through what felt like an endless labyrinth of appeals. I collected more evidence, becoming very aware of how hard pursuing a claim must be for most vets. As a professional scholar, I know a lot about searching archives and marshalling evidence and stating cases, but most guys have no sense of what to look for or how to find it. I gathered materials and consulted with veterans' representatives and wrote detailed descriptions. I spoke with my congressman. I went before a panel of psychiatrists, and as I got up to leave the interview one of them commented on my difficult childhood. I knew I was sunk—they were going to say that my problems all stemmed from my life before the war. My claim was again denied. I simply worked harder and searched out more effective help.

Then the Vietnam Veterans Legal Foundation provided me with a lawyer who'd been an Air Force flier in Vietnam. *He* understood what I was talking about, and he knew how to find records I wasn't even aware of, including some crucial statements from my unit's commander. A referral led me to a consulting psychiatrist who, purely by chance, had been in the Air Force medical corps during the war and had treated fliers. He, too, understood what I was describing and specifically contradicted some of the conclusions the VA doctors had reached. And then I hit pay dirt.

I tracked down the pilot who'd been our detachment's executive officer through the Navy's pension office. They forwarded a letter I'd written, asking whether he recalled the Hainan incident and could make a statement about it. He said he had roomed with one of the pilots who'd flown that mission and had heard the story in detail. Now a lawyer, he intuited what I needed and provided me with an elaborate affidavit, describing exactly what had happened on that eventful mission. When I appeared before a full appeals board in Washington, with ample documentation and an experienced attorney representing me, I was rigorously questioned; I prevailed. Finally, after 4 years of struggle, I received a 30% disability rating for PTSD.

It shouldn't surprise anyone to hear me say that this process, intended to compensate veterans for harm they suffered in the war, ultimately wound up inflicting a great deal more pain and suffering. I have little reason to doubt that the process was at least partly designed with the intent of scaring people away from submitting claims, and what is more, I suspect that I wouldn't suffer as badly as I do today if I hadn't been subjected to it. Back when I was battling with them, it was reported in the news that the VA paid its claims officers bonuses based on how many claims they rejected.[7] It's hard to understand how an institution that has played such a central role in developing the basic concept of the PTSD diagnosis and seems to be so familiar with it also seems to do so much to foul up its treatment. This may well be because different branches of the VA—the claims offices and the medical centers—are organized to deal with PTSD in different ways.

DOUBT AND DENIAL

The recognition that war can do long-term damage to people's psyches is at least as old as Homer's *Iliad,* but the modern notion that victims of trauma could seek financial compensation seems to date from the early days of railroading. Awareness that accidents can lead to substantial traumas unobservable to the naked eye, according to anthropologist Alan Young (1995), has been accompanied from the outset by deep concerns that these sorts of traumas can also be faked. Any system meant to provide help or support to victims seems to generate policies and procedures designed to prevent fraud. This is understandable, I suppose, but it is also counterproductive. As I know from firsthand experience, the apparatus developed to keep people from submitting and winning claims also serves to cast doubt, and it works to ensure that every step of the claims process leads some of those making claims to doubt themselves and drop away. It is precisely what we mean when speak of adding insult to injury.

Congress has repeatedly tried to streamline and enhance the VA's claims procedures, but as long as institutionalized disbelief and fear of fraud are built into the system, anyone dealing with it is likely to find themselves doubting their own experiences and whether they deserve any compensation. Given that doubt and fear of fraud are so deeply embedded in the VA's claims system, and that treatment for the vets who ultimately clear all the hurdles placed before us is then provided by the same agency that has tried to strip us of our dignity, it is hardly surprising that many are dubious about being treated for their PTSD.

It isn't clear to me that the two processes can be separated from one another, and I suspect that American combat vets seeking both compensation and treatment will forever be caught up in the fundamental contradictions inherent in this system. In recent years, in fact, Congress has mandated treatment for anyone who has been in combat, whether the VA has processed a claim or not, and this is an advance, but given the lasting effects of combat trauma and issues of financial compensation, these changes hardly solve the larger problem.

For me, one of the harshest injuries this system inflicts is the problem of thinking that I won't be believed. Everything that happened with the VA aggravated this fear, but it has a life of its own distinct from the damage done by the VA. The most vivid example I know of this is probably B. J. Burkett's *Stolen Valor* (1998). Burkett's goal was to demonstrate that the guys prompting negative stereotypes of Vietnam vets weren't vets at all, or that if they were, they were lying about what they'd experienced in Vietnam. He was in many ways attempting to do exactly the opposite of what I'm trying to accomplish here. He believes the United States fought the war in Vietnam for a noble cause and that the American side fought chivalrously. He insists that most vets came home from the war with few problems and were then able to integrate themselves seamlessly back into American life. And he's sure that most Vietnam vets see things in pretty much the same way he does.

My own views are far more complicated and nuanced, but what most interests me is the main theme of his work, which is to show that the guys who claim they suffer from bad things in the war are mostly lying about what happened to them and about their problems. He makes an impressive case, actually, and if I were to believe what he says, I would wind up doubting myself even more than I already do.

More of a problem for me, though, is Burkett's failure to tell us about the cases he investigated that turned out to be more or less valid. There *are* a significant number of cases of people making false claims about service in Vietnam (and other conflicts)—reports of these appear in the news when the individuals involved are prominent politicians and business leaders, and in some cases even military officers who have claimed decorations they have not earned. But then politicians and business leaders and military officers, like the rest of us, are human and engage in personal reinvention with startling frequency. The fact that Burkett has shown us that individuals make these false claims doesn't tell us much about the relative frequency of these incidents. He's found some unsavory cases, I readily admit, but I'd hate to draw any generalizations from them about people who speak of harm they experienced in the war or in living their lives following the war.

Most significant, though, is the fundamental contradiction that leapt out at me as I read almost every page. If, as Burkett says, the reputations of Vietnam veterans have been sullied by impostors seeking sympathy and/or glory, why then would they claim to be Vietnam vets when Vietnam vets are held in such low regard? There's a basic problem here, one that I don't think he recognizes. His book strikes me as stumbling over its own feet. If Vietnam vets have become as disparaged and discredited as he seems to think they are, claiming to be a vet hardly makes sense as a means of gaining sympathy. There may be an answer to this conundrum, but if there is, it lies more deeply than he delves.

I feel so strongly about this because one of the biggest pieces of baggage I carried back with me from the war is an ingrained conviction that a real man can handle the stress, which leads to my sense that if I was indeed affected by the war, and continue to be afflicted by it, I'm not very manly. That is, that my problems are my own from the get-go, results of my character and makeup, not the war. They jibe nicely with the views of the VA psychiatrists who told me my problems were the result of my childhood, not the war. These are ways of thinking about how I experienced the war that I have to overcome anew each day, each time the war comes to mind. So much of me still doesn't believe that what ails me can be traced to the war. I'm making it all up, a very loud voice inside me shouts insistently. It's a classic case of denial.

Then, amid all this stress, and undoubtedly as a consequence of it, came the next big hurdle.

DRYING OUT

I stopped drinking. It was in January of 1992. Grace was 4 years old, I'd been struggling with the VA for years, and my battle with them was still underway. I'd started drinking as a teenager, well before I left home. I became a daily drinker at the Canteen tavern in Santa Barbara after I ran away, I drank whenever I had the opportunity while I was in the military, and when I turned 21, just as I was discharged, I returned to drinking every day in another local tavern, the Seven Seas (an appropriately-named place for a sailor just home from the sea). In reconstructing my drinking history—my "drunkalogue," as we call it in Alcoholics Anonymous—I can see clearly that there was barely a day in the 25 years since I'd returned from the war that I hadn't done a lot of drinking.

The only time I didn't drink every day was when I was on Pohnpei, where booze wasn't available in the village, and where I replaced it with kava, bitter juice squeezed from a mildly narcotic plant that Pohnpeians prepare and drink ritually every evening. Drugs hadn't been around during my brief time in high school, and by the time I began college and it seemed that everyone was smoking pot, I wasn't very interested in it. Though I experimented with LSD, mescaline, and a few other things, they never appealed to me—I felt paranoid when I used them—and I stuck with alcohol: beer, wine, whiskey, gin, I enjoyed them all. What I didn't realize, until I stopped drinking, was how deeply dependent I was on them. I'd been engaging in the classic behavior psychologists call "self-medication." And it worked *really* well for me.

During the time I was nursing Gracie in the middle of the night, though, I understood that if I drank myself to sleep the way I normally did I wasn't going to hear her wake. I limited myself to a single drink each evening, and this had two quite contrary effects on me. I was very much aware of how hard it was for me to do this and recognized that alcohol was far too important to me, but I also rationalized to myself that my drinking wasn't *that* much of a problem because I'd been able to cut back when I needed to. With these thoughts in mind, I made a pact with myself.

If ever I could see that booze was becoming a real problem for me, I told myself, I would quit. Having made this promise, I felt free to continue drinking. I'd like to say that I continued drinking as much as I wanted, but this isn't how it was. I have more than an ordinary allocation of will power, and I almost always kept myself from drinking as much as I wanted, which I knew was too much. Although I drank a lot every day, I rarely got drunk and my drinking didn't seem to have much impact on my work. I'm not sure exactly how it affected my family life, but I know that it did. In effect, my emotional life was wrapped in a heavy layer of gauze; I was there, but just barely.

At last, though, I reached the conclusion that booze was a problem for me when I realized that I was entirely incapable of cutting back on how much I drank; it was this that forced me to acknowledge I was going to have stop drinking entirely. After puzzling over this for a few weeks, I decided one Sunday afternoon, while watching football, that I'd had my last drink. I could envision no good coming from this—imagining how I'd be able to live without booze was beyond me. But the alternative was just too dire: I'd promised myself that I would quit if I could see I had a problem and I'd finally acknowledged that I had a problem. If there's an aspect of my character I rely most heavily on, it's my candor and sense of honor. I knew I couldn't live with myself if I broke my promise and continued drinking.

And so I honored that which I held most sacred, my integrity, and haven't had a drink since then. It was a momentous decision, and it set off a cascade of other changes. At the outset, I couldn't comprehend living without the filter alcohol placed between me and the world. The self-destruction hadn't been obvious and it wasn't dramatic, but when it became clear to me that I couldn't manage without being in an alcohol-induced haze, I knew I was losing control of my own life. When I admitted to myself that booze controlled me, I knew that the only way I could live with myself—live, period—was to wrest control away from it, and that I could do that only by letting go of it entirely.

Life without alcohol, I quickly learned, was even harder than I imagined. One of the notions I've heard my AA comrades express is that in sobriety we hit many speed bumps, but they're not remotely as destructive as the brick walls we crashed into when we were drinking. That holds true for many recovering alcoholics, but it wasn't my experience. I soon discovered that I had in fact been self-medicating pretty effectively. The haze I maintained was carefully calibrated: I could do my work and care for my family, which helped keep me preoccupied during the day, and let me keep the war at a safe distance. I drank only at night. As the war had begun edging closer, though, I sensed that I was going to have to up the dosage—drink more heavily, that is—and risk progressing toward a condition that would keep me from doing the things I needed to do. The irony is that I was right for the wrong reasons. When I abandoned that protective mist, the war returned to me with such force and immediacy that at times I've barely been able to function.

I do not exaggerate. The war began troubling me emotionally—as opposed to intellectually—following Grace's birth, but its relentless assault on me really took off when I stopped drinking. I got my first taste of this just a few months after I quit, when I moved our family to Puerto Rico to teach for a year. Faculty housing at the University of Puerto Rico in Rio Piedras lies directly beneath the approach path to the San Juan airport. Small turboprop jets flying on local routes were continually descending right over my head. To me it was exactly the sound of aircraft making carrier landings, and I heard it constantly. The sound and the vibrations wore on me and I grew increasingly agitated. Then one night the National Guard staged a "predawn vertical insertion" on a drug- and crime-ridden housing project directly behind our building. Through most of the night helicopters hovered overhead. Helicopters had been problematic for me for a long time, but they'd always quickly passed by. Now they held their stations.

The sound of a helicopter, especially as its rotor blades change pitch, has long been one of the most troubling sources of agitation for me. As you step out onto a carrier's flight deck and head for your aircraft before a launch, the choppers are lifting off. There are usually two of them, known as plane guards or angels, one for each side of the ship. They're there to pick up anyone blown off the deck or who survives a crash during the take-offs and landings. Although they're meant to provide security, the fact is that even now the sound slices into the center of my being and stirs up in me an awareness of just how risky everything I did was. There is for me something visceral about that sound—when I hear it I'm immediately drawn back into in one of the worst parts of the war.

When those choppers spent much of the night hovering above my apartment building in Rio Piedras, I came as close to falling apart as I can ever recall. Every nerve ending in my body was exposed and raw. I was entirely unprepared for my reaction—I had no idea it was going to happen to me and no idea how to deal with it. That's when I began to realize what sobriety held in store for me. I could no longer mask the war with alcohol.

And it grew worse when we returned to New Jersey. Near our home were a county airport, a sprawling National Guard armory, and corporate headquarters with helicopter pads. I was constantly recoiling from the sound of passing choppers.

More of a problem, though, was driving. Flying in an airliner is like riding in a bus for me and it's not the flying itself that agitates me. But driving in a car, especially noisy ones with jittery suspensions like those I've owned, replicated some of the experience of flying in a Fudd. For a time, driving at night was especially problematic. I would sometimes see headlights and taillights as antiaircraft fire punctuated by tracer rounds, and the sensation would grow increasingly intense until I'd have to pull my car off the road and pull myself together. I would find at times that I was so certain something terrible was about to happen that I couldn't pull out from a side road onto a larger road—even if I could see no other cars, I was convinced that I'd experience a collision if I pulled into the road. For years, whenever I drove I found myself raising my right arm continually up to the roof, grabbing for throttles, as if to give the engines more power as we approached our carrier. And for a long time, I suffered when Grace sat behind me in her car seat, playfully kicking at the back of my driver's seat. I reacted viscerally to anything touching me while I was driving or otherwise concentrating.

Dozens of small things set me off and I was agitated more and more of the time, but it built up so gradually that I wasn't entirely aware of how disturbed I'd become until the Fourth of July three years after I'd stopped drinking. It began pleasantly enough. That evening I'd gone with my family to a nearby park to picnic and watch the fireworks. As twilight dimmed and darkness settled in, I suddenly and unexpectedly sensed that I was going to experience the overhead explosions as an antiaircraft barrage. I'd been watching fireworks my whole life without being disturbed by them, but something had changed in me, and in my bones I felt massive dread looming up.

Without thinking much about what I was doing, but only knowing I was in danger, I told my wife I had to escape and asked friends there with us to get her and Grace home afterwards. I rose from the grass and strolled toward the parking lot. My pace quickened involuntarily and soon I was running headlong for my car. I raced the mile or so toward home, parked, and ran down into our basement, where I hid till my family returned.

I'd never experienced anything quite like it. I'd been reduced to not much more than a quivering mass, frightened and puzzled and without any sense of what I was going to do. How could I protect my family, how could I continue being a man of the sort I felt I must be, if something as simple and unthreatening as fireworks could frighten me so? That was in 1995. I'd returned from Vietnam in 1967, more than a quarter-century earlier.

I'd become pretty much a loner by that time, especially during the summers, when I didn't teach or see my colleagues at the school, and I wouldn't have known what to do with my fears if I hadn't been attending AA meetings regularly. I spoke at one a couple of days later, telling my comrades there about what the fireworks had done to me. It wasn't easy to express what I'd been reduced to but it seemed that I had no choice. I'd reached my wit's end. I described the scene to the others and acknowledged my fears, and my overwhelming sense of defeat. I had no idea what to do.

And then AA did for me what it does best. One of the guys at that meeting told me he knew a therapist, Bill Hay, who'd worked with Vietnam vets at a VA hospital and who treated substance abuse. He thought Bill had the knowledge and skills to tell me what I needed to hear, and gave me his number.

When I saw him, Bill did indeed tell me exactly what I needed to hear, and I remember parts of the conversation distinctly. I explained that I'd been to therapists and veterans groups, that I'd tried talking about the war, but that instead of the talk helping, it seemed that I was getting worse—that the war seemed to be catching up with me. I was at a loss about what to do. He asked me how long it had been since I'd stopped drinking. About three and a half years, I said.

That's when he explained the notion of self-medication to me. That may have been the first time I'd heard of the concept, but I understood immediately what he was talking about. I saw that that's exactly what I'd been doing ever since I'd returned from the war. Alcohol's numbing effects hadn't ended the moment I stopped drinking, he said. They were only gradually wearing off. And as the years without the anesthetic effects of the booze accumulated, the war experiences stored up inside me were gradually reasserting themselves, pushing closer and closer to the surface of my consciousness. He told me that simply talking about them wasn't going to make them go away. He said that the potency of my war experiences had allowed them to penetrate deep inside of me. And then he used a word I've never forgotten. He said those experiences had become "organic." They'd become, that is, literally part of my physical being, not simply stored up ideas or memories. They were part of my body and had to be treated as such.

It was a new concept for me, but I grasped it immediately. It made complete sense to me, and I felt a wave of relief in having the demon inside of me named. If I knew what had seized control of me, I hoped, I might be able to do something about it. It's as if Lucinda Williams, in her song "Compassion," is singing a line meant *exactly* for me: "You do not know what wars are going on down there where the spirit meets the bone."

Bill explained that while AA and recovering alcoholics tend to distrust any medications that affect the psyche, I was in need of a prescription drug that would address the organic troubles that beset me. Prozac, he said, could do that for me. I claim no clinical knowledge, but I know that Prozac and Zoloft (and later buproprion/Wellbutrin) have indeed helped me. They're intended to moderate symptoms of depression but seem also to work well on PTSD. They worked for me. In a short time many of the fears and anxieties that beset me started to lift.

I was unwilling to continue taking a drug without some psychotherapy, though, and I had to search around for a time. Since I got my prescription through the VA I tried to find a VA therapist I could work with. When I had nearly given up hope of finding someone I trusted, I met Dr. Sally Wright, a psychologist who had begun working at the VA's new Trenton outpatient clinic.

My experience with Sally Wright is a saga in its own right, one that I'm mostly going to pass over here, but I can't ignore a few things from that relationship. Sally is the only VA mental health practitioner I've worked with who related to me with palpable emotional engagement. I felt immediately that I was talking with someone who cared about me. I have no idea whether other VA practitioners are capable of this, but it's my own sense that VA protocols and procedures discourage emotional attachment. I suspect this varies somewhat among VA Medical Centers, depending on who's running them, and who supervises their clinicians, but none of the others exuded anything like Sally's warmth. It's also the case that although Sally initially said she'd continue treating me for as long as I needed, she soon told me she'd been instructed to terminate my treatment in a matter of months. She fit me into her lunch breaks at times, and tried other strategies to keep us working together, but eventually she had to stop treating me.

I repeatedly told Sally how I doubted that my condition warranted treatment. Like most combat vets, I think, I felt there were others worse off than me who needed her help more than I did. Her response was always the same. I had served, I had earned my right to treatment, and she was going to provide it. There was never any judgment.

The most telling part of all that happened with Sally came right near the start. After listening to me express my agitation as I began one of my first sessions with her, she said, "We can't do much with the war in Vietnam, Glenn, until you deal with the battlefield at home." I emphasized my commitment to my marriage, and she let the matter drop, but she'd planted a seed; six months later V and I were in marriage counseling. I came to see that something needed to change and I announced a trial separation. I moved out of our home not long afterwards. Although I found a place close by and had joint custody of Grace, moving out was one of the hardest things I've ever done. In moving out, I felt like I was abandoning Grace, and was flooded with guilt.

I've never felt much of anything like guilt for running away—that was purely a matter of saving my own life, and I left because I was sure no one there cared much about me. Leaving the house when I separated, though, involved two people who I knew cared about me. But my biggest concern was Grace and my ability to care for her. In moving out I was doing something akin to running away, in the sense that I had to save my own life in order to care properly for her. Once I was out of *that* house, though, there was never really a moment when I felt that I'd made a mistake.

For me, feeling guilt merges imperceptibly into responsibility for having made mistakes. I don't think I fully understand how to distinguish between these. I was once trying to explain to a friend the nature of the guilt I feel for having fought in the war. She was in turn trying to convince me that guilt was uncalled for. She prodded me for a more coherent description of what I felt, and that's when I found myself explaining that *I should have known better*, that I feel I should have somehow understood that the war was wrong before I went, though it's obvious that I didn't. The war was wrong, I said, and I know now that I shouldn't have fought in it, and that's a big part of why I feel so guilty.

Did I hold those who fought alongside me, and all the others who fought, equally responsible, she asked. Should they have known, and are they guilty? No, I said, I know better than that. Then why, she continued, do *you* feel so responsible? If you excuse and exempt those who fought with you, why don't you give yourself the same benefit of the doubt? And you know what? I didn't, and I still don't, have an answer to that. As an AA buddy tells me, "Sure, we Jews invented guilt. But it took you Catholics to drive it into the ground."[8]

MORE WARS

I speak of all this in terms of how surprised I was when the war ambushed me after Grace's birth, but I'd actually had some warning, a foreshadowing that I'd failed to heed. Shortly after we married, V's doctoral research took us to Nicaragua. This was in the mid-1980s, when our country was fomenting civil war there, and the US military seemed on the brink of invading. There was a point in the fall of 1984, while we were living in a barrio outside Managua, the capital, when it appeared that an American invasion was imminent. I respected the Nicaraguan people's struggles to remake their fractured society after they'd expelled the American-imposed and -supported Somoza dynasty, and had much sympathy for them as they weathered the hardships the US-sponsored "contras" added to their suffering. Though invasion threatened to bring them to their knees, I could see that many were—like the Vietnamese—ready to resist at whatever the cost.

I agonized about what I would do if my own country's troops attacked while we were still there. Would I pick up a weapon and oppose them? It wasn't an idle thought, but one I was reflecting on constantly. We left Nicaragua when V had gathered the data she needed to complete her research, but our departure was hastened by the threat of invasion; in the end, the United States didn't invade and my question wasn't answered.

After we'd returned home from Nicaragua and found the United States growing increasingly involved in Central American conflicts, the two of us traveled to Washington for a protest march. By chance, New York City's contingent was assigned to rendezvous in a park on the Mall directly across the street from the Vietnam Veterans Memorial. This wasn't long after the memorial had first opened and I hadn't yet visited it (I'd passed by but hadn't been ready to approach it). In a mildly agitated state, I wandered over to the Wall, and then, without thinking about what I was doing, I sought out the directory to the names chiseled into it. I located the guys who'd served with me on *Bennington*, fellow fliers, and who had been killed there in the war.

With my fingers, I traced the letters of their names on the polished basalt, then turned away. I'd pinned a "No More Vietnams" button on my cap, and a man whose job seemed to be to keep an eye out for folks like me asked softly, "You were there, weren't you?" I must have nodded yes. "You were with them?" Yes. He held his arms out to me. I let him enfold me as I broke down and wept, sobbed, really. For a long time. Finally, V led me back to the park, where I cried in her arms for another 15 or 20 minutes before joining the march. I'd never before felt true emotion about the war—rather than intellectual rancor—so strongly that I failed to hold it in check. I was laid low by it, and it happened quite unexpectedly.

I had for a moment glimpsed the war in a purely emotional way and it was the first time I'd experienced that rawness. I was standing in the middle of our country's capital, in that awful depression in the ground that cradles the Vietnam memorial, bawling. It wasn't a few teardrops running down my face, it was body-wracking sobbing. I didn't know what to do with it, whether to be embarrassed or to embrace it, and I had no desire to experience it again.

I'd been able to live with the war as long as I was able to imagine that my country, my people, had, like me, learned something meaningful from our collective mistakes in Vietnam. But as the US government poured arms and support into obviously repressive regimes and counterrevolutionary movements in Central America and lied about it, and the news media echoed this official line while we drifted closer and closer to an invasion of Nicaragua, I found myself confronting the realization that if we *had* learned something, we were now on a short and rapid route to forgetting it.

That was in the mid-1980s, and the US military had in fact not forgotten the lessons of Vietnam. Try as they might, President Reagan and a handful of loutish officials working for him were unable to completely thwart the military and Congress, who in the end would not countenance another reckless invasion. As distressing as those events were for me, they kept me sane for a while longer. The time I spent in Nicaragua, and my vague awareness that I'd been ready to pick up arms and resist a US invasion there, allowed me to believe that something worthwhile had indeed come from my experiences in the war. Both our military's aggressiveness and my fears were kept in check for a while longer. It took another decade and half for the US military to forget entirely what it had learned in Vietnam, and to recommit itself to playing the world's policemen. And that's what would finally do me in.

FATHER AND DAUGHTER

When Grace was 10, I taped to the wall near the dinner table a news clipping about Hugh Thompson, the helicopter pilot at My Lai, in South Vietnam, who had ordered the chopper's door gunner to turn his machine gun on the American troops there if they would not stop killing old people, women, and children. That man, I said to Grace, now *he* is truly a hero, willing to stop his own people, by any means necessary, when they stumble far beyond any sort of moral bounds.[9]

It was a few years later that I first started talking with Grace, very reluctantly, about the war and its impact on me. I've never spoken much about it with her, and I'm not sure I can tell you why not, but some part of it must have to do with not wanting to place a burden on her: the war is *my* burden to carry.

Grace understands a lot about me. I once told her, quite spontaneously, to get dressed to go out to dinner, that we were going to celebrate something important. I would explain what the occasion was once we got to the restaurant, I said. I took her to the nicest place in our little town of Lawrenceville. As we sat down, she looked across the table and said, "I've done the math and figured out what we're celebrating. Today's the day I'm exactly the age you were when you ran away from home." I'd said nothing about this, but Grace understood how large that event loomed in my life and how important it was to me that we two had forged such close bonds. "Don't worry. I can't even imagine running away," she smiled.

In her early teens she concluded that even if I was uncomfortable discussing the war it was time to ask me about it. She'd been obliquely aware that the war was a problem for me, she said, and that I tried to avoid dealing with it. When she was younger she liked to surprise me by leaping onto my back. I don't know exactly what this triggered, but I know that when it happened, it required every ounce of my will power to refrain from violently throwing her off. I would steel myself, focus my emotions, and tell her to get off. Everything I had would go into remaining in control and speaking to her as calmly as I could. "Get off, Gracie, get off." It frightens me now to remember it. I don't know which is more telling, the degree of agitation I experienced when this small child leapt onto me, or the degree of control I had to summon in order to not fall apart when she did. As she learned not to do that, she realized that it had to do with the war. When she finally told me she was aware that the war was a problem for me, she made it clear that she'd been purposefully steering away from it. She said she knew that I carried something around with me, "But what did you *do* in the war, Daddy?"

And so I talked a little about what it was like working on a flight deck during flight operations, and about repairing our aircraft, and about flying our missions. It wasn't much, and we never talked much about it after that, but I'll never forget her response. She said, "If they made *me* do those things, I would have ran and found a place to hide." That sticks with me, and when I ponder it I recall what I thought at the time. That it simply never occurred to me not to do the things I did. They seemed so natural to me in my youth, such a part of what I'd sought out. My daughter, though, had been raised in another time, in another cultural and emotional environment, and without the testosterone-hardened steel shutters that I'd grown up with.

Perhaps the best way to illustrate this is with a story from when Grace was 10. We were visiting my sister, who'd moved to Santa Fé. It was our first trip there and it was in the midst of my divorce. I was in turmoil and because I had just moved out of our house and into a new place, I was particularly concerned about my relationship with Grace. As we drove from the Albuquerque airport to Santa Fé, I commented on some of the road signs, which named places I recognized from the early days of atom bomb testing. At some point, Grace leaned forward from the back seat and asked, "What's an atom bomb?" I looked at Ginny, stunned, then beamed and said, "That's one of the most beautiful things I've ever heard. My daughter's 10 years old and doesn't know what an atom bomb is." There's hope for humanity, I thought.

I still remember hearing the newscaster on the radio, when I was very small, speaking about fears that the Korean War was about to turn into World War Three, and about testing the hydrogen bomb. The notion that Grace had reached 10 without being conscious of these weapons overwhelmed me.

Grace simply hadn't grown up with the idea that war was a natural part of the world, or with any hint of my little boy's dream of going off to perform all the acts of heroic glory I'd watched in the films that illuminated my childhood. To this day, I'm somewhat amazed when I think about this; not so much that Grace wouldn't identify with my desire to prove myself in combat, as with the notion that in growing up the way I did I was so completely unaware of what I was taking for granted. To take something for granted means that we're oblivious to it, of course, but what I'm talking about here is something as all-encompassing as a death wish, my need to prove my manhood by risking my life in combat. No, it's not even proving myself, it's a matter of becoming myself. In order to become a man, as I understood it, I would have to do these things.

One way to explain this is to speak about how I've changed as I've raised her. I found myself wanting to know, and to understand, who she is, and what she needs as an individual in her own right. It was clear to me even when I was young that my own father had little or no sense of me as a distinct and separate individual who needed to be attended to. And so from the very start I not only paid attention to her, I *listened* to her. To listen to someone, and to truly hear them, though, one must keep not only one's ears, but also one's heart and spirit, open to them.

Keeping my emotional channels open remains a constant challenge for me, and I do it neither well nor comfortably. To the extent that I can manage it at all, though, it's because of the efforts I made as I parented my child. And to some extent I can see how the ways I experienced the war made this possible for me. I could see what I needed to do—what I *had* to do—in order to raise my daughter in a way that didn't replicate what I'd experienced with my own parents. And because I am nothing if not dedicated when it comes to doing my duty, I tried to open myself to Grace.

There's a conundrum here. To my mind, a father's task is to protect his child and at the same time allow her to experience enough of life's drama to develop her own strengths and insights. How do I protect my daughter from the war? I would ask myself. She needs, to my mind, to believe in and to be able to depend on her father's strength to protect her. But as I worked to keep my emotional channels open so that I could know my daughter, after striving so hard to keep them shut, I was also reexposing myself to the war's turmoil. This disorder was new to me, in the sense that I'd spent my life hiding from it, and I had no idea how to deal with it, how to process it, how to integrate it into my being. I couldn't pass this raw material directly on to my young child. And yet I also had a duty to provide her an example—a role model—for dealing with emotional stress and confusion.

I expected to protect her. I expected to teach her. To achieve these two entirely opposite goals at the same time seemed beyond my scope. Because I made an effort at it, though, she was at least aware that the war deeply troubled me. She steered clear of it until she felt ready to engage, and only then began to probe.

I'm not entirely sure how the prodigious responsibility I took on during the war transformed me, but it did. I wasn't merely willing to take it on, I sought it out, pursued it, and struggled to get it and hold it. After I left the war and much of the load—the most pressing parts, the actual responsibility of being in combat with so many people's lives at stake—was lifted off me, *then* I was able to soar. The irony of this is that for the most part I wasn't very conscious of what I'd been through or how I'd been changed by it. I knew I could handle the radar. I knew I could control aircraft in combat. I knew I could run a maintenance shop. I was shaped by all this, but I'm struck by how little awareness I had of it. And more to the point, I'm struck by how little conscious meaning it held for me and by how quickly I set these accomplishments aside and set my sights on new ones. This isn't a bad thing in and of itself, to be sure. There's nothing wrong with pursuing goals. The problem lies, at least for me, in *why* I do it, and especially in my inability to find much meaning in them once I've achieved them.

I don't believe that this is something at all peculiar to me—it's common in our society. What *is* significant is the chaos of the war—the existential noise and confusion—and the intensity, the sense that death may be looming around every corner encountered in this headlong pursuit. It's a part of why we—or at least some of us—fight.

What I'm talking about here is the sense I've always had that I have to work three times harder than everyone else. This has characterized everything I've done, in every aspect of my career. As long as I'm driving myself, working hard, worrying about what's next, what else I can do, and never feeling secure, then I'm okay—I'm preoccupied and focused and driven full-tilt boogie. I've always told myself that if I stopped this I wouldn't exist. It was exactly what brought me into combat and allowed me thrive and survive. I carried it away with me afterwards, and I just kept on doing it. [10]

NOTES

1. The extensive scientific and clinical literatures on this include, for instance, Habib and Lancaster (2006); Lundy (2002); Scism and Cobb (2017); Gritters (2020).

2. Vet Centers are small counseling operations funded by the Department of Veterans Affairs but run separately from it. They were established in the 1970s in direct response to readjustment problems Vietnam War vets were facing. They developed the "rap group" model, which allowed combat vets to work mostly with each other, and it was in this context that the VA's awareness of post-traumatic stress as a disorder (PTSD) quite specific to the Vietnam War blossomed. In *Home from the War* Robert Jay Lifton (1973) provides an intimate look at the work he did with vets in this context, work that led ultimately to having PTSD incorporated into the Diagnostic and Statistical Manual (DSM).

3. In *Armed With Abundance*, Meredith Lair (2011) writes extensively about both how many REMFs there were in Vietnam and how they were regarded by the relative minority of troops who served on what were euphemistically known as the front lines.

4. Steve Gardiner's discussion (2013) of what he calls the "hierarchy of valor" and the "banalization" of war experience captures the essence of this contradiction among veterans of the US military.

5. In the Diagnostic and Statistical Manual-IV (DSM), released in 1994 and in the process of being refined at the time the VA was adjudicating my claim, the Posttraumatic Stress Disorder diagnosis begins "The essential feature of Posttraumatic Stress Disorder is the development of characteristic symptoms following exposure to an extreme traumatic stressor" (American Psychiatric Association, 1994, p. 424).

6. As I explain in Chapter 8, "the body keeps the score"—that is, all those experiences are stored up inside us, whether we're conscious of them or not.

7. "Under a system of employee merit pay, bonuses for turning out paperwork and loss of promotions for low output, the VA has long known that its claims adjudicators in 58 regional offices were under such pressures to clear claims that many were denied without investigation or notice to applicants that documentation was required. The agency employees thus earned 'work credits.'" "V.A. Powers Face Challenge at a Congressional Hearing" by Ben A. Franklin, Special to the *New York Times*, March 15, 1987, section 1, page 22, https://www.nytimes.com/1987/03/15/us/va-powers-face-challenge-at-a-congressional-hearing.html?searchResultPosition=26.

8. My Catholic school training has something to do with this, I know, but it also has to do with the rigidity of my German-Swiss upbringing, and with aspects of my personality and character I was probably born with. I especially recall, from when I learned the liturgy of the old Latin Mass as I prepared to serve as an altar boy, the portion known as the *Confiteor*, where we struck our breasts and cried "*Mea culpa. Mea culpa. Mea maxima culpa*" ("Through my fault. Through my fault. Through my most grievous fault").

> In some ways, the *Confiteor* says it all: I confess
> that I have greatly sinned,
> in my thoughts and in my words,
> in what I have done and in what I have failed to do,
> through my fault, through my fault,
> through my most grievous fault.

I learned that it's not just what I've done but what I've failed to do that makes me responsible. This lies within the essence of the Catholic morality I was steeped in. I still believe in the imperative of acknowledging responsibility for what one has done and what one has failed to do; it's central to living in human society. But it can easily be pushed too far.

9. My Lai refers to a small village—a series of tiny hamlets—in central Vietnam; it was in northern South Vietnam during the war. A US Army infantry company massacred approximately 500 civilians there, mostly women, elders, and children, in March 1968. Warrant Officer Hugh Thompson and his crew, in a helicopter overhead, stopped the killing by threatening to fire on their own troops. The Army covered up the massacre, but reporter Seymour Hersh was ultimately able to bring it to light. Only one American soldier, Lt. William Calley, was put on trial for the killings. A court martial convicted him of murder and sentenced him to life imprisonment; he was paroled after 3 years.

As is typical of nearly everything concerning the Vietnam War, there is a sharp division of opinion about My Lai. Some view the brutality there as typical of how the United States fought the war; others argue that it was quite out of keeping with the way US troops fought (Jones, 2017; Turse, 2013).

10. I've heard women speak of how they have to work so much harder than men in order to succeed. I don't doubt this, but it's also the case that many men—or at least working-class guys like me—*feel* the same way.

Chapter Seven

War and the Arc of Human Experience

The war had a forceful impact on me, but during the hiatus, the decades after I came back, my momentum—my race to build a career—held me oblivious. The change began when Grace was born 20 years after my return, as it gradually dawned on me that something *had* happened. By 1997 I'd gained enough insight into what I was dealing with, and medication and psychotherapy had had enough effect on my psyche, for me to acknowledge that the stress in my marriage had been keeping me from making much sense of the war. I told V that we needed a trial separation and that I'd be moving out. She did not take this news well, and the stress continued to escalate. Within months I filed for divorce. Walking out that door had echoes of running away from home, and that walk is as good a place any to mark the end of the hiatus.

I moved just two blocks away, to the far side of the park right across the road from our place. We shared custody and Grace spent half her time with me. By prying myself free from a marriage that was draining away my emotional energy, I freed myself to focus my strength and attention on my daughter.

I respect V and I won't lay the blame for our marriage's failure on her. The simplest thing to say is that I could no longer live with the differences that had arisen between us. There were no affairs, no one was cheating. There were no significant financial disagreements. But neither was there much in the way of warmth or support. There *was* a lot of arguing and screaming, and I sometimes sat in my basement office literally banging my head on my desk in frustration. We occupied the same house but not the same home.

I'd turned 50 just two days before I moved out. The stress I was dealing with wasn't related to my age so much as it was to the collapse of an array of defense mechanisms I'd put in place long before. Ever since the war, I'd

excelled at blocking out or ignoring strife and danger and had instead focused my energies on my work and my career. But I'd passed beyond the
point where that strategy worked for me. A psychologist once suggested to
me that as veterans mature the demands of everyday life—family and work
in particular—increasingly draw away energy from our "emotional budgets,"
that is, the energy we use to hold the war at bay, and that's why I begin a new
chapter here: I'd embarked on a journey to find out what was going on inside
me.

Much of what precipitated the split had to do with the medication and the
therapy I was getting. My VA therapist, Sally Wright, seeing how distraught
I was, and pushing me to talk about my frustrations at home, had me describe
our division of domestic chores. When I described who did what, and Sally
wrote the chores down in two columns, it certainly looked as if I was doing at
least as much, if not more, than my wife. This breakdown was, of course,
arguable, but the point is that I had a fulltime job and she didn't and I was
doing a very big share of the household tasks. I'd supported V through her
PhD and I'd assumed she was going to put it to use. Things felt distinctly
unfair to me, and yet she insisted there was no problem. That's when Sally
said, "We can't do much with the war in Vietnam, Glenn, until you deal with
the battlefield at home."

We made our way into marriage counseling and the experience confirmed
my sense that something truly was wrong. Within weeks I could see what I
had to do. A moment came when I thought to myself that I had two children,
one of whom was growing up, while the other would never grow up. It was in
fact my 10-year-old daughter's emotional maturity that saved me from the
worst of the guilt I was facing. The day I moved into my new place, Grace
grabbed a friend and together the two of them crossed the park separating
what were now her two homes. She came into my apartment, settled herself,
and announced that she would be spending the night with me.

I've mentioned people who in the past bailed me out of jams. Now my
daughter, sensing what I needed, and expressing her own very strong needs
as well, bailed me out. I soon learned that when I was no longer preoccupied
with defending myself in my marriage, I was able to devote my energy and
attention to Grace. Together, we created a calm, quiet, and supportive space
for ourselves. I didn't need to feel guilty for ripping her family apart, because
I'd made it possible for her to be part of a household that didn't continually
feel on the brink of explosion.

Two seemingly simple incidents from that first marriage will illustrate
some of the deep-seated emotional turmoil that I continue wrestling with
even now. In the early stages of the battle over my disability claim, V and I
went into the VA's Newark office to testify before one of the claims officers.
I recall V describing a characteristic expression of my PTSD, my idiosyncratic hypervigilance. I don't worry about securing the perimeter or spotting

improvised explosive devices (IEDs), both well-known forms of hypervigilance. But then I hadn't been manning a forward firebase in Vietnam. I'd been immersed in operating and repairing equipment on which my life and the security of the fleet depended, and my symptoms reflect this. I experience abuse or misuse of domestic equipment, especially in the kitchen, as an acute threat to my personal safety and security.

It was a version of this that manifested itself when we spoke to the VA. V had a habit of placing things on top of the toaster oven on our kitchen counter. She sometimes set plastic cups on top of it, and I freaked when I saw one melt while the oven was on. After explaining to her several times that setting anything on top of the toaster was a hazard and seeing that this failed to keep her from continuing to place things on it, including cups that quickly melted, I set a sign saying *"PLACE NOTHING HERE"* atop it.

She explained to the claims officer that I'd put up a whole series of signs around the kitchen, including one that detailed exactly how many inches away from the wall the toaster must be. At the time, I saw this as merely a matter of inexactitude, but in retrospect I see that it was much more a matter of fundamental differences in the way that we experienced the world.

At a Thanksgiving dinner we held not long after I'd stopped drinking, V had invited several dinner guests whose company I didn't much enjoy. I was uncomfortable at the table, and quietly slipped away a few times to watch football alone. Later, she accused me of acting like a child. The fact is, once I stopped drinking, I found myself barely able to socialize with anyone. This has been a fundamental source of much friction and distress in my personal relationships ever since I quit.

These two examples will strike some readers as inconsequential, I'm sure, but they reflect major issues in my life. And now I'm able to see where they come from. Important work by psychologists on the ways trauma masks itself (work I'll describe in Chapter 8), has helped me understand how it's possible for me to have been so unaware of symptoms like those, warning signs that express themselves all over the place, especially withdrawal from social relationships. This has had profound implications for me, but at this point I simply note that even as I look back and see how all this affected my first marriage and want desperately to avoid doing the same thing again, I know that these issues continue to exact a very high price from me.

Incidents like these were common, but I had no idea there was a pattern in them. They were problematic and unfortunate but seemed random and unconnected. When I started becoming aware of them it was too late. They were woven into the fabric of my marriage. I was getting treatment that reduced some of the pain and despair, but it had little impact on concrete behavior issues like these. I mark the end of the hiatus at the divorce because by then I was aware that the war *was* affecting my daily life, my everyday life.

My PTSD makes it difficult—if not nearly impossible—for me to handle important aspects of normal social life. My relationship with Grace stands out in this context, because it's what made me aware of the problem in the first place, and forced me to deal with it, but also because it makes me conscious of just how complicated and confusing things are for me. She's been at the center of life for me, but my relationship with her also makes me painfully aware of just how great a problem this all is. This leads in turn to my second marriage, in which all the tenderness and openness I've gained in my relationship with Grace run smack into the festering fears of emotional openness and closeness the war imprinted on my soul.

I worry that these will cause my second marriage to collapse for similar reasons. Understanding and accepting PTSD, that is, doesn't make it go away, nor does treatment necessarily do the trick. I depend overwhelmingly on the good graces of my wife, my daughter, my family, and others I interact with to tolerate my inability to socialize, and to put up with my general withdrawal from ordinary, everyday social life.

9/11 AND THE NEW WARS

I teach in midtown Manhattan. I was riding New Jersey Transit's commuter train into the city as usual on the morning of September 11, 2001, but when I tried to transfer in Newark to the PATH train that runs under the Hudson River and into the World Trade Center, I learned that PATH had just shut down. I got back onto the train to continue on instead to New York City's Penn Station. As we pulled out of the Newark station, the twin towers came into view; it was only minutes after the first airliner had flown into one of them. We had no idea what was happening, but those with cell phones (which weren't ubiquitous in those days) quickly filled us in. After the train reached Penn Station, I walked south toward school and stopped in Madison Square Park, a few blocks from campus. It was filling with people fleeing lower Manhattan, many of them in a state of panic. I watched, transfixed, as first one and then the other tower collapsed. The images of those two buildings "pancaking" as they fell are etched indelibly in my mind.

An image even more powerfully engraved in me is that of a young woman screaming in near-hysteria. I folded her into my arms, her face pressed to my chest, and held her until she stopped sobbing. I turned to others and began comforting them in any way I could. This sounds maudlin to me as I write it now, but I also understand something about what that searing experience wrought in me. I recall thinking that something good had actually come from having learned in the war about dealing with fear and danger.

I was struck not only by the cataclysm of the towers falling, but also by the sudden proliferation of American flags that followed; they were literally everywhere in the city for a long time after 9/11, and I saw in them the same sort of unreflecting Americanism that had gotten us into Vietnam (and I understand that this isn't how most New Yorkers thought of them). I could see no reason to further destabilize a country—Afghanistan—that had long been in the process of tearing itself apart. And I understood that invading Iraq was a disaster in every sense of the word—moral, political, and practical.

I thought to myself that although the United States had managed to refrain from invading Nicaragua and had carefully limited itself in the Gulf War and in other spots, we were now repeating precisely the mistake that we'd made in Vietnam. And then the Vietnam War began haunting me in a new way.

That experience of standing in the street watching the towers come down intersected with our government's willful obtuseness and ripped away whatever scar tissue had been masking my old psychic wounds. The fictions the government spread about weapons of mass destruction and "smoking guns" were far too much like the humbug we were told about North Vietnam's "unprovoked attacks" on American warships exercising innocent right of passage in their coastal waters.

The invasion of Iraq might, I suppose, have rolled off my back after an initial wave of indignation if it hadn't then blossomed into a full-scale occupation and stoked a lasting insurgency. I reacted with real alarm to the publicity stunt the White House staged aboard USS *Abraham Lincoln* a few weeks after the attack on Iraq. President George W. Bush landed in an S-3 Viking, the plane that replaced the S-2s I'd controlled in the Tonkin Gulf. He was a passenger, not the pilot, but he'd rigged himself out in full flight gear and posed for multiple photos with the crew in his warrior get-up. Then, standing in front of a huge "Mission Accomplished" sign strung up by his administration's operatives, he proclaimed that "Major combat operations in Iraq have ended. In the battle of Iraq, the United States and our allies have prevailed." Sheesh!

A *Wall Street Journal* writer recounted how she'd

> turned on the news. And there was the president, landing on the deck of the *USS Abraham Lincoln*, stepping out of a fighter jet in that amazing uniform, looking—how to put it?—really hot. Also, presidential, of course. Not to mention credible as a commander in chief. But mostly "hot" as in virile, sexy and powerful. You don't see that a lot in my neighborhood, the Upper West Side of Manhattan (Schiffren, 2003).

(I include that last sentence because Manhattan's Upper West Side is my neighborhood, too.)

Seeing the president "prancing" (as some described it) around in a flight suit on a carrier flight deck, along with reading of the impression he'd created, made it unmistakably clear that these wars were being pursued, despite the absence of any conceivable way of winning them, for domestic political purposes rather than for any viable military or foreign relations strategy (and perhaps for other reasons as well: W's father really had been a carrier pilot in World War II).

The interweaving of these elements caused a lot more psychic and moral injury than the simple sum of the parts should have done. The spectacle accomplished a lot more than just the usual war propaganda, acting out as it did, in the person of our leader, the government's lies about the war. Bush had avoided fighting in Vietnam. Now he was a leader impersonating the warrior that he hadn't been. He could have done what presidents going aboard ships have always done, that is, arrive in a helicopter, wearing a leather flight jacket over a business suit, but instead he'd wrapped himself in a carrier pilot's gear and draped himself with a sign that was literally a "big lie."

This is the point at which the contradictions between guilt and pride that afflict me began at last to heave their way out of my unconscious and up into full awareness.

The intensity of the pain I'd been feeling continued to ratchet up. In January of 2007, in agony as I thought about what was happening in Afghanistan and Iraq, and how gruesomely familiar it all seemed, I sat and wrote these lines in a burst of free association. I make no apologies for their rawness, in either emotional or literary terms.

> It seems a bit much, you know?
> to speak of this feeling,
> this feeling of rending flesh,
> of having my flesh stripped off.
> How would I know?
> How would I know what it feels like?
> But still, that is what it feels like.
> A bit like the little girl,
> skin napalm-enveloped,
> stumbling down the road,
> in fear, in pain, in shame, in despair.
>
> The war,
> my war,
> in Vietnam,
> it still so thoroughly permeates me, my body, my soul, my spirit,
> and all the eyes and ears through which I sense the world,
> that when I'm confronted with this other war,
> the one in Iraq, you know?,
> it bonds with my skin, with my body, my soul, my spirit.
> And then it rips,
> rips,
> rips at me,
> strips,

strips,
strips from me my paper-thin skin.

Be thick-skinned,
someone tells me.
But, I think,
I worked so long,
so hard,
to feel.
Should I turn back now,
just because of this new war?

Or can I scream?

TRYING TO MAKE SENSE OF IT ALL

Grace had gone off to college by this time and my personal isolation, stark even in the best of times, deepened. I moved back into New York City. I'd established nothing I'd call a friendship in nearly two decades living in Lawrenceville and I had few ties there, with the exception of the AA meetings I'd been attending for years. Although I've never socialized among fellow AA's away from the meetings, I had at least forged a sense of connection with the regular participants in the three or four meetings I attended each week. AA meetings had become my only source of human contact outside the university and my time with Grace. As my vulnerability grew, I had fewer and fewer resources to help me deal with it.

I understood how well alcohol had allowed me to blunt the pain, but also that I'd be likely to kill myself if I started drinking again. I gradually learned that the only relief I could find was in action—that is, in taking political action. Once during those years, when I was formally debating some Army officers over the status of reserve officer training (ROTC) at City University, a young woman, an Iraq veteran who was sitting alongside me on the platform, turned to me just before we got underway. "Do you *enjoy* this?" she asked with a mild quaver in her voice. "That's not the point," I said gently. "I can't sleep at night if I *don't* do this." And I felt her relax a bit.

In the spring of 2007 my efforts to find some sort of relief from this pain led me to begin agitating for veterans services on my campus. Then a Vietnam vet in the university system's central office asked me to organize a CUNY-wide conference on veterans services. I've never been a conference organizer—my dislike of social interaction has driven me to avoid this sort of thing throughout my academic career. But I found myself in a put-up or shut-up situation. I ran some meetings, in several different venues, to figure out how to proceed.

We held a big conference and at last got a full-time coordinator of veterans services for the entire university system. But I quickly grasped that if I continued to pursue this route I'd become immersed in academic administration, something I could not and would not do. I needed to do something, but I was still flailing around, trying to figure out what I *could* do.

That summer I returned to Pohnpei. Damian and Iuli had died since my last trip. They'd lived full lives and left large families, and I was welcomed with the same grace and respect their adult children had always shown me. But it was clear that without Damian there to guide to me, I was no longer certain of what I was doing. I missed the couple badly, and no longer felt tied to the community in the ways that I had been. I sensed when I left that I was probably bringing almost 35 years of ethnographic fieldwork to a close. I was nearly done with the book I'd been writing, an overview of all Micronesia's traditional societies (Petersen, 2009), and my energies and attention were about to be set free.

Shortly after I returned from Pohnpei I strolled across the street from my office to the neighborhood Subway sandwich shop to buy my lunch. This hole in the wall sits directly opposite the entrance to the 69th Infantry Regiment armory on Lexington Avenue and East 25th Street, and as I joined the line to place my order, my gaze settled on the soldier just ahead of me.[1] His camouflage uniform—his cammies—struck something in me. I'm not quite sure what it was, but it felt like a red cape thrust in the face of a bull; a sharp, piercing wave of anger about the wars rolled over me. I reeled backward in surprise and saw that he was hardly older than Grace. An entirely different emotion, a pulse of sympathy, welled up.

I stood there, stunned for a moment, and then felt a surge of vertigo. The two contradictory emotions, anger and sympathy, weren't cancelling one another out. Colliding, they instead stirred up turbulence, a dizzying chaos of competing currents. I was completely off balance.

Disconcerted and confused, I knew only that the damned war had clobbered me yet again. It's my habit to consider, in cases like these, what I need to be doing. What's the next action to take? I asked myself. I thought about all the many ways I'd tried to deal with the war over the years, talking with therapists and with other vets, taking medications, trying to organize services for our campus vets. Nothing was working—I seemed to be falling farther down a rabbit hole.

And then I realized that the one thing I hadn't tried was the thing that seemed the most natural to me. I'd never tried to grapple with the war as an intellectual subject. What, I wondered, would happen if I *taught* a course on war? And in that moment, seizing the initiative and my prerogative as department head, I called the dean's office and told them to cancel one of my classes for the spring semester and replace it with a "special topics" course on war and peace.

So I set off on yet another stage of my journey. Seeing my students' enthusiasm, I taught the course a couple of times on a trial basis and then braved the bureaucracy to make it a permanent part of the curriculum. I quickly discovered that as much as I wanted to emphasize peace, it was a lot simpler to spend time on war. I compensated by changing the title to the anthropology of peace and war, imagining that putting peace first would force me to spend more time on it, but this ploy didn't really change much. [2]

There's a lesson here: you can talk all you want about peace, but it's conflict that draws attention. The course gave me insight into just how attractive war can be. Here's the paradox in a nutshell: I'd like to argue that in intellectual terms, people tend to praise peace, but in emotional terms they're more interested in war. While there's more than a grain of truth in this, the matter is in fact much more complicated. Most of what's entailed in war isn't dramatic or cinematic action; for the most part, it tends to be a highly disciplined, well-ordered, and well-thought-out activity. It's intellectually challenging and has attracted many of history's greatest minds.

Peace, on the other hand, which almost invariably presents itself as the voice of quiet reason, draws at least as much on our mammalian, hormone-driven needs and capacities for love, nurturing, and tenderness. Love and passion, as playwrights and moviemakers understand, are compelling. This is, of course, why so many war stories dramatize the opposing pulls of love and duty. I've learned how hard it is to draw simple or straightforward conclusions about teaching war and peace.

I'd honed a brooding hostility to war over the years, in the course of opposing American interventionism abroad. I knew I wasn't a pacifist, but I had a hard time imagining myself thinking or saying anything positive about war in general. At some level, I suppose, I still do. But as I interacted with my students, I gained a much better appreciation for why war is so damned attractive. It not only provides dramatic action, it also promotes human qualities like spirit, duty, and honor and excites many people's imaginations more than being smart or kind or gentle.

As an anthropologist, I feel obliged to teach about the behaviors of our close relatives among the primates, the great apes, as well as the predilections of societies all across the long sweep of human history. Over the years I've come to believe that when we take all the comparative evidence into account, we can make almost any argument we wish to about human proclivities for violence and for the organized violence we call war. I know what I approve of and what I disapprove of, but my own deepest, personal sentiments sometimes come up against what I—as a scholar and teacher—think the data show, which is that humans are equally capable of engaging in violence and of avoiding it. In some times and places violence is more eagerly promoted and in others it is disparaged. But always there are great yawning gaps between what people have to say about violence and war and how they actually behave. My life's experience as an anthropologist has taught me that to be human means we're fully capable of saying one thing and then doing something quite different.

Always, I press students to pay close attention both to what's actually going on and to how people experience or think about what's going on. These can be wildly different. With this in mind, we discuss popular films, video games, the news media, sports, and books. A point I dwell on a lot—in both this book and my classes—is how difficult it is to draw firm conclusions from the contradictory things we all experience.

When I explore contemporary American culture and society with them, for example, we dig into my perception that there's no such thing as an antiwar movie. It's not that filmmakers aren't making movies with antiwar messages, but that in order to pay for the costs of making the movie, they must get audiences into theaters, and that means attracting more than a handful of entirely likeminded individuals. To turn a profit, they've got to convince a range of people to come see their movie, people who are going to have a range of reactions to it. In simplest terms, what *adults* are likely to see in a movie—the kinds of lessons they're going to take away from it—is going to differ strikingly from what *boys and young men* are likely to see in it.[3]

Drawing on my own youthful experiences, I show students that what we bring with us when we look at war plays a big part in what we see in it. We need to see that any lasting account of war, in any time or place, has to be complex enough for us to find all sorts of messages in it. Rarely, if ever, does anything treating human activity of any kind, but particularly emotionally-charged things like sex and violence, allow for just a single message or interpretation.

I can say this with conviction and at least some clarity now that I've worked my way through the course a few times. These concepts will probably strike some as obvious, or even commonplace, but they are neither easy to teach nor easy to learn, and I didn't see them at all clearly when I began. It was only in struggling through a series of readings, in continually connecting them to the daily flow of news and working hard to open this realm up to my students, that I forged the perspectives that underlie all that I've been writing here.

The only thing I was sure of at the outset was that we'd begin the course by reading the *Iliad*. Jonathan Shay's (1995) pathbreaking book *Achilles in Vietnam*, which describes how Homer's work helped him in his duties as a psychiatrist treating Vietnam vets, first got me thinking about teaching with it. I wasn't all that familiar with it—I'd read commentaries and summaries, but never the full text (I *had* read the *Odyssey*, because I'd figured it would be more exciting). After some poking around, I chose Robert Fagles's (1990) *Iliad* translation mostly because it begins with the same word the ancient

Greek original takes as its starting point, the word *menin*, or rage. "Rage—Goddess, sing the rage of Peleus' son Achilles." Some scholars say that that's the poem's original title: "Rage." And rage was what I was feeling at the time, and what I wanted both to explore and to express.

I've spent a lot of time reading and studying the *Iliad*, and I now have, if not a completely different perspective on it, a distinctly different one. In particular, I've come to see that it is no less a meditation on the human costs of war than it is a celebration of war and its glories, and that Achilles, who is often spoken of as "sulking in his tent" over slights to his honor and character, can just as well be understood as having taken a principled stand against a series of abuses committed by the Greek army's commanding general, Agamemnon, king of Argos.

In trying to grasp the *Iliad*'s sweep, I found my way to Caroline Alexander's (2010) *The War That Killed Achilles*. It was her exploration of the contexts surrounding not only the war between the Greeks and Trojans but the conflict between Achilles and Agamemnon that got me to see Achilles as heroic not just because he was a valiant warrior, but because of his struggles with himself, with the gods, and with the age-old tensions between duty, responsibility, and love. To whom is one responsible, finally? To oneself, to beloved family, to comrades, or to leaders representing the state or government?

And I then found in Leon Golden's (2009) *Achilles and Yossarian* a way to make much more sense of my own relationship to the story. *Catch-22* had not simply headed me toward flying in combat when I was a boy on the run, but provided a mindset, a way of seeing and understanding things, that allowed me to do my duty while not having my character undermined by the war. Golden points out that Achilles ultimately overcomes his rage when Priam, the aged father of Hector, the warrior Achilles has slain, comes to him in the night and pleads for his son's body, that he might give him a proper funeral. Reminded of his own father (who will soon lose *his* son), and of all he has sacrificed in his pursuit of glory, Achilles sympathizes with the old man and at last relents. In *Catch-22*, Yossarian likewise heads toward healing when he escapes the war by paddling a life raft to Sweden. He isn't simply deserting, though. He first heads to Rome, to rescue a young girl from poverty and danger, to take her with him and thereby redeem his antagonism toward the military with an act of loving mercy. (This crucial element doesn't appear in the movie, incidentally, only in the novel.)

When Golden asked Joseph Heller whether he was aware of the ways in which *Catch-22* paralleled the *Iliad*, Heller replied excitedly that the *Iliad* had always been his favorite book and that it had indeed served as a guiding template for his own novel. Redemption, it is clear, is a central, driving force in what are for me the two most influential stories of war. These works help me see how my own personal history with the war is enmeshed with my unrelenting need to atone for having fought in it.

Having set the stage for understanding the ambiguities of war and war stories, I move the class on to consider how physical violence among our nearest relatives, the apes, gets used to explain our own proclivities, and why some say our original nature is peaceful while others insist it is violent, drawing especially on the work of primatologist Frans de Waal.[4] We explore various assumptions about the roles war and peace play in the course of human history. And then we immerse ourselves in some of the ways war gets portrayed in literature.

SHAKESPEARE AND HEMINGWAY

Henry V

I came to understand that Achilles isn't simply angry. He's torn—torn between many different things. And then I turned again to Shakespeare, my companion since I first ran away. *Henry V* exploded in my hands. Scholars argue endlessly over what Shakespeare had to say about the young king but teaching his plays in a course on peace and war—knowing as I do something about the dissonances between what people say and what they mean when it comes to war—gives me my own insights. I focus in particular on a profoundly ambiguous scene when the king, in disguise, sidles up to a cluster of his soldiers stirring anxiously before the battle at Agincourt. With the first hint of dawn, one of them says uneasily, "we have no cause to desire the approach of day." To which a companion responds, "We see yonder the beginning of the day, but I think we shall never see the end of it." Hearing that his men fear they'll all be dead before night falls, Henry admonishes them by trumpeting his own bravery. "Methinks I could not die anywhere so contented as in the King's company, his cause being just and his quarrel honorable."

"That's more than we know," says one, and a second adds, "Ay, or more than we should seek after, for we know enough if we know we are the king's subjects. If his cause be wrong, our obedience to the king wipes the crime of it out of us." Here are medieval soldiers pondering aspects of what philosophers call just war theory that have at times reduced me to blithering idiocy (*Henry V*, 4.1).

Recognizing his men's fears about how badly the French troops outnumber them, Henry launches into a soaring sales pitch:

> The fewer men, the greater share of honor.
> God's will, I pray thee wish not one man more.

It is *this* that is the occasion for some of most stirring lines in the English language.

> We few, we happy few, we band of brothers;
> For he today that sheds his blood with me
> Shall be my brother;
> (4.3.60–63)

In exploring this rhetoric with students I've come to believe not that these lines mean one particular thing or another, but that Shakespeare, like Homer, wrote of war in ways meant for unbounded interpretation, filled with layer upon layer of meaning and nuance. He makes war sound supremely attractive even as he points out the duplicity entailed in portraying it in just this way. If I have been conflicted about the nature of war, and about the attraction war holds, Shakespeare assures me, I'm in the best of company.

Hemingway's Code Hero

The same task, however, can be accomplished without fancy speeches. Ernest Hemingway is celebrated for his quiet protagonists, called "code heroes." The code hero is distinct from a "hero," who is someone who does something expressly heroic, in a specific situation, one who acts with valor in combat, or does something else in a bold way that attracts the eye. What makes a code hero, on the other hand, has to do with the way an individual carries himself. He's a guy whose way of being in the world expresses a set of underlying, core beliefs about how a man should act. His heroic aspects are rooted in an everyday code of behavior as he deals with challenges to his sense of self, his manhood, and his integrity. He does what must be done when it has to be done, precisely because it must be done. "A man's gotta do what a man's gotta do," as the saying goes. The code hero doesn't make a big deal of it, he just does it. Nor is he trying to get himself killed, but if that's what takes, so be it. He shows, Hemingway said, "grace under pressure" (Young, 1952).

There's a quixotic quality to this manliness. We see it in the curtailing of emotion and in the heavy drinking. The two are, of course, closely related. For Hemingway booze was the "giant killer" (1971, p. 41). The code hero is likely to have experienced significant injury, but he keeps it hidden, and it's the repression of emotion, aided by alcohol, that allows him to do so.

There's long been a question about the degree to which the wounds—physical and psychic—Hemingway received from an exploding mortar shell in Italy impacted his writing. He changed his own position on this over the years, which makes complete and absolute sense to me.

In "Big Two-Hearted River" Hemingway's alter ego Nick Adams goes fishing alone. It appears to critics that Nick has put his energies—both his physical and his psychic energies—to work repressing something; that something is assumed to have happened in World War I. They suggest that the story reflects Hemingway's repression of his own war injuries. Others insist that because the war is never mentioned in the story, there's no evidence that this assumption is true.

When this notion that "Big Two-Hearted River" reflects Hemingway's efforts to suppress the war became commonplace several decades after the story first appeared, he acknowledged that this was indeed the case. But skeptics argue that this is no more than post-facto reasoning; if Hemingway hadn't been aware that he was doing this at the time he wrote, they insist, then he wasn't doing it. The fact that he later concurred with the idea, they say, is simply a rationalization (Lynn, 1987; Paul et al., 2014).

As I think about what I teach I've come to understand that the ways I deal with the war are hardly peculiar to me. To fight well, we've got to be tough. When young men fight, many different sorts of things happen; our experiences are not all the same. It's common for men who've fought to develop a degree of self-regard or pride in their skill, endurance, and toughness, yet it's equally common for them to experience fears, stresses, and neuroses. The issue here is not simply the traumatic stress itself, but our fear we're going to forfeit whatever credit we've earned for our toughness if we admit, either to ourselves or to others, that we've been impaired by our war experiences. We stand to lose exactly what we fought to earn and this can leave us flailing around in confusion.

My own return from war was marked by a complete lack of awareness that anything had happened to me, by my reliance on the oblivion alcohol brought me, by burying myself in work, and by a high degree of alienation from the people around me. I left California for New York City, and then headed off to the middle of the Pacific Ocean, escaping for years to a remote island. I did these things for many reasons, of course, but I think the pattern is clear. I worked at a feverish pitch to ignore the war, a strategy that succeeded so well that it hid the trauma well out of sight. Until, that is, my daughter's birth forced open a fissure in the dam, a seam that grew slowly until the dam burst.

I recall having heroic fantasies during the war. I wanted to be a hero in the classic mold. I wasn't, and I was disappointed. If I couldn't be a conventional hero, though, I could still be a code hero. Everything I did, from well before the war and all the way through it, actually entailed basic aspects of doing what had to be done while I was consciously telling myself that a man's got to do what a man's got to do. This meant, for me, flying my missions, working at all the dangerous tasks I took on, doing them without a whimper or—and this is the crucial element, I now see—even giving much conscious thought to the dangers I faced, especially climbing back into my plane after that flight into Red China. I did so with the tellingly simple thought that it's like getting back on a horse—if I don't do it right away, if I allow myself to consciously contemplate my fear—I won't be able to do it in the future. The point is that my main concern was with getting the job done, not with being a hero. That's what I fixated on, not threats to my own safety, and I drew deliberately on the cowboy images I'd grown up with.

Hemingway didn't give this to me—I had it before I ever read him—but he illustrated it in a way that gave me the framework I needed to organize it. I could see what it looked like, and hear how it sounded. And afterwards, when the fears did threaten to make themselves known, especially at night before I went to bed, I drank. I recognized a clear connection between what it took for me to sleep before going out on that next mission and the way I drank in order to sleep following the war. And alcohol was important to me for another, equally important reason. I needed it in order to deal with people, in order to engage in any sort of social interaction. When I finally stopped drinking, though, the code got me into trouble. I found there just wasn't much room for dealing with infants and children, or with wives, for that matter. I'd managed to ignore my wife, but I couldn't ignore Grace.

MORAL INJURY

I'd begun using Ron Kovic's (1976) extraordinary *Born of the Fourth of July* in my introductory anthropology classes long before I began teaching courses about war and peace. I present it to students as an ethnographic account of the United States in the 1950s and '60s and as a lucid story about why so many young men of my generation went willingly to war, and I've made it a centerpiece of my course on peace and war. The book is rarely mentioned in the context of war literature, or even important Vietnam War literature, but my working-class, mostly immigrant undergraduate students find it gripping. I never have to exhort them to read it; they tear right through the book. At its climax, in a firefight, Kovic is wounded. He continues pressing forward into heavy fire, and receives a second wound, this one to his spine; it's the one that puts him into a wheelchair for the rest of his life.

He tells us how good this felt in the moment. His wounds thrilled him, he says, because finally, "I was going to be a hero." How is it possible, I ask my students, for this man to tell us that he feels good inside when he's just been shot? Because, we see when we study the text, that's exactly what he set out to do. After watching war movies as a boy he'd go home and re-enact them in his yard. He'd acted out those fatal scenes long before he ever got to Vietnam. And he'd become a high school wrestler with the same thought in mind. "I wanted to be a hero," he said, and practiced being a code hero, "the great silent athlete" (1976, pp. 76 and 221).

And then I explain that this all reflects exactly the same sort of contradictions I dealt with during the war. The code hero is cool, but the camera's drawn to the action hero, the guy who's blasting away with his automatic weapon while bullets fly all around him. As much as Kovic and I admired the code hero, it just wasn't enough. We wanted more.

In time I came to see that I'd been using others' experiences to avoid exploring my own. Despite the very personal character the class has for me, I'd been wary of telling much of my own story. As I grew more comfortable with my students, though, and as we worked our way through discussions of some very difficult materials, trust and openness increasingly filtered into the classroom. I would occasionally describe my own experiences and my dilemmas and confusions and I found myself talking more and more about my own struggles with the contradictions that lurk among all the pride and guilt and atonement. I expressed frustration at not knowing how to unburden myself. And then one of my students pointed it out to me. "Professor," he said, "by telling us all this, and expressing what you feel and describing what you experienced and making us understand some of the reality of war, you are atoning. Teaching us," he concluded, "*is* your atonement." And I knew he was right.

As I came to see that there was real value both for my students and for me in digging into my struggles, I asked my friend and colleague, Glenn Albright, a psychologist who works with veterans, to teach with me. We created a new course, "War and the Arc of Human Experience." It is, in fact, where I've figured out parts of this book. (And Glenn has given me startling insights into the science of what ails me.) As I teach, I continually remind my students that the questions we're exploring have no simple answers. I share some of my own experiences with them, not just about combat itself but about the broader nature of war and about how I wanted to fight and how I've carried the war with me, explaining that it's not simply one or the other of these.

It's in teaching these courses, and in translating what I've learned from teaching them into this book, that I've managed to harness the anger that accompanies the guilt and the pride. Glenn has asked me, in class, why it surprises me that I experience guilt and pride simultaneously. I haven't really found an adequate answer to his question: I just do.

I'm often afraid of this anger, and sometimes troubled by it, but it's there and it's not going away, and so the best I can do with it is to put it to work. I see that the anger itself is only one side of the coin. On the flip side is the matter of who I direct my anger towards. More often than not, it's authority: those I experience in ways that evoke my father and the military. Leaders. I direct my indignation at them. It feels like I haven't much choice, really.

In his work on moral injury, Jonathan Shay, the psychiatrist whose work first pointed me toward Achilles and the *Iliad*, dwells on three *key* factors: (1) the betrayal of "what's right" by (2) those in legitimate authority (3) in a high-stakes (i.e., life or death) context or situation. Other factors include a second sort of moral injury that comes when an individual in the military "does something in war that violates their own ideals, ethics, or attachments." He speaks of his work with the Vietnam veterans whom he describes as his teachers: "they do not want other young kids wrecked the way they were wrecked in Vietnam" and he argues that it isn't PTSD per se, "pure PTSD," that "wrecks veterans' lives." Rather, "moral injury—both flavors—does" (2014, pp. 183–184).

I understand this sense of being wrecked, and I've experienced it at some level, but what looms larger for me is my sense that moral injuries haven't destroyed me. I struggle each day to deal with them. As far as I can tell, there is no resolution or complete healing. But by working each day, every day, by choosing to teach and to speak out and to put my body on the line in protests, I can live with what I've done. And I'm hardly alone in this: nearly everything I've said here echoes lines that appear in Nancy Sherman's deeply insightful works on moral injury, *The Untold War* (2010) and *After War* (2015). Among the Vietnam vets she speaks with is Bob Steck, who "is visibly anguished about his own generation's ultimate failure to inoculate future generations of soldiers." Bob, she says, is troubled by "the underlying fact that he can't psychologically or morally fully separate himself from the war he fought. Wars and warriors don't easily come apart" (2010, p. 51).

Folks in Alcoholics Anonymous place great store in what's known as the Serenity Prayer, a few lines penned by the politically astute and morally engaged theologian Reinhold Niebuhr: "God, grant me the serenity to accept the things I cannot change; the courage to change the things I can; and the wisdom to know the difference." It may not surprise you to hear that I've always had trouble with the first part, acceptance. Accepting things has its uses, I know. But I'm much more interested in having courage to challenge things, to speak out against things, and to change things. And that's the only antidote or symptomatic relief I know for the moral injury I live with.

I have deeply ambivalent feelings about my confrontations with authority. On one hand, it troubles me that I rise so often at meetings and challenge those in authority about issues I believe are genuinely important. There are those who think some of my points are spurious or overly dramatized, but it's also the case that colleagues usually stop by later to thank me for raising these issues. And then there's the fact that I simply enjoy calling authority to task. The question for me is *why* I enjoy it. I must get an unusual amount of pleasure from doing so, because I am often the only person who does it, the only one who's driven to rise and push back.[5]

Why am I so odd in this respect? I can only conclude that it offers me a bit of relief, in the moment, from the almost constant burden of anger at authority that I carry. In the moment, when I am standing and pointing out the error of their ways, I am striking back, shrugging off the abstract weight of betrayal, telling the betrayers not only that they are doing wrong, but insisting that they stop doing it.

I am, of course, rarely successful. But that's not the point. I'm using an open forum for airing grievances as a means of resolving, for the moment, my own grievances. I don't do it as a victim. I experience little if any sense of victimhood when I do it. I do it to manifest—to make known—my own strength. But more than that it is an affirmation of my thumos, my spirit. You are wrong to ask this of us, I say, and I will point it out to you. I may not achieve much, things may not change much as a result of my doing so, but I will do so nevertheless. In fact, I often liken it to tilting at windmills. Being quixotic is my duty. I once did my duty under false representations. Never again. Now I will spot the falsehoods, the inconsistencies, the bullshit, and point it out for what it is. It's more than my duty, it's my job and responsibility. It is my being, and in the moment it serves to take some of the edge off my guilt. Speaking up and speaking out are for me a kind of atonement.

I needed to achieve a sense of balance if I was to be fair to my students in my discussions of war and it was in locating it that I became increasingly aware of my own ambivalence. I began to appreciate how attractive being a warrior had seemed to me as a young man, and I gained new perspectives on the pride I'd felt about my accomplishments and the pride I feel even now at my youthful willingness to risk my life in combat. I also gained a little insight into my willingness to kill others—people living halfway around the world from my home who constituted no threat to either me or my family.

NOTES

1. This is the regimental headquarters of the same unit that was featured in *The Fighting 69th*, one of those films the nuns regularly showed us as they shaped our sense of history. I never fail to think of this when I pass by it or look out my office window for that matter.

2. Anthropological studies of war have a long history. More recently the subfield of "military anthropology" has established itself. Among the titles I've worked with are Catherine Lutz's *Homefront* (2002), David Price's *Weaponizing Anthropology* (2011), Erin Finley's *Fields of Combat* (2011), Kenneth MacLeish's *Making War at Fort Hood* (2013), Anna Simons's *The Company They Keep* (1997), Hugh Gusterson's "Anthropology and Militarism" (2007), Roberto Gonzalez's *Anthropologists in the Public Sphere* (2004), and Montgomery McFate's *Military Anthropology* (2018).

3. In *Guts and Glory*, an almost encyclopedic account of American war movies, Lawrence Suid makes much the same point. The movie industry lies to think of itself as opposing war, he says, and claims that it makes only antiwar films. Filmmakers, however, "have usually depicted the brutality and violence as exciting and as a means to win against implacable enemies without considering the impact and effect such images and messages may have on audiences" (Suid, 2002, p. 199).

4. Frans de Waal is a Dutch American primatologist who's studied the behaviors of chimpanzees, bonobos, and monkeys for more than 40 years. He's gifted researcher and a prolific writer. He has written at great length about family, emotional, and political life among groups of chimps in captivity, and especially about apes' capacity for empathy (2007; 2019). He does not attempt to hide chimps' penchant for violent behavior but he has focused much more intently on their capacities for peace-making and reconciliation. He has also shared video

footage demonstrating monkeys' concern with fairness, suggesting that significant aspects of human morality have their origins among our primate ancestors. https://www.ted.com/talks/frans_de_waal_moral_behavior_in_animals/transcript?language=en.

5. Truth be told, I do feel that I've made a bit of headway; some of my colleagues are showing themselves increasingly willing to stand and protest at our meetings.

Chapter Eight

Everyday War

My confusion about my own PTSD—about whether I have it or not—flows from something more than my inborn tendency to doubt everything. A skeptical hostility toward any and all varieties of war trauma is characteristic of America's culture of self-reliance and lodged itself in my being long ago. By the time Grace was born and my Vietnam experiences were pushing their way toward the surface, Americans' notions about Vietnam vets' problems had fused together around the post-traumatic stress diagnosis, but suspicions about just how widespread PTSD is were simultaneously staking a claim in our national awareness, along with claims of fraud and fakery. Each time I try to get some handle on what I experienced during the war, and how it might be related to the agitation I live with now, I run squarely into a persistent but quite opposite sense that I'm imagining the stress and any residue that might accompany it.

These mutually antagonistic mindsets are so tangled up within my psyche that it's nearly impossible for me to draw coherence out of them. How can I feel so strongly about something I'm not even sure exists? If, some part of my brain tells me, I can successfully deny that anything happened, then maybe it will stop bothering me and go away. This is a legacy of my carefully cultivated ability to block out danger, and of how well that trick served me during the war; I've never abandoned it.

I know for certain that simply trying to confront what happened hasn't proved all that helpful. I am no longer able to block the war out, and I lack the capacity to do much that's useful with the fragments of the war that come back to me. I'm stuck—I can't move forward or back. The moment I recall something, and try to make sense of it, I find myself trying to banish it.

The connections between war and alcohol—Hemingway's giant killer— seem remarkably vivid as I look back at what happened when I quit drinking.

I have a clear recollection from shortly after I started attending AA meetings. This was in early 1992, while I was still mired in my long struggle with the VA over my original PTSD claim. New Jersey's National Guard headquarters are literally alongside the church where I participated in a weekly all-men's AA noontime meeting, and there were often men in uniform at these meetings. One was sitting beside me as my turn to say a few words came one afternoon, and I quite spontaneously started talking about my reaction to his uniform, about the agitation it stirred up, and about how much my experiences in the war seemed connected to my drinking. And then I was immediately embarrassed to hear myself talking about this: I felt like I was seeking sympathy or trying to draw attention to myself as a vet.

This interior conflict never goes away. I often talk at AA meetings about the war's impact on me, because it seems so much a part of my drinking after the war. But I always feel awkward when I do, even though no one's ever responded to me with anything but respect and support. I can see no resolution to this conflict: I need to talk about the war, and it makes me feel uncomfortable to talk about it.

The same confusion strikes in other contexts. When I'm getting my physical therapy treatments at the VA hospital (for a variety of age-related aches and pains) I find myself pondering a contradiction. As the kind of guy who would be a vet, my self-image depends a lot on not acknowledging pain, on showing that I can take whatever the therapist dishes out. At the same time, though, I'm afraid that if I don't show a convincing level of physical pain, they'll think I'm faking it, that I'm malingering. This isn't an especially big deal, but it's something I'm always worrying about.

I once heard a vet crying out painfully in the PT ward in reaction to some of the stretches they were putting him through. It struck me that this was unusual, and I asked my physical therapist about it, knowing that she'd worked at other, nonveteran clinics as well. Did she find a difference in how patients responded to the rigors of therapy? She paused to think, and then said that it hadn't occurred to her before, but that yes, there is a big difference. Vets tend to be much more stoic than non-vets. When I've asked them, other therapists have concurred.

And the uncertainties continue to cascade through many parts of my life. Central to my experience with PTSD have been not only my own doubts that anything significant happened to me, but also the VA's early unwillingness to believe me. Recognizing these habitual suspicions plays an important role in identifying a problem with the whole matter of PTSD. Not only are combat troops conditioned to ignore trauma, but the VA was for a long time predisposed to deny it. The fact that I ultimately prevailed has done little to diminish my own doubts. Despite the documentary evidence and my own lived experience, I continually struggle to believe that I'm really dealing with the disorder.

I've been treated for PTSD in a number of ways. I've received medications and therapy. I improve for a time, think I'm better, leave the treatment, and find the symptoms returning. I'm not sure why I don't like taking medications, but I don't. They're helpful, and reduce some of my symptoms, but I identify relying on meds with weakness. Once I get comfortable I decide I can live without them. And then I'm crazy again.

For a time, Zoloft (sertraline) helped me a bit, until whatever relief it provided was overshadowed by its negative impact on my sexual performance. My sense of my manhood remains tied to my sexuality whether I like it or not. Shifting to Wellbutrin (bupropion) not only cleared up that problem but helped chase away many of my nightmares. [1]

I know some readers will ask why I call myself crazy. It's because the most obvious symptoms of my PTSD, for me, are my responses to stimuli that aren't present. I find myself back in the war, frightened and fairly sure I'm about to die. The fact that neuroscientists can explain this doesn't do away with the fact that one of the ways we define crazy is responding to stimuli that aren't present.

For nearly as long as I can remember, I've heard accounts of men making spurious claims about their exploits or service in Vietnam, telling stories that have later proved false. In *Stolen Valor* Burkett particularly focuses on phony stories told by marginalized men, but high-ranking military officers, politicians, businessmen, and others manufacture similar fables. I assume that this sort of fabrication has been more or less constant throughout human history. The phrase "war story" has multiple meanings, but at least one of them is essentially synonymous with "fish story," that is, a tale that blows things way out of proportion.

In that sense, there's not much new here. What makes Vietnam vets particularly prone to scrutiny is the way war's psychic damages have shifted out of the shadows and into the spotlight in the wake of Vietnam. Psychoneurosis and related diagnoses were familiar after World War I (Kardiner, 1941; Fussell, 1975) and were common in World War II, and treated sympathetically in films like *Random Harvest* (a 1942 film about a World War I veteran suffering from combat-induced amnesia) and *I'll be Seeing You* (a 1944 movie in which Joseph Cotten convincingly portrays a Marine suffering from "psychoneurosis" following combat in the South Pacific). For reasons I don't think we really understand, though, these sorts of medical diagnoses in time seem to become shameful and are soon hidden away. Whatever the cause, the diagnosis was brushed aside in the wake of World War II, into the realm of things we don't usually talk about in polite society. [2]

PTSD FRAUD

In American society in general, and in our military in particular, there has always been enormous ambivalence about the psychological consequences of war. We can see one of the peculiar offshoots of this conflict in my own fears about having my PTSD diagnosis doubted.

"Catch-22," the fictional protocol giving its name to the novel that prompted me to enlist, was in part directed exactly at the military's preoccupation with keeping troops from shirking their duties. At the center of Heller's story is the notion that if a flier is crazy, then he must be grounded. If, however, a flier reports *himself* as crazy—so that he won't have to fly more missions—then he's exhibiting an entirely reasonable and rational concern for his own safety. He thus demonstrates that he's not crazy and must therefore continue flying.

In the military, of course, this fear that troops might be malingering or gold-bricking, that is, finding excuses to avoid doing their duty, is intense. Stories of men shooting their own toes or legs as a means of escaping further exposure to danger are common. And since cowardice is an unacceptable excuse, there are those who logically resort to claims of trauma as a means of withdrawing from exposure to danger.

But the larger issue here has to do with paying financial compensation to those who have been permanently disabled in connection with their military service. This is what the VA calls a "service connected" disability rating, and it's a potent source of debate. I'm going to skip over most of the dispute here, but plenty of people think that paying disability compensation discourages veterans from getting better and then going to work.[3] I have no reason to think that these things don't sometimes happen but shutting down an entire system or policy merely because it can be abused doesn't make a lot of sense. I doubt that these critics would argue for doing away with the military just because a lot of its own troops are killed by friendly fire and training mishaps.

In *The Harmony of Illusions* Michael Young (1995) places this outlook in historical perspective. His book provides an anthropologist's account of a PTSD in-patient ward or "domicile" at a VA medical center, and it's relevant to my story in two distinct ways. First, Young's history of psychological trauma makes it clear that these sorts of diagnoses have always been doubted. Whenever there's a chance of benefitting from injury, possibilities of fakery and fraud lurk nearby.

What's more interesting is the fact that compensating people for injuries and losses is an ancient practice that originally had nothing to do with the military. And so are fears that the process will be abused. But these concerns become vastly more prevalent in societies like ours that measure nearly everything in terms of money. People who aren't receiving payments either feel that they should be included or are angered by seeing others getting something they don't. Insurance fraud, including Medicare and welfare fraud, is among a vast array of related scams that are major areas of crime in contemporary America. If there's money to be gained, we can be sure people are scheming to get illicit access to it.

In this larger context, fraudulent PTSD claims for financial compensation are probably a minor issue, but one that particularly angers many people, especially veterans, because it intersects with so many questions about legitimate claims to honor, to valor, and to medals.

Let me explain how this affects me. I appear, I know, to be a man in full. Or as Zorba says, "Wife; children; house; everything. The full catastrophe." I've had a successful career as a scholar and teacher. How can anything seriously ail me? I ask myself this almost every day, and I assume that there are plenty of other vets asking similar questions.

But that, after all, is the point. What I call the craziness inside me actually drives much of my outward success in the first place. It partly explains my ability to block out distractions and to focus myself entirely on what needs to be done. My reliance on alcohol to quiet and hide my turmoil well enough to socialize with the elders in my field, and to engage in the essential activity of modern professional life, networking, enabled me to learn where I needed to place my focus and how to navigate the shoal waters of academia. When it became clear that booze was no longer a helpful adaptation and I quit drinking, I quickly ran aground. I call it the contradiction of sobriety: becoming conscious of what was ailing me in turn exposed me to all sorts of troubles I'd managed to cover up by self-medicating.

Fortunately, I'd built up enough momentum and goodwill, and had enough innate savvy left to continue on when I quit. But now I struggle continuously with stuff I used to be able to skip past. I can barely manage to handle my professional obligations and I spend much of my time trying simply to survive. And yet the residual skills, toughness, and *thumos* that I carry from fighting the war are still there.

I ask again, how can I be disabled—receive compensation—when I'm productive enough to write this book? How can I function so well if I'm so screwed up? To be honest, I don't know, but one answer that occurs to me is another of my favorite Shakespeare lines, from *Hamlet*: "I am but mad north-north-west. When the wind is southerly, I know a hawk from a handsaw."

And that may be the best answer. When I need to, I can perform. That is, after all, what I got from the war. It's in the nature of what afflicts me that I deny the affliction in order to keep performing. And if I'm performing then it must mean that I don't have it. But that's exactly what confuses those of us who live with this. It's a direct product of the orneriness that allowed us to perform in combat, hiding the truth from ourselves; we just keep on doing what has to be done, despite what it's doing to us. We interpret the fact that we could do it during the war to mean that if it didn't bother us then, it shouldn't bother us now.

But there's another telling point in Young's account of the PTSD domicile. The professionals working with the vets there use a standardized model, one that draws on the underlying concept that some very specific, particular event traumatized each of these men. Treatment is organized around getting patients to recognize and understand what happened when each underwent his own individual traumatic experience.

Young's work was conducted with Vietnam vets some years ago and it may well be that things have changed significantly as the VA has sought to respond to our current wave of veterans, and treatment for PTSD varies by VA facility and by individual practitioner, so I don't want to generalize too broadly. But my knowledge and experience of approaches to the treatment of PTSD is that many practitioners still rely on the notion that its onset must be traced to some *specific* traumatic event. That is basically how the Diagnostic and Statistical Manual discusses PTSD: a particular event outside the normal realm of human experience causes traumatic stress. I don't want to deny that this is the case—who am I to challenge the experts?—but it's very much my own sense that in the context of war, this doesn't explain a great many of the cases, including my own. This leads to an aspect of PTSD I think of as "lamination."

LAMINATION

Inherent in what I've been calling everyday danger is something more, a process I call lamination. It is phenomenon akin to what clinicians refer to as "complex PTSD." When I was originally applying for a disability rating the VA insisted, in line with general perceptions of PTSD, that I identify—and more importantly, document—a *particular, specific* event that caused the trauma I underwent. In my own experience of the war there were specific events or stressors, to be sure, but none of them loomed as large for me, and to my sense of what happened to me, as the long, slow build-up of stress that came from the everyday danger inherent in the work I did on the flight deck, in the air, and in the shop.

I use this notion of lamination as a way to describe what is probably not all that unusual in certain types of situations. A combatant, for instance, does something very stressful as part of a regular routine. In order to do it again the following day, he or she represses or minimizes it. And then does the same thing again the next day, and the next; with each passing day layers of stress are laid down one on top of the other, like laminations. The weight of each succeeding layer presses down more heavily on the early layers as the whole slowly builds up.

I am drawing an analogy here with laminated wood, which is stronger than naturally occurring wood. Natural or normal wood has weak points along the grain. Because the grains run in different directions in the many layers of a laminate, however, these inherent weaknesses are cancelled out. Plywood, for example, is made up of multiple layers, with the grains running in multiple directions, and is much stronger than normal wood of the same thickness.

People in combat and first responders, for example, undergo this process of lamination, as I see it. They deal with stress each day, but it may not ordinarily be of an intensity or degree that would qualify for the DSM's definition of a stressor. Each day they set aside this stress, and the following day new stress is added as an additional layer and again set aside. In time, these daily layers of stress are compressed together, one atop the other, to create a deep and almost impenetrable slab of stress. The resultant trauma can prove to be nearly impervious to the sorts treatment that are designed to deal with a single stressful, trauma-inducing incident.

EMDR

So far, nothing has vanquished my doubts about my own condition, although one drastic treatment did give me some measure of respite from them. I'm speaking of my experience with a treatment called EMDR, Eye Movement Desensitization and Reprocessing. I first heard of it back in the 1990s, but it sounded sort of bogus to me and I put no stock in it. As the wars in Iraq and Afghanistan ground on, with both civilian and military casualties rising, my sanity seemed to be failing me. At times I was in such emotional distress that it felt like my skin was being flayed off, and my emotional state continued spiraling downward. There were times when I was so nearly catatonic that I couldn't leave the house. Medication and therapy weren't doing the trick. I was thinking about ways to end my life, as a means of escaping the pain. One night I expressed my anguish at an AA meeting and Larry, a Gulf War vet I knew from that meeting—a guy I had reason to trust—told me afterwards about the EMDR treatment he'd received and how it had helped him. I felt that I'd run out of options and so I set my skepticism aside. I began EMDR treatment with a skilled practitioner, Gina Colelli.

I recall saying "I'm desperate" as I first walked into her office. I should probably explain what I meant by that, but I'm not sure I know. I was losing my grip, it seemed, and feeling continually threatened. It wasn't paranoia, though—I didn't feel that specific people or things were threatening me. The danger, the threat, was inside of me. I simply intuited that I was about to fall apart. But even as I expressed this overwhelming sense of desperation, my doubts persisted. As always, a major chunk of what ailed me included the voices—patterns from within the culture around me—telling me I was making it all up. They told me that nothing bad had happened to me. That I should feel guilty for making false claims about what I was experiencing.

And in some ways, the single most helpful piece of the EMDR treatment was the inescapably clear evidence that I was *not* making it up.

EMDR treatment proceeds in several different ways, but the core principle lies in setting up a left-right separation between the brain's two hemispheres by using alternating lights, sounds, or touch. The person being treated calls to mind problematic memories associated with trauma and free associates about them. As I understand it, and I'm sure there's debate about this, the general idea is that this then allows the brain to shift memories from areas where it cannot properly process them to areas where it can. All I can tell you is what I experienced with it, which was so unsettling, painful, and scary that I could just barely tolerate it. My experience was idiosyncratic, I'm told, and others experience it quite differently.

What stands out most sharply in my recollections of the treatment are my physical reactions to it. My entire body spasmed violently. I rocked and jerked in my seat, and sometimes in response to the psychic pain I involuntarily flew up out of it. I was often ready to flee the room, and it was only by exercising every bit of self-restraint I had that I managed to stay in my seat. I went for a 90-minute session each week. Because I was so disoriented by the treatment, I can't even recall much of what happened. But I know that I was pushed nearly to the limit of what I could handle and that I was exhausted and disoriented after each session, sometimes for hours.

I stayed with Gina and EMDR for 3 years, though as time went on my physical responses quieted down and we did less and less of it and more basic talk therapy. Three things in particular stand out. First, and most memorably, my involuntary physical reactions to the EMDR process convinced me that my post-traumatic stress is real.

This sounds odd to me as I write it, but I don't know how else to phrase it. As I've said, my symptoms have always included doubt, but it was hard—impossible—for me to doubt what I was experiencing during the EMDR. I simply could not ignore or deny the spasming and flopping around. At last, I thought, I have clear proof that this is real, and not imagined. I would love to say that this erased my doubts once and for all, but now, a few years later, the doubts have returned. They're not as strong or pervasive as they once were—I now know the doubts themselves are false—but for me they seem, in the final analysis, to be a fundamental part of the traumatic experience itself.

Though I had long assumed that what I carried with me from the war wasn't solely about the war itself, I was wary of acknowledging this. Early on in my experiences with the VA, their psychiatric board told me my problems stemmed from my childhood, not from stress I'd experienced in the war. Their conclusion apparently rested on the presumption that these were separate and exclusive realms. Over the years I'd slowly been coming to see that the ways I experienced the things I'd done in the war, and the things that happened to me, were not simply consequences of the war, but also of what I brought with me to the war. My drive, my willingness to continually endanger myself, and my desire to do something heroic: these all shaped both what I did and how it impacted me. Gina soon pointed out that after I'd worked through and peeled away some of the ways the war had affected me, I was likely to find issues underlying the war. I was ready to deal with this, and that's exactly what we found.

Second, as Gina repeatedly explained to me, one of the neurological consequences of war trauma is the propensity to see danger everywhere and thus to be almost constantly in a state of heightened arousal and alert. This, she said, is like walking in the woods and mistakenly seeing every fallen branch as a poisonous snake. The trouble here, of course, is that you're so continuously aroused that you fail to spot the real snake when it appears.

The problem for me, I found, lies in the force with which the stress I experienced in the war imprinted itself on me. It's lodged in my soul, my spirit, in my flesh and bones. Whenever something triggers a sense of danger or threat and I feel anxiety, my senses respond to the stimulus as if it's something from the war. When something causes anxiety, my nervous system returns to war. I feel that I'm back in the war and the threat enlarges itself. I grow increasingly tense and wary. And even when the EMDR helped me clear away much of this distraction, I still carried the older, more deeply entrenched issues. When something triggers them, though, my nervous system immediately returns to wartime defense measures. In the same way that some of my early, formative experiences are always going to be with me, it looks like I will always respond to things that evoke the war as if they're threats to my bodily integrity.

Third, EMDR did clear away some of the physiological symptoms I deal with. The involuntary spasming, while horrible in itself, eventually moved bits and pieces of what had been stored up deep inside me to a more directly physical realm; this allowed me, in turn, to shed some of it. In the same way that earlier medication had allowed me to deal with fireworks and helicopters, EMDR allowed me to deal with simple aspects of daily life, like merely going out of doors. And I got past some of the anguish over the US wars in the Middle East. It felt as though some of the rage was being tempered.

WHY WE FIGHT

EMDR and medications have helped me stand back far enough and calmly enough, at least at times, to gain some perspective on just how the war that persists inside me imposes itself on my *everyday* life. I have some sense of why I fight every goddamned day.

There's a fairly common notion that understanding our emotional histories can lead quite directly to resolving them. I've discovered that's not the case—for me, at least. Instead, as I've dug into my experiences during the war, and come to see how blind I was to them and tried to make sense of them in terms of what I've been calling "everyday danger," the feelings rise closer and closer to the surface. Behavior and thoughts that I'd taken for granted—simple aspects of everyday life—I now understand quite differently. I see how the war lies in wait just beneath the surface, and how seemingly insignificant everyday disturbances keep the trauma alive.

It's taken me a long, long time to get to this point; over the years I've dug deeply into it, picking at layer after layer of scar tissue. This was at first objective and distant. I wrote simple and basic descriptions as I prepared my VA claim. Only later, when I took a memoir-writing class and shaped some of the simple descriptions into what I came to understand as everyday danger, did I begin to recognize the feelings. That's when I saw that my impulse to curl up in a ball, which often strikes when I'm feeling psychological stress, was about my experiences out on the flight deck and up in the radome, and my bodily postures there, not simply a fetal position.

Even now, more than 50 years later, two subtly different movements of my right arm bracket my experiences in the war, telling very different stories and at times haunting me almost continually. Many times each day, in my mind's eye my right arm swings up, either choreographing my saber salute as I present the brigade in boot camp or reaching frantically to add power as we're about to land on the pitching carrier deck. Wielding the saber reminds me of the respect the Navy paid me, and the rewards I earned there. Grabbing for the throttles conjures up the stress I experienced with every mission I flew.

As I wrote, some of what I'd done in the war began to take on a new light. I was slowly growing aware of how consistently I'd put myself into hazardous positions, and how often I risked my life. I realized that when I speak of how often I risked my life I'm not exaggerating. I was doing these things not merely on a daily basis, but often many times in a day. Day after day. Along with a growing awareness of what I'd done out on Yankee Station came an explosion of other issues. It's as if embers that I'd carefully banked and covered had been exposed to the air and burst into roaring flame. I was suddenly awash with doubt, guilt and pride, denial, comparisons with the experiences of infantrymen, and anger.

As I decided to leave the EMDR treatment I found myself ready, finally, to begin writing this book. I'd been scribbling bits and pieces of my experiences for a few years, but I was at last getting some sense of the whole. I knew what I wanted to do. I'd often read, seen, or heard things that made me want to explain what I'd learned, but I'd never found a path that would lead me through it. This time it was different, and it must have been the EMDR that made the difference. I knew where I was going. It seemed simple enough: the circumstances that led me into the war, the ways in which these shaped the way I experienced the war, and the ways these experiences shaped my life after the war.

I'd been caught in sort of a trap for 15 years after my divorce, driven in part by an existential contradiction that I was very much aware of. With the sole exception of Grace, who was at center of my life, I really didn't want to be with people. At the same time, though, I didn't want to be alone. I unceasingly sought out relationships with women, each of them failing in turn. Something wasn't working for me. But at just about the same time that I started with the EMDR, I met Annette, and this time something clicked.

Navigation, the Kitchen, Socializing—My Everyday War Continues

There are, of course, still more contradictions. They come in the shape of all the war neuroses that rise to the surface as I've immersed myself in writing and teaching about the war and wars. Again, I flail around in pain. I've become so used to it over the years that at times it's hard for me to see. But this time, Annette could see what the work was doing to me. She fretted, and pleaded, and chided, and ultimately insisted until I agreed to go back to the VA for medication. Between the support she provides me and the peace of mind the medication allows, I've managed to inch my way through this.

Annette is a lightning rod for some of the most visible, practical, day-in and day-out problems that I live with. Issues of guilt and anger seem so omnipresent that at times I take them for granted, but they rush quickly to the surface when I'm dealing with intimate relationships or with authority. They push me to resist, and they seem to shape many of my personal interactions. A series of recurring situations can and do have great impact on my marriage.

Navigation

I've told you of my plane's border incursion into Red China, not because it represents what everything I experienced in the war was like—it doesn't— but because it supplies vivid images for so much of stress that isn't otherwise visible. But that episode did impact the rest of my life. It made what is for most people a fairly simple activity that doesn't involve a lot of emotion into something that is loaded with meaning for me, *navigation*: finding your way from one place to another.

That China incident was one of the few times I became truly aware of being about to die. At the moment it happened, the likelihood of escaping seemed nil, and I had to deliberately, consciously drive the recollection of it from my mind if I was going to climb back into the plane for my next mission. It's a focal point of the entire war experience for me, even if it was a one-off occurrence. But there was more to it than just my stark fear of dying. I was also afraid that I'd be held responsible for what happened, since I bore the responsibility for the equipment that failed.

In terms of the incident's lasting impact on me, there's yet another piece to it. I was the navigator, accountable for where our plane was in a war theater where we continually brushed up against enemy airspace. When my radar failed and the pilot suddenly had to navigate, he couldn't handle it (partly because he'd become so accustomed to and reliant on my radar). It was a navigation error that got us into trouble; I was supposed to do the navigating; and even though it was the pilot's error, I felt responsible. In my moral and emotional calculus, I almost got us killed. It shouldn't come as a surprise that navigation remains a heavily charged activity for me.

One of the most basic points I've been trying to make in this book is that the ability to set aside or ignore danger successfully leads those who are able to do so to believe that this is a good thing. Repressing or ignoring traumatic experiences can grow into a habit. We continue doing it long after it has served its purpose. But there are areas of vulnerability where the trauma leaks out and we find our capacity for ignoring it challenged, and even overwhelmed. These days, navigating, especially while traveling in unfamiliar places, is one of the ways my trauma blasts its way through whatever equanimity I have achieved.

Not knowing exactly where they are while driving a car is for most people a minor inconvenience, especially now that phones and cars are equipped with GPS. For me, though, being lost rises quickly to the intensity of a life and death matter. I've seen this in the course of two marriages and realize now that it's not coincidental. The ability to read a map quickly and accurately and to focus automatically and simultaneously on the exact spot you're at, on your destination, and on the surrounding terrain feels to me like a necessary part of every adult's survival skills. When I'm driving and the person in the seat next to me—ordinarily my wife—can't immediately give me all the exact and correct directions I need, it isn't the minor matter of inconvenience that it seems to them. For most folks, this sort of thing is amusing. But I feel I'm going to die. That's not the conscious thought, but it's the underlying fear that makes me so desperate.

What exacerbates the problem is the extreme difference in how we experience the situation. I grow agitated, while my companion is puzzled. To them, my agitation is entirely out of proportion to the nature of the problem. I, however, experience the lack of concern about where exactly we are as a lack of concern for my life and safety. I grow even more upset. My involuntary and unconscious sense is that I'm going to get killed. And their inability to comprehend the threat I'm experiencing upsets me even more—how can any competent adult not grasp the dire nature of this life-or-death situation?

I've finally come to understand what's going on when this happens. But comprehending it doesn't really do much to alleviate it. And this is the crux of the entire problem of PTSD for me. I've spoken of my sense that there's a common notion, certainly not universal but nonetheless widespread, that gaining an understanding of the trauma and learning to accommodate its impact or to think differently about it can eradicate or at least alleviate the symptoms (and I'm referring to what I know of Cognitive Behavior Therapy). In some cases, this works, I'm sure. But even now that I understand why my emotional system quickly surges to intense fear and anxiety, and then dire agitation at having my life held so lightly, it doesn't make the problem go away.

When I try to explain this recurring scenario, what I usually hear is that we should be using GPS. Sounds like good advice, but we have a couple of them and they don't do me a lot of good. It's not just the concrete question of location, but the underlying emotions and the feeling that my life is threatened by the person with me—who doesn't really care that they're scaring the bejesus out of me—that are at issue.

At an elementary, practical level the problem is that I don't trust anyone else's navigation, and that includes a GPS. Trusting someone else seems likely to get me killed. I need to know not only where I am and my spatial relationship to our destination, but alternative routes and what the surrounding terrain looks like. I need to know what the possible escape routes look like. Experience has taught me not to believe many of the GPS's decisions. I want to have a full picture of where I am and where I'm heading, and I can't manage that while I'm driving in unfamiliar territory. It would be simpler, of course, if I trusted my companion's driving and I held the maps and GPS and did all the navigation. But I also don't trust other drivers; I want to be in control.

And this isn't limited to traveling by car. Even making my way through New York City by subway can bring the syndrome far too close to the surface. Something in me locks into a mode that insists on getting where we're going in the fastest, most efficient way. I experience anything that interrupts me in my need to navigate the subway system as efficiently as possible as a threat to my wellbeing. And while it's happening I can't really see it. I experience what is almost like the instinctual drive of, let us say, a salmon swimming upstream to spawn. Anything that disrupts my efforts to move through the system this way feels like it's intended to thwart me.

Sometimes I'm aware of what's happening to me. But when I'm caught in the middle of one of these simple travel incidents, I'm usually unaware of it. Only afterwards, when my wife and I have to sort out the tension that accompanied our trip, can we reconstruct the ways in which the stress flared up, and disrupted communication between us.

Add in my discomfort with sitting and talking to people, which makes me quite antisocial, and you can see why I drive my wife nuts. I depend on my relationship with Annette for nearly all my interpersonal interactions, and because I tend to get riled when we travel and irritable when we socialize, we have problems. If the abrasion were limited to only these sorts of scrapes, I'd say there were limits to the ways the war continually intrudes into my daily life. But in the same way that the incursion into China is really just the tip of the iceberg, in terms of the war's long-term impacts on me, it's the day-in and day-out stress aboard ship while repairing and maintaining our aircraft— what I've called the everyday danger—that pervades my daily existence now, not just that one big event.

In the Kitchen

On its face, the problem is hardly unique. Two adults with long-standing habits and preferences accommodating, with more or less success, to life together. This can seem minor and insignificant, and if the background rooted in the war weren't there, it really wouldn't be very significant. What I'm talking about here are differences in household domestic styles, especially in the kitchen. Where does one put utensils and the myriad other things that fill a kitchen? Who replaces supplies that have been used up? Each of us has idiosyncratic ways of doing things that can lead to small-scale chafing. Sound familiar?

The problem for me is that I experience aspects of everyday life through a framework created during the war. A couple of examples should make this clear. When Annette uses a kitchen towel, for instance, she tends to set it down where she's working. This is reasonable—she may want to use it again in a moment. But my experience from the war, working with shared tools and supplies for our equipment with other technicians who may be elsewhere at the time, or who work the opposite shift, is that everything has to have its place, so one knows where to find it in a trice. My habit is to not think of something until the moment I need it, and then to reach for it. I need it at that moment, and if it's not there, my rhythm is broken, my concentration broken, and I fear I can't do the job right. I habitually and unthinkingly return things to where they were when I started to use them.

In our kitchen, dishtowels hang from the handle of the oven. Unless, of course, Annette is using one, in which case there's not much likelihood that she's returned it there. For me, having to stop and look for the towel, although a very minor thing in and of itself, is actually quite disruptive. If you think this is such an insignificant matter that it isn't worthy of attention, you are mostly right. Except that for me, not finding an implement I need when I reach for it sets off alarm bells, and then a whole set of concerns about getting whatever task I'm engaged in completed in a timely, efficient manner. And when my thought process is disrupted in this way, I'm agitated. I can't do what needs to be done. How could someone disrupt the process, thereby threating the mission and endangering me and the others? In short, the war is always there, waiting to resurface.

I have a couple of small utility knives that I use for all sorts of non-culinary tasks. I don't use them for food because they're exposed to every sort of contaminant. When we merged our kitchens, I discovered that my wife's sense of order is different enough from mine that she doesn't discriminate in this way and is apt to use these for preparing food. After asking her several times not to use them for food and seeing that she simply couldn't remember which knives I was calling attention to and which purposes I was excluding them from, I figured out that if I wanted them to be kept away from food, I had to approach the matter in a different way. I placed them in a different drawer, hidden UNDER the clean dishtowels, where there are no other utensils. She simply doesn't see them and doesn't use them.

I don't think it would make a lot of difference if we used them indiscriminately. I recognize this as a minor fetish of mine, part of my overall sense of using the right tool for the right job. (One of the radio techs in my squadron spoke of this in an unforgettable way: "Don't force it," he'd say. "Use a larger hammer.") But the point here is that this seemingly minor disruption causes me enough anxiety, frequently enough, that I've had to find ways to reduce it.

I've grown enough to see that the problem is mine, not hers, and can take the steps necessary to avoid conflict. But this doesn't make the underlying cause go away, nor does it reduce the symptomatic expression. I simply remove the source of friction by adapting to it. My domestic life is full of these minor shoals and I have to do a lot of navigating to work around them. The state of awareness and behavior modification this calls for keeps me constantly conscious of the craziness. I can manage it, and live with it, only by remaining perpetually aware of it. And that's exhausting, especially when all the ingredients are sitting on the counter, the potatoes are hot, and the potato masher is nowhere to be found.

One more example, again nearly insignificant in and of itself: making sure that there are adequate supplies. When something starts to run low, well before it starts to run out, I have to make sure that there's a replacement supply in place.

In fact, the moment I open a new container, even of something that may last for months, I buy another (or three, if they're on sale). When I needed to replace a vacuum tube in order to fix a radar scope out on Yankee Station, I needed it right then. In the early days of the Kennedy administration, Defense Secretary McNamara's whiz kids in the Pentagon had introduced a complex set of administrative procedures that required everything to be documented and fed into to data bases. One consequence of this was that each replacement part had to be ordered with a standardized form, in quadruplicate, and processed. Once we had diagnosed a problem and figured out which part had failed, and were ready to replace it, there would be a long wait, sometimes days or even weeks, especially at sea, before we obtained the part. As I explained in Chapter 4, we learned how to order extra spare parts and keep them in the shop.

When we replaced a part, we did it with a part from our hidden stocks and then formally ordered a new one (or three). This is something that anyone in the military is familiar with and is essentially what people who work in sprawling organizational systems now call a "work-around." But when I reach for an ingredient in the kitchen and find out that my wife has used up our stock but not laid in a replacement, I once again experience it as a threat to completing the mission. For lack of a better word, I get ridiculously agitated by the notion that someone could be so thoughtless about completing the mission and about our safety. What seems like a minor household contretemps is for me a threat to my bodily integrity. (To her credit, she now tries to show me when she has laid in a fresh stock of something, so that I don't immediately purchase the same items.)

This seems like a simple enough misunderstanding, hardly one to fuss over. And at one level, it is. But it is equally the case that every time I use a particular item, I'm thinking about when I'll need to replace it, and thus about whether I need to factor in more data about how fast it's being depleted. And so, as I move around the house, from kitchen to bathroom especially, my mind is perpetually struggling with the problem of whether I should ask Annette if she's been using one product or another. It's difficult to convince her that I'm not being critical, and it's difficult to convince myself that I don't really need to know how fast we're using up the dental floss.

These are not flashbacks or intrusive thoughts, per se. They're feelings, and the feelings evoke situations in the war. I don't remember having these feelings during the war. I don't think I was usually conscious of these sorts of feelings—or any others, for that matter—during the war, but when I find myself in a situation that evokes them now, I conflate it with the war—that is, with the sense of imminent danger. Now, a half-century on, the war is still with me much of the time. This is a sort of everyday stress that just isn't well understood.

WHAT MY PTSD LOOKS LIKE

The popular image of a PTSD eruption is some version of reliving the episode. For me, it's not a matter of seeing myself in combat when a towel isn't replaced, but of a feeling that my security is threatened, and of feeling that my efforts to do what's necessary to protect myself are being thwarted. And at that moment the anger is directed toward my partner, not at the war or those who sent me to it. As a consequence, *we fight*.

As I've grown more aware of what's going on, the condition has gradually morphed. Now I understand that what I'm feeling isn't about my partner, or myself, but about the war. And that's when I feel I'm back in the war, which leads in turn to anger, rather than fear. "God damn you," I think. "Why did you do this to me?" I'm not really sure just who I'm talking to, which is why I quickly turn the anger on myself: "Why in the hell did you do this, Glenn? How could I have been so naïve, so stupid?" And so a misplaced kitchen towel—one of an array of minor things that happen many times every day—quickly escalates into a PTSD episode. *This* is why I spend so much time agitated and feel so crazy. The PTSD is so deeply embedded in me that the normal flow of everyday life repeatedly pushes it into erupting.

Think about this: I feel that no matter how hard I work, something's going to go wrong, and no matter how much back-up there's supposed to be, it will fail. And it's my way to take on responsibility for everything. So no matter what I do, I'm in trouble.

The raw material for all this originates in my childhood, but it's been forged in the fires of the war. I'm always on edge, ready for calamity to strike. And it's the simplest, most innocuous things that set it off. It's not nightmares and flashbacks that plague me so much as it is *everyday* life, filled with the residue of everyday danger.

This is the world I live in. It seems absurd to me. I don't defend it. I apologize to my wife when I get upset. She's behaving in a perfectly normal, reasonable way. *I'm* the one reacting in an uncalled-for way. But that's the way it is. This is why the war remains simultaneously so unseen and yet so powerful. It's always there, just below the surface, exploding into consciousness at the least likely moments. And when I do experience it, I'm back in the war again, trying to deal with danger. I could list lots of other things that set off this chain reaction, but I think you get the idea.

What I've come to see in the last few years, as I become increasingly aware of war's continuing impact on me, is something that seems truly bizarre. Something in some situation I'm dealing with, or in the environment I'm in, or simply in the chain of free association my mind is making, produces a feeling of anxiety. I'm talking about mild, general anxiety, the everyday, garden-variety that most people experience from time to time and that neurotics feel much of the time. But this initially simple sense of anxiety will summon up feelings I'd managed to hide or ignore during the war—which is what I most identify anxiety with. So a fairly normal, passing wave of anxiety brings the war to mind. Then I'm thinking about the war, and the war stokes even greater anxiety in me. And there I am, back in the war again. This sort of thing happens frequently.

This doesn't plague me unremittingly. It comes and it goes, though I'm not sure what brings it on. But when the dread is present and active, the war can flare up out of my bones and into my consciousness dozens, scores of times, during a day. It is debilitating. It affects not just my sense of well-being and composure, but how I feel about people around me, how I respond to them, and how I experience them as threats.

I have great difficulty being around other people, socializing with them. And a lot of it has to do with this rising and falling tide of war-driven anxiety. It's a phenomenon that no amount of pondering has clarified for me; I simply feel a strong, sometimes overwhelming need to defend myself when I'm in social situations. It's not paranoia. I don't imagine others are out to hurt me. And most of the time it doesn't have much to do with who's actually present. I can sometimes engage comfortably with people I've never met, and often have trouble dealing with people I know and like.

Some of this is a simple aversion to small talk, something many folks share with me. But there's more to it than that. It's not just that I have a hard time—that is, that I don't want to talk to people—it's that I become acutely conscious of the discomfort I'm feeling. And I get upset with myself. And the more critical of myself I am, the more conscious I am of my agitation. Within minutes, my mind becomes a seething cauldron of restless confusion; I feel like I may explode at any moment. I feel increasingly vulnerable, increasingly under threat of attack, and I start preparing to defend myself. I'm apt to find a wall to stand against. Threats I'm experiencing evoke, again, the threats the war once posed to my personal security. I'm not merely uncomfortable, I am beside myself with agitation. I want to escape, but I feel trapped by social convention. In the past 15 years or so I've found myself becoming increasingly reclusive. I don't want to be with other people.

I am articulate, engaging, and passionate. People want to talk to me, but I keep pushing myself away. This has the perverse effect of making me appear elusive and all the more interesting. I get angrier and angrier with myself. I try to engage, to find ways to socialize, but I haven't yet. Most of the time when I'm with people I'm thinking about being somewhere else. At some level this is a textbook case of introversion, I know. But it's introversion on steroids.

I've grappled with this notion of everyday danger for years now. But I never entirely understood why it's such a big deal for me. I could see that it's related to what I call the hiatus—to the decades when I didn't know what happened to me in the war because I couldn't see it, given what I'd thought war was supposed to look like. But now I understand another dimension. The war is always with me precisely because of the everyday character of the dangers I faced.

For me, danger is more likely to inhere in small things, things out of place, placed incorrectly, not paying close enough attention to where we are on the map, not focusing properly on our surroundings. When I reach for something and it's not there when I need it, I experience it as a threat to my life. It's not an explosion or the sound of the general quarters klaxon, necessarily, that summon up the war. It's reaching for something when I need it and not finding it that agitates me, but much more than that, it's that I feel an angry, moral surge: how could someone be so heedless as to put me into danger? The danger and the moral component reside in these trivial things. The body keeps score, as I'm about to explain. It wasn't the explosions and gunfire, but the war's seriousness, exactness, and ubiquity that carried over for me.

Once I started understanding everyday danger, and how it lodged itself in my body, I could try to explain how the day-in, day-out work on equipment in demanding, exhausting, hazardous conditions seeped into my body and soul. And, ironically, all this insight has done me some good. I've been able to express my agitation and confusion much more clearly. The VA recently reevaluated me and increased my disability ratings for both hearing loss (which plays a big part in how insistently I avoid social interactions) and PTSD.

THE NEUROBIOLOGY

I've held off saying much about scientific research on trauma and stress. I feel that I should tell you why, but I'm not sure I know why, other than to say that it hasn't felt like it's been called for . . . until now. I've told you that I doubt nearly every reaction or response I have to the war, and that these doubts add another layer to my confusion and discomfort. But as we've been teaching about war together my colleague, psychologist Glenn Albright, has introduced me to a wide range of research and I've been educating myself as well. This has helped me steadily gain insight into why I experience the war's impact on me the way I do.

An incredible amount of work has been done on a wide variety of war-related traumas, among other things. Several books have made an especially powerful impression on me, Judith Herman's (1997) *War and Trauma*, Bertel van der Kolk's (2014) *The Body Keeps the Score*, and Jonathan Shay's (1995) *Achilles in Vietnam*.[4] Van der Kolk's book draws on both clinical treatment and laboratory research and I'm going to use it to stand for the findings of all three.

Van der Kolk roots his approach in the proposition that trauma is by definition "unbearable and intolerable." Troops who've experienced combat trauma try to drive it from awareness, but it takes enormous amounts of energy to hold it at bay (2014, pp. 1–2). Men in combat are placed in untenable positions; their flight/fight/freeze responses are thwarted, natural biochemistry and neurobiology are compromised and overridden, and the brain's neural pathways are permanently disrupted (p. 30). Following trauma, an individual's nervous system has distinctly altered perceptions of risk and safety (p. 86). As a consequence, he says, "*the body keeps the score,*" that is, our bodies register threats, while our conscious minds remain oblivious (p. 88, all italics added).

Among the ways people who've been traumatized compensate for these changes in their neural makeup is by focusing intensely on their work or studies, thus allowing them to ignore the injury (pp. 9–10, 200). These individuals are also apt to numb themselves, and to avoid interpersonal contacts and relationships. Van der Kolk describes, for example, *men going numb* at their children's birthday parties and at family meals (p. 85). And when these strategies don't work well enough, they *turn to alcohol and drugs* (pp. 94, 99). The *birth of a child* can heighten the conflict, as calls for nurturing collide with emotional distance and habits and behaviors that are used to dull emotional connections (pp. 15, 76).

At the same time, he says, being able to feel safe with other people is probably the single most important aspect of mental health (p. 81). In this sense, vets with PTSD often have *difficulty with any sort of socializing,* which reinforces the condition's effects.

Van der Kolk also notes that "*pre-existing temperament*" can shape responses to trauma (p. 78). In particular, *adults who've experienced trauma as children* may adapt very differently than adults who deal with traumatic events in adulthood (p. 257). In comparing soldiers' traumatic stress disorders in the wake of World Wars I and II with what's happened since the Vietnam War, he found that the disorders have expressed themselves in very different ways, leading him to conclude that "*culture shapes the expression of traumatic stress*" (p. 189). The brain, he insists, "is a cultural organ—experience shapes the brain" (p. 86).

Veterans are liable to respond to even small cues or triggers *as if they were still in battle.* Flashbacks and related reactions can be so unsettling that these veterans "*organize their lives around trying to protect against them*" (p. 67). "*Symbols related to the original trauma,* however benign in reality, are thoroughly contaminated and so become objects to be hated, feared, destroyed if possible, avoided if not" (p. 200). His choice of words here is key: symbols, not the real thing (because, after all, you're no longer in a war zone) provoke reactions because the traumatized mind processes them as objects—that is, reality.

Others may read the same situation entirely differently than a vet with a stress disorder. And the *vet himself may see things for what they really are at the same time that he experiences them as battlefield threats.* People who've been traumatized can *"superimpose their trauma on everything around them* and have trouble deciphering whatever is going on around them" (p. 17). Research shows that people can experience physiological responses to past events even as they're aware of where they are and what's happening around them (pp. 42–43); psychologically speaking, it's possible for us to be in two places at once, to be aware of the reality surrounding us even as we relive a past traumatic experience.

Van der Kolk tells us that in working with veterans groups he sometimes sees this playing out in seemingly bizarre ways. Soldiers "told horrible tales of death and destruction," but at the same time he could see "their pride and a sense of belonging" (p. 238).

While the various parts of the human brain have evolved to work in harmony, the rewiring that trauma causes can mean that *the rational or cognitive parts of the brain no longer communicate with the emotional brain* (p. 47). Some parts of the brain where the impact strikes are so deeply-seated that they are preverbal: traumatized people often cannot speak clearly about their experiences, or even speak of them at all (pp. 43, 183). The VA has a history of rejecting PTSD claims precisely because the *vets are unable to articulate what happened to them* (pp. 246–247). In fact, *the conscious brain may well have no awareness at all* of what's going on in other regions of the brain (pp. 66–68). Though internal alarms clang loudly, *any insight a person may have gained* into what's happening *is of little or no use in shutting them off* because the rational parts of the brain can't eradicate the stored trauma (pp. 64, 207).

Van der Kolk rejects what he says is the most common explanation for why many vets seem not to respond to treatment: "that receiving a pension or disability benefits prevents people from getting better" (p. 35). In reviewing the history of combat-related traumatic stress since World War I, he finds that both the British military/medical establishment and the Germans quite deliberately tried to erase all notions of shell-shock. In the United States, after World War II, doctors in the veterans medical system shaped the ways in which patients expressed their symptoms: "When a patient complains about terrifying nightmares and his doctor orders a chest X-ray, the patient realizes that he'll get better care if he focuses on his physical problems" (pp. 189–190). Following World Wars I and II, there were repeated "backlashes" against admitting "the reality of trauma" (p. 191).

Van der Kolk describes one of the patients he's worked with as "frazzled, explosive, and on edge," but with *"no idea that these problems had anything to do with what he had experienced in Vietnam."* It wasn't *until his son was born that he sought out treatment* (p. 229).

And finally, in discussing the tension between being rendered inarticulate about the trauma and the need to express it in order to deal with it, he addresses the problem of being met by silence when one eventually tries to speak. He mentions something the great theorist of attachment, psychologist John Bowlby, said: *"What cannot be spoken to the mother cannot be told to the self"* (p. 234).

When I superimpose van der Kolk's account over my own direct, personal experience, all sorts of things that have mystified me suddenly make sense. At last I glimpse some of the physiology underlying the ways in which I experience so many things, the things that make me feel crazy. His work offers me a sense of validation and confirmation, and a degree of solace; I am not alone, I am not imagining this; what I live with is a predictable outcome of what I went through. But it also reminds me that even as I gain insight and understanding into what causes so much of my agitation, I still deny it. Fundamental to this sort of trauma is the mind's steadfast refusal to acknowledge it. It's there and it's not there at the same time.

One of the scariest things about a traumatic event, van der Kolk tells us, can be experiencing it alone, given that the first thing young humans do in distress is to turn to others for help and support. Engraved most deeply into me—occupying that space where the spirit meets the bone—are those situations where I was alone, either up in the radome or out on the flight deck in the dark. What leaps out at me immediately and with great force as I write this is how absolutely alone I was. And it wasn't simply that I was alone so much as it was that I had to force myself to keep dealing with these situations again and again. This is the heart of what I call everyday danger. This may be why I find these incidents more of a problem than the flying itself; in the air I was part of a crew. That and the everydayness, in the sense that no matter how scary these tasks were, I did them routinely, amid the general exhaustion of the maintenance work, and they just didn't seem out of the ordinary at the time.

Every day, out on Yankee Station, I worked at a host of life-threatening tasks. In order to do them, I had to ignore and override my fight/flight/freeze responses. Here and now in the present, I can't even imagine how I managed to creep to the edge of the heaving flight deck with 110 pounds of radar scope on my back, in the absolute blackness of combat readiness conditions, knowing that I couldn't see the deck's edge, that the scope's momentum would hurl me forward, that there was nothing to catch me, that no one would see or hear me, and that I wouldn't be missed for hours. I simply did it, night after night.

Here's the puzzle: I remember doing it, but I don't remember feeling any fear. So how could I have been afraid? And that's what van der Kolk explains to me, the disconnect between the parts of my brain (the amygdala/"smoke detector" and the medial prefrontal cortex/"watchtower"), and how, in forcing that disconnect, I channeled stress hormones into spots where they built up so intensely that they rerouted the wiring. And now the trauma is lodged there, just barely hidden from my thinking brain, haunting me.

I don't want to dig into the huge subject of comparing World War II and Vietnam War responses to war trauma, but I do want to emphasize van der Kolk's comments that "culture shapes the expression of traumatic stress" and that the brain "is a cultural organ—experience shapes the brain." I actually grew up with contradictory images of what a hero should look like. I learned about both heroic action and about code heroes, I now realize, and this confused me.

A very loud voice kept telling me that engaging in some cinematically heroic action was central to being a hero. Creeping through the dark with a bulky piece of equipment on my back in no way fit that image. I wasn't heroic, I thought, and if I wasn't heroic, then nothing could have happened to me.

I was in fact performing in the best code hero fashion, but in the dark, literally, and *I* couldn't see it.

When I got back from the war I had a well-crafted personal formula for keeping any sense of trauma hidden from view—both my own and others. I found that my tight focus on whatever task was at hand worked really well as an adaptation. I concentrated on my studies and on my career with laser-like intensity and I excelled. As long as I could keep working full-tilt, I remained oblivious. The other viable course to take was to numb myself with alcohol, and so for the next couple of decades, that's pretty much all I did, work and drink, and there was actually quite a bit of synergy between them. I did both of them quite well, under the circumstances; it wasn't until Grace was born that the wheels began falling off.

I live simultaneously with layer after layer of traumatic stress built into my nervous system and with the bizarrely paired notions that nothing happened to me and that even if something did happen to me, a real man would not show it. So part of me insists nothing happened to me, while another part superimposes my trauma on everything around me. The traumatic stress returns in response to the smallest of symbols. A simple cue or trigger like a misused or misplaced knife upsets me, makes me feel threatened. Getting lost drives me nearly around the bend. I can see where I am, and know rationally that I'm in no danger, but my nervous system is convinced that death or life as a POW is imminent. No matter how many times I work my way through these scenarios, and understand what lies behind and beneath them, no amount of awareness is sufficient to flush them from my body.

I recognize that social relations are supposed to be crucial to my mental health, but being around people, even people I know well and love, is utterly draining. I'm continually on edge, frightened even, though I don't like to admit that fear is what I feel when I'm with people. Social interaction grows increasingly problematic for me. For decades, I solved the problem by drinking, by numbing myself, and it worked really well. It wasn't till I stopped numbing myself that I had to deal with the pain entailed in interacting with others. Now even something as simple as a dinner seems beyond me, and I feel there's something terribly wrong about me because of it.

When I first got a sense that something was wrong, after Grace was born, it was because I couldn't deny the bonds of intimacy springing up between us. As painful as these were, they touched some part of my soul that would not deny them. Opening up to Grace forced me to begin opening up to an emotional realm that I'd shut down. Now all this turmoil is exposed, but it's still rooted down deep. I can sometimes take the edge off it, but nothing makes it go away. As van der Kolk explains, the rational part of the brain can't eradicate stored trauma, try as it may.

What seems in some ways to speak the loudest is van der Kolk's point about being reduced to inarticulateness about the trauma, his notion that we need to express it in order the deal with it. One of the most insidious aspects of PTSD, he says, is being met with silence when we try to speak about it. In an earlier chapter I described what happened when I tried to tell my parents that I was beginning to get a sense that something happened to me in the war. "I don't want to hear about it," my mother said. Or as Bowlby put it, "What cannot be spoken to the mother cannot be told to the self."

GUILT

It's not just the trauma that beleaguers me. At a conscious, intellectual level the war makes itself known as a form of moral injury or, more to the point, *guilt*. I've figured out how to deal with guilt: I act. But the war's legacy is more problematic in the insidious—that is, hidden—ways that my every day wartime experiences continue shaping my everyday life.

I can't say exactly when I first understood that the greatest burden I carry from the war is my guilt, but I have a general sense of feeling it grow, and it was in some way tied to my decision to become an anthropologist. I initially chose anthropology as a form of escapism, a way to hide out on a remote island. But I was far too practical to jump without looking.

The cultural context in which I began studying anthropology had a huge impact on my thinking. It was at the height of the antiwar movement, near the movement's epicenter in the Bay Area. The Oliver La Farge stories that first exposed me to the idea of being an anthropologist were set among New Mexico's Pueblos. Vine Deloria's (1969) slashing attack on white America's relationships with Native Americans, *Custer Died for Your Sins*, had just appeared at the time and I was doing ethnographic fieldwork projects with American Indian groups and working on California archaeological sites.

Though I spent only a couple of weeks on Morongo reservation in Southern California's San Gorgonio Pass, the research I did there had to do with the demise of their once-thriving fruit orchards and the collapse of a viable farming economy. Oakland, where I lived, was the home of the Black Panthers, and I worked alongside a couple of Panthers in the East Oakland supermarket where I supplemented my meager GI Bill funding as I was rushing through college. These sorts of influences reignited some of the fires within me.

Then there are the emotions that throbbed painfully as I watched the film *Little Big Man*; they remain fixed in my memory. I don't believe I've ever really thought through what was going on with me then. The crucial scene for me came as Col. George Custer's cavalry swept down on a sleeping Indian camp, slaughtering nearly everyone, women, children, and elders, as well as fighting men, and I was so deeply troubled that I could barely remain in my seat—I nearly walked out of the theater.[5] I've always thought of it in terms of feeling some mixture of rage and guilt and embarrassment as an American. But now I see something more there. A part of me felt that I was one of those soldiers, visiting death on a peaceful village. And the village was in Vietnam.

That was in the fall of 1970, just as the My Lai court martial was convening, three years after I'd come back from the war. At the same time I read Dee Brown's just-published *Bury My Heart at Wounded Knee* (1970), a history recounting the endless stream of massacres American Indians experienced at the hands of the US Army. As Hampton Sides's foreword to the book's 2007 edition notes, many who read it at the time immediately saw parallels with My Lai (2007, p. xvi).

This was also the moment when I decided to do my doctoral research in Micronesia and to work toward ending American colonial rule there. And it wasn't long before I was exulting in getting arrested as I protested the war; it's pretty obvious that my behavior reflected both my guilt and my need to atone for it. All those many strands wove themselves together tightly enough to yank my agitation close to the surface. While the guilt shape-shifts at times, and pulses in intensity, it's always been there, influencing nearly everything I do and clouding a very large part of my soul. My sense of guilt is as fundamental to my character and to my persona as anything else in my makeup, and it's time to take a closer look at it.

When I read about veterans' guilt, I usually see it tied to killing, to atrocities, or to surviving when comrades did not. Although I was deeply involved in the bombing and coastal interdictions that killed people, my own plane was unarmed. When we were shot at, we turned tail and ran. I personally committed no atrocities, and I have no sense that the bigger, more penetrating parts of my guilt come from having survived the war.

My guilt is instead rooted in the role I played as an integral part of the bombing of North Vietnam, along with all the other pieces of the war, when there was no call for any of it. I traveled, willingly, the breadth of the Pacific to bring death and destruction to people of Vietnam. They deserved none of this. My sense of guilt is heightened by my belief that I should have known better.

I don't know how many other Vietnam vets feel this way, but it's central to my own sense of decency. Yes, I was very young when I enlisted. And yes, there wasn't much of an antiwar movement at the time I joined, before the Tonkin Gulf Incident ignited the flames. I could easily let myself off the hook, I suppose. But so many of my generation, guys just like me, opposed the war and refused to fight in in it; how is it, I ask myself, that I missed all the signs that should have been readily apparent to me?

I've told you of being asked why I don't let go of my guilt and forgive myself for fighting in Vietnam, given that I don't hold others responsible. My answer, finally, after an incredible amount of introspection, is that I *choose* to hold onto my guilt. My guilt is so strong, and frankly, so meaningful to me, because it spills across emotional, intellectual, and moral realms. It's not that I haven't tried to let go, but that I won't, and I think I've finally figured out why my efforts to do so fall short.

Years ago, I attempted to explain my understanding of what troubles me this way: When I expressed my guilt about fighting in Vietnam, people would often tell me not to blame myself, saying "You were sent there. You were just doing what you were told to do. You can't hold yourself responsible for that." In reply, I'd explain that I grew up in the shadow of the Holocaust, the Nuremburg Trials, and Adolf Eichmann's trial in Jerusalem. We—or at least I—learned that claiming you were "only following orders" was not a legitimate excuse. In those days it was common to hear people say "I vas only following orders" in a joking manner with a guttural German accent. How could I honorably shrug off responsibility when I was so thoroughly steeped in a moral code that said it was impermissible to deny it?

It's also the case, I say, that in a democratic society everyone bears a degree of responsibility for the country's actions. This means as a corollary, of course, that most Americans bear an element of responsibility for what the United States did in Vietnam. This is not a message everyone wants to hear. But it's one I hold to. And it's not just Vietnam. I bear some degree of responsibility for America's treatment of the Indians—we stole the country from them—even if many of those crimes were committed centuries ago. The same for slavery and for the theft of half of Mexico from the Mexicans and of Hawai'i from the native Hawai'ians. In that sense, Vietnam is just one more case in point. I don't get much traction when I say this, because most folks aren't ready to take on so heavy a burden.

JUST WAR THEORY

And then there's the problem of just war theory. Exactly what responsibility *do* soldiers bear when they fight in an unjust war? What difference does it make if they know or believe at the time that it's unjust, or whether they've been conscripted to fight under pain of death or imprisonment? And again, what difference does it make if the soldiers are in the armed forces of a democracy, where at least in theory they have some say in the fight? Philosophers argue these points ad infinitum, but very few philosophers, at least these days, fight in wars. The fact that these arguments have raged for at least 1,500 years (assuming one traces them back only as far as St. Augustine) suggests that no clear-cut answers are going to be reached soon.

The service academies employ philosophers to school their students in these debates, but I suspect that any instructor who spent a lot of time suggesting that the US military has been fighting in unjust wars, or fighting them in unjust ways, or that our troops should put much effort into worrying about these issues would not last long on the faculty. As much as I admire the work of a discerning scholar like Michael Walzer (2015), whose dogged work on just war theory is the most insightful I know, it can be hard to take just war theory very seriously when, almost by definition, every country that makes war does so insisting, like King Henry V, that its "cause is just."[6]

In important ways, then, the intricacies of just war theory don't do me much good. In the end, I believe I fought in a war that should not have been fought, and that was fought in ways that were uncalled for. And for those who are incredulous that I would imply that a war not be fought with every means available to win, I point out that a key element of just war theory, even as it's taught in our service academies, is "proportionality." Bombing thatched huts in peasant villages with massed B-52s flying at 30,000 feet or so and defoliating vast tracks of land with poison chemicals just don't seem proportional in my book.

And so I feel guilty, but—and this is a big but—my sense of guilt is two-faced. I'd be lying if I pretended there isn't a part of me, some self-righteous part of me, that enjoys the guilt. This makes for a certain self-regarding, self-satisfied, holier-than-thou attitude. Much weightier, though, is the agony that comes with the guilt, the self-recrimination and the self-doubt that never let up. I hold onto the guilt because it feels like the right thing to do, but it means continually inflicting pain on myself.

Some part of me wants to feel like a victim, but a much larger part of me resists this and insists instead that I inflicted all this on myself. At some level, I chose to go to war. That wasn't my purpose in enlisting, but when the bombing began, I pursued every opportunity I could to do something I perceived as valiant, if not heroic. I was ready and willing to fight in Vietnam. To use a cliché I usually try to avoid, I put my life on the line there. To use a technical term, I had *agency*: I was a willing actor, a willing participant, an agent of my own destiny.

And yet I did all this because I'd been deceived. Or to put it more emphatically, I was *betrayed*. And this confuses me. Would I have been willing and eager, or as willing and eager as I was, to do what I did had I known the truth about the Tonkin Gulf Incident? This may sound like an obscure matter, but for me it's momentous. Though the Incident wasn't a major event in any conventional sense, it was a crucial turning point; it led immediately to the bombing of North Vietnam and changed the entire course of the war from relatively low-key anti-insurgency operations in the South to conventional air warfare in the North.[7] It was the foreseeable consequence of covert but entirely deliberate provocations by the US Navy. I was in the Navy when it happened, I believed that it was an unprovoked attack, and I took it personally. I welcomed it in a way that mirrors the classically duplicitous way of militaries wherever they are. My first thought was that it might spring me from boot camp sooner than expected. My reaction wasn't much different than that of military officers known for looking eagerly at the beginnings of conflicts with their eyes attuned to the main chance: opportunities for command and for career advancement. Soldiers decry war and explain to civilians that they hate it because they know just how horrible it is. This isn't entirely a lie, but it certainly isn't the whole truth.

In the same way that police need crime to keep their jobs and psychologists need neurotic people to keep theirs, the military needs war. I hadn't gone into the military to make war, but when it came along I readily accepted the opportunities it offered me. And I didn't just take them, I sought them out. My underlying desire—lingering in the background—to be a hero of the sort I grew up admiring leapt to the fore. No longer was my time in the service simply about training and travel. Now I was going to have a real chance to emulate Yossarian and Davy Crockett and all the others who'd been my role models.

I made a quick switch from the peaceful, pragmatic reasons why I'd enlisted to a radically different set of interests. It would be an exaggeration to say that I became bloodthirsty, but the aggressive, saber-rattling side of me (and the image I retain of me as a 17-year-old waving a saber in the air remains a big deal for me) was unleashed. Had I been doing this to protect my community from a direct and obvious threat I wouldn't experience the sort of guilt that plagues me today, I don't think. But I was lied to, I was betrayed, and I have refused to get over it.

It's the sense that I unleashed my own aggressiveness in response to the lies and dissembling of our leaders that troubles me so. I keep telling myself that *I should have known better*. I'm not sure that that's true, but it's what my conscience keeps saying. Let me end this book by explaining how and why this sense of betrayal looms so large for me, which means looking a little more deeply at what happened when the Navy began bombing North Vietnam. I return again to consideration of why I fought.

NOTES

1. Here are some websites readers can consult for information on PTSD treatment:

Veterans Affairs/National Center for Post-Traumatic Stress Disorder
https://www.ptsd.va.gov/index.asp.
Medications for treating PTSD
https://www.ptsd.va.gov/understand_tx/meds_for_ptsd.asp.
https://www.uspharmacist.com/article/a-review-of-pharmacotherapy-for-ptsd.

2. The film *Patton*, released in 1970, near the high point of the Vietnam War and opposition to it, captured a lot of this ambivalence in a scene when General George Patton physically attacks a young soldier clearly dealing with traumatic stress, screaming that he won't have cowards under his command. The 1957 film *Paths of Glory* probes much more deeply into this topic; it tells of French soldiers in World War I executed following charges of cowardice that were plainly leveled to cover up the malfeasance of superior officers. Abram Kardiner explored these issues in the 1920s and published his work in *Traumatic Neuroses of War* in 1941, just as the United States was about to enter large-scale conflict for the second time in a generation.

3. Psychiatrist Sally Satel (2004, 2011a, 2011b) has written a great deal about the notion that providing vets with disability compensation for PTSD is counterproductive. She argues that these payments simply encourage them not to readjust. Bertel van der Kolk (2014), a psychiatrist whose work I describe at length later in this chapter, quite specifically rebuts these sorts of arguments.

4. In *Home from the War*, Robert Jay Lifton (1973) describes his early work with Vietnam vets at the precursors of the Vet Centers. He was prescient in his understanding of what the larger veterans health establishment would only come to learn much later about what these vets were experiencing.

5. The film was based on Thomas Berger's 1964 novel *Little Big Man.* I'd read the book during the war and I find myself wondering what sort of impact it had on me then.

6. Walzer has been revising *Just War Theory* regularly since its first edition in 1977, and he began the work as a means of exploring the Vietnam War and the responsibilities of American soldiers who fought in it.

7. Approximately half the money the US government spent making war in Vietnam supported aerial operations. Thomas Thayer has argued that in terms of resource allocations the war was first an air war and second a ground war of attrition (Thayer, 1985; Tilford, 1991).

Chapter Nine

Why We Fought

Why, I'm still asking after all these years, did I fight in Vietnam? Why did I head off so readily to war? And why do I so persistently, and agonizingly, regret having gone? Why, in other words, am I so bewildered by all this? I'd like to draw this very confusing story to a close that displays at least some clarity or finds some kind of sense in it all. But I also feel that if I'm to do my job as an ethnographer properly, I need to leave my readers as confused as I am: my task is to provide some sense of what my war looks like from the inside.

I've tried to convey a mix of competing and conflicting emotions, because there's no simple way to answer questions about why we fought, or why we're still fighting. More to the point, though, confusion about what first leads us into war can leave us, finally, in even greater chaos when we try to make sense of what happens *after* the fact. If we're not certain about why we went to war, do we have much chance of making sense out of our feelings about having gone to fight? I have far too many conflicting thoughts to say anything straightforward about the war. I live with guilt, pride, anger, wonder, and the bitterness of betrayal, among other things.

BETRAYAL?

To better explain the moral underpinnings of my outrage I return briefly to an historical overview here.[1] Americans who continue to reflect on the Vietnam War are never going to agree about why we were fighting there, but over the years historians *have* reached a fairly broad consensus about what happened in the Tonkin Gulf in early August, 1964, when the air war in North Vietnam—my war—got its start. I don't expect that everyone will concur with my summary, but I also don't think it's very controversial.

Small boats from South Vietnam, directed by the United States, were staging deliberately provocative raids on North Vietnamese coastal sites (coded OPLAN34), including radar installations, while USS *Maddox*, a destroyer laden with specially tailored electronics, steamed a few miles off the coast monitoring the North's radar frequencies and communications (an operation with the code name DeSoto), a tactic that often foretells a full-scale attack. *Maddox* was for a time well inside territorial waters claimed by North Vietnam. Responding to these raids, a local North Vietnamese naval commander directed a group of light patrol boats toward *Maddox*, which opened fire on them. The boats returned fire and launched torpedoes from a distance well outside their normal range. *Maddox*, struck by *one* machine-gun bullet, called in strike aircraft from a nearby US aircraft carrier; the North Vietnamese craft were hit and badly damaged.[2]

The US government immediately denounced the episode as an unprovoked attack on an American ship exercising the right of innocent passage in international waters. There was confusion and uncertainty in the White House about what exactly had happened, but there was little doubt that the US Navy had provoked the attacks.

Two days later, while *Maddox* and a second destroyer, *Turner Joy*, were patrolling the same waters in a deliberate show of American resolve, their crews misread radar and sonar signals, mistaking weather effects and their own wakes for a second torpedo attack. Strike aircraft were again launched but they sighted no North Vietnamese vessels. The confusion and uncertainty notwithstanding, US leaders for the most part understood that the North Vietnamese had not made a second attack.

President Lyndon Johnson privately acknowledged that nothing of real substance had happened, saying to his advisors, "Hell, those dumb, stupid sailors were just shooting at flying fish!" but he nonetheless dispatched aircraft from two carriers to bomb a series of North Vietnamese sites in what he claimed was retaliation. And he used the opportunity to implement plans already drawn up and being held at the ready. Months earlier, his staff had drafted a resolution, waiting for the right moment to present it to Congress. It was this Tonkin Gulf Resolution, passed by both houses with little discussion or dissent, that authorized him to attack North Vietnam as he saw fit and then served as charter for the war that ensued.

Johnson was deep in a reelection campaign at the time, running against Senator Barry Goldwater, a war hawk. LBJ pursued a delicate course: he wanted to appear less belligerent than Goldwater, while still portraying himself as firm enough to protect American interests. The folly in the Tonkin Gulf gave him just the platform he was searching for. Johnson's dilemma reflects a contradiction inherent in security policy. The military (or police or fire departments, for that matter) is obliged to convince taxpayers that dangers are great enough to warrant budgeting ample funds, and to convince them simultaneously that they're quite safe precisely because these funds are well spent. Policies formulated as a response to a threat (or a perceived threat) must navigate between what we might call the Scylla and Charybdis of threat and response.

Though he knew that the United States had provoked the August 2 episode and that there'd been no attack on August 4, LBJ managed the affair as political theater. Many in the Navy had some sense of what had actually happened, but this made little difference to admirals eager to see the Navy seize a larger piece of the action in Southeast Asia. Major bombing operations in North Vietnam, known as Rolling Thunder, soon got underway and continued with occasional lulls or temporary halts until 1972.

Johnson and Robert McNamara, his defense secretary, initiated the bombing under false pretenses. The record shows they understood that a strategic bombing strategy was unlikely to accomplish its stated purposes. There were many reasons for the war, but the United States began the bombing in the north primarily as a means of shoring up LBJ's credibility at home as he pursued an activist domestic political agenda in Congress. Johnson was ambivalent about going to war, and his decision to press forward was a difficult one. His own uncertainties led him to take the war personally, and he spoke quite openly about it in terms of proving his manhood, and privately of how he agonized over it. Both he and McNamara recognized early on that the war could not be won militarily; it was from the outset a primarily political matter. *This* is what I am referring to when I speak of betrayal.[3]

As I understand this history—and I readily acknowledge that others comprehend aspects of it differently—I was sent to fight in Vietnam *after* the men who sent me had concluded that their strategy had little chance of achieving success. We were meant to provide our leaders with political cover. I was part of operations that, as has often been reported, rained down more tons of explosives than all the bombs dropped in World War II. I played a role in killing millions of Vietnamese. I participated in these operations, risked my life each day, and nearly died, in good faith. But it was all a lie.

Yes, I know politicians lie. But there are lies, and then there are the lies that kill millions.

I cannot get over this betrayal, precisely because I served so damned willingly. I naively trusted those leaders, but now I berate myself for having been so naïve. Had there been no domestic opposition to the war, no one pointing out the government's deceptions, I might find a way to let myself off the hook. But I was eager to participate in the war and ignored mounting evidence that what we were doing was both futile and wrong. I should have known better but fighting in the war was serving my own purposes.

I readily acknowledge that some part off me was still hellbent on proving myself to my father—outshining him, in fact—and that part of me identifies this sense of betrayal by my government with my sense of betrayal by my father. My role in the war, as I've tried to make clear, had what can be called without much exaggeration, an oedipal component.

WHY WE'RE CYNICAL

War resists neat categories like rational and irrational. Theorists like to think that it follows predictable patterns, but it's clear that it does so only occasionally. Strategists like to think bombing will force people to submit, but bombing civilian populations seems more likely to shore up their resolve than to break it down (a notion I discuss below). More to the point here, troops facing intractable conditions out on the line may at times doubt their leaders' wisdom, but it's at least as likely that combatants risking their lives every day will instead hold tightly onto almost any argument that makes their suffering seem worthwhile. (And these two seemingly contradictory perspectives are by no means incompatible with one another.)

I think this can explain some of the cynicism that is so characteristic of the military. Soldiers need to decouple their own judgment and observations from the official story. The habit of doubting everything allows them to do their jobs without reflecting much on their responsibility, or for that matter, on their lack of responsibility. Though I don't recall hearing the phrase in the Navy, troops in-country during the Vietnam War often said of whatever was going on around them, "It don't mean nothin'." Being cynical provides a way of distancing yourself from the chaos that surrounds you, and that's exactly what all that ironic detachment we lived with in the Navy allowed us to do. We were able to do our jobs while denying any sense of personal involvement or answerability.

It's difficult to closely examine your doubts when you're putting your life on the line each day. At some level, you need to believe that what you're doing is right in order to take the risks. I understand that. And I was, after all, still a man-child. I can, if I want, find endless excuses for what I did. But in the end, I see that I dealt in death and destruction and did so without pondering what I was doing or why I was doing it. It's this that drives my conviction that I must atone.

MORAL INJURY

There's an element within all this chaos and confusion that especially confounds me. My plane dropped no bombs, but we were an integral part of the bombing, playing multiple roles in the attacks on North Vietnam and on coastal shipping. It's clear in retrospect, however, that the bombing accomplished little—if any—of what it was intended to achieve. And we now know that even while they had us dropping the bombs, our leaders understood that their strategy wasn't working. More to the point, many of those planning the attacks had been closely involved in studies of World War II bombing and knew just how dubious the effects of those earlier operations had been.

The impact of World War II's strategic bombing campaigns has always been controversial, and even if, for the sake of argument, we agree that these might have accomplished some of their goals (destroying fuel supplies in particular), it was still understood at the time that those strategies weren't relevant in Vietnam. North Vietnam was not an urbanized country where strategic bombing had even a marginal possibility of achieving results. There was little industrial capacity for the bombs to destroy. Strategic bombing— that is, bombing to ravage cities and factories and workers—was meant both to weaken popular morale and to damage or eliminate resources, transportation, and the production and distribution of arms and supplies. With the notable exception of the two atom bombs dropped on Japan, it did neither.[4]

Rolling Thunder, the long-term bombing operation in the North, was intended to be vindictive at least as much as it was meant to achieve strategic success; it was intended to punish the North Vietnamese for having the audacity to oppose the United States. It's neither foolish nor naïve of me to believe there's a different moral tenor in a campaign intended to express displeasure at the enemy's willingness to resist than there is in one with an explicitly military objective. The intractability of my guilt over the part I played in Rolling Thunder is in many ways rooted in this distinction and its moral weight.[5]

I'm not really sure how we distinguish guilt from moral injury, except in terms of who did what to whom. If someone does something that causes me moral harm, then I suffer a moral injury. If *I* did something I think is wrong, then I feel guilt. But we're talking here about the intersection of these two trajectories. I was complicit in actions that I now believe were wrong.

More to the point is the fact that I now see how the war transformed me into something I wasn't when I entered it. I went to fight willingly, but I was hardly bloodthirsty at the outset. (My major goal in enlisting, after all, was to get off the assembly line where I was working.) By the time that I tried to attack and destroy the *Phoenix*, laden with medical supplies for North Vietnamese civilians injured by our bombs, though, I'd become something quite different.

Among the principles I've chosen to guide my life over the past couple of decades is a line of Friedrich Nietzsche's: "He who would fight with monsters must beware lest he become a monster himself" (1886). It seems to me that a fundamental claim of nearly everyone who makes war their profession is that one of their first and highest priorities is to save lives. In asserting this, they then feel free to kill as many on the other side as they can, and sacrifice as many of their own troops as necessary to do the job well. There's a famous line from the fighting in South Vietnam, a US infantry officer explaining that his unit had to destroy the village in order to save it (Arnett, 1968). Some scoff at this as hyperbole, but there are ways in which it captures the essence of all wars.

I was caught in the middle. I helped kill as many Vietnamese as possible and was entirely ready to be killed in the process of doing so. These aren't abstract ideas to me, they are the reality of my war experience. I internalized the notion that my job was to help kill as many as we could. I let go of it soon after the war, but the enormity of what we did, the scale of the bombing, the mercilessness of it, the stupidity of it, the vindictiveness of it, all of these, when added together, make it far too great a weight on my soul for me to simply shrug off. PTSD therapists have told me that all I really need to do is take the world off my shoulder, as if simply saying this could make it possible. And now, reflecting on it, I realize why it pisses me off. If we don't accept responsibility for mistakes on a grand scale like this—feel truly bad about them—how the hell can we work effectively to prevent ourselves from repeating them, which is what keeps happening?[6]

I don't care how often or how emphatically high-ranking military officers tell us they hate war, they still understand that without a combat command it is difficult to get promoted. I'm not suggesting that this necessarily means that they don't hate war. They are, after all, humans, and humanity is nothing if not full of contradictions. But when they say they hate war, then, this in no way means they haven't also sought it out. In this sense, I suppose it's a lot like sex. It scares the hell out of a lot of us, but that in no way diminishes our appetite for it. It may, in fact, enhance it.

And high-ranking officers are hardly all alike, anyway. Some are cautious and conservative about starting wars, some aren't. Some have learned, some haven't.

I speak of this because it's integral to my sense of why the war won't leave me alone. I'm an intellectual by habit and by trade. I have to think about things, and study them. I can't leave them alone. And the more I learn, the more I feel implicated. I wasn't innocently taken advantage of, I wasn't cruelly forced into anything. I sought it out. And I pay the price for this.

GRACE UNDER PRESSURE

But the war's meaning for me isn't intrinsic to myself, that is, located entirely within me, nor is it entirely something out there beyond me. It's a product both of what I brought to the war and of what the war gave to me.

Amid all my floundering around in the mire of guilt, yet another thought strikes me. As I try to teach students about the ambiguities of warfare and the ambivalence of warriors, I run up against my own ambivalence, and I see that something else is going on, something that has to do with my growing appreciation of my willingness—my readiness—to accept guilt. It has to do with exploring with them the underlying notion of grace under pressure. Grace not only under fire, but in its wake.

And so, even as my anger grows, I've been startled to find myself experiencing a measure of pride in my performance, in both what I'd done and how I did it. I can see that I'd been tough, that I'd done everything I'd been asked to do without hesitation. I'd sought out and taken on important responsibilities and handled them with aplomb. It's meaningful to me, too, that as young as I'd been, I did a great deal more than I'd been expected to do. I hadn't flinched or recoiled from danger. I'd been as dedicated as I could be.

I realize that even though I hadn't done anything classically, cinematically heroic, which is why I thought nothing had happened to me, I had in fact been fulfilling my ideal of the code hero. I had put myself in harm's way, done what a man had to do, and maintained my composure as I did so. I had shown grace under pressure.

That was the first step: to appreciate how I'd handled things. Then, as I focused on all that I'd taken on during the war, I began to think about how *much* of it I'd taken on and how I sought out new tasks and responsibilities. I was one of only a few willing to fly off carriers, and I took on the enormous responsibility of controlling aircraft in combat. I can't recall ever shirking, and I have no reason to think that I ever did. And because I took my responsibilities in the air so seriously, I was equally dedicated to keeping the equipment operating, working as hard and effectively as I could aboard ship, for as long as necessary, in order to ensure that our equipment was operational for the next mission, whether I was flying it or not.

I've heard career soldiers speak admiringly of the person who *runs toward the fire*, as opposed to those who run *away* from it. When I reflect on what I'd done in the war, I see that that's exactly what I'd been doing. It makes me uncomfortable to say this, because it's open to sarcastic interpretation. It sounds like a silly cliché to some, as an admission of stupidity; who in their right mind wouldn't run away? But in the military, especially among leaders who emphasize the importance of leadership (and military leaders seem to do an awful lot of that), it's seen as a good and glorious way to be, in that ancient sense of *Dulce et decorum est, pro patria mori* ("It is sweet and fitting to die for one's country").[7]

There are problems with this. The last thing the code hero wants to do is brag. If you beat your chest and tell people that you run toward fires, you're being self-defeating, undermining exactly what you want to be proud of.[8] It's one of warfare's perpetual paradoxes: the toughness you need to do your job keeps you from saying much about how tough it is. But it's also my own essential dilemma. I want to call attention to myself; I do things to call attention to myself; but if I call attention to myself, the things I do lose much of their meaning and resonance. This is closely related to a Taoist precept I often draw upon when I'm doing my ethnographic work: "He who knows does not speak; he who speaks does not know."

And then there's what I've been calling lamination, the piling of one layer of stress atop another. Many people experience traumatic stress in the course of living normal lives. It can result from car crashes, the deaths of loved ones, and sexual assault, among other things. But in the military (and for those we call first responders), especially in war, there's something markedly different. You deal with traumatic stress but there's no respite from it. You know that the next day you'll have to do the same things and experience the same stressors. And you do. In order to carry out your duties day after day, you repress the fear and stress. And you do it again and again, week after week, piling up layer upon layer of stress and repressing each in its turn. Your traumatic stress isn't merely the product of *an* incident, it's a thick, rugged, high-tensile aggregation of stress and response. There's a world of difference between working through the stress of a particular incident and living with this thickly laminated block of stress.

WHEN GUILT AND PRIDE COLLIDE

The code hero aspects of my character stood between me and any awareness of what I was subjecting myself to, and my pride in doing what I did kept me from acknowledging the trouble my experiences were causing me. My troubles grew stronger as I grew more and more oblivious to them. More recently, in the painstakingly difficult grind of coming to some sort of understanding of what I'd done and what had happened to me, I stumbled across the perverse pride I took in doing this to myself. But this in turn forces me to ponder the question of how it is that I can take pride in something that I've regretted doing for so long. This is not an easy question to answer, for me at least.

I know vets for whom this is a no-brainer. They served honorably at the time, they say, in a cause they believed in at the time. Later, their views about the war changed, but this hasn't affected how they feel about their service. I've also encountered people who are aghast at the idea that I might simultaneously feel pride and shame about the same thing. And then there are the people who have never even considered the issue.

Let me dissect this a little more fully. How can my feelings of both pride and guilt be rooted in the same thing, that is, fighting in a war that I believed in at the time and have subsequently come to revile? How do I live with these profoundly contradictory emotions? They are indeed emotions, but they are at the same time something more. They sit on either side of a moral equation. My pride (most people's pride, I think) comes in part from doing something that I think of as good or performing well. By the same token, guilt comes as a result of doing something I think of as bad or performing poorly. This presents a conundrum on the face of it. Yes, when I thought I was doing a good thing, I was proud of it, and when I came to think that thing was bad I felt guilt. But doesn't the guilt I've felt almost constantly since the war erase the pride I felt? No, it seems not to. Why not?

I've long hoped that philosophers who deal in ethics or psychologists who deal in ego psychology might provide me a resolution to this paradox, without finding one.[9] Not long before I finished writing this, though, I finally found an answer that makes sense to me in the work of Elizabeth Anderson (1995), a philosophy professor at the University of Michigan. The puzzle I've posed, she says, is "an example of the kind of pluralism of values and how they are tied to diverse and conflicting emotions" that she's been exploring. She writes (2019):

> For me, values are embedded in the relations we have to people, including ourselves. To feel guilt is to feel that one has wronged someone else and must atone for that. That emotion is *directed toward others*. To feel pride is to feel that one has measured up to a certain standard of excellence—for example, courage. It is an emotional relation one has *toward oneself* or people connected to oneself (one could also be proud of one's children, for instance). Because these feelings are in relation to different people, and different standards of evaluation, they are consistent, even though they have different valences about the same conduct (fighting in the war) [my italics].

I've found this immensely helpful, and it makes sense to me in terms of what is called "category error." I've been confusing two quite different sorts of values, and this clarification goes a long way toward reducing my anxiety, but it hasn't yet made it vanish entirely.

In the end I choose to satisfy myself by returning to a theme I've touched on throughout this work, my thumos, or spirit. My sense of myself demands both that I be honest with myself and that I behave in ways that allow me to live comfortably (but not too comfortably) with my conscience. At the end of my touchstone, *Catch-22*, the chaplain tells Yossarian, the story's antihero, as he finally withdraws from the war, that he'll have to live with misgivings. Yossarian replies that he wouldn't want to live *without* misgivings (Heller, 1961, p. 441).

My thumos demands that I atone. I cannot live a proper life unless I first acknowledge that I participated in things that never should have happened, and then go on to atone for them. This is where I trace the long line connecting the pride I felt in acting bravely at the time with the pride I feel in acting appropriately now.

There's no set of simple answers for me. At an immediate, gut level, it has always seemed illogical, if not impossible, to have two such entirely different feelings about the same thing. As an anthropologist, on the other hand, accustomed to gauging people's actions in terms of the cultural patterns and social mores they've grown up with, I find this a bit easier to grapple with. But then I invariably run full force into the problem I've talked so much about. My generation's young men are better-known for resisting the war than for acquiescing in it. It's true, of course, that more went along with the war than openly opposed it, but it nevertheless remains that I came of age in a cultural and social environment where there seem to have been complementary and nearly equal but opposite expectations about going off to fight in Vietnam.

Glenn Albright, who teaches with me in our honors seminar on war and the arc of human experience, has asked me, as I speak to the class about the incongruity I feel between guilt and pride, to explain why it baffles me so. The contradiction strikes him as an entirely normal part of life. I appreciate his perspective, and wish I could make it my own, but something in my makeup or upbringing has remained steadfastly uncomfortable with the contradiction. I cannot simply will my confusion away.

AND STILL I FIGHT

In order to make sense of all this I have to set aside these sorts of arguments and approach the problem with a different mindset. The answer I've reached, after an absurd amount of banging my head against walls, is this: my opposition to the war, though belated, and my long commitment to atoning for having fought in it, spring from the same parts of my character that both fostered my willingness to serve in the first place and the commitment with which I served. This is what I've been calling my *thumos*, my spirit.

My need to atone is an integral part of a whole: the spirit and dedication that entail doing my best to do my duty (to quote the Boy Scout oath I recited as a boy). I've spent most of my life working in one way or another to atone. I take pride in accepting this responsibility. And I recognize that this is neither more nor less than that same willingness to accept responsibility that I had when I was young and possessed a different understanding of what my responsibilities were. I still carry the burden now, and run toward fires, because that's who I am, and it's who I was then as well.

When my university's faculty union calls for bodies to protest at demonstrations, and especially to get arrested, I'm front and center. When something must be called out, I rise and speak as forcefully, and I hope, as articulately, as I can. I'm still a fighter.

In writing this, I see it clearly. In exactly the same way that I took pride in doing my utmost to do what had to be done during the war, and in doing it as well as it could be done, I now take pride not only in being outspoken and putting my body on the line. I want to do it well. I want to do it well enough to have an impact, to make a difference.

This is a particularly difficult thing to do in the classroom. It's in teaching that I find my greatest satisfaction. I like to say that teaching a good introductory anthropology class to business students is the single most socially useful thing I can do. The problem, of course, is that to do so I must communicate my passion without being overbearing. This is not an easy thing to do. I wrestle with it every moment I'm in the classroom. And in my struggle I'm guided by exactly the same moral compass that guides my struggles with guilt and pride. It's in my nature to struggle. I have to *act*, to do things, and I have to be keenly aware of the contradictions that inhere in the actions I take.[10] The war and what I did in it and why I did it are always just below the surface and sometimes they break through. I am preternaturally conscious of the basic contradiction between taking an active, committed role and being at the same time aware of my own fallibility, that is, the difficulty of being certain about the rightness of my actions. I doubt myself and everything I do, even as I'm acting on my beliefs. This strikes me as resonating with what I've heard described as our modern predicament: we humans are stuck living in the space between what we know and what we feel.

These things aren't new—they've been aspects of my character for a long time. But as I've become aware of what happened to me in the war, and studied the contradictions inherent in war, I've come to appreciate them in new and different ways. I accept that struggle as my own particular lot, because there is no shared or basic Vietnam veterans' view of the war. Each of us seeks our own way through the swamp.

Because I choose to hold onto this guilt, I have to wrestle with yet another puzzle. When I grow too agitated, I go for treatment: medication, EMDR, or some form or another of therapy (most recently, Interpersonal Psychotherapy and Dialectical Behavior Therapy). These offer me temporary relief, and for a time I can stand back and observe myself. I see the changes in my behavior and feel the differences in my emotions. For lack of a better way to say it, I'm mellow. The problem with this is that I fear I'll lose my edge. My rage and distrust have served me like a suit of armor and I feel naked without it.

A relentless contradiction lies in my sense that unless my anger is near the surface, I'll lose some important aspects of my character. I know myself in good measure through my rough edges, my need to push back and speak out. Without these, who or what would I be? I wonder.

When I engaged in the EMDR treatment I felt fully aware of what was going on. It was so difficult and so painful, I believed, that it had to be good for me. "No pain, no gain," I kept telling my therapist. In some respects, it was so successful that I can't even recall how badly I felt before I got started with it. What I do remember was walking in that first time and telling her I was "desperate."

All this is directly connected to my issues with guilt and responsibility in general, and to not seeing myself as a victim. I find that I can only bear my afflictions if I push back, by trying, that is, to change things, the sorts of things that caused them in the first place.

Woven among the guilt, responsibility, and pride, which cause me so much confusion and ambivalence, come two more hurdles, my tendency to deny that anything happened to me and my refusal to see myself as a victim.

As I've tried to explain, the image of the code hero that I latched onto when I was young makes it difficult, if not impossible, to acknowledge that something happened to me. And so I deny that anything happened. As evidence mounts that something did indeed happen to me, and that I have to do something with it, the same code feeds my refusal to see myself as a victim.

My teachers' generation fought in World War II, and I sometimes heard my professors speak of how the war shaped their scholarly perspectives. On the other hand, in the conversations I've had with the handful of scholars I've met who are also Vietnam vets, I have no recall of having heard them mention how the war shaped their intellectual outlook. It occurs to me, of course, that that's exactly what this book is about. Can I in fact boil down the war's impact on my anthropology into a few sentences? Let me try.

The first thing is that it wasn't the war per se that's had the biggest impact on me, but my reaction to having fought in it. I've always seen my work—both on the Micronesians' drive to decolonize their islands and in my classroom teaching—as a form of atonement.

But strictly in terms of how I work and how I think about the things I work on, what stands out most sharply as a legacy from the war are my doubts about abstract thinking. Theories are okay, but I don't place much trust in them. I've always described myself as a resolute empiricist. That is, I need to *see* what's happening. What this means for my work is that my sense of myself is as an ethnographer. I go out and look. I sit down and observe. As I think about this, I realize that's one of the earliest expressions I learned in the Navy: "Hide and watch." And this is of course why I've written this book.

I'm not sure I've ever gotten over my fear of failing as I directed an interceptor toward a bogey. All I had to go by were the quickly fading images on my radar screen, and those tracings never felt sufficient to put so much at stake. I want to see and feel the things themselves, not images very much akin to Plato's famous shadows on the cave wall, which is what the blips on a radar scope resemble. I know my senses can fool me, of course, but relying on them cuts the margin of error way down.

Comparing the ways soldiers characteristically write about the wars they've fought in, Samuel Hynes (a literature professor who'd been a World War II Marine pilot) finds that a sense of victimization commonly plays a big part in the stories Vietnam veterans tell (1997). It's not an especially unusual phenomenon, actually: people who have trouble dealing with the consequences of things they've done often find refuge in identifying with their victims. The perpetrators excuse themselves by explaining that they too are victims, forced into doing whatever wrongs they were involved in.

In pondering these insights I've had to think, too, about the problem of unintended consequences. To my way of thinking, what the military euphemistically calls "collateral damage" in war—that is, unintended injuries to people who weren't meant to be attacked—is still damage we've inflicted and are thus responsible for. If we're aware in advance that there's a likelihood we'll kill or injure those we do not mean to harm, then we bear responsibility for the damage, whether it was intended or not.

This means to me that in the same way that I share responsibility for having fought in the war, and for what was done in the name of my country, I also bear some responsibility for the damage I inflicted on myself. I don't mean that others are without responsibility. Not at all. But it's how I respond to what I experience as betrayal. My feeling—and this is one of the times when I'm telling you how I feel, not about the logic of the thing—is that along with those who betrayed us, I have to accept some responsibility for allowing myself to be fooled.

As time goes by, my confusion doesn't clear up—it continues to grow. At this very late date I've begun to question my attitudes toward men of my generation who didn't serve.

Because I've long looked back at the war as a mistake, something that should never have been undertaken in the first place, I've always sympathized with those who avoided it. Some men who speak of how they managed to avoid Vietnam expect hostility from me and are surprised when I say I bear them no ill will, that I think they made the right decision. For a long time I made a point of assuring them of this. But recently I felt a wave of anger and bitterness welling up inside me at an AA meeting as I listened to a guy talking with self-satisfaction about how he avoided the draft. It isn't that I no longer think that this was a reasonable thing to do, so much as it reflects an age-old question, the one James Fallows (1975) addressed in "What Did You Do in the Class War, Daddy?"

Fallows points to a problem that still makes me uneasy. If *you* didn't go, he says, then somebody else went in your place. I know there are logical fallacies in this, but I'm talking about feelings here again, raw emotions. This is one of the most potent examples of my confusion, of the profound level of contradiction involved in my feelings about the war, the things I can't sort out. I think the war was wrong and I admire those who resisted it. I admire and respect those who organized protests, fled the country, went through the process of achieving conscientious objector status, etc. They fought in their own ways. Instead, I'm talking about those who simply tried to avoid the draft because it was inconvenient, or who wanted, like a president from my generation, to preserve his political viability. I have no answer to this, except to speak of something that happened in the classroom recently.

I had tears in my eyes, and only by mustering every ounce of restraint I possess was I able to avoid breaking down into full-throated sobbing. I took the students in my peace and war class through a *New York Times* essay by Jay Wellons (2020), a pediatric neurosurgeon in Birmingham. He was recounting an episode from nearly 20 years ago, when he got a call from an emergency room 100 miles away, concerning a badly injured child. She was in danger of permanent brain damage and it was imperative that she be transferred to his hospital within 30 minutes or so, but bad weather had grounded the medical helicopters.

"Are those Blackhawk helicopters still stationed at that base near you?" I asked the emergency room doctor.

"Yes but . . ." he trailed off. Then back again, "Yes! Those guys will fly in anything."

"You get the Blackhawks. I'll let our operating room know."

Events moved quickly after the girl's arrival. In the pediatric trauma bay, two of the soldiers who brought her through the storm, still in their wet flight gear, worked alongside our nurses.

As we packaged the child up and headed off to the elevator up to the operating room I turned back to them. There they stood amid the residual chaos of the trauma room, torn paper packaging and discarded blue gowns strewn about. They watched us roll into the elevator. I locked eyes with the closest soldier. He gave the briefest of nods just before the doors closed. Then he and the chaos of the trauma bay were gone.

I explained my tears to my students: for all the doubts I harbor towards war and the military, I understand exactly why things like valor and service, and a willingness to get the job done no matter what it takes, still stir me.

NOTES

1. For the general Vietnam War histories I've drawn on, see note 3, Chapter 2.

2. The Tonkin Gulf Incident and the Tonkin Gulf Resolution have been explored by nearly every work on the history of the war. To my mind the most comprehensive account—and there are those who disagree with some of its conclusions—is Edwin Moïse's (2019) *Tonkin Gulf and the Escalation of the Vietnam War*, revised edition. Documents from the Defense Department's analyses and planning during this period, with discussion by Neil Sheehan (who was the *New York Times*'s Pentagon reporter at the time), are published in the *Pentagon Papers* (*New York Times*, 2017, pp. 241–390).

The Navy's own confusion about what happened in the Gulf in August 1964 persists. Some sense of this can be gained from a series of articles appearing in its *Naval History Magazine* and *US Naval Institute Proceedings* (Andradé and Conboy, 1999; Patterson, 2008; Vasey, 2010; Marolda, 2014).

Two points in particular strike me as most relevant here. In introducing its Tonkin Gulf Resolution to Congress, the Johnson administration vehemently denied knowledge of any connection between OPLAN34 and Desoto operations. As Lloyd Garner (1995, p. 136) documents, however, Secretary of State Dean Rusk "appeared delighted with the results" of the DeSoto raids. "'We believe that present OPLAN34 activities are beginning to rattle Hanoi,' he cabled [US] Ambassador [to South Vietnam] Taylor the day after the first attack, 'and *Maddox* incident is directly related to their effort to resist these activities.'" John McNaughton, Assistant Secretary of Defense and one of the main architects of the bombing in North Vietnam, in an early 1965 memo to Secretary McNamara apportioned American aims in Vietnam (*New York Times*, 2017, p. 442). In his view, the war had very little to do with the South Vietnamese people's wellbeing, which is what we who were doing the fighting were told was the reason for the fighting.

70%—To avoid a humiliating US defeat (to our reputation as a guarantor).
20%—To keep SVN [South Vietnam] (and then adjacent) territory from Chinese hands.
10%—To permit the people of SVN to enjoy a better, freer way of life.
ALSO—To emerge from crisis without unacceptable taint from methods used.
NOT—To "help a friend," although it would be hard to stay in if asked out.

3. In the context of feeling betrayed by the Johnson administration's lies about the Tonkin Gulf Incident, I note that writers have pointed to an earlier misrepresentation that encouraged their lack of candor. In the wake of what's called the Cuban missile crisis, the Kennedy administration never informed the American public about the true nature of the crisis's resolution. In return for the Soviets' removal of their ballistic missiles from Cuba, the United States agreed to pull its nearly obsolete Jupiter missiles out of Turkey. This sleight-of-hand allowed American leaders to present themselves, and, more significantly, to think of themselves, as much tougher hombres than they were. It led them to believe that an unyielding show of force, rather than negotiation, was the surest route to resolving international conflicts. It was this false bravado, as it were, amplified by the government's refusal to be open with the American people, that facilitated the Americans' decision to play tough by bombing North Vietnam (Bird, 1998, p. 241, Alterman, 2004).

4. As with any aspect of warfare, there's an immense literature considering the efficacy of strategic bombing in World War II and to a much lesser extent in Vietnam and an unending debate on the topic. At the risk of straying into the territory sometimes known as testosterone autism, that is, the middle-aged white male's fascination with every aspect of World War II, I cite a few thoughtful discussions: Richard Overy's *The Bombers and the Bombed* (2013); Max Hastings' *Bomber Command* (2013); Michael Sherry's *The Rise of American Air Power* (1989); Freeman Dyson's *Weapons and Hope* (1984). With regard to the bombing of North Vietnam, see Mark Clodfelter's *The Limits of Airpower* (1989) and Earl Tilford's *Setup: What the Air Force Did in Vietnam and Why* (1991). An especially detailed historical account of President Johnson's political struggles with both Congress and the Joint Chiefs of Staff, and of Defense Secretary McNamara personal struggles over the bombing is in Brian VanDeMark's *Road to Disaster* (2020, pp. 336–410).

5. I'm hardly alone in experiencing this. See, for instance, a very similar discussion of guilt experienced by young Japanese American troops who fought in Vietnam that appears in Toshio Whelchel's *From Pearl Harbor to Saigon* (1999, pp. 27–29).

6. Others have expressed this confusion as well. In the obituary for Francis Kennedy, who served as an artillery spotter in the Korean War and experienced guilt about the deaths of those who died in the ensuing barrages, his son is quoted: "He believed he would never be able to get into heaven because of all the deaths he caused by calling in artillery strikes. I'd say, 'Dad, think of how many lives you saved.' But to his last days he carried that with him" (Thrush, 2020). On the other hand, compare the response of McGeorge Bundy, the president's national security adviser in the Kennedy and Johnson administrations and one of the chief architects of the bombing of North Vietnam, when in later years he was confronted with the policy's failure. Bundy was asked, "But Mac, you screwed it up, didn't you?" He replied, "Yes, I did. But I'm not going to waste the rest of my life feeling guilty about it" (Thomson, 1996). It's not easy to generalize about guilt, I think.

7. I'm referring here to lines from Wilfred Owen's poem "Dulce et Decorum Est." Owen was a British infantry officer in World War I, killed in action days before the Armistice. He is

recognized as one of the war's finest poets, and this is one of his most celebrated works. The final lines read:

> My friend, you would not tell with such high zest
> To children ardent for some desperate glory,
> The old Lie: Dulce et decorum est
> Pro patria mori.

The Latin can be translated as "It is sweet and fitting to die for one's country" and is a quote from the Roman poet Horace. The phrase is inscribed over the entrance to the Amphitheatre at Arlington National Cemetery.

8. A stock figure in theatrical comedy since ancient Roman times is the character known generically as Miles Gloriosus, a warrior/buffoon who loudly sings and wildly embellishes his own praises. He is the butt of jokes precisely because he draws attention to own martial accomplishments.

9. The eminent philosopher Bernard Williams, among others, has explored this conflict of moral obligations, but he does so in terms that are beyond my reach (1985, pp. 175–76).

10. In her thoroughgoing examination of how Aristotle used the concept, Marguerite Deslauriers said of *thumos* that "it gives rise to a love of honour, a desire to defend that honour (understood both individually and collectively), and a capacity for action, all of which are vital to political life" (2019, p. 73); this is a part of why I find that speaking in terms of *thumos* helps explain me to myself.

Appendix

Below is an op-ed piece I submitted to the *New York Times*, commenting on the news that the US military and the CIA had worked with psychologists to use our military's SERE programs to develop and enhance torture techniques that would later be used on captives held in our own POW camps in the wake of the 9/11 attacks. It was not published.

I note in passing that I am unable to type the word "torture" without making typos.

"Our Stolen Honor"
Glenn Petersen

When I was 18 years old I went through the US Navy's Survival, Evasion, Resistance, and Escape (SERE) "school" before deploying with my squadron to Vietnam, where I flew combat missions off the USS *Bennington*. I was the radar controller in an E-1B reconnaissance and surveillance aircraft. Ours were not bombing missions, but we continually risked crashing in enemy territory and my plane once strayed into the Peoples Republic of China, where we came under intense fire and barely escaped. At the time, I thought it a very good thing that the SERE program had prepared me to deal with capture, imprisonment, torture, and brainwashing.

Reports from a variety of sources are now making it clear that these SERE programs served as proving grounds where U.S. intelligence officers learned to perform water boarding and most of the other forms of torture and abuse they have subjected prisoners of war to in the past few years. These revelations represent a fairly clear-cut case of adding insult to injury—a final insult to a long ago injury—at least for those of us who were willing victims of torture in the SERE programs. We agreed to undergo this abuse out of a sense of honor, and we now find that our government has stolen our honor away from us.

As part of the introduction to our SERE program instructors explained that the U.S. military established these programs in the wake of American troops' poor performance in North Korean POW camps; too many had broken down and confessed to war crimes, they told us. Our military saw that Turkish troops possessed an esprit that enabled them to better withstand POW conditions, and the program we were going through was designed to train us in ways that would enable us, like the Turks, to honorably survive and resist. (I don't know how much of this was actually true—but I do know that it's what we were told.) I place the emphasis here on honor. While the program was certainly meant to prepare us as individuals to survive, the main emphasis was in fact placed on preparing us to uphold American honor—we were being trained to withstand torture so that our troops would not look so bad once again.

In the years following my return from the war I came to regret having played a part in the war and in inflicting so much grief upon Vietnam. I still bear a great deal of guilt. (I'm not suggesting that others should do so, but my Catholic school upbringing inculcated in me both a deep sense of sin and my culpability for it, whether appropriate or not.) Unable to seek refuge in what I think of as the Nuremburg defense, that I was only following orders, I have spent much of my adult life seeking ways to atone for the war and to redeem myself. It is only in recent years that I have begun to reflect on the simple facts that I served honorably when called, that I was courageous enough to volunteer for extremely hazardous duty, that I risked my life on a daily basis, and that I underwent torture so that I could uphold America's honor if I were shot down and captured.

Now I learn that all that happened to me, all those experiences I've been trying to mine in order to reclaim some tattered sense of honor, was ultimately put to use developing and refining techniques that my government has been using on prisoners of war. We were taught unequivocally in the SERE program that as Americans we were morally superior to those who would torture us if we were captured, and that by undergoing this practice form torture at home we would increase America's store of honor. But instead I now find that I was used as a guinea pig, allowing my government to develop exactly the skills our enemies were condemned for. The CIA and others honed those skills as a consequence of my willingness to have them experiment on me. Where's the honor in that?

A full-page ad in the Times (5/14/2009) asserts that because "Our own troops are subjected to waterboarding as part of their training," it cannot be torture, and that the U.S. media have therefore "been misleading the world that the United States condones techniques of barbarous cruelty." This sounds perilously close to Richard Nixon's claim that if the president does something it cannot, by definition, be illegal. That is, if my comrades and I underwent this torture, it cannot, by definition, be torture. And with a semantic wave my country is thus exonerated.

In calling up the ghost of Richard Nixon, I find myself hearing another voice from his era, Joseph Welch's celebrated plea to Senator Joseph McCarthy. "Have you no sense of decency, sir? At long last, have you left no sense of decency?" I ask, please, don't use the brutality we underwent back in sixties as a specious rationale for permitting the torture of prisoners today. 5/14/2009

LINKS

What follows are links to several items regarding the American Psychological Association's response to reports about the role American psychologists have played in the development and application of torture protocols.

- *New York Times*: "Outside Psychologists Shielded U.S. Torture Program, Report Finds," by James Risen, July 10, 2015, https://www.nytimes.com/2015/07/11/us/psychologists-shielded-us-torture-program-report-finds.html.
- American Psychological Association: Report of the Independent Reviewer and Related Materials, https://www.apa.org/independent-review/.
- A summary of much of this history can be found on the Andy Worthington website: "The Dark Desires of Bruce Jessen, the Architect of Bush's Torture Program, As Revealed by His Former Friend and Colleague," http://www.andyworthington.co.uk/2011/03/28/the-dark-desires-of-bruce-jessen-the-architect-of-bushs-torture-program-as-revealed-by-his-former-friend-and-colleague/.

Glossary

Agency: In the context I'm using it here, agency comes from the same root as "act," that is, to move or to do something. It means that one does something, that is, one acts, on one's own, not as the result of someone else's orders or an external impetus. It implies acting by free choice and accepting responsibility.

Airborne Early Warning/AEW: Since World War II many military forces have employed a wide variety of aircraft, including planes, blimps, and helicopters, to put radar systems high the air. This enables surface forces to see much farther. In both the North Pacific and the North Atlantic the Navy flew much heavier aircraft on long "barrier" routes that provided the same sort of protection over the seas that the radar installation of the DEW Line (distant early warning) provided in the Arctic. Some AEW systems are designed to control fighter aircraft and surface-to-air missiles to intercept potential attacks. The E-1B and its replacement E-2 were both designed expressly to provide AEW to the Navy's aircraft carriers. https://en.wikipedia.org/wiki/Airborne_early_warning_and_control

Air Group: Also an air wing. All the aircraft aboard a single aircraft carrier. Its commander is known as CAG.

Air Medal: The military changes its criteria for awarding the Air Medal from time to time, and different branches have different criteria. In Vietnam, the Navy's yardstick had to do with flying off Yankee Station. These sorties were designated combat missions; twenty combat missions on Yankee Station earned a flier an Air Medal. For each additional twenty missions a gold star was added to the ribbon. There were significant differences between the

Navy's criteria and that of other services, creating confusion when the Veterans Administration evaluates service records.

Alcoholics Anonymous (AA): AA means many things to many people and *is* many things to many people. I've attended meetings all over the United States and in many parts of the world, and been a long-time member of groups in three different places over the course of more than a quarter-century, and I've found the basic similarities to be much more robust than the differences among them. That said, I know the meetings from my own standpoint, and what I have to say about them is hardly the same as how others experience them. Some people deride AA as a cult or as too rigid, but I find the meetings themselves, as opposed to the program's twelve steps to recovery, to be the most helpful. Sitting and talking with others who find living life without the alcohol's mediating haze works for me, and we share with one another our experiences in beating booze's hold on us. When I think of the folks in AA, I think tolerant, kind, and supportive. For those who find whole thing too religious, many places now have agnostic and/or humanist meetings. If you're uncomfortable at first, try a few different meetings. I think it's well worth the effort. https://www.aa.org/

Arresting Wire: Heavy duty steel cables, usually a set of three or four, stretching laterally across the flight deck of an aircraft carrier. When a plane's tailhook catches one of these wires its forward progress along the deck is halted.

Avionics: A contraction of aviation electronics. Avionics includes all the specialized electronic equipment a plane carries, including the radios, navigation devices, radio altimeters, and in my case, all of the radar systems.

Barrier: A mission flown between a carrier battle group and the direction from which it is most likely that an enemy attack will come. Often flown as a "racetrack" pattern, a long back-and-forth route. Barriers are flown by AEW aircraft and their accompanying BARCAP, "Barrier Combat Air Patrol."

Bingo: When a plane is unable for some reason, having to either with the plane itself, its fuel status, or with deck conditions aboard ship, it heads for an alternate landing point. On Yankee Station, our standard bingo destination was the Da Nang air base near South Vietnam's northern border along the demilitarized zone (DMZ) that separated it from North Vietnam.

Birdwatcher, birder, ornithologist: In short, these are informal terms reflecting matters of skill or degree. Birdwatchers enjoy looking at birds. Birders are obsessed with finding and identifying them. Ornithologists are professionals who study the science of birds.

Bogey: An unidentified radar contact, potentially hostile.

Bolter: When an aircraft's tailhook fails to catch an arresting wire and it continues rolling forward and off the carrier's angle deck. Animated diagrams of bolters can be viewed at: https://en.wikipedia.org/wiki/Bolter_(aeronautics)

Cannibalize: The process of pulling parts or equipment out of one component or plane in order to repair another. Usually, a piece of equipment that's already out of service is used as the source.

Chief petty officer: The Navy uses the term "rate" in place of rank when referring to its enlisted personnel. Without going into detail, there are multiple rates or grades of "seaman" (or in my case airman), petty officer, and chief petty officer. While officers make decisions, it's the chiefs who actually run things. In my 4 years in the Navy I advanced from seaman recruit (E-1) to airman apprentice (E-2) to airman (E-3) to Aviation Electronics Technician 3rd Class (E-4) to Aviation Electronics Technician 2nd Class (E-5), the equivalent of a sergeant in the army. In Navy shorthand, I was an ATR2 (AC).

Cognitive dissonance: The discomfort or stress a person feels as a result of holding two opposing or contradictory views simultaneously. Theorists like to assume that individuals work to resolve these contradictions, but my own sense is that people are often oblivious to them. Scott Fitzgerald famously said, "The test of a first-rate intelligence is the ability to hold two opposed ideas in mind at the same time and still retain the ability to function," but it seems to me that many of us do this much of the time.

CVS: In the US Navy's nomenclature CV stands for aircraft carrier. For several decades in the 1950s through 1970s, some of the old World War II–vintage Essex class carriers were assigned anti-submarine warfare duties (ASW) and designated CVS to distinguish them from the attack carriers (CVA) charged with bombing. CVN designates carriers driven by nuclear propulsion; today, all the Navy's carriers are designated CVN.

Delousing: One of the tasks of carrier AEW. When aircraft were returning from bombing strikes to their carriers, it was potentially feasible for North Vietnamese MiG attack aircraft to tuck themselves in directly behind them

and thus slip undetected into range to attack the US ships. Screening home-
ward bound flights for hidden MiGs was delousing.

Detachment: Aircraft carrier air groups include certain types of very specialized aircraft in only small numbers. A larger squadron sends subunits to each
carrier in the fleet as separate detachments. My squadron, VAW-11, sent
detachments, designated by letters, aboard each carrier in the Pacific fleets.
My unit, assigned to USS *Bennington*, was VAW-11 Det. Q. Our detachments had three, four, or five aircraft (depending on the carrier's mission), 10
or 12 pilots, six or seven radar officers, and 45 or so enlisted maintenance
personnel, and were headed by an officer-in-charge.

E-1B/Fudd: The E-1B was a propeller-driven airborne early warning aircraft
designed and built by the Grumman Aircraft Engineering Corporation. It was
formally a "Tracer," but because an earlier nomenclature system designated
it as the WF, it became known to all as the Willy Fudd. The Fudds began
serving with the fleet in 1958 and were phased out by the early 1970s,
replaced by Grumman's E-2 Hawkeyes, which still fly as a part of today's
carrier air groups. The Fudd carried a crew of four. In simple terms, it was
the flying platform for the AN/APS-82 radar.

Enlisted/Non-Commissioned/Commissioned: All US military branches follow older European and British military traditions in dividing their personnel
into three overarching categories. Officers receive commissions from Congress and are by definition "gentlemen." (There is a small component of
officers who receive warrants rather than commissions.) The remainder are
"enlisted"; they are divided into two categories, noncommissioned officers
(called petty officers in the Navy) and enlisted personnel. During periods of
conscription, troops who are drafted into the military, rather voluntarily enlisting, are still referred to enlisted. In British terminology, enlisted troops are
known as "other ranks."

Essex class: Beginning in 1943 the US Navy commissioned 24 "fast carriers," the largest aircraft carriers to serve in World War II, over the span of
three years. They carried multiple aircraft squadrons in air groups and crews
of approximately 3,000. They were the mainstay of the US fleet in World
War II and Korea and half of them participated in the Vietnam War. They
also served as recovery ships for space capsules in the early years of the US
space program. All but one of the carriers now serving as museums are Essex
class.

Gung ho: Overly or unnecessarily enthusiastic or committed. It can be used as either praise or derision in the military, but in my time in the Navy I don't believe I ever heard it used as anything but a disparaging remark.

Hypervigilance: A common symptom of PTSD. It is characterized by extreme alertness and a sense of imminent danger. Those experiencing hypervigilance are continually on the lookout for threats to their safety and may be prone to overreaction. The condition can be exhausting.

Kava: Pohnpeians make a beverage from the kava plant (*Piper methysticum*) by pounding its roots into a pulp and adding a bit of water. In the Pohnpeian language it's *sakau*, but it's the same word, ultimately, and the same drink found in many parts of the island Pacific. It's sold as a dried powder in many places and advertised as a mildly tranquilizing concoction. But fresh the ground, it packs a wallop. On Pohnpei, adults gather together to prepare and drink it almost every night, and it has traditionally served as the island's main source of entertainment and social cohesion. I describe kava's place in Pohnpeian culture at length in "The Complexity of Power, the Subtlety of Kava" (1995).

Launch: Aboard aircraft carriers a plane's takeoff is termed a launch. Fixed-wing aircraft (as opposed to helicopters) are launched with the use of a catapult. Today's catapults are steam-driven (though electromagnet systems are being introduced); on older carriers the catapults were hydraulic. *Bennington*'s catapults were never converted to steam.

Liberty: The day-by-day time periods when sailors are permitted ashore, either off their ships or the bases where they're stationed. Depending on circumstances and locales, liberty may be granted until rollcall the following morning, or only until some specified hour, often midnight, which is known as "Cinderella liberty." Ships in the US Navy are "dry," that is no alcohol is allowed aboard, and liberty, at least in my time, was associated with bars, pool halls, night clubs, dance halls, womanizing and the reckless, profligate, and abandoned behavior sailors ashore are famous for. "Leave" generally refers to longer periods of time, the equivalent of vacation.

Margaret Mead: The United States' preeminent anthropologist in the second half of the 20th century. Mead had a profound impact on the ways in which anthropological views were adopted by and integrated into the country's popular culture. She was best-known for her book on adolescent sexual behavior, *Coming of Age in Samoa*, but she tackled a great many important issues dealing with youth, gender roles, and family values, and wrote a critique of the draft that influenced my thinking when I first began college.

As the Columbia anthropology department's South Pacific expert, she served on my doctoral committee.

Meatball: The nearly universal term for the landing signal lights. These are a series of lights, reflectors, and lenses used to guide carrier pilots onto the glide slope that will enable them to land safely aboard an aircraft carrier's flight deck. The pilot radios "Ball!" to signal that he is properly lined up to make his landing safely.

Micronesia: A vast area of islands in the Central Pacific Ocean, comparable to the adjacent areas of Polynesia and Melanesia. Many of the key battles between US forces and Japan during of World War II were fought there and following the war the United States took the islands from Japan, claiming them as a strategic trust territory ostensibly overseen by the United Nations. Most Micronesians preferred to be no one's colony and they struggled for self-government and independence for many years. Today the former trust territory has split up into the nation-sates of the Marshall Islands, the Federated States of Micronesia, and Palau, and the Northern Marianas, a US territory. The adjacent island nation of Kiribati, which has a different colonial history, is in ethnological terms a part of Micronesia.

My Lai: My Lai refers to a small village—a series of tiny hamlets—in central Vietnam; it was in northern South Vietnam during the war. A US Army infantry company massacred approximately 500 civilians there, mostly women, elders, and children, in March 1968. Pilot Hugh Thompson and his crew, in a helicopter overhead, stopped the killing by threatening to fire on their own troops. The Army covered up the massacre, but reporter Seymour Hersh was ultimately able to bring it to light. Only one American soldier, Lt. William Calley, was put on trial for the killings. A court martial convicted him of murder and sentenced him to life imprisonment; he was paroled after 3 years. As is typical of nearly everything concerning the Vietnam War, there is a sharp division of opinion about My Lai. Some view the brutality there as typical of how the United States fought the war; others argue that it was quite out of keeping with the way US troops fought. See:

- Jones, Howard (2017). *My Lai*. Oxford University Press.
- Turse, Nick (2013). *Kill Anything that Moves*. Metropolitan Books.

Peacenik: A term that appeared in the early 1960s, used first to describe pacifists and opponents of the Cold War, and by the mid-'60s applied to opponents of the Vietnam War. Some used it derisively or dismissively, but many in the antiwar movement happily called themselves peaceniks.

Pohnpei/Pohnpeian: Pohnpei is a small volcanic island in Micronesia's Eastern Caroline Islands, a few degrees north of the equator and approximately half-way between Hawai'i and the Philippines. The Pohnpeians speak Pohnpeian. Rainfall there averages over 200 inches per year and the island is densely vegetated. Pohnpeians traditionally live in tiny, isolated villages hidden among the forests, although today a great many of them have immigrated to the United States. Hospitality and generosity are among their highest cultural values and they readily welcomed me to live among them. They taught me a great deal about being a proper human being.

Post-traumatic stress disorder/PTSD: This diagnosis formally entered the American Psychiatric Association's Diagnostic and Statistical Manual of Mental Disorders (DSM-III) in 1980. War trauma and its aftermaths have been recognized throughout history and technical terminology for it is not new. In the twentieth century terms like "shell shock," "war neurosis," "psycho-neurosis," and "combat fatigue" were used to discuss it. Causes and symptoms have long been debated and in some medical and military traditions these symptoms are attributed to failures of character rather than medical conditions. Something about the larger impact of the Vietnam War on American society pushed the medical professions to formalize the diagnosis. The US Department of Veterans Affairs' National Center for PTSD provides an overview: https://www.ptsd.va.gov/index.asp

R&R: "Rest and recreation," "rest and relaxation," or "rest and recuperation." During the Vietnam War, this referred to time when ships would leave their duty stations and sail to a friendly port, where crews were granted liberty, that is, time ashore. Ground troops were granted something similar.

Rolling Thunder: Operation Rolling Thunder refers to the bombing of North Vietnam by the US Air Force and US Navy from 1965 to 1968. Attacks were launched from Task Force 77 on Yankee Station and from Air Force bases in South Vietnam, Thailand, and Guam. I flew as an early warning component of Rolling Thunder. The bombing of North Vietnam resumed in 1972 with Operations Linebacker and Linebacker 2.

S-2F/Stoof: A propeller-driven, dedicated antisubmarine warfare aircraft built by Grumman. It was officially designated as a "Tracker," but was universally known as a "Stoof." Stoofs flew from anti-sub aircraft carriers from 1954 to 1976. They carried a crew of four, an array of submarine detection gear, and were armed with a variety of ASW weaponry. Many of them have been converted to fire-fighting service.

Sea Dragon: US Naval operations along the coasts of North and South Vietnam, intended to intercept small-craft shipments of war materiel from the North to the South. Operations included both surface vessels and aircraft.

Self-medication: I use this term in a nontechnical way to refer to consuming substances that are in one way or another psychoactive, as means of reducing various discomforts or afflictions, often psychological in origin, without medical advice or oversight. There's a debate about whether people should be free to diagnose and treat themselves, of course, and it's possible that self-medication is ultimately no more dangerous than the drug-pushing large pharmaceutical companies engage in.

Service-connected disability rating: Veterans may qualify for compensation in the form of monthly payments if they were injured or otherwise disabled in the course of their duties while in the military. It is possible to have a service-connected condition recognized by the VA that is given a 0% rating, but most disabilities are calculated on a scale ranging up to 100%, which merits a monthly payment of $3,057 in 2019, with additional allowances for dependents. The VA's compensation site and disability scale: https://www.benefits.va.gov/compensation/index.asp

Smoke light: Technically, a marine location marker. An illuminating flare dropped from an aircraft to mark a specific spot in the water below. It releases fiery sparks and smoke and is activated by contact with seawater. Some patrol and AEW aircraft have launching devices. They were jettisoned by hand from the E-1B.

Squadron: An essentially self-contained unit of aircraft, the pilots and crew who fly them, and the enlisted maintenance and service personnel who keep them in flying condition. Ordinarily, they are dedicated to a single role and operate a single type of plane. In the case of carrier-based ("tailhook") aircraft, they are based on naval air stations when the ship they are assigned to is in homeport and move aboard the ship when it deploys overseas. An air group or wing is ordinarily composed of several types of aircraft and is attached to a specific ship.

Surface-to-air Missile (SAM): Perhaps a third of all the US aircraft shot down in the Vietnam War were hit by SAMs. These are radar-guided ballistic (that is, armed) rockets fired from launching pads on the ground. They fly much faster than planes and are not easily avoided.

Tailhook: An extremely heavy-duty metal hook that swings down from the rear of carrier-based aircraft. The hook catches one of the arresting wires/

cables stretching across the carrier's flight deck in order to stop the plane as it lands on the deck. In Navy parlance, "tailhook" can also refer to anything having to do with ship-based aviation, in particular the aircraft squadrons attached to carriers.

Thumos: A Greek word (θυμός, also spelled thymos) that expresses the concept of "spiritedness" (as in "spirited stallion" or "spirited debate"). The word indicates a physical association with breath or blood and is also used to express the human desire for recognition.

Yankee Station: A general location (as opposed to a specific point) in the Tonkin Gulf, approximately 90 miles off the coast of North Vietnam. The ships of the US Navy's Task Force 77 took up position here as they mounted attacks on Hanoi and other parts of North Vietnam. a point further south was designated as Dixie Station and used for launching attacks on targets in South Vietnam. Newsreel of US Navy on Yankee Station: https://www.youtube.com/watch?v=xB0L7UHgU6c

VAW-11: Carrier Airborne Early Warning Squadron Eleven. A large post-World War II Navy squadron flying EA-1Es, E-1Bs, and E-2s. It placed a detachment of three to four planes on each carrier in the Pacific fleet, providing them with early warning capabilities. In 1967 the detachments were redesignated as individual squadrons.

Vietnam Veterans Memorial: A site run by the National Park Service on the Mall in Washington, DC, between the Capitol and the Washington Monument. It's a V-shaped wall that runs uphill on either side of its center point in a shallow depression in the ground. Dedicated in 1982, it is made of polished black granite and the names of 58,000-plus Americans who died fighting in Vietnam are carved into it. "The Wall," as it's known, was funded by private donations and designed by a young American architecture student, Maya Lin.

References

Alexander, Caroline (2010). *The War That Killed Achilles*. Penguin.
Alterman, Eric (2004). *When Presidents Lie*. Penguin.
American Psychiatric Association (1994). *DSM-IV: Diagnostic and Statistical Manual of Mental Disorders*.
Anderson, Elizabeth (1995). *Value in Ethics and Economics*. Harvard University Press.
——— (2019). Personal communication.
Andradé, Dale and Kenneth Conboy (1999). The Secret Side of the Tonkin Gulf Incident. *Naval History Magazine, 13*(4), 27–33.
Andresen, Lee (2003). *Battle Notes*. Savage Press.
Armistead, Edwin (2002). *AWACS and Hawkeyes*. Zenith.
Arnett, Peter (1968, February 8). Major Describes Move. *New York Times*, 14. https://www.washingtonpost.com/archive/opinions/2001/12/01/lbjs-secret-war/c479bf13-a76e-4422-a014-4e75bcd91db6/?utm_term=.ad8e6a8b5175.
Baskir, Lawrence and William Strauss (1978). *Chance and Circumstance*. Random House.
Berger, Thomas (1964). *Little Big Man*. Dial.
Beschloss, Michael (2001, December 1). LBJ's Secret War. *Washington Post*.
Bird, Kai (1998). *The Color of Truth*. Simon & Schuster.
Bird, K. and L. Lifschultz (eds). (1998). *Hiroshima's Shadow*. Pamphleteer's Press.
Bradley, Doug (2019). *Who'll Stop the Rain*. Warriors Publishing.
Bradley, Doug and Craig Werner (2015). *We Gotta Get Out of This Place*. University of Massachusetts Press.
Brown, Dee (1970). *Bury My Heart at Wounded Knee*. Holt, Rinehart & Winston.
Burkett, B. J. (1998). *Stolen Valor*. Verity Press.
Charlton, Michael and Anthony Moncrieff (1978). *Many Reasons Why*. Hill and Wang.
Clodfelter, Mark (1989). *The Limits of Airpower*. Free Press.
Deloria, Vine (1969). *Custer Died for Your Sins*. Macmillan.
de Waal, Frans (2007). *Chimpanzee Politics*. Johns Hopkins University Press.
——— (2019). *Momma's Last Hug*. Norton.
Dorfman, Ariel and Armand Mattelart (2018). *How To Read Donald Duck*. OR Books (Original 1971).
Dyer, Geoff (2014). *Another Great Day at Sea*. Pantheon.
Dyson, Freeman (1979). *Disturbing the Universe*. Basic Books.
——— (1984). *Weapons and Hope*. Harper.
Fagles, Robert (translator) (1990). *The Iliad*. Penguin.
Fallows, James (1975, October). What Did You Do in the Class War, Daddy? *Washington Monthly, 7*(8), 5–19.

Falstein, Louis (1950). *Face of a Hero*. Harcourt.

Finley, Erin (2011). *Fields of Combat*. ILR Press.

Flynn, George (1993). *The Draft, 1940–1973*. University Press of Kansas.

Francillon, René (1989). *Grumman Aircraft Since 1929*. Naval Institute Press.

Fried, Morton, Marvin Harris, and Robert Murphy (eds). (1968) *War: The Anthropology of Armed Conflict and Aggression*. Natural History Press.

Fussell, Paul (1975). *The Great War and Modern Memory*. Oxford University Press.

——— (1988). An Exchange of Views. In *Thank God for the Atom Bomb* (pp. 27–28). Ballentine (Original New Republic, 1981).

——— (1990). *Wartime*. Oxford University Press.

——— (1998). Thank God for the Atom Bomb. In Kai Bird and L. Lifschultz (eds.), *Hiroshima's Shadow* (pp. 211–222). Pamphleteer's Press.

Gardiner, Steve (2013). In the Shadow of Service: Veteran Masculinity and Civil-Military Disjuncture in the United States. *North American Dialogue, 16*, 69–79.

Gardner, Lloyd (1995). *Pay Any Price: Lyndon Johnson and the Wars for Vietnam*. Ivan R. Dee.

Garner, James and Jon Winokur (2011). *The Garner Files*. Simon & Schuster.

Golden, Leon (2009). *Achilles and Yossarian*. Author House.

Gonzalez, Roberto (2004). *Anthropologists in the Public Sphere: Speaking Out on War, Peace, and American Power*. University of Texas Press.

Graham, Thomas (2008). *Remembering Revell Model Kits*. Schiffer Publishing.

Graziano, Michael (2018). *The Spaces Between Us*. Oxford University Press.

Green, Justin (2009). Binky Brown Meets the Blessed Virgin Mary. McSweeney's Store (Original 1972). https://archive.org/details/BinkyBrownMeetsTheHolyVirginMary/page/n5/mode/2up.

Gritters, Jenni (2020, May 5). This Is Your Brain on Motherhood. *New York Times*. https://www.nytimes.com/2020/05/05/parenting/mommy-brain-science.html.

Guardia, Mike (2013). *Hal Moore*. Casemate Publishers.

Gusterson, Hugh (2007). Anthropology and Militarism. *Annual Review of Anthropology, 36*, 155–175.

Habib, Cherine and Sandra Lancaster (2006). The Transition to Fatherhood: Identity and Bonding in Early Pregnancy. *Fathering, 4*, 235–253.

Harmetz, Aljean (2002). *The Making of Casablanca*. New York: Hyperion. (previously published by Hyperion as *Round Up the Usual Suspects*, 1992).

Harris, Marvin (1968). *The Rise of Anthropological Theory*. Crowell.

Hastings, Max (2013). *Bomber Command*. Zenith Press (Original 1979).

——— (2018). *Vietnam: An Epic Tragedy, 1945–1975*. Harper.

Heller, Joseph (1961). *Catch-22*. Simon & Shuster.

——— (1998). *Now and Then*. Knopf.

Hemingway, Ernest (1938). *The Short Stories of Ernest Hemingway*. Scribners.

——— (1971, December 20). An African Journal. *Sports Illustrated*, 40–46.

Herman, Judith (1997). *Trauma and Recovery*. Basic Books.

Herring, George (1994). *LBJ and Vietnam*. University of Texas Press.

——— (2013). *America's Longest War*, 5th ed. McGraw-Hill.

Homecoming II Project (1990). Homecoming II Project, 15 May 1990. Riordan, John Michael. https://www.pownetwork.org/bios/r/r369.htm.

Hornfischer, James (2011). *Neptune's Inferno*. Bantam.

Hunter, Chuck (2018). Quora: What Is the G-Force Experienced by Pilots When Their Aircraft Is Catapulted Into the Air by the Aircraft Carrier? May 14, 2018. https://www.quora.com/What-is-the-g-force-experienced-by-pilots-when-their-aircraft-is-catapulted-into-the-air-by-the-aircraft-carrier.

Hynes, Samuel (1997). *The Soldiers' Tale*. Viking.

Jones, Howard (2017). *My Lai*. Oxford University Press.

Kant, Immanuel (1991). Idea for a Universal History With a Cosmopolitan Purpose. In H. S. Reiss (ed.), *Cambridge Texts in the History of Political Thought*, 2nd ed. (pp. 41–53). Cambridge University Press.

Kardiner, Abram (1941). *Traumatic Neuroses of War*. Paul B. Hoeber Inc. Martino Publishing (Reprinted 2012).

Karnow, Stanley (1997). *Vietnam*, 2nd ed. Penguin.

Kazantzakis, Nikos (1953). *Zorba the Greek*. Simon & Shuster.

Kerouac, Jack (1957) *On the Road*. Viking.

───── (1958). *Dharma Bums*. Viking

───── (1962). *Big Sur*. Farrar, Straus and Giroux

Kovic, Ron (2016). *Born on the Fourth of July*. Akashic Books (Original 1976).

Kramer, Michael (2017). *The Republic of Rock*. Oxford University Press.

Lair, Meredith (2011). *Armed with Abundance*. University of North Carolina Press.

Lembcke, Jerry (2000). *The Spitting Image*. New York University Press.

Lifton, Robert Jay (1973). *Home from the War*. Simon & Schuster.

Loewen, James (1995). *Lies My Teacher Told Me*. New Press.

Logevall, Frederik (1999). *Choosing War*. University of California Press.

───── (2012). *Embers of War*. Random House.

Lundy, Brenda (2002). Paternal Socio-Psychological Factors and Infant Attachment: The Mediating Role of Synchrony in Father–Infant Interactions. *Infant Behavior and Development, 25*, 221–236.

Lutz, Catherine (2002). *Homefront*. Beacon Press.

Lynn, Kenneth (1987). *Hemingway*. Harvard University Press.

Machin, Anna (2018). *The Life of Dad*. Simon & Schuster.

MacLeish, Kenneth (2013). *Making War at Fort Hood*. Princeton University Press.

Manchester, William (1980). *Goodbye, Darkness*. Back Bay Books.

Mansfield, Harvey (2007). *Manliness*. Yale University Press.

Marolda, Edward (2002). *The U.S. Navy in the Vietnam War*. Brassey.

───── (2014, July). Grand Delusion: U.S. Strategy and the Tonkin Gulf Incident. *Naval History Magazine* 28 (4).

Marolda, Edward and Oscar Fitzgerald (1986). *The United States Navy and the Vietnam Conflict*, Vol. II. Naval Historical Center.

McFate, Montgomery (2018). *Military Anthropology*. Oxford University Press.

Mobley, Richard and Edward Marolda (2015). *Knowing the Enemy*. Naval History & Heritage Command. https://www.history.navy.mil/content/dam/nhhc/research/publications/publication-508-pdf/KnowingtheEnemy_508.pdf.

Moïse, Edwin (2019). *Tonkin Gulf and the Escalation of the Vietnam War*, revised edition. Naval Institute Press.

Moore, H. G. (1992). *We Were Soldiers Once . . . and Young*. Presidio Press.

Murphy, Robert F. (1971) *The Dialectics of Social Life*. Basic Books.

Nayman, Adam (2020, January 29). "1917" and the Trouble With War Movies. *The Ringer*. https://www.theringer.com/movies/2020/1/29/21112768/war-movies-1917-dunkirk-saving-private-ryan-apocalypse-now.

Nelson, Janet (2019). *King and Emperor*. University of California Press.

New York Times (2017). *The Pentagon Papers*. Racehorse Publishing.

Nichols, John (1987). *On Yankee Station: The Naval Air War Over Vietnam*. Naval Institute Press.

Nietzsche, Friedrich (1886). *Beyond Good and Evil*.Cambridge University Press.

O'Brien, Tim (1990). *The Things They Carried*. Houghton Mifflin.

Osborn, Shane (2001). *Born to Fly*. Broadway Books.

Overy, Richard (2013). *The Bombers and the Bombed*. Viking.

Parke, Ross (1981). *Fathers*. Harvard University Press.

Pasulka, Nicole (2016, October 16). The American Boat That Sailed to Vietnam During the War, Then Disappeared. *Atlas Obscura*. http://www.atlasobscura.com/articles/the-american-boat-that-sailed-to-vietnam-during-the-warthen-disappeared.

Paterson, Pat (2008, February). The Truth About Tonkin. *Naval History Magazine, 22*(1).

Petersen, Glenn (1990). *Lost In the Weeds: Theme and Variation in Ponapean Political Mythology*. Center for Pacific Island Studies, University of Hawai'i, Occasional Paper 35.

—— (1992). The Vietnam War as an Exemplar of American Culture. *Dialectical Anthropology, 17*, 217–23.

—— (1995). The Complexity of Power, the Subtlety of Kava. In N. Pollock, ed. *The Power of Kava*. Special issue, *Canberra Anthropologist, 18*, 34–60.

—— (1999a). Politics in Post-War Micronesia. In R. Kiste and M. Marshall, (eds.), *Anthropology in American Micronesia* (pp. 145–197). University of Hawaii Press,

—— (1999b). Strategic Location and Sovereignty. *Space & Polity, 2*, 179–205.

—— (2004). Lessons Learned: The Micronesian Quest for Independence in the Context of American Imperial History. *Micronesian Journal of the Humanities and Social Sciences, 3*, 45–63.

—— (2005). Important to Whom? On Ethnographic Usefulness, Competence and Relevance. *Anthropological Forum, 15*(3), 307–317.

—— (2009). *Traditional Micronesian Societies*. University of Hawai'i Press.

—— (2012). Finding a Moral Compass for an Anthropological Career. *Anthropology Now, 4*(3), 75–84.

—— (2013, September 6). When Santa Barbara Was My Paris. *Santa Barbara Independent*. https://www.independent.com/2013/09/06/santa-barbara-was-my-paris/.

—— (2014). The Possibilities of Violence and the Skills to Avoid It. *Anthropologica, 56*, 315–326.

—— (2015). American Anthropology's "Thailand Controversy": An Object Lesson in Professional Responsibility. *Sojourn, 30*, 528–549.

—— (2018). The Abyss Stares Back. *As You Were*, vol. 9. http://militaryexperience.org/as-you-were-the-military-review-vol-9/the-abyss-stares-back/.

—— (2019) Micronesian Ethnography from a Disordered Soul? *Anthropology and Humanism, 44*(1), 112–126.

Petersen, Glenn, V. Garcia, and Grace Petersen (1998). Field and Family on Pohnpei, Micronesia. In J. Flinn, L. Marshall, and J. Armstrong, (eds.), *Fieldwork and Families* (pp. 84–95). Honolulu University of Hawai'i Press.

Pogge, Thomas (2007). *John Rawls: His Life and Theory of Justice*. Yale University Press.

Polmar, Norman (2010, April). Elmer Fudd's Flying Cousin. *Naval History Magazine, 24*(2).

Poyer, Lin, Suzanne Falgout, and Laurence Carucci (2001). *The Typhoon of War: Micronesian Experiences of the Pacific War*. University of Hawaii Press.

Price, David (2011). *Weaponizing Anthropology*. Counterpunch.

Raeburn, Paul (2014). *Do Fathers Matter?* Scientific American/Farrar, Straus and Giroux.

Rand, Ayn (1964). *The Virtue of Selfishness*. New American Library.

Rawls, John (1998). Fifty Years After Hiroshima. In Kai Bird and L. Lifschultz, (eds.) *Hiroshima's Shadow* (pp. 474–484). Pamphleteer's Press.

Roszak, Theodore (1969). *The Making of a Counter Culture*. Anchor Books.

Salinger, J. D. (1951). *The Catcher in the Rye*. Little, Brown.

Satel, Sally (2004, March 5). Returning From Iraq, Still Fighting Vietnam. *New York Times*. https://www.nytimes.com/2004/03/05/opinion/returning-from-iraq-still-fighting-vietnam.html?searchResultPosition=22.

—— (2011a, February 1). PTSD's Diagnostic Trap. *New York Times*. https://www.hoover.org/research/ptsds-diagnostic-trap.

—— (2011b, August 11). The Wrong Way to Help Veterans. *New York Times*. https://www.nytimes.com/2011/08/20/opinion/the-wrong-way-to-help-veterans.html.

Schiffren, Lisa (2003, May 9). Hey, Flyboy. *Wall Street Journal*. https://www.wsj.com/articles/SB105244292810654300.

Scism, A. and R. Cobb (2017). Integrative Review of Factors and Interventions That Influence Early Father–Infant Bonding. *Journal of Obstetric, Gynecologic & Neonatal Nursing, 46*, 163–170.

Shay, Jonathan (1995). *Achilles in Vietnam*. Simon & Schuster.

—— (2003). *Odysseus in America*. Scribner

Sherman, Nancy (2010). *The Untold War*. Norton.

—— (2015). *Afterwar*. Oxford University Press.

Sherry, Michael (1989). *The Rise of American Air Power*. Yale University Press.

Sherwood, John (2004). *Afterburner*. New York University Press.

Sides, Hampton (2007). Foreword. In Dee Brown, *Bury My Hear at Wounded Knee*. Henry Holt.

Simons, Anna (1997). *The Company They Keep*. Free Press

Snarey, John (1993). *How Fathers Care for the Next Generation*. Harvard University Press.

Steinbeck, John (1942). *Bombs Away*. Viking.

Suid, Lawrence (1996). *Sailing on the Silver Screen*. US Naval Institute Press.

———— (2002). *Guts and Glory*. University of Kentucky Press.

———— (2005). *Stars and Stripes on the Screen*. Scarecrow Press.

Thayer, Thomas (1985). *War Without Fronts*. Westview.

Thomson, James C., Jr. (1996, September 22). A Memory of McGeorge Bundy. *New York Times*. https://www.nytimes.com/1996/09/22/weekinreview/a-memory-of-mcgeorge-bundy.html?searchResultPosition=1.

Thrush, Glenn (2020, May 21). Francis Kennedy, War Hero and Restless Inventor, Dies at 95. *New York Times*. https://www.nytimes.com/2020/05/20/us/francis-a-kennedy-dead-coronavirus.html.

Tilford, Earl (1991). *Setup: What the Air Force Did in Vietnam and Why*. Air University Press.

Tucker, Spencer (2000). *The Encyclopedia of the Vietnam War*. Oxford University Press.

Turse, Nick (2013). *Kill Anything that Moves*. Metropolitan Books

VanDeMark, Brian (2020). *Road to Disaster*. Custom House.

Van der Kolk, Bertel (2014). *The Body Keeps the Score*. Penguin.

Van Ronk, Dave (2005). *The Mayor of MacDougal Street*. Da Capo.

Vasey, Lloyd (2010, August). Tonkin: Setting the Record Straight. *U.S. Naval Institute Proceedings, 136*(8), 66–71.

Wald, Elijah (2015). *Dylan Goes Electric*. Dey Street Books.

Walzer, Michael (1988). An Exchange of Views. In Paul Fussell, *Thank God for the Atom Bomb* (pp. 23–27). Ballentine Books. (Original New Republic, 1981).

———— (2015). *Just and Unjust Wars*, 5th ed. Basic Books.

Whelchel, Toshio (1999). *From Pearl Harbor to Saigon*. Verso.

Wellons, Jay (2020, February 29) From a Doctor, a Reminder to Keep Pushing On. *New York Times Magazine*. https://www.nytimes.com/2020/02/29/opinion/sunday/doctors-medicine-military-emergency.html?searchResultPosition=10.

Williams, Bernard (1985). *Ethics and the Limits of Philosophy*. Harvard University Press.

Woodward, Bob (2015) *The Last of the President's Men*. Simon & Schuster.

Young, Alan (1995). *The Harmony of Illusions*. Princeton University Press.

Young, Philip (1952). *Ernest Hemingway: A Reconsideration*. Harcourt, Brace.

Zinn, Howard (2006). *Just War*. Charta.

Index

A-1 bombers with radar pods (Guppies), 97, 98
A-4 bomber, 137
Abraham Lincoln, USS, 199
accountability, 106, 107. *See also* responsibility
Achilles, 204–205, 206, 210
Achilles and Yossarian (Golden), 205
Achilles in Vietnam (Shay), 204, 233
Afghanistan, 2, 63, 143, 168, 198, 200, 221
Afterburner (Sherwood), 96, 98
After War (Sherman), 211
Agamemnon, 205
agency, 265
Airborne Early Warning (AEW), 49, 57, 265
Airborne Radio Code Operator (ARCO) school, 47
aircraft carriers, 5, 49, 52, 96, 137;
  Bennington, 71, 72, 76, 80, 86, 89, 90, 92, 93, 94, 101, 104, 105, 133, 137, 146, 188, 261; catapult launch from, 84–88; landing on, 88–91. *See also* flight deck
Air Force, 5, 9, 14, 15
air group, 265
Air Medal, 94, 99n4, 133, 265
air raid drills, 17
Alamo, 23, 24
Albright, Glenn, 210, 233, 254

Alcoholics Anonymous (AA), 182, 183, 185, 186, 201, 211, 215–216, 266
Alexander, Caroline, 205
American Anthropological Association, 170n9
Anderson, Elizabeth, 253
anthropology, 134–136, 158, 159, 161, 170n8, 170n9; ethics of, 8; military, 212n2; Petersen's career in, 1, 2, 35, 130n5, 136, 142, 158–159, 167–168, 202–210, 212, 238, 253, 255, 256; war and, 2, 10n1. *See also* ethnography
antisubmarine warfare (ASW), 71, 113
Apollo program, 137, 139, 169n2
APS-82. *See* radar
arc of human experience, 2; "War and the Arc of Human Experience" courses, 210, 254
Army, 9, 14
arresting wires, 89, 91, 92, 137, 266
atom bomb. *See* nuclear weapons
Audubon Society, 32, 33
Australia, 133, 134, 169n1
Australian National University, 175
authority, 210, 211, 225
avionics, 46, 266

baby boomers, 144; Vietnam War and, 3, 5
Baez, Joan, 124
Barbasch, Annette (second wife), 198, 225, 227–229, 230–231, 231

About the Author

Glenn Petersen ran away at 16, joined the Navy at 17, began flying off aircraft carriers at 18, and fought in Vietnam at 19. Nowadays, he's professor at the City University of New York's Baruch College and Graduate Center, where he teaches anthropology, international affairs, and geography. He's worked as an ethnographer in the islands of Micronesia for more than 40 years and has represented the Federated States of Micronesia at the United Nations. His books include *One Man Cannot Rule a Thousand*, *Lost in the Weeds*, and *Traditional Micronesian Societies*. In 1966 to 1967, he served as a radar intercept controller and flight technician, flying from USS *Bennington* on Yankee Station in the Tonkin Gulf.